“*You’re Every Sign!* is a wonderful … ou know nothing about astrology, this bo … nd. And it’s entertaining as well. I wholeh … to you.”

—Louise Hay
author of *You Can Heal Your Life* and *Empowering Women*

“Phyllis’s book is a star among the stars. The uplifting keys found within its pages can assist anyone to better understand themselves and grow into the person they were meant to be.”

—H. Ronald Hulnick, Ph.D.
president, University of Santa Monica

“Our journey here is to know the True Self. This definitive and exciting book offers very useful and dynamic revelations to help us along the way to who we truly are! Enjoy!”

—Leigh Taylor-Young
Emmy Award–winning actress

“*You’re Every Sign!*’s descriptions are written with such clarity, simplicity, love and humor, that I found myself thinking, *I couldn’t have described myself better!* I was even further impressed with the simple yet effective strategies Phyllis recommended for empowering myself in my work, relationships and spiritual life.”

—B. Remus
management consultant

“Phyllis has so masterfully succeeded in bringing the spiritual aspect of astrology to life! Reading this book is a truly fun and enriching experience!”

—Agapi Stassinopoulis
lecturer and author of *Conversations with the Goddess*

“The advent of quantum physics implores us to reconsider all that we have come to believe about our physical and psychical worlds. *You’re Every Sign!* offers us a rich tapestry of symbols and invisible forces from which we can ponder, in an enlightened way, the metapsychology of our human essence.”

—Allen B. Weiner, M.D.
psychiatrist, Los Angeles, California

You're Every Sign!

Using Astrology's Keys to Create Success, Love and Happiness

Phyllis Firak-Mitz, M.A.

Health Communications, Inc.
Deerfield Beach, Florida

www.hci-online.com

Library of Congress Cataloging-in-Publication Data

Firak-Mitz, Phyllis, date.
You're every sign! : using astrology's keys to create success, love and happiness / Phyllis Firak-Mitz.
p. cm.
ISBN 1-55874-963-2
1. Astrology. I. Title: You're every sign!. II. Title.

BF1708.1.F57 2002
133.5—dc21

2002068673

ISBN 1-55874-963-2 (trade paperback)

Publisher: Health Communications, Inc.
3201 S.W. 15th Street
Deerfield Beach, FL 33442-8190

Cover and inside book design by Larissa Hise Henoch
Inside book formatting by Dawn Von Strolley Grove

Contents

Acknowledgments

This book is dedicated to my clients. Their expression and candor about their life's journey, including their triumphs and pain, have taught me volumes about how every sign grows and blossoms. It's an honor to be their astrologer, and a privilege to be privy to their innermost secrets.

Although members of every sign helped me write this book, there were some who went the extra mile. I want to thank and acknowledge them for the time, interest and direction they offered.

To Laren Bright, for not only serving as my first editor, but also for extending his Cancer Sun's powerful support. He "mothered" me (even though he's a father), and buoyed me with confidence and enthusiasm throughout this project's creation.

To my HCI editors, Lisa Drucker and Susan Tobias, Aries and Libra, respectively, who gave me tremendous freedom and latitude in every aspect of this book's creation. Their wordsmith abilities made my manuscript sing!

And to Cancer Kim Weiss, who nurtured this project along by opening door after door for me.

To Reed Bernstein, who gave me terrific guidance and advice, including the Capricorn credo, "Take your time and get this right!" Those were words I lived by.

To Scorpios Philip Sedgwick, Stacy, Zoë and Nancy: As only Scorpios can, they challenged and motivated me to keep digging deeper to identify just what I wanted to say. Their insightful reviews of my manuscript let me know not only what worked, but also what needed clarification. Sometimes, their silence about something was all they needed to "say." And to HCI art director, Scorpio Larissa Henoch, who generously extended her creativity and made creating the artwork for this book a joy.

To Peter Vegso, who, in typical Aquarian fashion, shocked me by offering me the golden opportunity to publish this book.

To Drs. Ron and Mary Hulnick, whose Spiritual Psychology Program at the University of Santa Monica taught me how beautifully psychology and spirituality can be intertwined. Much of what I learned from them is reflected thoughout this book.

To my Sagittarian friend, Reverend Cathy Norman, who not only kept me laughing and optimistic, but also designed the concept for the book's cover according to my heart's desire.

To my parents, Taurus Millie and Gemini Joe, who encouraged my interest in astrology by making astrological conversation a normal household occurrence (as it should be).

To my beloved spiritual teachers, John-Roger and John Morton, who continually hand me wisdom on a silver platter. Indeed, they are every sign to me. I thank them, and my soul thanks them.

To Muriel, whose Libran balance and clarity kept my astrology practice flowing and organized, even when I was not.

And especially to my awesome husband, Richard. True to his Aries nature, he was the first to envision the idea for this book, and constantly encouraged me to run with it. His unwavering support and clear direction provided me the strong foundation from which I wrote. Truly, he is my hero every day.

Introduction

This book is *all* about you. It describes you in great detail. It may not mention you by name; still, you will recognize yourself in it. And, if you check it out, its information about you will help you to be even more successful, happy and loving.

That's because *you are every sign* of the zodiac! Never heard that before? You've probably never had your chart read by a professional astrologer. They can tell you how that works.

I'll explain it really simply. At the moment you were born, every sign of the zodiac was somewhere in the sky. The position of each sign in relation to you determines the area of your life that it influences. For example, you might express the qualities of one sign in your relationships, the qualities of another sign in your career, and still another at home with your family.

In addition to that, each planet in the solar system was also in a sign when you were born—often a different sign from your Sun Sign. Those signs' influences will also be pronounced in your life. So you're bound to express at least a little bit of the characteristics of each sign in at least one, if not a few, areas of your life.

Here's the secret to astrology: Since the position of the zodiac changes literally from moment to moment, each person is born with a combination of astrological energies all their own. That's why members of the same sign can be so alike in some ways, yet totally different in others—they are as unique as the sky was at the moment they were born. Just as you are.

Of course you'll want to learn everything you can about your Sun Sign. That's because it has a tremendous influence on who you are and almost everything you do. In fact, your Sun Sign even points to your life's purpose. *You're Every Sign!* describes the gifts, drives and personality traits of your Sun Sign, and how to use them to achieve your life's mission and to live the most satisfying life possible. The more you understand how to channel the power of your sign, the more you can flourish.

However, since you are much more than your Sun Sign (eleven signs more!), you'll gain even greater insight about yourself as you read about each sign. You probably won't have all the traits of every sign (few people do), but there's bound to be something in each sign that you resonate with and can benefit from.

Let's face it: Life is about learning. Some even say that this Earth is a schoolroom, and each of us has certain kinds of lessons we've come to learn. Each sign of the zodiac teaches a certain lesson, or life theme. You might consider your Sun Sign your "major" or what you are primarily intent on learning. But you are surely taking the courses offered by the other signs as well. *You're Every Sign!* gives you a head start in finding out what your lessons are and the resources you possess to master them. In doing so, you become more empowered and fulfilled.

Each chapter explains one sign in detail. For the sake of expediency and just plain simplicity, I have described the signs' influences as they relate to a person of that Sign. So, when I say "Aries are . . ." or "Cancers tend to . . . ," what I really mean is, "The part of *you* that's like Aries is . . ." or "The part of *you* that's like Cancer tends to . . . ," etc. That way you remember it's you, not them, I'm talking about.

You will also find (because I know you're interested) how to attract and work in relationships with people of the different signs. Knowing why the people in your life act the way they do can help you to better get along with them. It can also show you how to bring out the best qualities they possess. I've added a section about love and romance because, as life is a schoolroom, there are some classes we all look forward to.

And since spirituality is so much a part of good astrology, I've also included how to tap into and enhance your spiritual gifts. Although who we are spiritually is vastly more than anything astrology can fully explain, each sign hints at how our spirits can be better understood. With this book, you can explore how you can align more effectively with your Higher Nature, or potential, and step away from your Lower Nature, or your sign's weaknesses.

Some people believe that the challenges that go with their signs are something they have to just accept and suffer through. But that's not the case. The stumbling blocks of each sign are actually stepping-stones to learning how to strengthen the positive attributes each sign offers. *You're Every Sign!* gives you specific, step-by-step ways to do that.

I've been a professional astrologer for over two decades, during which time I have counseled thousands of people from all walks of life. I've watched how some people make the most of their abilities to create success and happiness in their lives, and how others have created lives where they feel stuck and frustrated. Usually, it's just a slight difference in their approach that makes the difference. This book describes the way you can use the qualities of *every sign* to approach life to get the most meaning and success out of it that you possibly can. In doing so, you'll be glad that you've got every sign working for you!

Whether you know much about astrology or not—or are even particularly interested in astrology or not—you can enjoy and find value in this book. After all, you *are* every sign, and this book *is* about you!

Author's Note

Your Sun Sign (or Sign) is the Sign of the zodiac the Sun was in when you were born. Sun Signs change from month to month. To find out what Sun Sign you are, check the dates at the beginning of each chapter for the period in which your birthday falls.

You may notice that the dates listed at the beginning and the end of each sign differ somewhat from those listed in newspapers or on the Internet. The reason for this is that these dates vary from year to year, depending on where the Sun really is. For clarity's sake, I have used the dates most commonly accepted for each Sign. Much of the time, the Sun goes out of one sign and into the next on the last day noted in the book (i.e., on each chapter opener page).

Chapter 1

Aries

(March 21–April 19)

Aries is the quality in you that is self-promoting and competitive, seeks to conquer new interests, and enjoys being the first (and the best) in all you do. It's also the part of you that's learning to find the essence of your "True Self."

It might be said that Aries rush in where angels—or anyone else—fear to tread. It's not that Aries folks are necessarily foolhardy—it's more that Aries are fast . . . and often impatient. So, hurry up!

Acting on the essence of being the very first sign of the zodiac, Aries seek to be the first and the best at all they do. They are incredibly spontaneous and immediate: If something sparks their interest (many things do), Aries charge right for it, using their confidence and determination to lead the way. Initiating projects is what Aries excel at. They can spot opportunities long before others do, and they use their self-motivating skills to get things going. In doing so, Aries continually distinguish themselves as trailblazers and innovative leaders, achieving things that set new standards for others to reach. But since Aries are easily bored with what's already established, the minute things are up and running, they start looking around for the next new project to tackle.

Aries are Conquerors at heart. They enjoy doing battle and emerging triumphant over anything or anyone that challenges them. Nothing satisfies Aries more than winning: Their competitive spirit is undefeatable, their spirits are resilient, and they do what it takes to be number one. Aries are resourceful and quick to adapt. So, if one approach doesn't work, Aries will swiftly resort to another, intent on winning the "gold."

The Aries Mission: Finding the Inner "I Am"

All of us are learning what Aries are born to discover: There is an essential "I" which truly runs our show. Some call it the Higher Self, others call it the True Self, still others call it "The Big Me." Whatever it's called, Aries are driven to discover the "I" that is themselves. The way most Aries attempt to do that is by jumping fully into life. Aries figure the more they experience themselves living life, the more they will discover about themselves. And that's true . . . up to a point, at least. But there comes a time when Aries need to turn inward to find what really makes them tick.

Aries don't need to keep making things happen in order to attempt to know themselves; they can know themselves no matter what happens. Then, Aries overcome the distracting impulses of the "little me" and tap into the power and the wisdom of their "I" that is great, expansive and truly heroic. That also shifts Aries out of any feelings of being alone, to a grand experience of feeling connected to "the force." From there, Aries lead themselves and others to activities that expand and reflect their nature, and conquer those lower passions that led them astray.

The Aries Challenge: Diving in the Deep End Before They Remember Whether or Not They Can Swim

Often, Aries decide to give the wisdom of their Higher Self a try because they end up getting into hot water when they don't. If Aries impatiently drive after the impulses of their Lower Nature, they can hurry and create situations they wish they hadn't. For example, Aries can let their warrior qualities incite them into dominating and conquering others with a spirit of "againstness" or anger, which can leave them feeling terribly lonely. Or Aries could become so headstrong and determined to get what they want that they end up risking losing what they truly value. Another scenario is that they can even self-reliantly push and force matters, only to crash into a brick wall. This urge to experience before thinking things through is Aries' greatest teacher. It points to the fact that an important ingredient in everything they do needs to be the presence of their wise Self.

When Aries realize that it's important to look ahead to the possible results, including possible problems they may create by doing the things they're tempted to do, they begin to open to their inner wisdom. In doing so, they start to distinguish between their Lower Nature, which prompts them to do things out of self-interest and combativeness, and their Higher Nature, which encourages them to do things that expand them and lend support to others. It's that Higher Nature they're seeking. In finding it, Aries can create a life that is one long stream of excitement and accomplishment, wherein they and others are greatly benefited and amazed.

The Aries Key: Take a Breath, Then Look Before You Charge into the Burning Building

The key for Aries is *patience.* If Aries could manage to take just enough time to consider their actions before doing them, they give themselves a chance to tap into and align with the direction of their wise inner essence. From there, Aries can better recognize what is really worth jumping into, and what's best left alone. Another benefit of being patient is that it gives life a chance to unfold in a way that might be far better than had Aries forced it.

As one Aries who learned the value of patience once said, "When I'm patient, it gives the Universe time to work its magic and help me out!" With that approach, he realized that patience wasn't non-action (which is what Aries fear it to be); rather, it was a distinctly active (and smart) approach. But Aries will learn about patience through experience. No one can force them to be patient.

The Battering RAM

The Ram is the symbol of the sign Aries, because in many ways Aries behave like rams. Just as a ram charges forward to meet its challengers head-on, so do Aries charge to confront life's challenges. Actually, Aries are head-on about everything they do: If something catches their interest, Aries surge right for it.

Aries are head*strong:* They have clear intentions of what they want and they courageously set out to make it happen. Like rams, Aries are fierce contenders. They thrive on competition and are quick to butt heads to assert their dominance. And, if you've ever watched how a ram fearlessly fights, even to great physical peril, to establish itself as the leader, you'll know how Aries fearlessly fight to conquer anything or anyone in their drive to establish themselves as the head man or woman.

Many Aries even look like rams. Their head tilts forward as if they are butting their way through life, and their foreheads and eyebrows seem to have the swoop of the ram's.

Fiery FIRE Sign (Can Be Hotheaded, Too)

Aries are Fire Signs, which means they are Fiery by nature: If they decide they want to do something, they do it *right now*. Fire gives Aries excitement: Just as a little spark can turn into a bonfire, so does a little interest of Aries blaze into a consuming passion. Aries will get fired up and enthusiastically plunge into any new project, idea or relationship that comes along, investing themselves fully until they get what they are after. But just as fire can burn out, so does Aries' interest in a matter the minute it gets too familiar or the least little bit boring.

Aries' unique expression of Fire is their ever-present, burning desire to discover and express themselves. Aries will seek to discover themselves by asserting themselves in every situation they encounter, with an intention of "conquering" it. That conquering can be through learning its secrets, establishing themselves as the best, or dominating the others who are involved. Fire prompts Aries to do all they do with a passionate sense of "I." Always they consider "Who am I (in this)?"

Of all signs, Aries are the most spontaneous and immediate. They live *in the moment*. They are focused on right now: what they want right now, who they believe they are right now, what they are doing right now. That translates to Aries being fully present in their every activity, and prepares them to take full advantage of what's offered. But, when the moment changes, so do Aries, and their Fiery passions can easily shift away from one subject, to feeling passionate about the next.

Aries' emotions are also quite immediate. Aries intensely experience whatever they feel in the moment. When they are happy, they are really happy; when they are mad, they are really mad. But like everything else about Aries, their emotions are fast-moving. Aries usually manage to release their feelings in a flash, the minute they express them. They aren't given much to introspection or emotional probing. Aries don't need to go to great depths to try to figure why they have a certain feeling—they just know they do, they experience and/or express it, and, then, it's over and on to the next.

Being the first of the Fire Signs, Aries' passions are sparked by all things new. They live life creating a constant stream of new experiences, new projects, new ideas. Aries keep themselves new as well. Instead of defining themselves according to past experiences or triumphs, Aries keep changing and growing, ready for the next adventure that might give them another clue about who they are.

Fire also blesses Aries with an undying optimism. They insist on looking at the glass as part full—even when it's close to empty. If there is just the slightest chance that something can happen or be made good, Aries are eager to try it. This optimism feeds Aries' enthusiasm and helps them to make the absolute most of whatever possibilities and opportunities they are given. So, instead of letting themselves get discouraged or sour if things get tough, Aries use their gumption to improve matters. That's why you'll hear countless stories of Aries triumphing over even the harshest conditions, and making something magnificent out of themselves and their lives.

Aries' optimism also makes them exciting to be around because they don't wait for matters to be fun and adventuresome, they bring fun and adventure to whatever they do.

Aries' Fiery optimism leads to one of their greatest assets: their distinctly positive charge. It's Aries' positivity that invites the best things in their lives to happen. Positivity also makes Aries magnetic: Others want to be a part of their open and expansive vision. And Aries' positivity is downright contagious. They are so sure that matters are good that everyone around begins to see it, too.

Aries' Fiery energy fills them up with so much drive—so great an urgency to experience—that they want to jump headfirst into any and every experience. They are challenged, therefore, to be wise about their actions by taking a moment to check in and see what part of themselves is urging them forward. As Aries learn to direct their powerful enthusiasm toward experiences that will truly promote and uplift them, they can let the other ones—enticing as they might seem in the moment—move on by.

The CARDINAL Quality of Aries: Dynamically Initiating (Everything, All Over the Place)

Aries is one of the four Cardinal Signs (Cancer, Libra and Capricorn are the other three), which makes them quite dynamic, with a drive to initiate. Because Aries is the very first of the Cardinal Signs, Aries' urge to initiate is intensely essential: They initiate everything. New missions, new relationships, new approaches—new, new, new is what Aries is all about.

When initiating, Aries experience a surge of power, enthusiasm and commitment that helps them bring new ideas into form. Indeed, getting matters started is the elixir of life for Aries, and nothing is more heady and exciting. Their keen foresight and intuition spots what is possible, and their confidence and determination make it appear. But once things are established, Aries lose interest and are on to initiating something else. Aries' Cardinal energy becomes cranky and impatient with details or structure—those are for someone else to oversee, not Aries. Their job is to make things happen.

Aries also express their Cardinal energy by being direct and clear about how they feel the moment they feel it. If something should set an Aries off, they can hardly bear to hold it in, even for a few seconds. They've got to express it and get it fixed—now! So, instead of taking the time to reflect on finding just the right words to convey their concerns (like Air Signs do), or allowing hurts to smolder until they've become exaggerated out of proportion (like Water Signs do), Aries say distinctly what's wrong—and what they want instead. Although others might find Aries' confrontations uncomfortable, Aries consider it to be honesty and "just telling it like it is."

Aries is what's known as a **Personal Sign.** That means that their primary life lesson is about developing and caring for themselves. This complements the Aries' mission of discovering their True Self. Personal Signs seek to satisfy their need to know themselves in whatever they do and in whatever happens around them. They are learning to follow the advice, "To thine own self be true."

Personal Signs needn't change the world, they simply need to awaken and understand themselves. But as they do that, their spirits shine so brightly, that they do, indeed, make a tremendous impact on others.

The challenge that goes with being a Personal Sign is particularly critical to Aries: figuring out just who the True Self is. Aries are sorting out what part of their nature is their True Self (and should be developed) and what part of their nature is their False Self (and should be released).

This can be a lifelong lesson. One key for Aries (and the rest of us) is to look beyond the ego's demands and personality traits for clues about who they truly are. That's because personalities and egos are simply tools to manage this world. It's their *Spirit* that Aries are truly hunting for. When they tap into that energy, Aries are brilliant, wise and powerful.

When Aries use their intentions to be true to themselves by being true to their Spirit, they are naturally expansive, and unceasingly optimistic. Life is one fun adventure when Aries are in touch with their True Self, because they realize that no matter what they do, *they* are there. They understand that they have the fullness that overflows to understanding and supporting others, which they will do in the most creative and insightful ways.

But if Aries simply develop their ego, or personality, they risk becoming extremely selfish and self-involved. They will be consumed by their little "I." When that happens, everything becomes about Aries: "I want this," "I think that," indeed, no other sign can emphasize the word "I" like Aries. This constant focus on themselves leaves Aries very little room for recognizing others' needs, considerations or even contributions to their lives. That kind of selfishness keeps Aries immature and reactive, unable to deal with matters if they don't go their way. But worse, it robs Aries of what they are truly after: the truth of their essence.

If Aries realize they are being selfish (or someone tells them they are), they can expand into their greater essence by remembering that their spirits are great enough to encompass other people and their needs. Indeed, by acknowledging others' needs, opinions and gifts, Aries can learn more about life, and, in doing so, discover even more about themselves.

The MARTIAL Influence

The sign Aries is ruled by Mars. Mars governs self-promoting actions like assertion, competition, dominance and sexual drives, and Aries can express these qualities fully. Mars gives Aries an undeniable urge to assert themselves and get what they want out of life. There is nothing patient about Martian energy—it wants what it wants when it wants it. And that pretty much describes the Aries nature. They want their needs and desires fulfilled *right away.*

Mars gives Aries a relentless, enduring passion for life, which they express through their confidence, sexuality and feistiness. It fills them with high energy that sets them on their way to wring the absolute most out of life. Aries never, ever wait on the sidelines. They are completely involved, usually to the point of becoming the dominating leader, in whatever they do.

Mars makes Aries direct. They go from point A to point B in the quickest, most efficient way possible. Aries walk directly, talk directly and look others directly in the eye. If Aries likes you, they will be direct (indeed, very direct) about it. If they don't like you, they'll be direct about that, too. This directness gives Aries a kind of simplicity: They are interested or they're not, they are involved or they are not, they are in love or they are not. Aries don't take the time to reflect on the "rightness" of something—they feel it instinctively . . . or they do not.

Since Mars rules speed it makes Aries fast. They are fast thinkers, fast movers, and fast to know what (and who) they want and don't want. Aries do everything in a speedy fashion, from the way they drive their cars, to the way they decide their careers, to the way they tend to conquer a project.

While others are still lacing up their running shoes, Aries have already run around the track a few times.

Aries' best use of their Martian speed and directness is to go quickly toward and straight for first discovering, then expressing, their Higher Nature. Why fool around with anything less?

Mars is named after the Roman god of war, and Aries have a warrior quality about them. They use their headstrong will to slash through any obstacles and slay any contenders that stand in the way of their getting what they want. Mars gives Aries a taste for battle, which they demonstrate in their zeal for competition and their willingness to fight to establish themselves as primary in their every endeavor.

Many Aries choose careers in the military or sports as a way of expressing their warrior energy. But Aries will express their Martian aggressiveness in any career they choose by making sure they are the dominating leaders.

Mars also gives Aries a temper, and many Aries have to deal with feelings of intense anger, even rage. Mars' anger isn't a slow-burning kind of anger, either. Rather, it's a fast burst of fire. It's there—all at once—and Aries (and others) have to deal with it. Most Aries express their anger quickly, and get it all out. Then, for Aries, it's forgotten.

However, the recipients of Aries' anger might be left quite scorched. They can be deeply hurt and offended by Aries' outbursts, and foster continuing feelings of resentment, as well as fear that it might happen again. That surprises Aries: They figure they were just expressing themselves, they got over it, why doesn't everyone else? Aries have to realize that others aren't as resilient as they are—or as fireproof. They need to understand that there can be blisters that need healing from their temporary blast of anger.

Many Aries use the powerful energy that comes from anger to fuel their actions. If mad, Aries can be fearless and intensely directed. Anger can seem like sheer power to Aries, and they can channel it into making things happen. However, Aries risk getting "addicted" to the power and passion of Mars' anger energy, and use it as their primary motivator. Instead of Aries connecting with the power and determination that comes from their wise inner core, Aries will ride on angry feelings of "againstness" and pit themselves against anything, anytime.

As powerful as this may seem to Aries, it actually throws them off track. Anger contracts Aries, and severely limits their overall view of the big picture. They not only sacrifice their creativity and openness while angry, they also cut themselves off from all kinds of support that could be available to them, from their own inner truth to the love and assistance of others. But mainly, anger causes Aries to relinquish their number one greatest asset: their positive take on life.

The Aries Archetypes: Follow Me! (Whether You Want To or Not)

In their mission to discover their True Selves, Aries (and those who are Aries-like) will demonstrate the archetype of the Conqueror, the Leader and the Trailblazer.

The Conqueror

Aries will demonstrate the Conqueror archetype with their intense drive to "do battle" in an attempt to vanquish anything (and anyone) that challenges them. This "doing battle" is Aries' great motivator. They are excited and compelled by the notion that they could overcome any obstacles and then emerge triumphant. Aries have a need to prove (to themselves, mainly) that they have the power and the ability to attain whatever goals they set their sights on. As my Aries client, Agapi, says, "Darling, I want to bring home the trophy!"

Aries' Conqueror likes to make life into a series of missions. They set goals, and then use their considerable determination to reach (i.e., conquer) those goals. Aries set themselves on missions in everything they do. They will make it their mission to achieve highest honors at work, but they'll also make it their mission to find the shortest line at the grocery store. And when Aries are on their missions (which they are every minute) that's all they care about: Their focus is singular, their intention to succeed is clear, and nothing, but nothing, can distract them. Their attitude is, "This won't get the best of me—I'll get the best of it." Missions inspire Aries to be the valiant Conqueror who will prevail.

Aries' Conqueror archetype is intended to inspire them to turn any "I can'ts" into "I cans," and gives them the confidence and the determination to achieve their dreams.

In doing so, Aries' Conqueror can make them downright heroic. They will display tremendous courage, foresight and creativity, and pull off feats that astound everyone, including themselves. If someone tells an Aries they can't do something, just watch their Conqueror prove that person wrong. Aries' Conqueror has the indomitability of an army of soldiers driven toward victory.

However, Aries are in charge of maturing and directing their Conqueror energy. If they don't, it can run them ragged. Untamed, Aries' Conqueror energy turns combative and makes life one long series of battles. Instead of conquering their own fears and Lower Natures, Aries will instead use their conquering energy to "go against" life and people. They will set out to destroy something or someone just for the sport of being the victor. Anger and irritation will likely be Aries' motivating power, and they will search for people or things they can dominate or fight with. In doing so, Aries become negative and defensive, which is a shame because it thwarts Aries' expansive, heroic disposition. Instead, they remain reactive and mad, feelings that hold Aries back from achieving the prize they truly want: aligning with their Higher Nature.

It also keeps them alone. When Aries feel they have to conquer the world, they'll even try to conquer those who are offering them friendship and love. But Aries won't see that. They'll be blinded by their projection that there's a war on, and they interpret everyone's actions as somehow against them. Aries will frequently justify that others are against them because they're "just jealous" of them. The truth is, they are fed up with Aries trying to conquer them.

Instead, Aries are learning to use their conquering energies to vanquish and release the limitations of their Lower Nature. These energies give Aries the ability to triumph over those things that hold them back—like reactiveness, impatience and self-involvement—so there's more room for Aries to express their Higher Nature, which is courageous, generous and grand.

Winning—at anything and everything—is very much a part of the Aries' Conqueror nature. Aries' Conqueror has a simple interpretation of life's order: Either they are the winner or they are not. And Aries really, really want to be the winner.

Aries' Conqueror energy gives them a drive to dominate. They want to be the one on top of everything they tackle. They want to be the "-est" of whatever they consider important: the strong*est*, fast*est*, smart*est*, rich*est* or sex*iest*. To Aries, "second best" means loser. They want to be out front, better than *everyone* else, and they will do whatever it takes to achieve that. This urge to dominate can motivate Aries to reach deep into their nature to discover and develop their greatest assets.

Aries' Conqueror also seeks to dominate by controlling everything that *involves* them. Aries have very clear ideas of what they want in every circumstance, and they'll set out to make that happen. In many cases, Aries are able to achieve dominance simply by carrying on doing what they envision with such self-confidence and assurance that others are tempted to follow. But if someone else is controlling the scene, Aries will attempt to wrestle the reins out of their hands so they can steer matters according to their vision.

Aries also like to dominate by having the best ideas. In other words, they absolutely love being *right*. (Well, don't we all?) But Aries will promote their ideas, point out when their ideas are superior, and continue to hammer away with their arguments to prove that their ideas are the ones that should be adhered to. Truly, however, the only ones they need to convince are themselves.

If Aries carry this too far, they will insist on having everything their way to the point of trying to dictate the actions of everyone around them. They'll bark orders and impatiently demand that others do exactly as they say.

Predictably, when using their Conqueror energies to dominate others, Aries will cut off a few heads. Aries will set themselves on one, clear-sighted track to get what they want, and if someone happens to be in their way, or tries to thwart them, they will be treated as a foe. Aries will do or say something so quickly, and so powerfully, the other person is cut to shreds, thrown to the wayside, and Aries are back on their way. This cutting people to shreds isn't necessarily something Aries intend to do—and many times they don't even realize they've done it. All they know is what they want, and if—oops!—someone got in the way, well, they shouldn't have been there in the first place.

Aries' Conqueror energy loves the adrenaline rush of confrontation. Aries thrive on the power and sparks they feel from facing a contender. Instead of trying to downplay any differences they have with others (as Libras do), Aries enjoy bringing them up, and having an in-your-face discussion. Aries are able to channel any tension, fear or righteousness from a confrontation right into their personal power bank and recycle it as raw energy.

So, whereas fights can deflate and discourage some signs (Cancer, Pisces and Libra especially), Aries can be enlivened by them. One thing is for sure: most Aries don't avoid them. After all, like Rams, Aries are confident when going head to head with another. They intend to do their best. At the very least, they will stand up for themselves; at the very best, they'll consider that they "won."

Aries' Conqueror thrives on competition. In their need to distinguish themselves as the dominating best, Aries will compete with anyone and everyone, anytime, any place. They'll compete with their boss to see who's *really* in charge; they'll compete with their best friend to see who can get the first promotion; they'll even compete against a traffic light to see if they can "beat" it!

Competition can bring out the very best aspects of Aries' Conqueror. That's especially true if they approach competition the smart way—and use it to bring out their personal best. When Aries use the challenge of competition to compel them to discover and develop what they're made of, they are all the more expanded and enhanced by their competitive experience. In other words, if Aries use competition *for* themselves instead of *against* anyone else, they can expand. Many times, Aries will tap into qualities and traits they didn't even know they had, until their competitor brought it out in them. When riding on the heady energies of competition, Aries move far out of their comfort zones, using their determination and creativity to access their highest potential.

However, competition can just as easily bring out the very worst of Aries. If Aries approach competition like it's a "fight" where winning means that someone else must *lose,* or even be "crushed" or dominated (even if it's just the defeated's ego), Aries can turn their determination into ruthlessness. When winning has an "againstness" quality to it, Aries can become quite negative and combative. Worse, Aries squander their energies and creativity on trying to bring their competitor down, rather than channeling their energies to building up their own personal strengths. In the end, Aries might triumph, but their positive spirit is sacrificed. That way they lose.

Aries' competitive nature is so strong that many times they don't even know they're competing. One way they can detect if they are is if they feel separate from others. The negative use of competition puts Aries at odds with others. It might prove that Aries are on top, but that top might be very lonely.

I once counseled a brilliant Aries woman who facilitated personal growth seminars. She complained to me that she was frustrated because the women in her seminars seemed to continually distance themselves from her and resist her input. That decreased her effectiveness measurably. She guessed the cause of this problem was that women were jealous of her because she was so beautiful. (Aries consider themselves gorgeous.) I asked her if she was putting out any competitive energy, because that could surely turn people off. She replied,

"No. There's really no need for me to compete with other women because I am always the prettiest woman in the room." But that very response exposed that she was, indeed, competitive. She wasn't just confident in her looks, she was comparing herself with others, and coming out the winner.

Aries can keep themselves from even the temptation of misusing competitive energies when they resolve to simply compete with themselves. When Aries set an intention to continually challenge themselves to find and further develop their own gifts, regardless of what everyone else is doing, they are directing their energies in the way they were intended: toward expanding their own lives.

Aries' Conqueror energies draw them to careers that call for the excitement of self-promotion. Aries' Conqueror isn't attracted to one career path over another. Rather it supports Aries' careers by giving them a drive and an intention to be the very best at, and work to the very top of, any profession they choose. However, because Aries' Conqueror energy finds it difficult to be told what to do, it's best if there's a degree of independence about whatever careers Aries choose.

Parents will see their Aries child's urge toward dominance/competition right off. Aries children use the authority and the power of their parents (the father, usually) to develop their own. They will do that by challenging every parental policy, competing with Mom and Dad for who's right and who's in control, and basically setting themselves up against their parents' rules. Although this can be annoying—at least for Aries parents—they are in a position to teach their Aries child the rules of fair play in competition, as well as to reveal the fact that they cannot, and need not, dominate everybody.

The Leader

Aries demonstrate the Leader archetype because they are driven to be the first, and the best at whatever they do. Aries have a natural urge to step to the front of the line and lead the way. They are, in fact, most confident and direct as leaders. Aries know exactly what they intend to accomplish (their mission, after all) and they use everything they've got to get there. Aries' leadership style is simple: their way or the highway.

In fact, there is a loner quality to Aries' leadership. They depend only on themselves to get where they are going. The tag line "army of one" very much describes Aries' leadership approach. So, instead of seeking support or consensus from others, Aries use their own enthusiasm and determination to propel them toward their vision. Aries act as if they were born to lead. And they were.

Aries can apply their leadership skills to whatever careers they choose. But they do have a penchant for wanting to do their own thing. So, the Leader archetype might help Aries choose careers in which they have their own practice or business. If they are part of another's business, or a corporation, they will demonstrate their leadership skills by wanting to be the manager, the boss, the CEO—any position that lets them call the shots, at least for themselves, if not for others.

But not every Aries is a Leader of others. What Aries choose to lead depends on how they see themselves. If Aries only identify themselves with their individual self, they will feel charged with leading only themselves. In doing so, they give themselves missions to accomplish, and concern themselves solely with whether or not they are being personally successful.

However, if an Aries' identity includes something or someone else—like their family, their corporation or a world situation—they will set out to lead them with the same fervor and direction as they do themselves. Then, Aries come up with missions those people or situations should achieve, and lend their leadership skills to make it happen.

Interestingly, Aries don't lead from a vision of what's right for everyone (unlike other leadership-oriented signs like Capricorn, Leo and Scorpio). They usually don't care about that. Rather, Aries lead from a vision of what's right for themselves and their ideas of what should happen. Any others involved are considered assets to help Aries in carrying out their mission. Aries never assumes to know what's best for others. They figure that's their business.

When Aries lead, they lead. They are quick decision makers, fast executers, and expect others to keep up. They dictate the orders, and expect others to carry them out—now! They refuse to hold others' hands, or check in to make sure others can work as fast as they. If they can, fine; they are part of Aries' team. If they can't, they are not. Aries don't have time to wait.

Aries are groundbreaking Leaders. They don't care whether or not something has been tried before, it's all the better if it has not. Nor do Aries feel intimidated by attempting to do what thousands of others have already tried and failed at. Aries trust in the superiority and creativity of their own direction. They are confident that they will be the one that figures out the way to get the gold.

This confidence, however, does not come from Aries' careful

planning or extensive research. They don't lead that way. The truth is, Aries usually have no idea how they are going to achieve their missions. They just set out after the objective, trusting that, as they take one step, the next step will show up. And usually they are right. Aries have uncanny instincts and intuition, which recognize avenues of opportunities the moment they appear. This can make others nervous until they witness Aries pulling off amazing feats, time and time again.

However, Aries aren't always right. At times their leadership energy is so impatient, and so driven to *make* things happen—their way—that Aries lose touch with their instinctive wise core. Then they become deaf to important feedback, either from others or from life, that they are off track, and that their leadership is not working. Aries' confidence turns into headstrong arrogance, and they assume they are on target, even when they are off.

One way Aries can tell if they are driving off course is if they think they have to push or force matters or people. When Aries try to get what they want by dominating, suppressing or ignoring others, chances are their leadership is coming from their overblown ego, rather than their wisdom. Aries will rant and rave impatiently, demanding that others "get with it," instead of using their instincts to flow with what's right. Aries can become intensely determined that matters be carried out their way, and their way only. They'll dismiss, undercut, even destroy other people's ideas and contributions, even if—or especially if—they are good ones. Aries can even forgo their natural honesty, and stoop to manipulating and scheming. Neither one is an Aries strong suit, which is a sure sign they are not in alignment with their truest power.

If Aries realize they are leading in an inappropriate way (or someone tells them they are), it works best if they reset their intention to do what is for the highest good for all concerned. Although this might seem a tad too lofty, or even global for many Aries, it works anyway. Intending to do what is for the highest good aligns Aries to lead with a greater mission than they alone can envision themselves. And it allows them to tap into the "force" which can then lend support to their leadership, making it truly more effective. In fact, when Aries are in alignment with that clear intention, there is a seamlessness, a type of grace or ease, that allows them to carry out their visions in the best possible manner. In doing so, others are able to express and make contributions to Aries' leadership, which is a plus for them, as well as for Aries.

Regardless of whether Aries lead a country, a dental practice or just themselves, the root of their leadership drive is an urge for self-discovery. Aries learn about who they are by experimenting with life, and leading and influencing matters is part of that. And because Aries especially love new experiences, leading ensures they can always penetrate into new territories that provide new experiences.

In truth, it's self-leadership that Aries are truly after. They are learning to apply their leadership skills toward leading themselves in positive directions, and staying true to themselves and their Higher Nature. In doing so, Aries are loving and fun and fulfilled while accomplishing the simplest acts in life. Self-leadership also entails Aries leading themselves away from any temptations of their lesser expressions, such as mere willfulness, impatience and selfishness. Being trusted leaders to themselves helps Aries in their mission of discovering their highest essence.

As part of their destiny of learning self-leadership, Aries are likely to go through periods when they feel very alone. And, at times, they very likely are. In (rightly) answering the call to be true to themselves, Aries can come to times and places in life where no one can follow. Or, in pursuing a dream that they know they must follow, Aries might necessarily have to depart from loved ones. That teaches Aries more about being true to themselves and standing in the confidence of their spirit. Times of aloneness can strengthen Aries like nothing else can.

However, some Aries make a habit of feeling alone, unsupported, even when they don't need to be. If Aries carry their self-leadership too far they can assume that no one could possibly relate to them, help them, or love them the way they need to be. They (mistakenly) think, *I have to do everything on my own!*—and believe they should rely only on themselves. Period.

But that's only a projection. What's actually happening is that Aries have isolated themselves by closing down their ability to receive. Chances are they are afraid to seem vulnerable, and believe that needing others is a sign of weakness. Because of that, Aries will dismiss other people's attempts to love and support them.

Aries need to remember that an important part of self-leadership involves receiving love and support from others. Aries are learning that being vulnerable, or receiving the input of others, isn't weakness at all. Rather, it's a kind of strength that opens doors for even more growth and self-knowledge. It's true that Aries need to rely on themselves. But part of that is relying on themselves to ask for assistance and companionship, which can help Aries to grow and develop even more. In doing so, Aries can still be the leader, but they can have a support team that spurs them on even farther.

The Trailblazer

Aries demonstrate the archetype of the Trailblazer because they are absolutely driven to discover or accomplish something—anything—that's new. What's already known or what's been already done holds no interest for Aries. They have an innate need to push through established barriers and find out what else there is. Once again, it's the Arian ever-present drive to be the first and the best that motivates them: If Aries trailblaze and become the first at something, well, they're automatically the best.

Aries' Trailblazer energy is courageous and relentless in pursuing this new, unconquered territory. Aries are excited and motivated by the fact that they are doing something no one else ever has before. And they are creative and clever about finding avenues where they can be innovative. It's not so much that Aries sit and think to themselves, *Hmmm. What can I do that's never been done before?* Their trailblazing isn't that contrived. It's more that Aries go about doing whatever they do by always looking to test the limits, to test themselves, to challenge themselves to succeed even further. It's also true that Aries are just plain attracted to doing things that haven't been accomplished before. So, an Aires Trailblazer might be the first one in their family to get a college degree, or it might be an Aries who is the first woman president of the United States.

When Aries trailblaze, they feel fully alive and captivated. Moving into new territory is both compelling and perhaps a little scary to Aries. When Aries have thoughts like *What's going to happen next?* and *I hope I can pull this off,* it makes for an emotional cocktail of thrilling, heady excitation. That's the fun of it for Aries. The great adventure of "not knowing" keeps Aries present and on their toes. In doing so, they can tap into their essence and discover even more of who they truly are.

Aries trailblaze in every aspect of their lives. It's not something they do every once in a while. Trailblazing is their personal policy.

Aries' Trailblazer is attracted to professions in which there is always something new do to, hopefully every day. Trailblazers are attracted to any field and career that allows room for growth, experimentation and Aries' own stamp of individual approach. No matter what career Aries picks, they'll use their Trailblazer energy to try new things, push to the limits of what's been done (and accepted), and set new standards of what can be accomplished.

One of the ways Aries might trailblaze is by challenging themselves to keep pushing past the already established levels of their personal best. If they can do fifty pushups, they challenge themselves to do sixty. If they can sell two houses a month, they shoot for selling four. Or, Aries might trailblaze by pushing past other peoples' best. If the champion at an Aries' fitness club can do 1,000 pushups, an Aries might shoot for 1,001. If the top salesperson in an Aries' real-estate office sells nine houses a month, the Aries coworker might set a goal to sell ten.

Aries also trailblaze by constantly searching for, and finding, things to do that they've never done before. As my Aries client, Steven, says, "Hey, I'm up for trying anything, at least once!" So, they'll skydive one week, then it's scuba diving the next. The promise of forging something new inside themselves as they conquer each new experience is what spurs Aries on.

Furthermore, Aries trailblaze by finding new and innovative ways to do what they're doing. Instead of taking the route that's agreed upon by most, an Aries will think, *I can do better than this,* then devote their creative skills to finding a superior approach. For example, the same client Steven was a Trailblazer in his medical profession. Long before anyone else recognized how significant insurance companies and HMOs were going to become in healthcare, Steven saw it. He got busy and established relationships with most of the major insurance companies, so they would refer clients exclusively to his practice. The other doctors thought he was nuts. But Steven's foresight allowed him to tap into a very successful and lucrative niche.

This foresight and innovation is a huge part of Aries' Trailblazer archetype. Aries not only have the drive to do things in a new way, they have the instincts to figure out what that new way is. If there is an opportunity, or a good idea, or a new possibility, Aries are on it.

Aries' Trailblazer thrives on, needs and continually creates new projects to work on. One time I asked an Aries friend what made him happy. "New projects," he said. When I asked him what he feared the most, he said, "No new projects." Aries need something to work toward. This isn't because they are industrious (like Virgos and Capricorns) and need to continually produce something. It's more that they need something to *tackle.*

Here's an important point about Aries' tackling something: When they do, they're done. Once an Aries discovers the secret of something (or someone), or gets good enough at something, they are satisfied.

That's because most Aries have short attention spans. Unless something continually challenges or excites them, they quickly become bored. And once Aries' passionate interest wanes, they're gone. Although they want to be the best at something, Aries don't want to be the best if that means enduring prolonged periods of boredom or predictability.

So an Aries who wants to be a champion figure skater can stay with the sport most of her early life because there is always a new level she can achieve. But most Aries don't want to be the champion if it's going to take that long. They want to get into an interest, take their best shot, and, if it doesn't hold their attention, they are out of there. Pronto.

Countless are the Aries who have books written up through chapter three, a closet full of canvases of half-painted pictures, or professional licenses that have expired because they just lost interest.

This need to stay stimulated can tempt Aries into quitting something before they truly receive the rewards that it offers. Sometimes that's okay. Aries don't need to be proficient at everything they try—there's just not enough time. But, if Aries show promise at something, it might be wise if they use their Conqueror's resolve to resist their urge to move on, and pursue what they're doing even further.

Andrew's decision to resist his urge to stop playing the piano really paid off. When he first came to see me, Andrew told me he was getting antsy and bored with the piano, even though he was just starting to get really good. He was considering dropping it and taking up the drums instead. But since his chart indicated that success was coming in a year, if he was prepared for it, I urged him to hang in there, at least for that long. In a little less than a year, Andrew was invited to play the piano in a jazz band. He absolutely loved it. Had he deserted playing the piano, he would have missed out on that opportunity. He also might have missed meeting the lead singer, who later became his wife.

Boredom is one of the greatest challengers of Aries' Trailblazer energy. Because they are so wired to trailblaze, Aries can think something is wrong if there is nothing new in their lives to pursue. It can be excruciating for an Aries to stay in a job, a project or even a relationship after they have found out what they want to know about it. There's no new territory to explore. So many Aries live their lives moving from project to project, house to house, or relationship to relationship, trying to satisfy their trailblazing desire to find the new. But eventually that can get tiring and boring itself, even to Aries.

What works best when Aries find they are bored, distracted and tempted to bolt is to trailblaze their *approach* to the matter. If they find there are absolutely no new ways they can do their job, for example, Aries can trailblaze taking a new *attitude* about it. In doing so, Aries might find a whole new world of possibilities right inside their own consciousness.

Ellie had great results when she changed her approach to her job. She was bored in her job as customer-service rep and wanted to move on. But because there were no new job prospects, she was feeling quite trapped. So Ellie decided to change her approach to her job by challenging herself to be the best service rep in the store. That turned Ellie from a sour, snippy customer rep to Employee of the Year.

One trap is that Aries' Trailblazer energy can get Aries addicted to *doing*. And all their doing and exploring might get Aries distracted from their main purpose, which is self-discovery. Sometimes, Aries just need to *be* with themselves, and doing ordinary, familiar things can be a good forum for that. When Aries turn their trailblazing urge toward discovering new vistas within their own consciousness, they are using it for its highest purpose. Then, they can move past who they thought they were, and forge even deeper insight into who they truly are. That is truly rewarding for Aries.

The Aries Gifts: Self-Determination and Resiliency of Youth

One of Aries' most relied upon gifts is their **Self-Determination.** It gives them the clear-sighted, singular-focused, stop-at-nothing drive and intention to go for—and get—what they want. Aries' determination is so primal, so intense, they sometimes describe it as having a mind of its own; it's almost as if their determination drives the Aries instead of the other way around.

Sandy confessed her Arian determination almost cost her her marriage. She had fallen in love with, and was determined to buy, a penthouse in the city. The problem was that her husband did not want to move there, and no amount of salesmanship or badgering from Sandy would change his mind. So, in her red-hot determination to live where *she* wanted, Sandy resolved that she would just buy the penthouse herself, and her husband could join her or not. Sandy didn't realize she was setting up a divorce; her focus was just so intent on what she wanted.

Fortunately, thanks to the calming intervention of her friends, it eventually dawned on Sandy that she was making her determination more important than her marriage. She backed down. It was hard for her to do then, and it's hard for her today. But she says she now uses her determination to hang on to what she values (her marriage) over her determination to get what she wants (the penthouse, even though she still would like it).

Most Aries experience the same kind of challenges with their self-determination as Sandy did. They have to evaluate whether or not their determination is driving them to achieve something that promotes their bigger vision or important values in life, or if their determination is just a herd of wild horses taking them to a destination they haven't truly thought through.

Fearlessness is another Aries gift. Mars fills Aries with so much adrenaline to make things happen that they can seem—and be—downright fearless. They say and do things the rest of us wouldn't dare to, and they make it look like it's the most natural thing in the world.

In reality, Aries have fears and insecurities like the rest of us, but they relate to them differently than most. Whereas most signs let their fears and insecurities hold them back, or at least caution them, Aries are loath to consider that they might make them "wimpy." They can't bear the thought that their fears might control them. After all, they won't let anyone in life hold them back, so why should they let their fears? As a result, Aries use their fears as motivators. If Aries feels intimidated to speak publicly, they'll sign up to do a talk. Or, if Arians fear they won't be up to a project, they'll volunteer to be its organizer. If an Aries dreads telling her mother-in-law that she hates the present she bought her, Aries will call first thing in the morning and tell her so. No fear is going to get the best of Aries.

Aries also have the gift of **Innocence.** Being the first sign of the zodiac, they appear to be seeing, or doing, things for the very first time. That gives Aries a fresh approach to whatever they do. Instead of getting jaded or presumptive about how life is, Aries have a way of taking each moment for what it is. Not only does this keep Aries alert to the fun and opportunities that are in every situation, it also adds to Aries being able to take an innovative approach to even the most established of situations.

Aries' innocence also makes them seem constantly **Renewed, Young, and "With-It,"** no matter what their chronological age. That granny you see in a sports car is an Aries enjoying life.

This innocence leads Aries to be **Self-Reliant.** They will try things others would never think of, let alone do. Instead of worrying about whether or not something will work, or if others have tried and failed, Aries will jump in and see for themselves whether or not they can pull something off. Aries want to learn through their own experience. So they tend to dismiss other people's guidance, even their warnings about life, and instead discover for themselves what works and what doesn't. As has been pointed out before, this approach can lead Aries to crashing into brick walls. But unless they had the experience, they wouldn't have believed those walls existed. That same "trying for themselves" approach leads Aries into priceless discoveries, both about life and themselves.

Aries also have the gift of **Honesty.** Aries feel compelled to "say it like it is," even if that "is" is only what's true in that moment. That means that Aries are lousy liars, and usually feel pretty crummy about themselves when they attempt to. Aries are usually honest about their intentions, too: Instead of scheming or manipulating, (which takes too much time and forethought anyway), Aries will be direct and open about getting what they want. If others don't like it, they can lump it.

Aries can have loads of **Sex Appeal,** which they definitely—and unapologetically—use to their advantage. Aries have a tremendous confidence in their ability to attract others, and they like to do so, just for sport. They are as direct about their sexuality as they are about everything else. Aries don't bother with acting coy—if Aries find someone attractive they let them know it, certain they'll feel the same about them. Mars gives Aries a lusty, feisty sexual appetite. They'll use their sexuality in everything they do. Not in a seductive "come hither" way (like Scorpio)—more in a "let's spark each other up" kind of way. Flirting, winking, giving others "a look" thrills Aries, and keeps them stirred up and feeling alive.

One of the greatest Aries' gifts of all is their self-assurance in their appearance: Aries always feel gorgeous and "hot" no matter what they look like, or what shape their bodies are in. So much so that they can't help but unabashedly admire themselves in the mirror, should they come across one. Actually, Aries are so self-assured of the superiority of their sexual appeal that they can many times be convinced that others are lusting after them, even when they are not.

Aries have the gift of **Resiliency** in that, no matter what challenges they are faced with, Aries seem to make the most of them. Instead of letting life beat them, they set out to beat life. Part of Aries' resiliency comes from their optimism and positive charge. They don't truly believe that things are bad, or if they do, they're sure matters are going to get better real soon. That attitude keeps

Aries on the lookout for "the break," and ensures they'll exit their tough situation the minute a door opens for them to do so.

Aries' **Optimism and Positivity** also get them to look for the blessing each situation holds. Deep inside, Aries refuse to feel they are victims. Therefore, they are determined to focus on the good in life. So, even if it's a tiny thread of opportunity or hope that a situation holds, Aries grab on to it. Usually, however, Aries' difficulties offer more than just a tiny thread of goodness, many times there are reams and reams of blessings. Aries see these because they look for them. Because of that, Aries can bounce back from times of insecurity or sadness faster than most others can. Even after facing tough situations, Aries can renew and refresh themselves by viewing their rough spots as learning experiences. They consider themselves better people for having triumphed over whatever challenged them.

Aries are also resilient because no matter how hard they fall, they pick themselves up and try again. Part of that is their ability to stay in the moment. Just because they were down in the last moment, Aries don't feel they have to carry it over to the next. They always have hope and enthusiasm that they will prevail. And, most important, Aries get up and start prevailing.

The challenge of Aries' resiliency comes when they don't learn from their difficult situations and instead just muscle through them, anxious for them to "go away." When that happens, Aries might be in denial that they had anything to do with why things are tough. Then, they don't learn from their experiences—even if they happen over and over.

Mattie had a knack for using her Aries confrontive energies to get in knock-down screaming fights with her friends. Mattie always took the approach of "I don't know why my (ex-) friend became so angry—jealous, probably," and blew off the friendship. Always, it was the other gal's fault. Mattie would go on to make a new friend, only to have a big fight and separation with her. Eventually, Mattie came to believe that females just don't like her, and limited her friendships to only males. Too bad. Mattie's friends liked her, they just didn't like Mattie's competitiveness temper being directed at them.

Mattie would have benefited by adding a little self-reflection to her resiliency. That way, she might have realized that she had a hand in her predicaments, and could thereby start to try some different ways of behaving that might have allowed Mattie to have rewarding relationships with her galpals.

The Aries Fears: "Who Remembers the Silver-Medal Winner?"

Incredibly, Aries can **fear being inconsequential.** With all the conquering, leading and trailblazing that Aries do, they might still fear that deep down they're nobodies. Aries might compensate for that by doing more of the conquering, leading and trailblazing to prove to themselves, and others, that they are, indeed, of consequence. But that can lead to Aries getting involved in situations that are unnecessary, and take up valuable time they could spend doing things that are more true to their purpose.

Aries might find it a better strategy to quell fears of being inconsequential by digging deeper into their sense of Self. Instead of looking to prove themselves of consequence in the world, Aries are more satisfied by doing those things that have true consequence to their spirit. Things like meditation and self-reflection might not seem compelling at first to Aries, but they might reveal to Aries their True Self. And, believe me, that's of consequence! (To those Aries who are right now shaking their heads in disbelief, I say, "Give it a shot!")

Aries can also **fear seeming weak or wimpy,** like the ninety-pound weakling who others pick on. That would be unbearable for Aries. So they set out to make—and keep—themselves strong. Aries might work to create a strong body, or a strong bank account, or a strong ability to promote and defend themselves. All those assets are useful in showing Aries that they aren't weak at all.

However, it's also important for Aries to develop their own inner strength, or else they might bow to the world's ideas of what's considered strong or heroic, and sell themselves short. If Aries don't develop inner strength, they might compensate by feeling the need to prove they are strong by getting involved with things that make them look cocky or daring or powerful, but, in truth, they are not what really satisfies Aries. And it could prompt them to take risks that could threaten what they have built.

It works best when Aries seek to find the strength that comes from being true to themselves. When Aries learn to do what's right for them, they prove to themselves that they are the captain of their ship. Now, *that* takes power. By doing those things that truly satisfy Aries, regardless of whether they impress others or get their approval, Aries strengthen what they were born to empower: their alignment with their own Spirit.

Aries can also **fear becoming deflated by boredom.** Nothing new to do, conquer, learn or be takes the wind out of Aries' sails, and leaving them listless and aimless. This fear can serve Aries by keeping them on the lookout for opportunities from which they can grow. But it can also prompt Aries into taking on tasks and experiences just for the sake of keeping boredom at bay. When that happens, Aries end up distracted from their better choices, not to mention their inner essence—just in an attempt to do *something*.

Aries can wisely manage this fear by approaching times of ordinariness or boring familiarity as opportunities to have an inner adventure, challenging themselves to go about even the most ordinary moments with a curious pose of "Who's the *I* that's doing this?" In doing so, they might discover their True Self shining through. That could make a walk to the mailbox an enlightening experience. And truly, that's what Aries are after (enlightening experiences, not walks to the mailbox). Instead of needing exciting outer experiences to define themselves, Aries are looking to the expansiveness of their inner experience to know who they are.

Aries in Relationships: "First in Every Way"

Aries are as quick and direct in pursuing relationships as they are about everything else. When Aries are attracted to anyone—a possible friend, a potential lover or simply the waiter—they go for it. They want to consume that person and connect with them fully and passionately. But when Aries are no longer attracted, they are tempted to leave.

What keeps Aries attracted is excitement. They want to know that there is always something unexpected, challenging and passionate that is going to happen between them and anyone they are in relationships with.

Aries insist on being number one in any relationship they are involved in. They want to be the best friend, the best lover, the best employee, and they'll use their charm and attentiveness to make it so. Aries themselves want loads of attention—and they want it right now. It's not the best policy to tell an Aries friend you'll call her in a few weeks, or put off making love with an Aries spouse until the house is cleaned. Later is an eternity to Aries, who interpret having to wait as, "I'm not number one." Aries will feel hurt (and they'll mope) or jealous (and they'll blow), and start to wonder if you even like or love them at all. If you're genuinely busy, and can't interact with your Aries, it helps if you remind them how important they truly are to you, and give them a certain time when you'll be all theirs. Then, they can happily wait for you by entertaining themselves with a mission or two.

In love, Aries are passionate and involved. Their Conqueror energy melts into a very romantic lover and they devote themselves to being the hero in their loved one's life. They are very attentive in their affections, and sexuality is extremely important to them; it renews their creativity, encourages their ego and awakens their Spirit.

Although Aries enjoy playing the field to see whose heart they can conquer, once they finally select their beloved (and it is usually Aries who do the selecting because they are not about to wait around), they are most loyal and devoted partners.

Aries enjoy a good pursuit, and they are not intimidated if they have some competition. They know they are exciting and irresistible, and they figure it's only a matter of time until they win their beloved. They love to conquer, so let them have the impression that they are conquering you. But no game playing—Aries lose patience with dishonesty or complicated head games. Rather, give the impression that you know you are one hot prize, and they can win it if they try.

A gorgeous face or hot body can easily attract Aries' attention—and it does, regularly. Aries are extremely visually stimulated. At first, Aries might even choose partners based on physicality alone. But that could ultimately prove to be frustrating, because the true foundation for sharing and caring might be missing. (Aries will learn that from experience.)

Aries can also be attracted to someone who engages competitively with them. This can be thrilling, because it gets their juices up, with their love of winning. But Aries fall in love with the one with whom they can surrender and become their vulnerable selves with.

In truth, Aries are happiest with someone who encourages (never squelches) their enthusiasms, doesn't fall apart over the risks they take and isn't threatened by their competitive need to win. They really need someone who can stay neutral about it all. It's really great when Aries find someone with whom they feel calm, because that brings to Aries the peace that they seek.

If you are trying to catch a female Aries' eye, do something that gets her attention, and you can do that by *giving* her attention. Let her know you're noticing her, that she's appealing to you (she knows it, but appreciates your saying so), and that you would like to find out more about who she is. Then take her to fun and interesting places where she's never gone before. Remember, she loves the new.

All the while you're doing this demonstrate your personal power and your strengths, because she's looking for a partner who can match her energy and power. Don't do this in a puffed-up way where you attempt to make her feel like the "little lady." She isn't one, and she'll have no part of it. Actually, Aries women have a masculine quality that can out-male males, and she'll compete with any man who tries to take her over.

Instead, show her that you have the power and the wherewithal to respect and trust yourself, and take care of matters, and still have plenty left over to attend to her. That works because Aries women are seeking a partner who is strong and reliable enough so she can relax and yield. She yearns to express her vulnerable side, but she needs to make sure that she can trust her partner enough to open up. If she feels you're making any attempt to control her, she'll resist, and her vulnerability will close right up. If, instead, you encourage her to be herself in all her power and glory, she will make it her business to please you like you have never been pleased before, if you get my drift.

Importantly, Aries women are looking for chemistry, so let your hormones flow. She doesn't want to date a "good friend." She wants a passionate lover who helps her bring out her femininity. If you're good-looking, you'll get a faster response than if you're not. But that's just initially. If you can let an Aries woman experience your compelling inner presence, she'll think you're Fabio no matter what you look like.

If you're trying to catch the eye of an Aries male, appeal to him visually—at least at first. Wear something (in a shade of red) that broadcasts your availability, and let your sexuality show. Aries men resent uptight people, and he will be flattered by someone letting him know that they think he's hot (although he already thinks he is). Aries men are looking for someone who satisfies their passions, first and foremost. He wants to be fully engaged, wowed and made drunk with excitement. (Don't worry—if he loves you, that can happen when he watches you get up to get a glass of water.)

Aries men are at first (distractedly) attracted by physical beauty, or a sexy body, but what he's really after is chemistry. He wants to be with someone who makes him feel all man and alive. If you can do that, he'll consider you Venus herself, no matter what you look like. Compliments, sincere acknowledgments of what he's done right and well, soften him, and make him want to give even more. (This applies to sexual matters, too—perhaps even especially so.)

Because they are very masculine, Aries men love a partner who is very feminine. They love—and need—a soft touch, a loving smile, a caress that says, "You're special to me." Many Aries males crave nurturing. It helps them to relax and receive. But they hate being controlled, corrected or put-down. That makes them defensive and takes the romance out of everything. He needs a lover, not a manager.

An Aries male in love will see the Goddess in his beloved. In the world, he will be the chest-pounding Conqueror. With his partner, he will be a mush-ball of love.

Remember: An Aries male's heart is all or nothing. If you're dating an Aries who keeps dating around, forget him. If you don't bring the "all" out in him pretty quickly, it's likely you'll end up with "nothing."

The Last Word on Aries

Aries, being the first, see the world through the perception of "I Am." What they learn is that the "I" they refer to is the one of their Higher Nature.

Chapter 2

Taurus

(April 20–May 21)

Taurus is the quality in you that's stable and loyal, seeks to create security, and enjoys the rich comforts of life. It's also the part of you that's learning to recognize that you always have the resources to create true security and self-value.

When you think of Taurus, think of stable. Not the kind of stable that a bull (their symbol) stays in; rather, think of people who are very solid and steady.

In addition to being stable, Taureans are blessed with strong wills and determination, which they use to achieve whatever goals they set for themselves. Once they identify something (or someone) they desire, they steadfastly pursue it. They are patient, and instead of expecting instant results, Taureans reach their goals step-by-step, knowing that things worth achieving are worth working (and waiting) for.

Taureans are natural cultivators. They have a powerful urge, coupled with innate know-how, to make things grow and prosper. In fact, Taureans are much like farmers at heart: They pick a spot in life where they see potential for growth (for a business, maybe, or a relationship) and go about planting, then nurturing the seeds for success. Like farmers, Taureans carefully watch over and protect whatever they're cultivating, ensuring it can grow and flourish.

Taureans are also one of the most loyal and devoted signs of the zodiac. Their hearts of gold give them a tender sweetness that attracts others to them. In turn, they stand by their loved ones through all tests of time, creating a safe haven of protection and caring for them.

The Taurus Mission: Learning the Value and Security of Self

All of us are learning what Taureans are born to discover: The true essence of security and value is within us, not out in the world. And, in fact, everything they truly need will always be provided for.

The high state of Taurus is one of experiencing a fullness that comes from valuing themselves and being grateful for their lives. From there, Taureans recognize that no matter what seems to be happening around them, they possess the inner resources to be safe, secure and create plenty.

Being farmer-like, Taurus is charged with cultivating security and value, both within themselves and in the world. The key to living well for a Taurus is recognizing and using the resources that are always available. Hence, Taureans have a particular affinity for abundance: They have a tremendous ability to locate and develop value. Their practical nature is always asking, *What is available for use here?* In recognizing and making use of both their inner resources and resources of the world, Taureans are able to provide security and comfort for themselves and loved ones.

The Taurus Challenge: Learning Abundance Through Lack

Surprisingly, one way Taureans learn about the truest meaning of security and abundance is by experiencing inevitable times when they believe they lack . . . anything. Exactly what Taureans think they lack can vary depending on what's happening in their lives: lack of material security, apparent lack of worthiness, or lack of feeling lovable. Whatever Taureans feel they lack at the moment, it's scary to them. But really, lack is the most powerful teacher for Taurus. When Taureans feel lack (and note I'm emphasizing *feel* because usually it's unfounded in reality), it is a call for them to find their way out of lack. As they do, it awakens them to the truth of their existence: When they (or we, for that matter) are experiencing the innate abundance, abundance is everywhere.

Feeling lack can actually be a powerful motivator for Taurus to find the resources, both in themselves and in the world, to realize and cultivate plenty. In doing so, they eventually learn that they always have what they truly need. This is something that Taureans need to learn from experience—no one can convince them of it but themselves. As they do, they strengthen what they are here to learn: That they are already full, and that the security they seek comes from within.

The truth is, most Taureans have exactly what they need every single moment. But that doesn't mean Taureans always have what they *want*—and that's why they think they are lacking. Taureans can be blind to the fact that they have what they need because they want even more, or something else. **It really helps for Taureans to practice *wanting what they have.***

Taureans are also learning that, instead of needing things to go their way in the world in order for them to be satisfied or secure, they can be satisfied and secure within themselves—no matter what is going on around them. For example, Taureans are learning that they are worthy regardless of their bank account; or that they are lovable, whether or not anyone in the world seems to care.

The Taurus Key: Gratitude Opens the Door

Gratitude is really the secret to happiness for Taurus. It's not only the fastest antidote for feelings of lack, it reminds Taureans of the plenty they do have. Gratitude helps Taureans recognize (and better receive) the things around them that are already available. Then, gratitude takes Taurus one step further by opening them to the abundant flow of the universe. When Taureans feel grateful for what they have, they are better attuned to a higher state of awareness, which is so resourceful, it might even be called Resource Consciousness. From that state of awareness, Taureans spot the opportunities and openings where they can apply their many abilities to make things grow.

When Taureans seeks to find inner worth and inner security, they are going after their essence. When they discover that, they are truly rich. The more often Taureans choose to step out of feelings of lack or insecurity into gratitude and resourcefulness, the better and faster they get it. They will increasingly anchor into their consciousness a state of abundance and fulfillment, which is their birthright.

As Unstoppable—or as Immovable—as a BULL

The astrological symbol of Taurus is the Bull, and Taureans are indeed bull-like. They have powerful determination and strength, and they tend to make things happen by pushing and pulling them along. Like bulls, Taureans are deliberate and surefooted, preferring to take their time in everything they do. Just as it's nearly impossible to push a bull into hurrying or doing anything it doesn't want to do, Taureans resist any pressure to rush or move in a direction they don't want to go in (or even one that they do). And, just as bulls enjoy grazing contentedly in their safe and protected fields, Taureans take pleasure in their surroundings. But, if a bull—or a Taurus—thinks their territory is threatened, look out! They both will snort and stomp and push aside anything or anyone in order to protect what's theirs.

The horns of the bull signify the ability of Taureans to receive of plenty. *Receiving* is one of Taureans' most important life lessons. When they allow themselves to be open to receiving with gratitude in their hearts whatever the Universe offers them, Taureans are lifted and awakened to the magnificence of life. Taureans are able to recognize the constant flow of abundance available to them, and accept that abundance as something they deserve.

Every Taurus is destined to receive some kind of abundance. Some Taureans are destined to receive material or financial abundance. (Every Taurus reading this will be praying it's them.) Other Taureans will receive an abundance of loving relationships. But, in truth, there are countless avenues of abundance for Taureans: like the abundance of opportunities, creativity or Grace. For example, I know one Taurus musician who lives in awe of the abundance of melody that always flows through his head.

Whatever form of abundance Taureans have in their lives, they are at their best when they allow themselves to fully receive of it, without conditions, simply with gratitude. But, sometimes, Taureans feel they have to first do something to *deserve* receiving. That might prompt Taureans to knock themselves out trying to give, thinking they have to earn what they want to receive. Giving is great, but it's not necessarily a prerequisite for receiving. Just being who they are is the only requirement, and it's Taureans' job, and lesson, to understand that.

If Taureans do feel unworthy of receiving, they risk blocking themselves from doing so by ignoring, or overlooking, what others—and life—are offering them. They might refuse to look at all that's being made available, fearing that if they do check, they will find nothing there. That's painful for Taurus. What might work better is if they simply create a place in themselves that is fully *willing* to receive. (Gratitude sets them up for that.) Doing so opens them to the generosity of the Universe, and all the clever ways and avenues the Universe uses to deliver the goods. It's also important for Taureans to remember that it's as valuable to receive as it is to give. That helps them to better recognize—and accept—what's being offered to them.

Salt of the EARTH and Solid as the Rock of Gibraltar

Taureans are Earth Signs, which means they are primarily interested in (and good at!) practical, worldly matters. Taurus's Earthiness gives them the ability to manifest whatever they deem worthy, be it a bank account, a business or loving relationships. They will set a strong foundation by sticking to the basics, then build and expand upon it to manifest their goals step-by-step, inch-by-inch.

Taurus's unique expression of Earth energy is their urge to establish a comfortable, secure lifestyle that insures they and loved ones will be taken care of. They aren't as interested in the prestige or acknowledgment that success brings (like Capricorn), as much as simply wanting the stability it will provide. And they don't care how perfectly or elegantly things get done (which motivates Virgos or Libras), they just want them done. They'll tromp through the mud and everything else in their path to make matters secure.

The Earthiness of Taurus translates to a practical, black-or-white approach to life. Either they want something or they don't. They like something (or someone) or they don't. And Taureans are practical: They have little interest in considering ideas they can't prove or experience through their senses. If something works, show them, don't talk about it. Taureans lose patience with abstract concepts or ideas, especially if they can't see how they can work. They value something according to whether or not it can make their life better or more comfortable.

Mainly, Taurus expresses Earthiness by thoroughly loving and enjoying all things physical: bodies, material things and sensual pleasures of all sorts. Much of their reward in life comes through things or acts that provide physical satiation. They want to feel, hold, smell and taste all of life's offerings. Taureans love scrumptious food, soft and luxurious things, wonderful smells and the beautiful way music makes them feel.

Most of all, Taureans love touch. They need touch—crave it, really—and they want to give it and get it. Caressing, massaging, even a soft touch on their hand opens Taurus's spirit. And they love sex. They are one of the most sensual and sexual signs of the zodiac. (Scorpio is intense about sex; Taurus is sensual about it.) Sex not only gives them pleasure, it also helps them feel they are valued. Whereas some signs might use sex for power (Aries or Leo, for example), or persuasion (Scorpio), Taurus uses sex for pleasure. Simple as that.

Steadfast in the Positive Expression, Stubborn in the Negative

Taurus is one of the four Fixed Signs (Leo, Scorpio and Aquarius are the others), which means they desire to firmly establish and anchor themselves in whomever and whatever they are involved with. Fixed energy is extremely strong and determined: It helps Taureans remain focused and to ably deflect any influences that interfere with them and the path they've chosen. Being a Fixed Sign also prompts Taureans to commit themselves wholly and deeply, willingly investing themselves and their resources to support whatever they're involved in.

Taurus's specific expression of Fixed energy is their ability to establish avenues of security. They devote much of their time and energy creating whatever it is they believe would produce value, comfort and safety. One way they do that is by seeking stability, and they use their Fixed energy to create it.

Taureans tend to feel most comfortable and happy with a familiar and predictable status quo. It gives them a solid framework from which to operate. Indeed, a Taurus can be counted on to be there through thick and thin, holding matters together and keeping things safe. They don't mind unvaried routines or long-term commitments—in fact, they seek to create them.

Taureans are solid folk: They do what they promise, call when they say they will, and act as a rock of security and reliability for those around them. However, if Taureans take this urge for stability too far, they will try to resist the inevitable changes of life. They will fear that any change means losing security or something they value, which, to them, is a terrible thought. They'll dig in their heels, and stubbornly resist any movement or action that threatens what they seek to preserve. Taureans can miss out on exceptional opportunities because they are focusing on what they think they will lose rather than using their resourceful consciousness to recognize what they might gain. When that happens, their need for the stability of their comfort zone can get them stuck in no-growth situations because they're afraid to risk moving.

One way Taureans can differentiate between being stable and being stuck is to evaluate whether their situation is expanding them or limiting them. Are they learning anything, or just sticking to what's familiar? Stability has a nurturing and growing quality to it, even if it is very subtle. Being stuck has resistance to it: a stagnation that comes from trampling down any sprouts of new life.

If Taureans do discover they are stuck or in a rut, they needn't make gigantic changes all at once; that's usually not their nature anyway. It works better if they take a series of small steps, or perhaps just change their attitude. Eventually, those small steps lead to great distances in improving their lives.

Staying Power is a gift of Taurus's Fixed energy. Flexibility is their lesson. Taureans are challenged to know when to release their willful determination and allow for flexibility or a change in approach to keep learning and growing.

Ruled by the Love and Beauty of VENUS

Taurus is ruled by the planet Venus. (Libra is as well, but it expresses Venus altogether differently.) Venus imbues Taurus with an urge for love and beauty, as well as the gifts for creating both. Love is one of Taurus's strongest needs, as well as their most compelling motivators. Taureans crave love of every kind—romantic alliances, caring and bonded families, and deep and lasting friendships. They yearn for the comfort, the affection and the security relationships offer. Being alone and independent has little appeal for most Taureans. The sacrifices love demands are nothing in comparison to the value Taureans find in the presence of love.

Taurus is one of the most loving and affectionate signs of the zodiac. Touching, hugging and holding loved ones are the elixir of life for them, and they enjoy being on both the giving and receiving end of affection. Because love is so very important to Taurus, they have a natural vulnerability to it. When someone shows a Taurus they like them, they are deeply touched and grateful. They just melt. They think, *Me? You like me? Oh, thank you!* However, this doesn't mean Taureans are easily wooed away from established relationships. They are not. Taurus is extremely faithful and committed and does not stray.

Taureans express the love aspect of Venus by being affectionate and giving, and striving to protect and provide for everyone they care for. They become quite attached and seek long-term, lasting alliances. Perhaps more than any other sign, their commitments endure through even the hardest of times and setbacks. They believe that the love they have is worth it. Once they give someone their heart, that's it. They are comforted in believing they can rely on their partners and friends, just as they, themselves, can be relied upon.

Because love is so important to Taurus, and because they feel very vulnerable in relation to it, they can get quite hurt when relationships don't go well. As a way of defending themselves against hurt, Taureans can build a shield of protection that is virtually impenetrable. Others' attempts at reaching out to the insulated Taurus just bounce right off and go unnoticed or unvalued. These Taureans would prefer to feel nothing than to feel hurt.

But this insulating themselves rarely keeps Taureans from feeling hurt. It works better if they create a safe space within themselves, and treasure and value themselves no matter what others seem to do. From there they can be much more willing to actively work out differences with others, and find ways to heal hurts that happen, rather than simply block others out and hope another hurt never comes their way. (Good luck!)

In addition to a loving quality, Venus also gives Taurus a sweet and gentle disposition (unless their security is threatened, in which case they turn into snorting Bulls). They have a balanced nature, and mostly express themselves in a calm and steady way. Although Taureans feel things very deeply, they usually don't go in for huge waves of emotional expression. Rather, they prefer to express their feelings in a matter-of-fact way. And, although Taureans are quite passionate, they ultimately choose to behave in ways that are practical, rather than go off the deep end. Except in love—Taureans love going off the deep end there!

Venus also imbues Taureans with an ability to receive immense enjoyment from nurturing: be it for babies (anyone's), spouses (their own, of course), family or their cherished friends, Taurus feels tremendous satisfaction from being able to provide sustenance and affection. They lend rock-solid reassurance and support to their beloveds, and do whatever it takes to make their lives comfortable and safe. A Taurus will cook a yummy meal for a loved one, then fluff up their pillows and rub their feet, enjoying every minute of this kind of providing. And they welcome that kind of affection in return. (Well, who wouldn't, but Taurus especially does.)

Venus also gives Taurus an appreciation for, and gift of creating, beauty. The kind of beauty Taureans love and create is a hands-on, sensual beauty, the kind you want to touch and take comfort in. Pottery, textiles and other tactile mediums are Taurus specialties. Even if Taureans aren't personally creative, they will take pleasure in the creations of others.

Venus imparts excellent taste to Taureans: They recognize good design, adore elegant materials and demand good, solid craftsmanship. (They will instinctively walk up to the most expensive suit in the store.) No matter what a Taurean's budget, they usually manage to live the good life by using their resourceful ingenuity to find ways to surround themselves with comfort and elegance.

Venus also imbues Taurus with the gift of *Music.* Many Taureans are professional musicians. Because Taurus rules the throat, Taureans tend to have especially distinctive voices. Singers and radio announcers are likely to have Taurus prominent in their charts.

Taurus is what's called a **Personal Sign,** which means their sign's primary focus is on themselves. That is so they can learn to develop their Higher Nature or tune into their Spiritual Self (as compared to other signs which tap into their Higher Nature via being involved with others or the community). It's a life lesson for Taurus folks to learn to take good care of themselves, develop themselves and be good to themselves in ways that expand their loving, appreciative nature. The more Taureans do that, the more they grow spiritually.

But if, instead, Taureans just focus on their needs, wants and personal desires (or what they feel they are lacking), they risk simply developing their Lower Nature, or ego. Then, instead of becoming expansive and expanded, they become selfish and self-centered.

Sometimes, it's hard for Taureans to recognize they've become overly self-involved. One clue is if they perpetually feel unfulfilled or demanding. If a Taurus only develops their personality, they can be consumed by desire and considerations of what they want without appreciation for what they receive. This can create a catch-22 because they will focus on the one thing they currently don't have while being oblivious to the ninety-nine other things they wanted and *do* have—and they will insist they are in lack.

I have been in family counseling situations where a Taurus will say, "For once I have to think about myself," and the mouths of every other family member drop as if to say, "You are constantly thinking about yourself!" Sometimes, a Taurus will think they failed to present what they want as clearly as they should; when, in fact, they have, but haven't been appreciating—or even acknowledging—what's been given. However, as Taureans develop their Higher Nature, they learn they are fully capable of filling themselves up (or loving themselves) and don't need others to satisfy them.

The Taurus Archetypes: The Farmer's in the Bank Vault (with His Friends!)

In order to learn more about self value and inner security, Taureans (and those who are Taurus-like) will demonstrate the archetypes of the Security Seeker, the Cultivator, the Loyalist and the Conservator.

The Security Seeker

Taureans live the archetype of the Security Seeker because they are absolutely driven to establish inner and outer security. As they do, they awaken to their "Resource Consciousness," wherein they are fulfilled by an understanding and recognition of the constant presence of abundance.

One of the primary ways Taureans seek outer security is through material means. Financial security is extremely important to them. Savings, investments and possessions are the foundation of Taureans' sense of well-being because they need to know they are provided for at every moment. Consequently, Taureans take a keen interest in their financial status. They know at any given time exactly how much they are worth (down to the penny). And because they are perpetually aware they can have "more," Taureans spend their time considering other ways they can build their financial means.

Since money is so important to Taureans, they are careful to manage it wisely. Many Taureans are quite thrifty: They don't want to part with any money they don't have to (like Cancer and Capricorn). Because Taurus is the sign of value, Taureans have an uncanny knack for getting the maximum return on their dollar. They search for "good deals," scour the sale racks and discern the real value from a mere cheap imitation. (If there is only one treasure at the flea market, Taurus will find it!) Because they appreciate long-term security, most Taureans live well within their means, and sock their cash right into savings and investments. They derive great pleasure in cultivating money itself, as well as security.

However, there is one certain "spender" kind of Taurus who adores money in the bank, but doesn't want to be the one who puts it there. This type of Taurus prefers to live well and spend freely, even if it's beyond their means. To these folks, wonderful possessions make life worth living. Their feeling of security comes from the things their money can buy, so they find possessions as important as savings—probably more so. Being surrounded by nice things helps these Taureans feel good about themselves; when they have the *trappings* of abundance, they feel abundant. They are just as concerned about their future security as the more thrifty types of Taurus, yet their drive to accumulate stuff overrides any budget. Sometimes, this kind of Taurus seeks a partner who can help support their material lifestyle.

However, being in debt is emotionally (and psychically) stressful for any Taurus. They worry and fret about going broke and being left with nothing. So, although having nice things can be initially satisfying, unless they are truly affordable, they can also be the source of anxiety. It works well for the "spender" types of Taurus to treat themselves to a few good things, while staying within their budget. Sometimes going out and just trying on the expensive dress, or test-driving the sports car, can help them "act as if" they have the wealth they crave, and can motivate them to go out and create it.

Because money and luxurious possessions thrill Taureans, they are well suited for careers that involve such things, like banking, investments, financing or real estate.

Here's the challenge: Regardless of how much money or how many things Taureans may have, there are bound to be times when they worry that they don't—or won't—have enough. When this kind of "lack consciousness" kicks in, Taureans scare themselves with thoughts of not being able to provide for themselves. (This is true of Taureans of every financial status. I've counseled multimillionaire Taureans who suffered sleepless nights worrying all will be lost.)

One sign that Taureans are trapped in "lack consciousness" is when they start withholding—from themselves, as well as others. Instead of taking stock of what they do possess, and assessing what they can afford to spend, they believe they can't afford anything, even if in truth they can. Taureans then get overly attached to their money or possessions, valuing them above even their relationships. They become miserly and greedy, thinking they have to hang on to every penny and asset, because eventually they will desperately need it.

When feeling lack, Taureans might also become unavailable emotionally. They can get into a kind of survival mode wherein they only feel capable of attending to their own needs. Instead of being fulfilled by their ability to provide for others, they can become stingy and resent having to share.

What's ironic is that Taurus's fear of lack can actually create it. It can shut Taureans off from their natural connection with the flow of abundance. They become so focused on what they *won't* have, they fail to recognize what they *can* have, and miss opportunities because they don't believe they exist. Worse, instead of receiving joy from their possessions, they become trapped by them, because they're constantly worried about how lousy it will feel when they lose them.

It is at times like these that Taureans are learning to step back into their "Resource Consciousness" (by practicing gratitude) and expanding their awareness by remembering that they always have the resources necessary to create security for themselves. This relaxes them and helps them open more to the flow of life's abundance so they can once again partake.

When Taureans *prefer to* have material security, but don't *need* it to measure up or be secure, they are at their healthiest.

Not all Taureans seek outer security via materialism. Some seek the kind of security that comes from devoting their lives to something they deeply value, whether or not there's a big paycheck involved. Some Taureans get value from devoting their lives to nurturing and supporting others; other Taureans seek value through pursuing their art or music; still others value taking care of the environment.

What's important is for Taureans to value what they do.

Sometimes Taureans' Security Seeker energy will convince them they have to remain in situations that are limiting, even unhealthy, just because they offer security. They can believe they have no other means of support, even if that is rarely the case. It takes a lot for Taureans to finally get to the point where they'll leave a limiting, but secure, situation. A *lot*.

I have counseled countless Taureans who have stayed way too long in stifling jobs or unfulfilling relationships just because they feared there was no other place they could find support. But when they finally had the courage to leave, they discovered there were, indeed, other ways to support themselves.

Taureans need to discover for themselves that there are many avenues of support. They learn from experience that when they make decisions that say "no" to what they don't want, they are much more likely to get what they do want. In doing so, Taureans gain more confidence and security because they further realize the many resources available inside of themselves and in the world. One important decision is for Taureans to decide they are worthy of success and happiness.

Some Taureans seek security via committed relationships. Instead of establishing security for themselves, these Taureans expect their security to come from another. This puts a lot of pressure on finding the Right One, because love can easily be confused with security. Instead of waiting for the beloved who brings out the best in them, these Taureans settle simply for someone who was around, which provides them with a false sense of security. Eventually, that becomes confining because it is not the true security Taurus seeks.

Cultivating self-value is an important means of developing inner security for Taureans. It is also a key for Taureans to connect with their Higher Nature. Taureans' psychological health stems from recognizing their innate value, no matter what their outer circumstances. Instead of seeking security or self-value from possessions or relationships, Taureans are at their best when they declare that they are enough and lovable just because they exist. When Taureans value who they are, just as they are, moment to moment (sacrificing thoughts that they should have or be more), they lift themselves and tap into an inner sense of fulfillment.

If Taureans don't develop self-value, they suffer from feelings of unworthiness. In truth, all signs struggle with unworthiness, but Taurus folks can react to feelings of unworthiness by not standing up for themselves. They can give up—or never start—asking for what they want out of life, or they might give others power over them. (That sure doesn't work. When have you ever seen a Bull that was content to let others run it around?) And, if Taureans don't cultivate their own self-value, their relationships can suffer.

Sometimes, Taureans mistakenly believe they are unworthy of love. When that happens, they don't recognize love, even when love is being offered. This is particularly painful because love is such a primary need of the Taurus nature. This is another reason why cultivating self-value is so important: Taureans can't fully accept love from others unless they accept it from themselves. (This is, of course, true for everyone, however it plays out in this particular way most dramatically for Taurus.)

Or Taurus can go in the other direction and try to get self-value from the validation of others. In the throes of feeling unworthy, Taureans can become controlling because they believe that if others loved them, they should behave in the ways Taureans expect them to.

But trying to get others to act in these ways rarely works (for long, at least) and can actually leave Taurus feeling even less secure. The remedy is, of course, for Taureans to love themselves and value themselves. When they do, it becomes far easier for them to accept whatever way others choose to demonstrate that they love them.

Sometimes, in an attempt to win love, Taureans might try to "earn" it by over-providing for others. They will generously bestow their intended with stuff galore. But there are strings attached. These gifts aren't so much acts of giving as of investing, wherein Taurus expects a very specific payoff of love, loyalty, affection or sex. But for these things to be genuine, they can't be bought, and that's a lesson Taurus may have to learn the hard way.

My client, Evelyn, did. She wanted to marry Chuck so badly, she pulled out every stop. She lavished him with gifts that she could barely afford, like Rolex watches and expensive suits, in an attempt to win him over. But Chuck held out from marrying Evelyn for one last condition: He wanted equal ownership of her flower business. That was daunting for Evelyn. She single-handedly built that business and used it to support her three children. (Taurean parents are great providers.) But she gave in. Chuck married her, took over the business and promptly drove it into the ground. Worse, he divorced Evelyn right after that. Evelyn was left with nothing—at least, nothing in the asset department. But she told me that experience made her richer because she would never, ever believe she had to buy a man's love again. Finally, Evelyn realized she was worth much more than that.

Self-esteem is another aspect of Taureans' cultivating inner security. They develop self-esteem by choosing actions that demonstrate good self-care: saying yes to what they want, standing up for themselves, attending to their own needs instead of waiting for others to, and counting their blessings instead of focusing on what's lacking. Also, remaining loyal to their practical needs helps Taureans feel good about themselves. This includes things like staying out of debt, fulfilling their commitments, and eating and sleeping wisely.

Sometimes, if Taureans don't value themselves, it can affect their ability to connect with their spiritual essence, and they can even imagine that God doesn't value them. Usually, this happens when matters aren't going the way Taureans think they should, or when they notice that others have something they don't. Taureans can erroneously project that since others seem to have more, it means God loves them more. Of course, that's not true—everyone has their unique lot in life; it has nothing to do with their inherent worthiness. God's love is always unconditional for everyone all the time.

In truth, it isn't God that's not valuing these Taureans, it's themselves. Projections that they aren't loved by God are one of Taureans' greatest challenges and most potent teachers. When they can acknowledge that God does indeed love and value them, *especially* during times when they are having trouble valuing themselves, they are able to awaken spiritually. But Taureans have to choose to open. God won't force them to. Opening up is part of their spiritual course.

When Taureans have gratitude and appreciation for everything around them, they tap into a peace within themselves, recognizing that, in truth, nothing is lacking. That's when Taureans find inner fulfillment. From there, they can proceed in building outer fulfillment and abundance from a mindset of enjoyment. Every step along their way is interesting and valuable, and their assets become a joy. Their consciousness is relaxed, better able to spot the opportunities and relationships that really serve them. They become truly successful in their aspect of Security Seeker.

The Cultivator

Taurus will activate the Cultivator archetype by bringing to flourishing life whatever they set their sights on. They derive rich satisfaction from making things grow and prosper.

Exactly what each Taurus cultivates depends on the aspects of their unique astrological chart. This can be anything from a child to a garden, from a business to a viable solution to world hunger. But the underlying reason Taureans cultivate is to create deep roots, and a sense that whatever they devote their time to will bring them lasting value and, most important, security.

Taureans might use their Cultivator archetype to create successful careers. They are hard workers, putting in the extra hours, careful planning and devoted loyalty that ensures their job will provide long-term security, so they can support themselves and their loved ones.

Generally speaking, Taurus Cultivators choose careers based on job security. Instead of entering exciting, yet unstable, careers, they will choose to cultivate ones that are dependable. Many Taureans consider things like pension plans and retirement packages even in their twenties. Because they promise long-term security, you will see many Taureans faithfully putting in years of dedicated service and loyalty to jobs in the government, corporations or stable industries that can be counted on being in existence decade after decade.

Many Taureans have tremendous business savvy. Their Cultivator archetype intuitively understands how to work with supply and demand to make a profit. Taureans keep their eye on the cash: They watch to see who's paying how much for what, and they figure out ways to provide something others will pay for. You will find Taureans in every aspect of business. They are loyal, dependable employees eager to prove their worth to those in charge. Taureans make excellent bosses because they can spot whatever resources others have (like Scorpio can) and help cultivate them.

Many, many Taureans own their own businesses. When they do, they work tirelessly to make it profitable. Indeed, Taurus can consider their business to be the most important thing in their life and keep it central in their thoughts at all times. It's not only their source of security, it is their creative outlet as well. Taureans love the thrill of finding ways to make it grow and thrive. Family, spouses, even their own health may have to wait in line while Taurus attends to business. To Taureans, that is as it should be because the business provides for everyone. They don't want to risk it failing and letting their loved ones down.

Whatever career Taureans choose, it's important that they find value in what they do. When they recognize the inherent value of what they have to offer, they open themselves and enjoy the opportunities that they are given. And, when Taureans are in a state of appreciating their skills in the marketplace, they tend to attract others who want to partake of their gifts and services as well.

Taureans are also likely to cultivate a satisfying personal life. They crave the comfort of what a home and family circle can bring (even if that family involves just them and one pet). They enjoy relaxing in their own space, and love the intimacy and support of having beloveds there with them. Taureans want to create a solid foundation from which everyone can grow and flourish. So, they do their best (which is considerable) to cultivate an environment that's nourishing, supportive and loving.

Taureans really *live* in their homes! They need a retreat from the world, and burrow in at home to be renewed and refreshed. That's where they will most often choose to spend their quality time. Even Taureans who enjoy a glamorous and active social life need to go home, put on their slippers and curl up on the couch to recharge.

Taureans' homes themselves are usually cozy, yet luxurious. (Of course, that depends on their budget and how old their children are.) Taureans' practical side chooses furnishings that are useful and durable, and built to last a long time. They want to get their money's worth. Yet Taurus's Venus influence also needs a lovely environment. Even those on a modest budget are able to put things together in a clever and beautiful way.

Taureans usually enjoy doing the things that cultivate a homey atmosphere. Doing a load of laundry relaxes them (they love the smell of freshly laundered clothing), cooking a savory meal rewards them, even getting on their hands and knees in the dirt while gardening can be an uplifting, almost spiritual experience for Taureans. They are grateful to possess things that need caring for.

Taureans also cultivate pleasure. Being one of the most sensual signs of the zodiac, Taureans seek to make life feel good. They find ways to satisfy their need for creature comforts and activities that will nourish their senses, and make their bodies feel good. This can be anything from lingering in a warm, scented bubble bath, to getting and giving massages, to staying at the finest resorts. Whatever Taureans' budget, they will make sure part of it is spent on pleasure.

And the Taurus Cultivator loves to accumulate things. What kind of things depends on their unique personality (and their pocketbooks), but whatever Taureans collect is of good quality. Be it clothes, cars or rental properties, Taureans receive great enjoyment from their possessions: They love the act of acquiring things, as well as looking them over and feeling fulfilled that they are the owner.

Along with cultivating *things,* Taureans benefit greatly by cultivating *trust*. They have a natural innocence about them, a childlike quality that allows them to take things at face value. Rather than analyzing or probing to expose some hidden meaning that may or may not exist, Taureans believe what they see or feel is truth enough. This simple approach can be terrifically refreshing and comforting to others, particularly those who get anxious about abstract possibilities. The earthy, "see and feel" wisdom of Taurus can simplify things down to the very basics.

However, if Taureans don't cultivate trust that they will have the resources necessary to deal with life, they can feel they have to use their considerable strength to exert control over how things happen. They will become pushy and forceful, believing that, if they don't, they'll lose out on what they really need. Although this can be quite effective in helping Taureans manifest what they desire, it could backfire. They might end up creating something that isn't truly right for them, and push a lot of people around in the process.

It works better if Taureans cultivate trust in themselves and the universe by looking for the good and beneficial prospects offered in every situation. When they intend to use everything to their advancement and growth, Taureans put their energy on using what is present—which takes the focus and worry off what might not be present. That's a much more realistic, powerful and productive stance. They can use their natural innocence to be curious, rather than anxious, about life.

There are all kinds of ways and avenues for Taureans to use their Cultivator archetype to make things grow and prosper in the world. Because whatever they put their attention on tends to grow, it's important Taureans choose wisely what they devote their cultivating efforts to. If they don't, Taureans might find they are cultivating attitudes and actions that don't serve them, and undermine their sense of fulfillment.

Taurus is a sensitive sign, and prone to feeling let down by the thoughtless acts of others. Taureans may feel they give so much to others, they can be disappointed when others don't give to them the way they expect them to. One way Taureans can respond is to build up a deep case of resentment (or its cousin, blame) against whomever they think has done them wrong. Taureans can use resentment as a shield to keep whoever's hurt them out of their heart. Although this hurts the Taureans as much as (or more than) it hurts the one who's resented, Taureans sometimes think that's the only way they can protect themselves. I had one Taurus mother tell me, "I resent my son because if I don't, I'll let him take advantage of me again."

But resentment closes off that which feeds Taurus the most—the flow of giving and receiving. And it doesn't solve the problem. Not only that, the people who are resented or blamed can feel bewildered, because usually Taureans refuse to tell them what's wrong. No one wins.

What works better is for Taureans to use their Cultivator archetype to take actions that create and promote healing and understanding in all their relations. They might do that by talking things out, perhaps letting others know how they interpreted their actions as hurtful (remembering that it was *their interpretation* of what happened that hurt them, not the other person's actions), and what they would prefer to have happen. Importantly, Taureans need to forgive judgments they have of others in order to open the door for healing and the return of loving. That's wise cultivating.

The spiritual essence of the Cultivator energy in Taurus is to awaken Taureans to the abundant generosity of the Divine. As Taureans feel fulfillment in the act of providing for themselves and others, they connect with the supreme fulfillment of the Divine One's care, learning the true meaning of providing.

The Loyalist

Taureans live the archetype of the Loyalist because being loyal to who and what they value is a big part of their self-definition. Loyalty gives Taureans a moral compass that helps govern their actions. Living loyally increases Taureans' self-esteem. It also brings structure and meaning to their life. Taureans will gain courage from their loyal intentions, and valiantly stick to something or someone no matter how great the pressure to do otherwise. However, the real lesson for Taureans is to learn to be loyal to themselves first. From that inner loyalty they can express loyalty outwardly.

Taureans are incredibly loyal to their loved ones. Once they give someone their heart, that's it. They don't look around wishing they were with someone else; they stay focused on whom they've picked.

Perhaps more than those of any other sign, Taureans remain true blue to their relationships. This is an incredible asset, not to mention a luxury for the beloveds of a Taurus.

If Taureans do not operate from loyalty to self first, they risk confusing loyalty with "giving in" to others' (possibly unreasonable) demands. Taureans are empowered by being able to provide for the needs of others. But, sometimes, this can be tipped out of balance, and Taureans can let others take advantage of them, thinking that is a requisite of being loyal.

Taureans are also loyal to their word. If they say they are going to do something, they do it, even if what they promise ends up being considerably harder than they anticipated. In those kinds of situations, Taureans can use loyalty to their word as a power tool to drive past the obstacles and setbacks that stand in their way. They want the self-satisfaction of completing what they set out to do.

But because life is full of surprises, sometimes Taureans discover that what they say they will do really doesn't work for them. That's when they need to remember that they can renegotiate their commitments. Taureans needn't stick to agreements that send them down the wrong path because that's not being loyal to their True Self.

Principles are another area in which Taureans can express loyalty. If they believe something is right or good, it serves as a guidepost for their behavior. No matter how others try to convince—even seduce—them away from what they hold as righteous, Taureans will firmly resist.

But, sometimes, Taureans can resist feedback that they are off course. They'll stick to being loyal to their commitments, instead of sticking to being loyal to what they feel inside. They might consider this as a noble act, when sometimes it's resisting their higher calling.

An example of this is my Taurus client James, who was a gifted artist, yet born into a family that owned a huge grocery empire. Although painting and sculpting were his passion, he accepted that being loyal to his family meant taking the reins of the business when his father retired. So James put his art aside, got an M.B.A., and invested his efforts into helping the family business thrive. However, even as the business prospered, he became depressed. No matter how much money he made (or spent), nothing satisfied him.

When James finally sought counseling, it was suggested that he return to his art and let someone else run the business. At first this was unthinkable to him because it meant a breach of loyalty to his family. But after a few more years of "sticking to it," his depression worsened.

Finally, James trained his cousin to manage the business, gave it up and moved to Montana to start painting. He felt like he started living for the first time since his M.B.A. days. Now James has his own gallery and makes a comfortable living as an artist. More important, he is content because he is being loyal to his own essential nature, first and foremost.

When Taureans are loyal to what is of real value to them, they are able to create a most satisfying life. If Shakespeare had been a Taurus he might have said, "To thine own self be loyal." (Or, maybe he did.)

The Conservator

Taureans also live the archetype of the Conservator because they seek to masterfully utilize everything they've been given. Their motto is, "That which is not used is abused." Taureans take care of possessions, relationships and anything else they deem valuable, making sure they get the longest and most productive life possible.

It breaks Taureans' hearts to see something—or someone—go unvalued or underutilized. That is a reflection of their need to develop their own personal assets, and not let them go unrecognized or underdeveloped.

Some Taureans are literally conservationists who seek to conserve the valuable resources of the Earth itself. They recognize there is a limit to what the Earth can provide, and work tirelessly to help protect and maintain ecological balance.

Other Taureans seek to conserve principles they find worthy, like family values or spiritual practices. Or they might seek to support institutions that serve to maintain what they value by fundraising or volunteering for hospitals or the political party they support.

One thing that all Taureans seek to conserve is what works in their lives. They value established routines that support their life's ease and pleasure. They feel secure in counting on knowing what's going to happen next. Because of that they can create a dependable, stable lifestyle for themselves and their loved ones.

But, sometimes, Taureans try to conserve what used to work, even when it no longer does. Instead of adapting to changing times, Taureans can try to maintain old ways, thinking they are conserving a lifestyle they enjoy. This tendency to resist change can be exhausting for Taureans and frustrating to those around them because change is always knocking at the door. If Taureans try to preserve stability by refusing to allow change, it can actually cost them what they're trying to keep.

That's what happened to Joan and Taurus Thom. Joan was at her wit's end because Thom refused to consider any of the changes she requested, both in their lifestyle and in their marriage, claiming that what they already had was good enough. But Joan felt confined and limited by this, and it drove her away from Thom. She eventually elected to divorce him, thinking that was her only option for breaking out of Thom's limiting control.

I've also met with Taureans whose Conservator energy is expressed as resistance to making the changes necessary to keep up with the changing climate of their careers. They felt that what worked once should keep working, and refused to keep learning and trying different approaches. That led to many of them being left behind—even fired—while other, more flexible coworkers rose up the ladder.

In both cases, Conservator energy was motivated by fear of, or resistance to, productive change. And the payoffs were not what the Taureans were seeking.

Taureans are smartest when they use their Conservator energies to hold on to what's of true value throughout the flow of changes in their lives. Using conservation, Taureans are able to shift and change as life does, while keeping sight of what's really important.

Taureans use their Conservator nature to their advancement when they approach change as if the universe is bringing something to them, not taking something away. This not only helps them enjoy the ebb and flow of life much more, it also helps them discover more of their innate abilities and resourcefulness. They then use their powerful energies to be proactive, not reactive against the inevitable.

The Taurus Gifts: Standing on Solid Ground

Taureans are imbued with the perfect gifts that help them learn more about the true essence of value and abundance.

One of Taurus's greatest gifts is **Resourcefulness.** Taureans have a keen eye (and nose) for assets and opportunities that can further their goals. They see value in things that others miss or even discard, knowing that a little polish here and a little adornment there will make them all shiny and valuable once again.

Taureans just know where and how to get what they need: They find the greatest bargains, or the one and only job that's available, or the day museums let everyone in for free.

Practicality is another gift Taureans use regularly. Taureans have the ability to target a goal, and then see the doable action steps to achieve it. (They might think everyone does this, but believe me, everyone doesn't.) They have a natural wisdom that discerns the difference between an attainable goal and a pie-in-the-sky scheme.

Once Taureans determine what they want to do or accomplish, they are **Methodical** in their approach; first things first, cultivating and nurturing each phase with **Patience.** Their approach: If it's worth wanting, it's worth waiting for. And, even when challenges or setbacks arise, Taureans apply their awesome **Perseverance.** Where others would be daunted and thrown off track, Taureans put their heads down and keep on plodding through the pasture to the barn . . . er . . . finish line.

In their pursuit of what they want, Taureans are **Realistic** about their capabilities. They are careful not to promise more than they can deliver, or to underestimate the time it will take to accomplish something.

Akin to these attributes are others that come in to lend support. Taureans demonstrate a **Deliberate** quality that keeps them grounded and dependable. They will rarely "jump without a net" or do something that throws them too far off balance. Taureans aren't gamblers. They simply aren't willing to trust their valued assets to a twist of fate. Instead, Taureans always calculate the return they will get for the efforts in which they invest.

Importantly, Taureans have the ability to **Deeply Enjoy the Simple Pleasures of Life.** Simplicity really serves them. Life needn't—and really shouldn't—be complicated for Taureans. All it takes for them to feel fulfilled is comfort and love. They derive deep joy from holding a baby, arranging a bouquet of flowers, whiffing a sensual aroma or working with a well-designed machine. An unhurried walk in nature expands Taureans' spirits and helps them to put worries in perspective. Even better, a yummy meal in the company of loved ones can send Taurus right to Heaven on Earth.

An aspect of determination, **Resistance** is another powerful asset of Taurus. While resistance isn't usually considered an asset, when threatened, Taureans can use the energy of resistance to keep themselves safe. This is a tremendously useful tool for blocking negative influences in pursuing their dreams. Taureans can use resistance to discount fears or insecurities so those things don't run their lives.

But, sometimes, Taureans can confuse the self-supportive kind of resistance with the kind of resistance that denies taking the steps in life they must. They might think they're being strong, for example, and maintaining the valued status quo; when, in fact, they are holding back necessary change.

Defensiveness is also something usually considered to be negative that is actually a gift Taureans can use to fend off threats to what and whom they value. It also assists them psychologically by helping them to shoo away limiting thoughts and emotions that can keep them trapped.

But if Taureans don't cultivate their own sense of power and resourcefulness, they might develop defensiveness as a way of protecting themselves. They will project power onto others, believing they can be controlled or taken over by them, and then use defensiveness to battle them. So Taureans needs to become adept at recognizing when they use their defensiveness as protection from real threats, instead of wasting energy on resisting an illusion.

One way for Taureans to use their natural defensiveness is by refusing to let their worries or fears have any "air time" in their thinking, by knocking them out with positive images of how good it's going to feel when they reach a desired goal. In that way, Taureans are champions to themselves.

The Taurus Fears: The Insecurity Factor

Because security is such a huge drive for Taureans, **losing security can be their greatest fear.** They can scare themselves with thoughts of going broke, being unable to provide a home, food—even the basics (much less the luxuries they adore) for sustaining life. Sometimes, Taureans allow this fear to run away with them, and they imagine worst-case scenarios that are truly gloomy.

When that shows up, Taureans do well to take a hard look at how likely that is to happen. And, whether or not it has happened (and odds are it hasn't), Taureans can use this fear of loss of security to propel them into action to make sure they do, indeed, find ways to provide for themselves and loved ones. It can give them the courage to reach out and do things way out of their comfort zone in order to fend off lack.

The more Taurus learns to step away from fear back to inner security, the more they anchor themselves in the security, and spend more and more time there.

Taureans might also **fear they are not as strong, or as worthy,** as others are. They might compare themselves to what they see in others and come up short. When they don't feel worthwhile, Taureans can fail to stand up for themselves, or allow others to take advantage of them.

But Taureans are strong, and they are worthy. And it's their job to find that out.

The ironic thing is that Taureans are incredibly supportive of other people. Taureans are generous with their support, as well as their ability to point out where others are gifted. So sometimes it's good for Taureans to turn the tables and allow others to support them by letting them give Taurus feedback about their gifts and strengths. For example, if someone reminds Taurus of the time they overcame this situation or that one, or accomplished something important, Taurus can remember, "Yeah! I guess I am pretty strong!" But in the end, it's Taurus that needs to know that they are strong, and they are worthy, for themselves.

Taurus in Relationships: A Prized Possession

Taureans are at home with love and (along with financial security) want it more than anything else in life. Being ruled by the planet Venus, they have a natural inclination for establishing close, affectionate relationships. Taureans are some of the most loyal and attentive people on the face of this Earth and are givers when they are in love. That can be in things or in physical support (like great dinners every night). And Taurus loves the sensuality of love. That might be sexuality, but it's more the touching, caressing and affection that go with intimacy that Taureans crave.

Love is so important to Taureans that, if they feel they're not getting what they want from others, it's important they get to the bottom of it. It may be true that they're getting the short end of the stick. That could be because they haven't asked for what they want, instead just assuming the other person should intuitively know. (Some people are mind readers, but most need to be told what's important to them.) Talk about these concerns and get them cleared up, because more than anything, Taureans *want to know they are valued in relationships.*

As security-minded as Taureans are, they nevertheless seek excitement from their mates. They usually choose someone who is more emotional, explorative or dynamic than they are, enjoying the edge of life their partners take them to.

By the way, if you're considering marrying or going into any sort of a partnership with a Taurus (or if you're a Taurus considering partnership of any kind), it's a really good idea for honest financial talks *before* the partnership. It is a critical subject with Taurus and, in order for the partnership to work well, Taurus needs to be satisfied with how the finances are worked out. Remember, money is a central issue with Taurus; treat this subject with clear intention.

Female Taureans are incredibly flattered when someone likes or loves them. No matter how accomplished or attractive they are, she'll feel, *Who me? You like me?* Court her by showing up on time and doing what you say you are going to do. And draw her out—she's a little shy, even hesitant, about revealing her true self. When she sees that you not only want to get to know her, but you *approve* of her when you do, her heart opens. (And, remember, when a Taurean's heart opens, it stays that way.)

And then here's a trick: Make sure you smell good. Glamorous Taurean women love refined, expensive smells. (I'm not necessarily talking about cologne—it might be the way your shirts smell, or the scent of something you groom with. The outdoorsy Taurus woman might adore the fact that you smell like you've been hiking all day.) Each woman is different. But find out what scents please her.

Regardless of their specific type, Taurus women like when you spend money on them. Not uneconomically, though. Remember that she's interested in getting the most for the money and wants you to do the same. But when you spend thoughtfully, like bringing her a bouquet composed of just her favorite flowers, she'll melt. Remember, there is a bottom line show-me-the-security thought with Taureans, and you need to demonstrate several things, the first two being the most important. Step one: Show her you value her. Step two: Show her that you can help her build her dream—whatever it is. Steps three through ten: Show her affection. Be gentle and sensual, and take your time. She'll reciprocate in more ways than you can imagine.

Male Taureans are also seeking value in their mates. Beauty is important, but more than that, a Taurus man is looking for a certain kind of "body feeling" around his partner. He's not seeking an intellectual match; he's seeking someone with whom he can relax. He wants to feel comfortable with himself when his partner is around. He wants to know his beloved will be loyal and won't take advantage of him. In other words, he needs to trust his partner, ethically, morally and financially.

Taurus men don't need their mates to be major earners, but they do need their partners to demonstrate good fiscal sense. Being a good sexual match is extremely important to Taurus men. They are very sensual and need to feel attracted to and comfortable with their partner's body. A Taurean's partner needs to smell good and match his ideas of good grooming. Taurus males love to be touched and soothed and massaged. Take your time. You're in for a treat.

The Last Word on Taurus

What Taurus offers is a sense of value and security, and the many ways of discovering that true value and security are found within each of us.

Chapter 3

Gemini

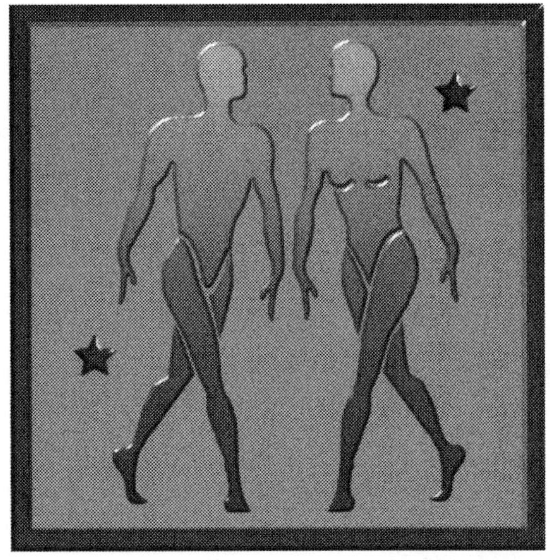

(May 22–June 21)

Gemini is the quality in you that is curious and multifaceted, seeks a wide range of experiences, and enjoys communicating and learning. It's also the part of you that's learning that the Divine is everywhere, all the time.

Just when you think you have figured out a Gemini, they turn into someone else. Not really, but Geminis are so multifaceted, and have such a wide range of interests and expressions, it can seem like they are two people living two lifetimes at once!

Geminis are unusually bright and curious people. They have a highly adaptable and changeable nature that they use to "try on" a variety of ideas and approaches to life. Students at heart, Geminis are eager to learn, even if it's just a little, about almost everything. They travel through life sampling whatever (or whomever) catches their interest, and usually juggle at least two pursuits they feel passionate about at any given time.

Geminis' versatility and adaptability allow them easy passage into a wide assortment of experiences and relationships. They don't watch from the sidelines of life—they jump right in and participate. With their clever wit and friendly nature Geminis know how to put others at ease. So wherever Geminis find themselves, they can make a new friend, or at least someone with whom to strike up a fascinating conversation. Geminis' ability to grasp, then cleverly communicate, all kinds of information makes them savvy contributors to any situation they're involved in.

The Gemini Mission: Learning That God Is . . . Well . . . Everywhere!

All of us are learning what Geminis are born to discover: Just as they have countless ways of expressing themselves, so does God. As Geminis travel and explore their many interests, they recognize that Spirit is there, no matter what they choose to pursue. Importantly, as Geminis come to realize that although this world, and even their own nature, has a duality about it—good and bad, light and dark, etc.—God is the unifying constant.

So, the Gemini lesson is a particularly expansive one: discovering how God is everywhere, in everything.

Throughout all they do and learn, Geminis are searching for that insight that can illuminate for them who they truly are, as well as the meaning of life. The trick of being a Gemini, though, is to learn to discover themselves through *any* experience, not *every* experience.

Although it's tempting to try to satisfy all of their interests all at once, it's not Geminis' best strategy. In doing this, they spread themselves too thin and lose touch with their inner core.

What Geminis are learning works best is to bring everything they've got to whatever they're doing at the moment. When they do that, they align with the vastness of their own nature and begin to live from the inside out. Instead of looking for life to stimulate them, they stimulate themselves into life, because there's a huge world of consciousness inside them that can keep them utterly fascinated.

The true lesson of being Gemini is to tap into the variety inside themselves and apply it to their experiences—not the other way around.

The Gemini Challenge: The Temptation to Be Everywhere

Interestingly, the way that Geminis can learn to discover themselves through *any* situation is by overcoming the tendency of trying to pursue every situation (and every person) that interests them all at once. Since Geminis seek self-discovery through experiences, they can imagine that the next experience, the one they haven't yet pursued, is the one that will awaken them to the "aha!" they seek.

This can keep Geminis leaping from one experience to the next before they invest enough time or attention to gain what was available in the first one. It can also prevent Geminis from committing themselves to even the most meaningful relationships or opportunities, because they fear they might lose out on the promise of what else might come along. So, as Geminis move from experience to experience they can have a disappointing sense that they're just distracted, not illuminated, and not learning what they yearn for. Usually, they are right.

The Gemini Keys: Focus, Focus, Focus

However, **if Geminis stay completely present with what they're doing in each moment, they can become attuned to the dimensions of themselves they are truly searching for.** Instead of getting side-tracked by all their possibilities, their single focus narrows the beam of their considerable intellect so they can discover more about their own essence. Geminis can thereby be truly awakened by their experiences.

Double Your Pleasure, or Double Trouble, with Gemini, the TWINS

Geminis' astrological symbol is Twins, symbolizing their dual nature. Although everyone has multiple sides, Geminis *really* demonstrate it. **The distinction between them and other signs is that they *fully develop* different sides and aspects of their nature and their interests,** so much so that they can seem like they are two people or living a few lives at once. Hence, the twins.

On the surface, Geminis' twin-like nature will be characterized by swings from being introverted to extroverted, from being aggressively masculine to tenderly feminine, from being warm and friendly to suddenly crabby and cold. It is also demonstrated by Geminis' ability (they might call it a need) to be simultaneously involved in many pursuits—including relationships. The saying, "Variety is the spice of life," was either coined by (or for) a Gemini.

But, for each Gemini, there is a deeper duality—their nature possesses a unique array of personas that they will fully develop and express during one lifetime. These multiple characters within them all are valuable aspects of their grandness—each persona contributes to their life in its own unique way.

Rather than compartmentalizing these characters, Geminis' lesson is to creatively synthesize all aspects of their nature, and work them as a symphony of self-expression.

Geminis are just chock-full of talents, interests and abilities; so, their challenge is finding ways to manage all of them instead of being pulled in several directions at once by them. One helpful guideline is for Geminis to keep their agenda limited to activities that somehow expand them—not just keep them busy or distracted. That keeps life interesting for Geminis without making them scattered.

Feet Planted Firmly in the AIR

Gemini is one of the three Air Signs (Libra and Aquarius are the others), which means Geminis' most comfortable function is thinking, rather than feeling or doing something practical. Geminis' facile minds easily move from subject to idea to intuition, able to conceptualize almost anything. They are extremely inquisitive and driven by a need to learn new things and find out what others are up to. Geminis are continually asking questions of life and people, looking for answers that illuminate and compel them.

Geminis' unique expression of the Air quality is through their pure love of thinking. Geminis' minds are incredibly active; always going, always evaluating (or judging), jumping from one subject to the next, covering all sorts of thoughts in such quick succession, it can seem as if Geminis are thinking of two or three things simultaneously. (And they might be.) One Gemini I know compares the thoughts in his head to a constant state of channel surfing: For a minute his mind will focus on one topic, then jump to something else, then to something completely different again. Geminis also have incredibly vivid imaginations that keep them and others constantly entertained with ideas, possibilities and creative acts.

Geminis absolutely love learning. Anything. All kinds of stuff. One year it's history, the next year it's windsurfing, then it's ancient religions. Somewhere in the middle of all that, they will study art and take a handful of trips. (No one is more fun to travel with than Gemini—as long as you like to keep moving and seeing all the sights.) Life is utterly fascinating to Geminis, and when something catches their interest (many, many things do), they eagerly investigate it. A little information goes a long way with Geminis: They can extrapolate the big picture just by learning the minimal facts.

Experience MUTABLE Gemini . . . for a Change

Gemini is one of the four Mutable Signs (Virgo, Sagittarius and Pisces are the others), which means Geminis are changeable and flexible, and able to adapt themselves to whatever situation they find themselves in. Geminis' unique expression of the Mutable quality is their ability to fluidly adapt their thinking and their persona so they can fit in and relate to whatever situation they encounter.

But Geminis have to watch going overboard with this ability. Taken too far, they can start to feel "schizy," instead of adaptable. Geminis can become so changeable, or so overextended, that they step away from the center core that's their essence. Instead of using the multiple sides of their nature to learn and grow, they can become confused about who they really are. Geminis should always take time to tap into their essential self, so they can remain stabilized through their many experiences. Making the time to *stop,* sit quietly, breathe, and meditate or contemplate, can go a long way in accomplishing this.

Geminis' mutability makes them incredibly active and curious, yet also easily bored. Geminis are the first ones in and the first ones out of a situation. They will quickly investigate any new person or opportunity that comes their way. If their interest isn't held, they're gone—just like that. Some signs judge that as superficial, and it might be. But do keep in mind that Geminis' quick minds can often gain as much in a quick swoop through something as other signs get only after a lengthy stay.

Geminis don't have the need to go poking round in the dark corners of people and situations. They prefer quantity of experiences to depth of experiences. They like to collect information about lots of things rather than have mastery over one thing. That's their nature. But Geminis need to watch that they are not running from something that could ultimately prove to be fascinating to them—even if it means they might have to face pain (theirs or another's) for a while.

Gemini is what's known as a **Personal Sign,** which means Geminis are primarily interested in their Self. Geminis don't need to change the world in order to be fulfilled, they just need to change themselves. In doing so at an essential level, they find out the many mysteries of who they are. But, remember, it's not Geminis' Ego Self they're learning to enhance, it's their Higher Self. If Geminis simply develop their Ego Self, they risk remaining immature and one-dimensional. When they seek to develop their Higher Self, Geminis will become truly wise, multidimensional beings. By doing that, Geminis can shine so brightly, they can—and do—have an impact on the whole world.

As Swift as MERCURY

Gemini is ruled by the planet Mercury, named after the Roman god who was the Messenger. Mercury took information from one source and gave it to another. That describes Gemini's strategy: They needn't come up with their own original thoughts and ideas because their gift is catching and collecting thoughts and ideas from various sources, then synthesizing and passing them on in useful ways. Geminis can hear a phrase or idea one minute then turn around the next minute and repeat it as if they've always known it.

In some ways, Geminis' minds are like tape recorders: picking up facts, thoughts, even words, and running them over and over and over. This enhances their memory and makes them a whiz at recalling and repeating information, even languages, they've heard. Because Geminis record even the smallest of nuances, they make great mimics and imitators of others. When Geminis see someone doing something interesting, they just have to "try it on for size" and experience it for themselves. They'll do what they observe being done, and say what they heard being said. Geminis can do this to entertain themselves and others, or they can use this as a way to learn from other people's success. They might learn by studying the successful strategies and thoughts of others, and adopt them for themselves to see if they'd work for them. But of course, Geminis will put their own creative spin on it.

Because the Gemini mind is so active, they need to find ways to take dominion over it, or it can drive them nuts. It can also be tiring for others, because Geminis might try to release their mental energy by talking, sometimes going over the same ideas or concerns again and again. Geminis need to remember that others don't have the mental stamina they do and will likely need a break from conversation, no matter how interesting the Gemini managed to make it.

Quiet time brings Geminis much-needed peace of mind. Although they might avoid it for fear it would be boring, quieting their mind is its own uniquely valuable experience. It actually enhances Geminis' intelligence to reflect on the meaning of what they've learned, rather than just running facts over and over in their consciousness. So, it's a good life strategy for Geminis to develop ways to calm their mind, or focus their awareness away from their thoughts, even if it's for just a few minutes a day. Meditation is really useful for helping Geminis tune down their ever-present thoughts, and so is exercise.

In short, Geminis' intellect is one of their greatest assets. Because Geminis' minds are such a prominent aspect of themselves, they might not realize that it's also important to develop and mature the complexity of their emotions or their hearts. Although feelings can seem awkwardly sticky to Geminis—less fluid than their thoughts, and harder to shake off—they help Geminis to understand more about themselves, others and the whole of life. And importantly, Geminis' hearts can transform their knowledge into true wisdom. But this only works if Geminis can still their minds long enough to tap into what their emotions and hearts have to offer.

Indeed, Geminis' greatest awakening might come when they actually leap from the thoughts of their mind into a place beyond thinking where the Divine can be experienced.

The Gemini Archetypes: The Many Mouths of the Tricky Twins

As Geminis live their destiny of discovering the many faces of God, they (and those who are Gemini-like) will embody the archetypes of Communicator, Quick-Change Artist and Trickster.

The Communicator

Geminis embody the archetype of the Communicator, because they are elegantly designed to pass information in some way. (Their nickname could be NBC: If you want to get the word out about something, tell a Gemini.)

Geminis simply adore the spoken and written word. It's likely they enjoy rolling fascinating words around in their head and off their tongue. They adore a new catch phrase and quickly adopt it as their own. On top of that, Geminis are witty, with the ability to string words together with clever and interesting twists that surprise and entertain their listeners. (Or if no listeners are around, they entertain themselves.) Geminis love puns, puzzles and word games that display their command of the language.

Conversation is the elixir of life for Geminis. Most Geminis are downright chatty. They love to talk, to exchange ideas, to learn from their encounters with people. Geminis know how to punch up their conversations with information they've gathered from all kinds of sources to make it more interesting. They will quote something they've read, report on a TV program they've watched, or recall a conversation they had with an authority on a subject.

Remember: Geminis are designed to communicate and they do that very well. If someone tells a Gemini a secret, it might not be a secret for very long! Most Geminis can't resist repeating what they hear to at least a few (dozen) others.

Geminis also tell great stories. They can embellish the driest subject with clever side thoughts, jokes and surprising bits of info, and make it compelling. In short, Geminis are interesting.

Geminis are also friendly. Whereas some signs seek others who have similar ideas and interests, Geminis' curiosity prompts them to reach out to strangers. They want to find out who they are and what they know so they can add it to their material to communicate. They can, and do, strike up conversations with almost anyone. Even if Geminis have nothing in common with someone, they can still find a way to have an interesting interlude. Because of that, sales, advertising or jobs where they serve as a communicator are great career choices for Geminis.

Geminis also enjoy the tools of communication. They can spend hours on the phone, surfing the Web, or studying up on the newest technological gizmo that helps get the word out. But, for Geminis, nothing compares to reading. They're usually voracious readers. They can have three or four books going at once and still hunt for something else to read. And Geminis retain what they've read. Years after reading an author, they can quote her or him line-by-line.

Because Geminis treasure information, both for the sake of the information itself and its value to them as grist for their communicator mill, *teaching* is one of their main joys and gifts. Geminis love to educate others and do so with enthusiasm and cleverness. Their special knack for making information exciting and accessible makes what they have to say interesting. Geminis explain things simply. They break down even the hardest, most arcane subjects to easily understandable points that are easy for their audience to grasp. This probably stems from Geminis' tendency to keep in the back of their mind as they live life how they would teach or write (or draft a screenplay) about what happens. In truth, as Geminis teach they learn, and as they learn they teach.

Geminis value teaching and education so much that something in that field would be a terrific career choice for them. Actually, many Geminis usually end up teaching in some capacity no matter what career they choose.

Geminis also tend to be gifted writers. Writing helps Geminis sort out all those crazy thoughts that are running around in their mind, giving them meaning and order. Even if Geminis aren't trained as writers (having been distracted by their ever-flitting mind during English class), they've still got talent. Many Geminis *have* to write: It's an undeniable urge. They are nourished by it, and good at it. Some Gemini clients tell me they would love to write, but just haven't taken the time or developed the discipline to sit down and do it. I encourage them to. It's likely they've got something very important to say—even if it's just to themselves. Careers in writing, publishing or related fields are excellent career choices for the Communicator Gemini.

Now here's an interesting twist: Some Geminis express communication through numbers. Numbers can say a lot, and they can be moved and manipulated to demonstrate a world of ideas. Accounting and finance can be very creative outlets for these Geminis' keen intellect.

Language is another forte of Gemini. Their mind can easily assimilate the different sounds, words and dialects of language, and capture its nuances almost immediately. Geminis' ability to mimic can also help them hear and repeat how language flows. They are likely to be interested in at least one foreign language, if not a few. Any field using languages is a good career choice for Geminis.

Because Geminis love to communicate, they can sometimes let it get in the way of necessary introspection time. They can spend so much time talking with others, they forget to communicate with themselves and check in to find out how they are doing or what they are feeling.

Geminis need to ask themselves if they are talking to communicate or just to fill the time. It also helps if they evaluate if they're communicating about *who* they are, not just some ideas they've heard and are mimicking. The secret to Geminis being lifted by their conversations is letting their heart and their feelings come through what they say. That way Geminis can learn and be transformed by what's being communicated, which is what they're truly after.

Sometimes, even though Geminis don't plan on being a communicator or teacher, Destiny calls them to it. Madeline is a Gemini who owned a roofing business for twenty years together with her husband. She deeply loved this man—they were both gregarious and had loads of fun together. But he became very ill, and she had to nurse him through a long and painful illness to which he finally succumbed. After he died, Madeline began to tour the country lecturing hospitals and other organizations about how to better handle the trauma that families endure from problems with insurance, as well as with each other. In her wildest dreams, she never would have thought of herself as playing that role until Destiny asked her to.

The Quick-Change Artist

Geminis live the archetype of the Quick-Change Artist because they can easily shift from one expression of their nature to another, each complete with interests and talents. It is as if there's a collection of people living inside of Geminis, eager to express and experience life. This isn't schizophrenia, or a *Three Faces of Eve* thing (although it can sure feel like it sometimes); it's just that Geminis can and do have lots of facets to who they really are.

Part of Geminis' Quick-Change Artist archetype is demonstrated through their different personalities. Depending on whom they're with, what they're doing or what stage of life they're in, Geminis will have a personality that fits that particular niche. Each of these personalities expresses something that Geminis can learn from, and has experiences that make Gemini whole. So if someone thinks they know a Gemini, it's more likely that they know *part* of them, but chances are there are other people who know a completely different aspect of the same Gemini.

Each Gemini experiences their multiple facets uniquely. Some say they behave completely differently with different kinds of people in different kinds of situations. Other Geminis report being one way by day—say at work—and another way at night, perhaps with family. Some have one set of interests and friends completely different from or hidden from another set of interests and friends.

Gemini Dan sure does express his multiple personas. When I first met him, he was a psychologist with a respected radio show in Atlanta (Gemini Communicator archetype). During that time he was also a member of a local motorcycle club that had some pretty daunting participants. He was also a Big Brother. And he was celibate. That was then. Now he's a musician who tours the country with his band. He's dedicated to his spiritual practices and also enjoys having sex every chance he gets. At first, I didn't believe he was capable of doing all these things; I thought he was making it up. So I started asking around and found out, yep, he definitely was. In truth, many Geminis have this many-lives thing going on in some way. It may be difficult for those of us who don't have this kind of extreme diversity going on to understand that a Gemini can do it all—but they can . . . and they love it!

There's another kind of Gemini who remains constant and consistent for years, perhaps decades, then wakes up one morning and decides to change their life altogether. (This usually happens when they're around forty years old.) Whatever the nature of Geminis' multiple sides, it's important they own them all as valuable parts of their being. When used correctly, these various parts of Geminis' nature help them to discover more about the meaning of life and their own purpose.

In living the archetype of the Quick-Change Artist there are few things Geminis *can't* do. Their love of, and need for, variety keeps them enthusiastically developing whatever gifts and interests they've got. Most Geminis are satisfied dabbling in their interests, just wanting a "taste" of what things are about, and then they're eager to move on. Other kinds of Gemini get wholeheartedly involved with their interests and fully exhaust all the possibilities of each.

One thing is for sure: Geminis will be involved in multiple interests at one time. They love the excitement and the variety of keeping lots of "plates spinning on sticks." Working on one relationship or project feeds their enthusiasm for their other relationships and projects. Whereas some people would get confused with all this activity, Geminis thrive because of it.

Another aspect of Geminis' Quick-Change Artist is their arsenal of creative talents. Geminis are usually quite artistic and clever: Painting, sculpture, styling and designing are among the activities they're likely to be good at and want to pursue. Geminis love the variety and surprise element of art. And, true to their nature, as soon as Geminis get good at doing something one way, they'll experiment with doing it another.

Then there's music. Most Geminis have learned at least a little about how to play an instrument (even if it's air guitar) and many are quite gifted musically. Geminis appreciate the lyrics and melodies that music offers, and are good at creating it themselves.

The sign Gemini rules the hands, and Geminis are exceptionally good with theirs. They have a need to keep them busy and useful. So, they find countless outlets for their nimbleness and dexterity: Pursuits like music, crafts of all sorts, knitting and carpentry can be fulfilling for Geminis. But Geminis don't stop at just one creative outlet: They are eager to try something new, and keep tinkering with what they already know.

Geminis are also natural actors. Their creativity, combined with their ability to mimic and imitate allows them to study, and then become different kinds of people with penetrating insight. Whether or not a Gemini is a professional actor, they are sure to act in their everyday lives. Geminis like to try on different nuances, attitudes, even appearance styles just to keep themselves interested and fresh, and to see what will happen when they do.

The Quick-Change Artist in Gemini needs to keep active and engaged. Projects, ideas, relationships, trips—all keep Geminis motivated and excited about life. But, if they attempt to explore everything that interests them all at once, it will scatter them and leave them without satisfactory knowledge in any area. Geminis need to remember that although their lives are about having many experiences, those experiences can, and should, happen over a span of time. If it's their destiny to do something, life will open the door for it.

So, it's fine for Geminis to go ahead and jump in with both feet with what interests them and allow themselves the joy of really exploring something fully. Then, when they've fulfilled one interest, they can go on to explore something else.

Geminis' multifaceted nature serves their spiritual growth by giving them the ability to approach their spiritual essence from many different directions. It's been said there are many paths to God. Geminis may pursue multiple spiritual philosophies, use what works for them, then move on.

The Trickster

There is also a side of Gemini that demonstrates the archetype of the Trickster. Geminis use their Trickster energy playfully, to have a good flirt, a satisfying spar or an unexpectedly fun interlude with someone. And they love to tease or play a good practical joke on someone—it might even be their way of showing affection. They'll wink as if to say, "Gotcha!"

Geminis are good gamesmen and find life interesting when they challenge themselves to see how well they play the game. They love twists and turns in life, and they'll do things to create them. Geminis will do the unexpected; they'll act like they're going in one direction, then take another, they'll say one thing while thinking another. They love to surprise others (and themselves) with doing things that catch them off guard. Exactly how or where Geminis express their Trickster energy depends on the rest of their chart.

Part of Geminis' Trickster plays out in their ability to guide people in directions they want them to go, many times without them knowing it. The Gemini intelligence generally allows them to be way ahead of other people's thinking so while others are still gathering facts and evaluating, Gemini has already sized up where matters are going and how that will impact them. If things aren't going to Geminis' liking, their wit and finesse knows just how to reroute circumstances so Geminis are more satisfied. They do this without being pushy or overt. Instead, Geminis are incredibly charming about it. Geminis have a gift of salesmanship: a knack for presenting their ideas in a way that entices others to want what they have or to follow their lead. Geminis don't need to be heartfelt, or even believe what they say. It's not exactly that they are deceptive, however; they will say whatever's needed in the moment, knowing all along that's exactly what they're doing. They figure life's a game and they will say what they need to win in that particular aspect of the game.

In business, Geminis' Trickster mind helps them to strategize and negotiate masterful deals. They can promote anything, coming up with sales campaigns that make even the most ordinary product gleam and glow. And no other sign can juggle numbers to make a deal work like Gemini. Their versatility thinks way outside the box and comes up with truly clever ideas. And they love it. Coming up with strategies that prompt people to do things is exciting to Geminis. It's a game worthy of their intelligence. They can't wait to see if it will work.

There are other times Geminis' Trickster energy might express itself in a naughty way or where it might downright take advantage of others. Hence the reputation Geminis have of sometimes being untrustworthy or con artists. Most Geminis don't set out to harm anyone, but sometimes they just can't resist a prime opportunity for a prank when it shows up. And, sometimes, they don't plan to be the Trickster—their wit just leads them to it.

This is something Geminis (and others) need to be watchful of because, though being a Trickster is in essence a neutral quality, it is all too easy to use it to manipulate or gain at someone else's expense. So Geminis might want to check as they enter into Trickster mode that their intention is to have fun, or at least that it is not to be hurtful to anyone. After all, ultimately, we get back what we put out, and Gemini might be putting something into action that's hard to deal with at payback time.

Geminis' Trickster knows just how to get information from people who wouldn't ordinarily give it. One way they accomplish this is by claiming to have plans or feelings they suspect another might have. For example, a Gemini might say, "I'm really intimidated by giving this presentation." When in fact they aren't at all, but they are fishing to see if the others giving presentations are, in fact, intimidated. Since it seems like Gemini is opening up to others, others open up to them. Geminis walk away knowing their secrets, yet they know nothing of Geminis' truth. Other times Geminis will use their salesmanship to entice another away from who or what they want for themselves. Off they go in another direction while Geminis pluck their intended prize. Or Geminis might just act like they know something, and get others to spill the beans before they realize the Gemini knows nothing of it at all.

Another Gemini trick is the one that embodies their dual nature: They will play on both sides of a situation, eliciting trust and secrets from all involved. This double-agent tendency can show up in lots of areas of life, from relationships to business, to understanding both the male and female sides of Geminis' sexuality.

Geminis' Trickster archetype can sometimes make them feel like they are impostors. Maybe that's because Geminis can play the part of one. Their remarkably changeable and chameleon-like nature prompts them to join into novel situations, and gives them the skills it takes to relate. Geminis' wit and ability to convincingly present knowledge, even with things they know very little about, allow them passage into many arenas. And then they learn even more by being there.

But, if Geminis actively promote themselves as something they're not, or pretend to understand something they don't, they may fool others, but they can't fool themselves. Inside they'll know they're faking it. It's one thing to do that for fun, and Geminis do. But if Geminis judge themselves as being bad for faking it, they could live with a fear that others will eventually catch on to their game. Or, worse, Geminis could get so entwined with little lies, they can forget who they are at their center core. Instead of knowing it's them *playing* a role, they might start convincing themselves they *are* the role and get confused about who their true Self is. Geminis can even believe there is something ungenuine about their very essence.

Needless to say, that makes intimacy or true friendship difficult—if not impossible—because there is something Geminis think they need to hide. As soon as others begin to get close, a Gemini might bolt, fearing they will be exposed as an impostor. It's better if they are up front about the fact that they are exploring a new situation or expression. People will adore their charm and the quickness with which they actually do learn, and then they will accept Gemini on their terms.

The truth is, most people feel like they are impostors from time to time, no matter what sign they are. That feeling is rooted in the fact that we are part human, part Spirit. Almost everyone feels they misrepresent themselves, knowing inside they are much more than they express. So, it is wise for Geminis not to judge themselves.

The spiritual opportunity Geminis' Trickster gives them is in learning to outwit even their cleverest negativity, their most insistent Lower Nature, and to allow themselves to slip away clean into their higher expression.

The Gemini Gifts: Multiplicity!

Geminis have so many gifts, it can take them a lifetime to explore them all! But here are some that they can use every day. . . .

Of all the signs, Gemini can be the most **Fun.** This is at least partly due to the many aspects and gifts they possess and present.

Geminis' ability to **Assimilate** is also one of their most essential gifts. They have an uncommon ability to adjust their persona, their attitudes and their thinking to fit in, then to contribute to almost any situation. Geminis are quick to recognize the dynamics of whatever social culture they find themselves in, and become adept at participating with that culture as if they've belonged their whole life.

Geminis' abilities of **Mimicking and Imitating** assist them part of the way in doing this. Their assimilation process might initially involve "faking it," or mirroring what they see. But as they're doing that, they are reaching into themselves to find a part that is like the others, and bring it out for expression. In doing that, Geminis develop true understanding of the genuine qualities they were at first mimicking. This is not con-artistry; it is true assimilation. While Geminis are part of that group, they are truly taking on their culture.

This gift allows Geminis to fit into countless unique and varied situations. When they're at an auction in the farmlands of Ohio, they're like the farmers who are bidding on the bulls. When Geminis are at the opera, they're loving the music, and mingling and conversing in a most knowledgeable way with those who have studied the art form for decades. And when the Gemini is at a Buddhist retreat, they are most contemplative, reflective and intent on getting free of their karma. In each of these situations, Geminis find within themselves what that culture values. That's how they learn.

With this gift, Geminis can do or be almost anything they put their minds to. They can work for years in one profession, then change tracks, quickly assimilate into the culture of another profession, and rise quickly to the top. They will be most welcome participants in all the areas they're interested in because they can make an interesting contribution to whatever the culture finds appealing.

Geminis assimilate knowledge at the speed of light. Whereas other signs may need some time and practice to understand a concept or idea, Geminis seem to capture the essence of an idea instantly. Geminis' minds make connections, draw conclusions and see inferences. Indeed, they can hear an idea one minute, then be teaching about it the next—complete with the accompanying lingo. I've gone to dinner with my students after one three-hour astrology class and watched the Geminis talking to the waitress about the characteristics of their sign with such clarity and insight it seemed like *they* were the astrology teacher. (I did not begrudge them.)

While Geminis are assimilating, it is important that they keep connected to their Inner Core. There is a Self that remains constant throughout every situation they will ever experience. If Geminis confuse assimilating, which adds to their repertoire of behavior and knowledge, with surrendering their Self, in which they let go of their core values and truths, they will become lost in a sea of actions and traits. The challenge for Geminis is to learn more about their Essential Self through their experiences, not give their essence over to them.

This ability to assimilate assists Geminis' spiritual growth by helping them to quickly develop their Higher Self, or more refined frequency, once they recognize it's there. Some Geminis study spiritual figures to assimilate the knowledge and transcendence they possess. Other Geminis assimilate spiritual knowledge through reading about it. Still other Geminis are able to assimilate knowledge directly from their Higher Nature, learning to progressively touch into and develop their Higher Essence. (That, of course, requires that they slow down, turn down the volume of their mind and open themselves to receive from the higher/inner levels.)

One of the great benefits of Geminis' assimilation gift is they are **Great Travelers** (one of their most favorite pastimes of all). Geminis almost immediately begin to pick up the culture of wherever they are, and copy it until it's no longer a mimic. Rather, Geminis genuinely understand and integrate the traits of the culture under observation. They will easily assimilate not only the language, but also the nuances of the culture: when it wakes and goes to sleep, how it eats and takes its coffee. Geminis are completely there, and they take on the new culture with gusto.

Assimilating also makes Geminis the **Fun Friend.** They grasp what people want and need in order to connect, and they bring that out in themselves in order to befriend them. Much as they do in foreign cultures, Geminis do the same with other people: They speak other people's language (so to speak), and quickly get into their world. Geminis fully enjoy what others enjoy and do what they do, at least for a little while. But if another's world ultimately doesn't prove exciting for Gemini, they'll move on—but they sure were fun and interesting while they were there.

Versatility is another one of Geminis' gifts, as well as one of their life's strategies. They have an uncommon ability, as well as a need, to approach life with a vast array of abilities, strategies and attitudes. For Geminis, there is never one set of ways things should be done. Repetition, or regimentation, even if they are effective, bore Geminis to tears. There's no spark in them, nothing to learn. Rather, Geminis' joy comes from trying new pathways and strategies in every aspect of life, from their work to their relationships, to how they feed the dog. (This changeability can drive the dog crazy—unless, of course, the pooch is a Gemini, in which case it's perfect.)

Geminis love **Experimenting** with life and seeing what happens when they try different things. This versatility expresses in both Geminis choosing to involve themselves in many and varied life experiences, as well as their ability to approach familiar situations in creative and novel ways.

Geminis have incredible **Mental Versatility,** which allows them to capture and entertain all kinds of ideas and concepts. They can fully develop one angle of an idea or concept, then switch their perspective and develop a completely different angle of it altogether. Then, they'll gather information that helps them spark a new approach again. If something doesn't work, Geminis will fluidly move to another idea that will. Geminis' minds love playing around with endless possibilities, many times entertaining them all at once. Just because they think something is true or right one day, doesn't mean they'll think so the next. Consistency isn't all that desirable to Gemini. Remember, to Gemini, variety is the spice of life.

Geminis are also **Versatile in Actions.** They will do something until they get good at it, or until they feel they've solved the mystery of it, then they'll try it another way altogether to see what happens. The challenge to Geminis' versatility is dealing with a situation after they've explored all its possibilities. They might think it holds nothing more for them, and fear boredom. That's when Geminis' versatility is truly needed. It's then when they have to apply the versatility to their *attitude* toward whatever they are doing. That serves Geminis in that they begin to recognize aspects of their own nature that can contribute to their awareness, which might have been lying dormant. By developing the versatility of their consciousness, as well as the versatility of their mind and actions, Geminis discover the awesomeness of their own essence.

In this regard, it certainly helps that Geminis have remarkable **Imaginations.** They can dream up all kinds of things that are worth trying or pursuing, and that gives them a creative edge to doing even the most mundane duties in life. Instead of being satisfied with something that's tried and true, Geminis' imaginations explore what other possibilities might work. In doing so they're most inventive and clever—and fun. No one—not even they—can predict what they'll come up with next.

Geminis also have the gift of great **Playfulness.** Their nature gives them an ever-youthful quality that loves having fun and fooling around. They're silly, funny and entertaining, and almost instinctively know how to get the laughs. No matter what kind of situations Geminis are in, they will look for ways to have fun there. (Leos love fun as well—Leos and Geminis are a great duo.) If matters start to get too heavy or stuffy, Geminis will use playfulness to lighten things up and make them interesting. But, if something isn't fun, and Geminis can't do anything to liven it up, they'll bug out.

No matter what their age, Geminis will often act like kids. Their curiosity draws them to wanting to know what something would feel like. So, when all the adults are standing around watching the children jumping through the water sculptures, the big kid running around with them is probably an adult Gemini.

Geminis' playfulness is attracted to games of all sorts. Along with their love of word games and puzzles, Geminis love to spar and play mind games with others. And they do so regularly, whether others catch on to it or not. Geminis also love games that challenge their dexterity, and challenge their motor skills. And no one, but no one, is a better poker player than Gemini. Every aspect of the game, from the keeping track of which cards were played, to the adventure of betting, to the acting it takes to keep a "poker face," makes use of Geminis' innate skills.

Geminis' playfulness is also expressed through their **Love of Entertainment**. They know how to capture an audience (even if it's an audience of one: the Gemini), and keep them intrigued and laughing. Geminis act, tell stories, make up jokes, do tricks, and are so incredibly charming and endearing that people can't take their eyes off them.

And Geminis love *to be* entertained. They search for people and forums that capture their fancy, make them think and laugh, and present the world in a refreshing new way. Because of that, Geminis can be found working or volunteering in most entertainment fields, either as the talent, or in a supporting role.

Geminis' playfulness can work as an effective coping mechanism for difficult or painful situations. They use comic relief as a way of easing intensity off themselves and others, even if it's just for a minute. It's not that they're disrespectful of what's going on; they just think any situation would benefit from a little levity.

Part of Geminis' playfulness comes from the **Ever-Youthful,** Peter Pan-like quality of their nature. In truth, most signs of the zodiac can have members that are Peter Pan-like, but Geminis wholly embody it. There is an "I don't want to grow up" aspect to Gemini that wants to keep life magical. It keeps them perpetually seeking, and full of hope. This Peter Pan seeks fun by having things be ever exciting, promising and fresh. That keeps their juices flowing. When matters are light-hearted and variable, Geminis are entertained and intrigued.

But because Geminis' Peter Pan quality doesn't want to face maturity, they can feel threatened if things become sober or demand responsibility. If a situation starts to ask too much of them, or takes a turn for the intense, Geminis can start to feel confined. They might think, *Uh-oh, I don't want to get caught here!*—fearing the situation might choke the life out of them.

If Geminis can't find a way to make a situation bounce back to something free and easy, they might bolt. They could do this by extracting their feelings from a situation, or simply become coolly intellectual and just surf the surface of what's going. Or they might leave the situation altogether. Sometimes, they'll do that just long enough for things to smooth out so not as much is needed from them. Then they will return as if nothing has happened, ready for more fun. But many times, Geminis will be gone for good, on to the next adventure, one that isn't so heavy.

This side of Geminis' nature serves them by keeping them from getting too enmeshed in situations they needn't participate in. But it can also keep their growth stunted, and their experiences limited. Geminis might mistakenly think that if they get too involved with the heavies of life, including commitment, they'll lose their freedom to move and breathe and investigate all of their interests. That scares them. They think they might miss out on something valuable or more exciting.

But in truth, if Geminis resist diving deeply into their own or other people's feelings and needs, they are likely to miss out learning and experiencing some of life's most fascinating offerings. The surface of matters can be interesting, but it's what is going on underneath the surface or what happens when the going gets rough, that brings out some of the most compelling aspects of Geminis and others.

If Geminis have the urge to bolt from a situation, it helps if they try using their curiosity to help them linger just a little more. Instead of fearing they might be confined, they might imagine ways they can be expanded or enhanced by what can happen. That will give them the courage to stick around. Geminis' versatility can then adapt to the situation, and show them ways to deal with it and learn from it.

One of the things that makes Geminis fun is their insatiable **Curiosity.** Being able to explore something that's piqued their interest is what gets them up in the morning—and it's what keeps them going all through the day. Curiosity is the basis of Geminis' learning: They are irresistibly drawn to people and situations that are new or novel, for they hold a promise that Gemini is going to learn something. And that something might just change their life, even in a little way. Geminis' curiosity keeps them alive and fresh, and interested in life.

The force of Geminis' curiosity can bring them courage. If they're feeling withdrawn, shy or sad, even unworthy, Geminis' curiosity moves them toward getting involved with whatever is present. The idea that they might learn something can be stronger than any need to withdraw. It keeps Geminis perennially interested in life. They can hardly believe it when people tell them life is boring. To them, life is an endless offering of curiosities that need examining.

Importantly, curiosity holds boredom (one of Geminis' worst fears), at bay. It provides them with a steady stream of situations that are worthy of exploration and participation, and that keeps life from becoming predictable and ho-hum. Indeed, curiosity is one of Geminis' key motivators. Their curiosity tells Geminis, *Now this is really going to be fascinating!* And their urge to learn goes after it.

Curiosity also keeps Geminis learning more about life, and how others live it. Whereas some signs develop their philosophy early in life and stick to it, Geminis' curiosity keeps them looking to update their viewpoint. They'll interview people about what they think on various subjects, perhaps pluck an idea or two from them, and then assimilate it as their own. Geminis are more open-minded than most other signs of the zodiac, always ready to consider another's point of view as interesting, if not truly valid.

Geminis' curiosity serves them spiritually because it keeps them ever alert, ever seeking the "what else?" in life. When this is applied to their consciousness, they can keep exploring the different facets of their human-spirit potential, climbing ever higher in their perceptions and understanding.

The Gemini Fears: Death by Boredom

Boredom scares Geminis to death! Since they thrive on being stimulated, they can fear that if they become bored, life will become unbearable. This fear of boredom can work against Geminis by convincing them that if matters become ordinary or predictable, there will be nothing they can do to make them interesting. Geminis project that they'll become trapped with no outlet for their considerable curiosity and intelligence, and energy. They fear that becoming too familiar with people or tasks will make life uninteresting, with no color or meaning. Boredom can seem like the ultimate prison cell.

These fears can keep Geminis from committing to or completely involving themselves in a situation. They will attempt to keep their options open by keeping one foot out of their experience, poised to step into another experience that might be more appealing. If Geminis are in one job, they'll investigate another to see if it would be more satisfying. If they are in one relationship, they'll keep looking around, even flirting, to see if there's anyone who's more interesting.

But in truth, that keeps Geminis from the fulfillment they seek, because they're not positioning themselves to truly learn what their situation is offering. In fact, they might be courting boredom by not allowing their involvements to reach levels they haven't yet explored. By keeping themselves riding the surface of situations, Geminis don't change or evolve. They remain the same, and just involve themselves in a series of experiences that in the end only take Geminis to the same place: the consciousness they had started from. That's because Geminis are not invested enough to be stretched or challenged by their experiences.

The irony is that boredom doesn't come from knowing something all too well—it comes from not being present with what is. So, by withholding their involvement, Geminis actually create the boredom they fear.

When Geminis learn the trick of bringing everything they've got to everything they do, whether in stunningly exciting or terrifically ordinary situations, they remain compelled because they are aligned with the endless aspects of who they are. That applies to activities Geminis become involved with or relationships they are in.

Geminis have to discover how to do this so it works best for them. I once asked a Gemini when he knew to leave one interest to pursue another. He told me he liked to let go of a situation just before he learns everything there is to know about it, which left a little mystery in it. He loved living life knowing there were still mysteries.

Geminis can also **fear confinement.** This might be physical confinement, wherein they might feel hemmed in by their environment, unable to move freely and enjoy new vistas. They need to be able to "travel" in some way. This travel could be to the park every day, or it might be a need to travel to other lands. (I know one Gemini who needs to get in his car and drive—anywhere—just to see the scenes flow by him.)

If Geminis are experiencing a time of life when they feel physically confined, they might be able to deal with it best by learning to travel the vastness of their own consciousness. They might be learning how to use their remarkable imagination as a tool to develop a rich inner experience. Or Geminis might be learning how to tap into their spiritual awareness and travel through levels of consciousness that are far more amazing than any physical location on Earth.

Geminis can also **fear intellectual confinement.** This can be when they are in situations where they're unable to express their ideas freely, or in which they don't have the opportunity or space to explore new and refreshing ideas. Indeed, the thought that they can't develop or express their thinking can be truly scary for Gemini! This fear can serve them by keeping them alert and impelling them to seek situations where they are, indeed, encouraged to develop their intellect. But it can also lead Geminis to darting away from situations that might challenge them to stand up for their ideas more.

If Geminis do find themselves in a circumstance that seems intellectually confining, they can still be plenty stimulated. They might take that time to develop their inner intellect—their ability to communicate within themselves, and develop the multiple facets of their own inner consciousness. In doing so, Geminis have the opportunity to develop aspects of their deeper intellect and intuition that they might not have had the opportunity to if circumstances were more open.

Geminis tend to also **fear emotional confinement,** or getting "suffocated" by feelings and needs—either their own, or someone else's. They might fear the "overwhelm" that emotions can bring, or the dependency that emotional alliances entail. Geminis can fear that other people's needs might ask too much of them, or their own needs may make them feel too vulnerable. Because of this, Geminis might have a tendency to disappear the minute the relationships start to ask anything of them. They will tell themselves they need to "break loose" and move on to a situation that isn't quite as intense.

At times that might work okay for Geminis; they don't need to experience every tense moment. But if it's a habit for them to cut out when things seem uncomfortable, either inside of them, or with another, they might be selling themselves short. They are robbing themselves of going to the deeper, more potent, levels of life. The very illumination Geminis seek might be available in situations from which they have tended to flee.

If Geminis are starting to feel a bit overwhelmed with emotions—theirs or another's—it might work best if they brought in their curiosity. They can ask themselves, *What's this about? How does this work? What are these feelings saying?* When Geminis' curiosity is activated they can move past fears of confinement, and instead focus on the learning and fascination that's present. In doing this they are adding to their repertoire of experiences.

Geminis' love of variety can also cause them to **fear commitment,** projecting it will limit their choices. And it will. But limited choices don't mean limited experience. Geminis will find that if they invest all of their cleverness into whatever situation they commit to, they will experience things that are much more profound and enlightening than if they skip from one thing to the next. Commitment allows Geminis to reach many levels and facets of themselves and others that could be lost if they were not completely involved. In other words, Geminis will gain in the richness from the quality of the single experience in place of the novelty from the quantity of many experiences. And, in fact, they just might find (okay, they *will* find) it's the richness they are really after, not the variety.

Commitment does not mean leaving some things out—it means bringing everything Geminis can to what they're doing. Being committed allows Geminis to develop all the angles of their perceptions and abilities in whatever they're involved with, and allows them to cultivate their capacities.

One of the more unique Gemini **fears is expressing their "evil twin."** Many Geminis report they have one side of their nature that is so dark, they consider it their "evil twin." When I point out that everyone has a dark side that surfaces occasionally, these Geminis insist that their dark side is with them *all the time.* They say they have to work hard not to let this dark side show, for fear it will be destructive, or cause them to lose what they value, and alienate those who love them. While it is probably not as ever-present as these Geminis fear, this side of them does exist, and does surface from time to time, sometimes at the most awkward of moments.

For example, Randy is a corporate coach who helps top-level executives sharpen their skills. Although he is usually very positive and inspiring, occasionally his so-called evil twin surfaces and he becomes angry and abruptly critical. Randy reports he has to put great effort into resisting his temptation to lash out at his clients, especially when they seem the most vulnerable. Upon reflection about this side of his nature, Randy realized that he fears his own vulnerability and feels scared when he sees it in others. Now, he understands that his evil twin has just been telling him he needs to face, and heal, his own fears about being vulnerable.

It's important that Geminis remember the evil twin side of themselves is there for a reason. Chances are it's not really evil at all, but simply a side of their nature that's at odds with what they've created in their life. It is probably made up of wishes and urges that they have pushed down or ignored, and that part of Gemini feels neglected and angry. They might want to bring it up for air, explore it and see what it really wants. It's possible the so-called evil twin has feedback for Geminis about what they are truly capable of in this life, and offers them talents and perspectives that can help them achieve something valuable. By acknowledging and loving that side of themselves, they might bring greater harmony to themselves and fulfill something in their life that's of value.

But, like all the signs, Geminis can just have a negative side. Because Gemini is learning about ways to bring what seems like the duality of life into a workable harmony, it might be that being aware of the negative aspects of themselves emphasizes their challenge to continually choose the light, or positive side of their nature. In that way, Geminis' temptation to express negativity strengthens and enhances their ability to choose and develop their Light.

Gemini in Relationships: "Variety Is the Spice of Life"

Geminis are incredibly social creatures and adore all kinds of relationships. They have a genuine interest in others and enjoy finding out what people are about. Most Geminis have a wide circle of friends that they circulate in and out of. What's interesting about Geminis' friends is that they come from many walks of life, have varied interests, and may actually be quite different from one another—but they all have something in common with Geminis.

Geminis are the first in—and the first out of—relationships. Their natural curiosity draws them to new faces, and their social skills allow them to befriend others quickly. But because Geminis can get bored very quickly, they can go from being totally smitten and devoted to becoming distracted, then gone, in a very short period of time.

What ensures a Gemini's continued presence is variety. Friends and loves of Geminis keep them around by finding ways to keep the Gemini interested. Geminis fall in love intellectually—it's the mind, not the body that attracts them: They can't resist someone who makes them think or laugh. So if you're in relationship with a Gemini, find little pieces of information that make for good conversation. And be willing to try new things. (If you are in a romantic relationship with a Gemini, trying new things sexually is very important, and Gemini will lead the way.)

But save your need to probe emotionally or indulge your emotional outbursts. That turns Geminis off, as do displays of neediness or possessiveness.

You might discover your Gemini friend or love disappears from the scene from time to time. Don't take that personally. They regularly step away from situations, even if they're good ones. A Gemini just needs to spread their wings. Sometimes, Geminis dart out of relationships because they're feeling very deeply, and fear the vulnerability of their affection. When that's the case, just keep yourself busy. Sooner or later, your Gemini will be back, fresh and renewed, acting as if nothing happened. But it's also possible your Gemini has found another attraction. More than any other sign, Geminis can juggle multiple relationships and not get overwhelmed. You will need to find out if you are Geminis' one and only, or if they have another beloved in addition to you.

If you are going to be in relationship with a Gemini, you'd better be ready for conversation. Constantly. They want to, need to, talk about every little thing, all the time. If you're the type that loves quiet time, or prolonged periods of silence, a Gemini might not be the one for you.

If you're trying to catch the eye of a female Gemini, do clever things that engage her wit. Send her well-written articles, take her to a variety of interesting places and flirt like mad. Hand holding, gentle kisses and brushing her hair away from her face bring out her passion more than more overt sexual moves. She's sexual, but prefers to lead up to it with lots of flirting and talking. Remember, you need to engage her wit before she will take you seriously.

If you're trying to catch the eye of a male Gemini, wow him with your wit . . . then leave! Let him wonder what happened to you. Male Geminis like to be lured in little by little; they love a bit of hide and seek. Importantly, they yearn for a great conversation, and discovering intelligence in another. Be tasteful—they don't appreciate lewd acts. Rather, try being breezy and flirting, and think up ideas for trips, excursions and new places: They bring out the romantic side of Gemini males. And remember—variety is the spice of life for him, so if you're the type who likes to be spicy in a variety of ways (if you know what I mean), all the better to keep your Gemini interested and coming back for more!

The Last Word on Gemini

What Gemini offers us is seeing the wondrousness of the world in all its diversity, and learning that we can use the variety we find either as a distraction from or an avenue to our own self-discovery.

Chapter 4

Cancer

(June 22–July 22)

Cancer is the quality in you that is sensitive and caring, seeks to create a safe and homey atmosphere, and enjoys providing what's needed to make life flourish around you. It's also the part of you that's learning the secret to the true essence of nurturing.

"Sit down, relax, eat, would you like a cup of hot chocolate?" If you want to do Cancer friends a favor, let them feed you.

Cancers have a deeply sensitive and caring nature, which they tend to use to nurture everyone, and everything, in sight. Cancers are like both a mother (even the men) and a child at heart. On the one hand, they are driven to protect and nourish, so all they take under their huge, loving wings can flourish. On the other hand, Cancers are vulnerable and innocent, eliciting and receiving nurturing care from others.

Cancers have a powerful drive to create security and connectedness, and their gut-level understanding of what's needed and how it's needed make them invaluable supporters in any situations. Cancers' changeable nature runs the gamut between quiet introversion and bubbly extroversion, and everything in between. Cancers are the homebodies and family lovers of the zodiac. But since the world is their family, they can also extend their uncanny instincts to sensing and providing what's needed in the marketplace or for the public in general.

The Cancer Mission: Learning It's Natural to Nurture

All of us are learning what Cancers are born to discover: The Highest Essence of nurturing is nurturing one's True Essence.

Cancers are in their highest expression when they are aligned with the "home within." This is a place of inner safety and nurturing inside themselves. When Cancers are in contact with it, they enjoy knowing that they are protected and safe. From this sanctuary, Cancers are able to fluidly give to and receive from life, understanding that the world, and all its inhabitants, are one big family.

The Cancer Challenge: Finding Security Through Insecurity

Interestingly, one of the ways Cancers learn about how to nurture themselves is by dealing with, and overcoming, feelings of insecurity. Insecurity is Cancers' greatest challenge and most powerful teacher. The form of Cancers' insecurity can change as often as the Moon (their ruling planet) does. Usually it involves some feeling that they won't have or be enough to meet the demands of life. Cancers can worry about money, or fear they don't measure up to the talents of others, or just have a sense that some tidal-wave-like catastrophe can take away all they love or have.

Whatever form Cancers' insecurity takes, it is in truth a call for them to tap into their inner resource of self-care and self-nurturing. They are learning to support and stand by themselves and reassure themselves that no matter what, they inherently have whatever's needed to take care of themselves and their loved ones. Insecurity can also teach Cancers to ask for assistance from the Divine Parent, and realize the countless ways they are, indeed, always cared for.

Insecurity also teaches Cancers another important lesson: trust. Cancers are learning to trust that the way things are unfolding is as it should be. They are learning that just as a loving parent tends to its child's needs, so does the benevolent universe provide what Cancer truly needs. The more Cancers learn to tap into trust (and stepping out of trust is a good way to learn to tap back in), the more trust becomes stronger and more consistent in their consciousness.

The Cancer Key: Nurture Yourself

Here's the secret: The way Cancers can access the essence of Divine nurturing is by becoming a good parent to themselves. That means doing those things that support them on every level—loving themselves no matter what, making choices that truly support them, and offering themselves (and taking) wise counsel, so who they are can thrive. In doing so, Cancers build a deep well of security, wisdom and creative power inside themselves. Then, in their fullness, they extend that same empowering support to others.

A CRAB, but Not Necessarily Crabby

Cancers' astrological symbol is the Crab, and they will undoubtedly recognize some of their characteristics in the behavior of that adorable crustacean. Just as a crab carries its home on its back, Cancers are learning to find that always-present inner home. Crabs can retreat into their shell to protect their vulnerability, as Cancers can "go into their shell" when needing to protect their soft side. Interestingly, just as crabs many times walk sideways, Cancers sometimes approach situations from the side, instead of going directly for what they want.

If ever you've seen a crab use its huge claws to clamp onto something it wants, then hang on for dear life, you'll understand how Cancers grab on to something, or someone—especially in an emotional relationship—and never let go. This determination is designed to help Cancers hang on tight to their spiritual center and not let anything in the world pull them away from it. But there will be times when Cancers want to hang on to other things, like their kids, their stuff (of which they have accumulated plenty), or the way things were. Those are things they will eventually have to release, however. And, let's face it, if Cancers let their bad moods take over, they become downright *crabby*.

WATER, Water Everywhere

Cancer is one of the three Water Signs. (Scorpio and Pisces are the others.) Being a Water Sign means Cancers' primary way of relating to the world is through feelings or emotions; they are most comfortable using them as their reference. Cancers have a very deep emotional nature, which they are learning to harness and guide so it supports their wholeness and expansion.

The unique Cancerian expression of Water is the way Cancers use their feelings and emotions to sense what's needed in a situation, so they can wholly satisfy their caregiving/caretaking needs. Cancers' depth of feeling also contributes to their compassion. They hate to see any living thing hurt and will use their considerable power to help make matters better.

Cancers' feelings are a rich part of both their experience and expression. They are the tools Cancers use in order to make heartfelt connection with others, and form the deep bonds of intimacy they crave.

Cancers' emotions and feelings are powerful. So powerful, in fact, they sometimes think they *are* their feelings, or that their emotions are their truest indicators of reality. Sometimes that's true: Cancers' feelings can give them uncanny insight into what's going on in a situation, or into a person's inner Self, even if appearances portray something different. They also help Cancers evaluate whether or not someone is safe or trustworthy, as well as whether or not something is right for them.

However, because feelings can sometimes be inaccurate, Cancers can sometimes be thrown off course if they give them too much power. The trick for Cancers is to check the impulses of their emotions with their minds and hearts. That helps Cancers get a clearer idea of whether their feelings are accurate, or if they are simply reactions. This can be challenging for Cancers because their feelings are so strong, they can convince Cancers something is happening (like a hurtful slight) when it is not. When this occurs, Cancers can expend loads of energy reacting to their feelings, even spending hours upon hours worrying about something, instead of doing what's really productive. That can keep them from making the most out of the opportunities that life offers them.

Cancers are learning how to channel the power of their emotions to serve the wisdom of their heart and the direction from their Spirits. In doing so, Cancers are better directed toward what's truly right for them, and they can use their passionate emotions as fuel to accomplish that.

Indeed, Cancers can ride on their emotional energy to make things happen in life. It provides immense energy from which Cancers can create. In using their emotions positively, Cancers are potent and wise creators. For example, instead of expending emotional energy worrying about whether or not an upcoming project would be successful, Cancers are wiser to use their emotions to start to "feel" excitement for their project, and perhaps even feel what it's going to be like when the project is a success. In that way Cancers use their emotions to lift and energize them, instead of discouraging them with negative images. Used this way, Cancers' emotions become well-honed instruments for discovering ever-greater aspects of their True Self.

Being a Water Sign means that many of Cancers' life lessons involve learning how to take positive dominion over their emotions, and use them in an expansive way. But if Cancers don't mature and direct their emotions, they can be run ragged by them. That's awkward because Cancers can feel out of control, and others don't like it because they never know when Cancers are going to go off.

Cancers' negative feelings can parade as, "I'm not good enough," or "No one loves me," or, sometimes, "I just want to run away and hide." To counter these feelings, Cancers might just need to acknowledge them. "I'm feeling unworthy" might be pointing to a place that needs loving or healing. These emotions might be trying to tell Cancers that something is amiss in the way they are behaving or treating themselves. "I'm angry!" might be a signal that Cancers are hurt about something and need to address it. Perhaps someone overstepped a boundary and Cancer needs to declare it. Then, there are those feelings that are pouty or whiny, which are signals that Cancers might be looking outward for the support they really can be giving to themselves.

Many Cancers think they're stuck with these defeating feelings because it seems as if they completely take over their mind and body, and there's nothing that can be done. But there is a lot that can be done—and should be done. Cancers have these negative emotions for a reason: They exist to help them learn to harness and direct their personal power by choosing to move away from them. As Cancers learn to redirect the negative energy of emotions into more useful expressions, they become more masterful creators.

It's exactly the times when Cancers are reacting like mad or their self-esteem is dragging around the ground that they are learning the lesson of being a Cancer: self-nurturing. When Cancers take dominion over their emotions, they demonstrate that *they,* not their feelings, are the captain of their ship. When Cancers bring the loving of their heart, and the understanding of their mind to nurture themselves and lift themselves out of negativity, they reconnect with the energy of their birthright. Some call it the Divine Parent, the Loving Universe, the Mother Mary. Whatever name they have for it, when they connect to it, Cancers know they are well cared for. The more they do this, the easier and faster it becomes. Over time, Cancers find negative emotions are no match for the loving power of their True Essence.

Plainly said, it's Cancers' job to bring maturity to their emotions in order to experience the best of what their sign has to offer. Just as raising a child involves differentiating what works from what doesn't, Cancers are learning to raise themselves emotionally, finding ways to use their feelings so they are lifted and expanded by them.

It's never a good idea for Cancers to attempt to control their immense and powerful emotional nature by simply denying their negative feelings, or trying to close off to feelings altogether. It would be a shame if Cancers masked over their vulnerability—it's one of their most endearing traits. Closing off emotions isn't mastery, it's just shutting down.

The best approach, if Cancers are to gain the greatest value from what they have been given, is to use the energy of *all* of their feelings to nurture and lovingly support themselves.

The CARDINAL Quality of Cancer: Initiating and Impelling Emotional Dynamics

Cancer is one of the four Cardinal Signs (Aries, Libra and Capricorn are the other three), which makes Cancers dynamic, with a driving need to initiate matters. Cancers' unique expression of the Cardinal energy is initiating emotional dynamics. Cancers like to keep the emotional energy of whatever they're involved in moving and active. Their own feelings are dynamic in that Cancers are always aware that they are feeling something. They might not always show how they feel (especially if they feel unsafe), but feelings are churning inside of Cancer nevertheless. Most Cancers need to "get it out" and express how they feel, just to give themselves some relief. Sometimes, Cancers' feelings are so close to the surface, they laugh or cry, whether they want to—or plan to—or not.

Cancers also enjoy initiating the expression of others' emotions. Intellectual conversations are fine only up to a point for Cancers—then, they want to get to the meat of the matter and find out what others *feel* about what they are talking about. And they know just what to say to elicit the response they're looking for. Cancers are the first to say something like, "How did you feel about somebody else getting the promotion?" Then, they give a look that says, "You can tell me. I'll understand." And they do. Whereas other signs (all the Air Signs particularly) might find emotional sharing unnecessary, or a distraction from the truth of the matter, Cancers find feelings fascinating and of the utmost importance. If someone needs to sort out their feelings, Cancers are always interested parties.

Sometimes, in Cancers' Cardinal need for action, they might create feelings that might not really be there. They can prod others to express what they feel, when, at the moment they don't feel anything (except possibly annoyance). Or Cancers can take a little feeling and blow it into a big feeling, and create a dramatic scene. Although that can sometimes turn out to be unpleasant for the Cancer (as well as others involved), at least something happened.

Cancers use their Cardinal energies to initiate circumstances that enhance their security. They are quick to get themselves a home, and quick to fill it up with a spouse and kids. Cancers also move and shake in their careers, as well as get actively involved in any organizations that interest them. When Cancers learn to redirect the impatient quality of Cardinal energy into courage and forthright determination, there is nothing they can't accomplish.

Cancer is a **Personal Sign.** That means their attention is directed toward their person, and their immediate environment. Whereas the Social and Transpersonal Signs need to affect vast numbers of people as a way of developing their nature, Cancers' job is to develop their Self as richly as they can. After that, they can attend to the multitudes.

Cancers' challenge of being a Personal Sign is to develop their True or Higher Self, rather than their Ego Self. If Cancers just focus on their personality, they risk becoming selfish or self-involved, which keeps them immature. When that's the case, Cancers become consumed by their own wants and needs. And they forfeit the joy of nurturing others, because they aren't aware of anyone but themselves. If, instead, Cancers direct their focus toward developing their higher qualities—such as loving, nurturing, tenderness and compassion—they are able to bring out the best of their Spirit.

There's a MOON Out Tonight

Cancer is ruled by the Moon. The Moon governs all things nurturing: feelings, emotions, home, family, women, motherhood, children and food. It also governs things that support or influence us—whether we know it or not—such as cycles, the unconscious and family heritage. It's likely these are very important areas of concern and interest to Cancers, and they might choose a career that involves one or a few of them.

The Moon is an extremely potent influence on humanity. This translates to Cancers being an extremely powerful force in their environment. Although Cancers are sensitive and tender, make no mistake: They are also very strong. Just as a mother is kind and nurturing, yet fiercely protective—not to mention an incredibly important influence in her family's life—Cancers' Lunar Energy makes them gentle, yet determined and valuable contributors to any situation they participate in.

The Moon is a Luminary because it reflects light. [The Sun is also a Luminary because it generates light. See chapter 5.] Cancers do the same in that they reflect the nurturing aspect of the Great Light: God. Cancers are also able to reflect others' feelings and thoughts in a way that helps them better understand themselves.

What's interesting about the Moon is that it changes signs about every two and a half days, traveling through the whole zodiac in twenty-eight and a half days. This means Cancers' moods and expressions can change every two and a half days. It's even likely they will reflect the different moods and attitudes of the sign the Moon is passing through. So, there's a changeableness about Cancers: They're fluid and multifaceted. If others want to get to the whole Cancer, they need to stick around for some time and see all the different expressions, moods and attitudes they express. (They should also go to their home. That's where Cancers are most genuine and powerful.)

Actually, moodiness is something Cancers deal with. Some days they'll be all bubbly, enthusiastic, full of smiles and open to all. Other days, Cancers become irritable and sullen, and not want anyone to talk to them. In truth, it's not just Cancers that have to deal with this moodiness. Those around them may have to contend with their ever-changing feelings as well.

Each of Cancers' moods and introvert/extrovert inclinations serves a purpose. So, it's important that Cancers search for the wisdom and messages that lie within their changing nature. But, even if "a mood hits" them, Cancers don't need to let it take them over. Cancers are still in charge of themselves and their attitudes, and can choose which mood to hang on to and which mood to let pass on by.

If Cancers don't take dominion over their moods, they will not only be controlled by them, they might be tempted to inflict their feelings onto others. If Cancers let their moods run them, they could become so reactive that others start walking on eggshells in their presence, trying to avoid a disturbing scene with them. (Cancers can rationalize that others need to be sensitive toward them because they are so tender. Not usually. They tread cautiously because they've seen that, if they do otherwise, their Cancer spouse/lover/friend might snap.)

The Moon also gives Cancers a deeply sentimental nature, which can express itself as an appreciation for things of the past. Cancers understand the importance of ancestors in the shaping of the world, and they probably enjoy learning everything they can about them. Cancers might study their family's history or world history. They can also be sentimental about their personal past—their childhood, their children's childhood, or what last year's prices were. In short, Cancer looks back. They can use their interest in the past to discover how the present was created. That will assist them in making good choices. But if Cancers become sentimental in the sense of boy-those-were-the-good-ol'-days, I-wish-they-were-here-now, they might be so caught up in the past, they will be distracted from the opportunities of their present.

Feeling Crummy in the Tummy

The sign Cancer correlates with the solar plexus. That makes Cancers sensitive in the tummy area, because it's the seat of much of their power. If Cancers find their solar plexus area is achy, or if they aren't digesting their food well, it might be a signal that they are not using or directing their power correctly. It helps if Cancers ask themselves if they are letting another control them somehow, even if it's by needing too much. If so, Cancers can redirect their flow of energy from their solar plexus area to their heart. That will increase their power, while helping Cancers to hold in a loving place toward themselves and others.

The Cancer Archetypes: Trust in God, Child, to Provide

In order to explore and express the nurturing aspect of God, Cancers have been given the energy of archetypes that help connect them to that essence. Cancers (and those who are Cancer-like) will live the archetype of the Nurturer, the Child and the Provider. These traits support Cancers' learning about life-sustaining energies, of both themselves and God.

The Nurturer

Cancers demonstrate the archetype of the Nurturer by bringing life and support to everything around them. Their natural tendency is to caretake: Nothing satisfies Cancers more than tending to the well-being of someone or something they love. Cancers instinctively know how to nourish and nurture. No one needs to show them how to tenderly feed a baby, make a garden flourish, or be a soothing and comforting confidante for a troubled friend. They are simply compelled to help things grow and they go about doing it in many ways each day.

One of the most likely ways Cancers demonstrate their Nurturer archetype is by being a parent. Cancers absolutely love and adore children and usually have a powerful drive to have at least a few, if not many, of their own. Cancers are doting parents who make their children the main focus, the central meaning and the greatest pleasure of their lives.

Parenting comes naturally to Cancers—from day one, they instinctively know exactly what their kiddos need. And a Cancer parent never considers their parenting job done: Even when their child is sixty, they still worry whether or not they are getting enough to eat, or if they should put on an extra sweater to keep warm.

Although Cancers make most excellent parents, not all Cancers are destined to be parents. Some are charged with parenting themselves this lifetime, and that's job enough. Other Cancers parent artistic creations, while others parent other people's needs. Many are the Cancers who parent their clients in some way as an expression of their nurturing.

Since family can come in any form, sometimes Cancers' families are made up of a circle of friends. Or, they might make a family of their beloved animals, or of nature itself. However Cancers create it, it's important that they have the experience of being part of a nurturing system, for that is the foundation of their well-being.

No matter who or what Cancers nurture in their lives, they need to make sure they don't go overboard and become downright smothering. Although Cancers want to protect loved ones from any possible hurts, they have to remember that everyone (including their children) needs to live their own lives. That includes making their own decisions, even if they're bad ones. If Cancers get feedback that they're overwhelming their beloveds, it's a great time to refocus on themselves. Maybe their worry about others has been distracting them from something within themselves that could use support and love.

One thing is for sure: Cancers' lives will involve a steady stream of various people and projects they parent. But it's important to remember the first assignment for Cancers is to parent themselves. That's why many Cancers aren't satisfied with how their own parents nurtured them: They are learning to do it for themselves. Parenting themselves is an act of alignment and cooperation with whatever is for their highest good. As Cancers learn to step away from those activities that don't serve them, and choose activities that do, they demonstrate responsible creating—the lesson and the highest expression of their sign.

If Cancers slack off on self-parenting, they risk underdeveloping the self-worth and the self-esteem it provides. They might find it hard to find their "center," that aspect of themselves that is crucial in their ability to deeply trust or respect themselves, as well as to assess what's right for them.

One red flag indicating Cancers might need to increase self-parenting is finding the world perpetually threatening. If they believe they need to be defensive, or assume that people will somehow use them or do them harm if they open their heart, it's likely that unhealed feelings are running them.

If Cancers are carrying painful memories of past hurts, it's important they do whatever it takes to heal and forgive them. Otherwise, Cancers' tendency to cling to the past, coupled with their sensitivity, will convince them that people are trying to harm them in the present, when they aren't. Cancers can "clam up" and hide their charismatic Spirit, and that puts a huge crimp in their relationships. Remember, when Cancers take good care of themselves, it's unlikely they will be victimized. Cancers are no wimps, and it's important that they don't assume they will be hurt if they open up.

Cancers love to be needed. They enjoy giving something of value to others, or providing them with something that fulfills them. And they find countless ways to do that. But they have to watch for the sneaky Cancer tendency of trying to earn love or self-worth by being needed by others. Cancers might attempt to become over-responsible—overly involved in others' lives—as a way of being useful, and therefore lovable. This is an illusionary need to be needed. It can keep them distracted from dealing with their own challenges and lessons—even for decades—while trying to be a solution to other people's problems.

Instead of being a good example of self-parenting, demonstrating so others see how to take care of themselves (which Cancers are really good at), Cancers might encourage others to stay in their weakness. Cancers might be tempted to try this with anyone, but it's likely they will pick the relationships closest to them. So, it is important for Cancers to check to see if they are encouraging neediness, especially from their kids or their spouse.

If Cancers find they are confusing being needed with being loved, it's just a signal they need to learn more about finding value within themselves. They do that by attending to their own needs, and doing those things that build their self-esteem. In that case, they can do for themselves what they are so good at doing for others: supporting themselves back into strength.

The marketplace is another arena for Cancers to use their nurturing skills. They can create a satisfying career doing things that involve helping things to flourish: children, adults, animals, nature, houses—whatever particularly interests them. Just as a mother knows what her children need, Cancers have instincts for what the world needs. They can use these instincts to know what's the next fad, the next need, or the coming interest of their community, and set out to get into the business that fulfills it. Cancer Energy is a natural at marketing products that involve helping families or their homes: home furnishings, children's products, kitchen stuff, or real estate itself, can all be interesting businesses for Cancers.

Cancers will nurture and sustain whatever livelihood they select. They will tenaciously put in long hours to make sure what they are creating is well cared for, so it can thrive. It truly doesn't matter what Cancers choose to nurture, as long as they do it.

However, because Cancers are rampant nurturers, they need to be aware of what they are nurturing inwardly. It's a great idea to consciously choose what they want for themselves and what they need to nurture in order to get there. **Qualities like inner security, self-loving, patience and wholeness are the kinds of things Cancers would do well to nurture, and they blossom beautifully. By focusing on intentions like these, Cancers provide a good guide to their powerful creative energies and decisions.**

Accentuate the Positive

If Cancers are not mindful of what they are nurturing, they could be tempted to nurture things that don't support them: like feelings of worry, hurt or inadequacy. Their sensitivity to others is deeply affected by them, and, sometimes, Cancers can get hurt by what others say or do.

Hurt feelings are a tendency of the sign of Cancer, so it's important they develop healthy strategies for dealing with them. If Cancers allow themselves to nurture their hurt feelings by doing things that sustain those feelings—like brooding, imagining the hurtful scene over and over, feeling sorry for themselves, or even considering themselves a wounded person—they are helping those worries or hurt feelings to flourish. Or Cancers might feel inadequate and build a case against themselves, comparing themselves with others and coming up short. That's the time for a good dose of self-support to redirect the nurturing energy into a positive direction.

If Cancers find they are nurturing things that don't lift them, they can shift their focus to nurturing those things that do. They can remember what a great person they are, how caring and considerate they are; generally just be good to themselves. Cancers have a most powerful capacity to be loving toward themselves. It's important for them to do it.

At the same time, it's important for Cancers to learn the difference between self-nurturing and self-indulgence. Self-nurturing supports their whole being, and sets a foundation for them to gain more inner strength. Self-indulgence, on the other hand, might look like nurturing, but it's really supporting some kind of weakness.

When I was earning my master's degree in psychology, there was a strong emphasis on developing self-nurture strategies. A group of six of the students in my class responded with an attitude of "All right!" and started treating themselves to Häagen-Dazs after every session, not to mention taking advantage of the huge brunches at a nearby hotel. (They were not all Cancers, but they all had Cancer in their charts.

Believe me, each sign has its indulgence.) After gaining a total of a hundred pounds between them, they began to see that, although good food is terrific, eating it didn't truly support them in their grander goals of what they wanted in life. If anything, it set their goals back a few months. So they switched their strategy for self-nurturing into things like getting plenty of sleep, asking for that long-overdue raise and setting aside quiet time for meditation. After that, they downright prospered.

Cancers are also learning to use "climbing into their shell" as a time to truly take care of themselves. It's very important that Cancers have plenty of time for themselves; time to withdraw from the demands of the world. Usually this happens at home. Alone time helps Cancers recharge their batteries. This is very different from climbing into their shell to hide out, not wanting to face the world or the life they have in it. Hiding out in their shell keeps Cancers from participating fully in life, and from learning the valuable things they have intended to this lifetime. Although avoiding the harshness of the world might have the semblance of safety and control, in truth it only causes Cancers (or anyone) to delay the success that comes from participating in the world.

Cancers need to be mindful of their tendency to withdraw. They can hide in their shell while in a room full of people by withdrawing their participation and expression. Or they could pull all of their feelings into their shell, never expressing them to others, thinking that's the way to keep themselves safe from hurt, or criticism, or exposure. This isn't self-nurturing; this is letting their fear of hurt or exposure run them.

If Cancers find they are retreating into their shells it's a good time to "parent" themselves and attend to that part that's withdrawn or scared. Chances are, their Inner Parent knows some creative ways to handle most, if not all, of their life's challenges. After all, their challenges are there for them to learn about their strengths, and we are never given a lesson without the resources to learn from it.

Cancers' Nurturing energy ultimately expresses in them *creating*. Each Cancer expresses this differently, but somehow they have to give birth to their ideas: I've seen countless artists, landscapers, actors, writers or simply the owner of the cutest house in the neighborhood all under the sign of Cancer.

Don't Mess with Mother (or Father) Cancer

Cancers' Nurturer archetype is incredibly protective. They do whatever it takes to defend anyone or anything that's of value to them.

Cancers can be ferocious when protecting. If they feel that someone or something in their charge is threatened, they can switch out of their Mama Bear disposition and become the Growling Grizzly. They will do whatever it takes to form an impenetrable barrier against whoever or whatever is impinging on their territory. This is a terrific asset: Whomever and whatever Cancers are responsible for can rest assured knowing they will go to the greatest lengths to keep it safe and thriving. Cancers do this, and it empowers them.

Cancers need to put limits on their protective nature, or it can tend to extend them too far! They might think that *they* need to protect anything and anyone that needs protecting. If Cancers try to champion every person who their sensitivity tells them needs protection, they will soon find themselves overextended, wiped out and resentful that no one's taking care of *them*.

In such situations, their lesson is to once again align with the first key to their power: Take care of themselves first so they can give to others from their overflow. It will serve them to remember that the Nurturing aspect of God provides each person with exactly what he or she needs to deal with their life's circumstances. Cancers needn't underestimate anyone's ability to handle his or her own challenges. And since Cancers don't know what another person needs to learn or what muscles they need to develop, it might not be the highest act for them to try to assist.

When Cancers wisely use their protectiveness it creates a safe space so they and what they are protecting can flourish. It works best when coming through the energy of loving and tenderness. But if Cancers let their protectiveness be driven by a fear that something terrible will go wrong if they're not 100 percent in control, they can become overbearing in their protection. Overprotectiveness not only gives a constricted feeling, it cuts Cancers off from the very source they are designed to connect with—God's Nurturing. Control makes Cancers forget the Divine One is overseeing everything, as well as providing everything and everyone with what they truly need to accomplish their destiny.

Taken to extremes, Cancers' protective side can even make them paranoid. They can become suspicious that others are after what they've got. They will project that others are undermining their power, or trying to steal away with something or someone the Cancer values. This negative perspective keeps Cancers defensive and armed because they've lost their ability to discern whom to trust. If this happens, it helps if Cancers return back to the part of themselves that knows that what's theirs is theirs and cannot be taken away. It also helps Cancers to put things into perspective by counting their blessings, and coming back into their powerful Inner Parent-center where they know that they can trust life.

The spiritual purpose of Cancers' nurturing gift is for them to nurture along their spiritual growth. They are designed to create a safe and loving space within themselves so their True Self can develop, flourish and express.

The Child

Cancers demonstrate the Child archetype by having a vulnerability about them that expresses in some way a need and a desire to be nurtured. Their mother is the first one Cancers are vulnerable to, and in many ways she will be a larger-than-life character for them throughout their lifetime. Most Cancers are incredibly attached to their moms, and devoted to them as well. The mother is the Goddess to Cancers, and that's that.

Not surprisingly then, Cancers are incredibly influenced by their mothers. Most are eager to please their mothers (unless they are reacting perversely, then they're eager to displease her). In order to do so, Cancers might be tempted to live their lives according to their mothers' plans, instead of being true to their own dreams and wishes.

Cancers' allegiance to their moms can sometimes lead to problems in their marriages. Because Mom is so central in Cancers' lives, spouses of Cancers can sometimes feel they're in second place. I heard one husband tell his Cancer wife that if he had just one-tenth the power over her that her mother did, he'd be happy.

When Cancers get along well with their moms, they should consider themselves kissed by fate, because that love will be an incredible support for them in this lifetime.

But when Cancers do not fare well with their mothers, fate might have kissed them as well. Although it was likely devastating not to have the kind of loving attachment they craved, not connecting to their mom might have been necessary for those Cancers to learn one of their life's greatest lessons. If Cancers do not get what they need from their mother (or a nurturing Dad), they are compelled to find nurturing in other ways. This looking for and finding other avenues of nurturing can awaken Cancers to the understanding that nurturing is everywhere when they have the eyes to see it.

Most important, though, is that Cancers are learning to recognize the nurturing they hold within themselves. Indeed, they are prompted to find their Inner Mother. Although it might seem unfair to some that they have to do that (while others get to have loving mothers), in truth it's a fantastic opportunity for Cancers to learn to touch into the high frequency of their sign. When they find the presence of nurturing in all kinds of forms, Cancers understand their mother is not the only source of loving support for their Child archetype. That's awakening.

The bottom line is that Cancers tend to work out much of their karma (life's lessons) with family, particularly their mothers. These lessons aren't really about their mom—they are truly about Cancers being the "Child" and having their own relationship with the feminine or nurturing aspect of God. If Cancers had problems with their mother, they might project that those same problems exist between themselves and God. If Cancers didn't think their parents took good care of them, they might suppose that God won't either. But that's an error in approach. That can lead them to not noticing all the good things with which they have been provided.

It's important to Cancers' emotional health to forgive any judgments they might have about their parents not doing things right in raising them. Chances are they were doing exactly what was needed for the Cancers' development. Cancers do much better to put their focus on allowing themselves to be nurtured and supported by the Divine Parent. I've known countless Cancers who report feeling the presence of the Divine Parent when they interact with nature. Others feel the Divine Parent moving through them as they participate in the arts. Many tell me that as they nurture their own children, they themselves feel nurtured by the Divine. However they do it, when Cancers allow themselves to connect with the plentiful nurturing of Spirit, their consciousness moves to a higher state.

Cancers' Child archetype gives them the disposition for what they are here to do: allow themselves to fully receive from God and others. Innocence is the key gift of this childlike quality. Innocence doesn't judge, guard itself or push life away. It assumes nothing. When Cancers are in their consciousness of innocence, they are open to understanding the true wonders of life. The openness of their childlike nature gives them a receptiveness and curious wonder about life. It gives them a youthful joy about the simplest of things, such as hugging a pet, or walking in the rain.

Cancers' innocence is also incredibly endearing. It quickly disarms other people's defenses, putting them instantly at ease. Then there are those times when Cancers become the magical Child, full of luminescence and capable of wondrous things that go beyond their normal talents. Those might be the times Cancers' innocence allows them to be a pure vessel for Spirit to create, lift or heal.

This state of innocence is a fantastic place for Cancers to return to during times of emotional upset. If they touch into that place inside that is innocent and doesn't "know" how things should be, they will be less hard on themselves, and less upset with their life's situations.

Childlike is different from immature, however, and it's important that Cancers don't overdevelop their childlike nature or underdevelop the maturity of their Parent aspect. If they do, they might demonstrate the lesser expression of their sign: neediness. Thinking they are unable—but really they're unwilling—to support and fulfill themselves, Cancers might look to others to fulfill their needs. They'll be tempted to cling to others for fear that if they leave them they will be stranded with nothing. Needless to say, life is very threatening then, because Cancers will be out of touch with their own resourcefulness.

In such cases they can get disappointed, thinking others aren't supporting or giving to them, when in truth it's not the job of others to do that. If Cancers forget that they are the receivers of the universe's bounty, and instead believe they are needy of certain other people's support (like their parents' or spouse's), they'll try to extract things from people that those people might not want to give. Or Cancers might get into relationships where they play the child and the other plays the authority, allowing them control in exchange for security. That might work for a while, but in truth it may cause the Cancer, and quite possibly the other person involved, to miss their higher calling. It's needless to be needy. In truth, Cancers are incredibly strong and resourceful.

The Provider

Cancers display the archetype of the Provider by making sure they deliver all the support and sustenance needed for themselves and loved ones to live a safe and fulfilled life. Whereas Cancers' Nurturer archetype wants to hold the world to their breast and protect it from harm, their Provider archetype wants to be able to give everything it takes for life to flourish around them. There is a need to give of themselves those things that are needed by or could "complete" others. This giving fulfills Cancers. Instead of tallying up how many favors they've done, or meals they've lovingly cooked, Cancers understand that by giving unconditionally, with no strings and no expectations, they receive.

Giving through Cancers' Provider energy puts them in harmony with the Divine One and fills them with an energy of connectedness and completion. When tapping into that energy, Cancers have a sense that there's nothing they couldn't—or wouldn't—provide for another. When they do this, they access the Universal Parent energy.

Security—in every form—is mainly what Cancers are driven to provide. They will tirelessly do whatever it takes to provide a foundation of home, family and loving support for themselves and their loved ones.

Emotional security is job one of Cancers' Provider archetype. It's extremely important for Cancers to know that they are surrounded with safety, love and support, and that those they love are, as well. "Am I safe?" is the very first question Cancers ask in any situation. "Am I safe to express myself?" "Will I be loved?" "Will I be cared for?" These are all conditions they survey before truly relaxing. Although this world doesn't always present safe situations, Cancers do their best to gravitate toward them whenever possible, and leave those exciting, but threatening, scenes to others.

Emotional security involves physical well-being: such as a safe and secure (read: paid for) home life, and knowing those immediately around them will support them. Cancers want their circle or family to be safe and complete. "Is everyone accounted for?" "Sleeping tight?" "Without distress?" "Is there anyone I need to attend to and comfort?" When that's established, Cancers look to make sure their feelings are safe: Will they be understood? Will others safely regard their feelings (so they can open up), or will others deny Cancers' feelings or hurt them (sending them off to their shell)?

It's not just a one-way street, however. Cancers are also likely to extend themselves so that others who might be asking the same questions can feel secure in their presence. They'll say the kind words, give the sincerest encouragement, show heartfelt understanding and in general do whatever is appropriate and necessary to get the job done. This is so instinctive in Cancers that they might not know they're doing it until they've done it. They just don't like to see anyone falter. Cancers are quick to fold their protective and loving arms literally or figuratively around anyone—or anything—who needs them, hoping to provide them with the support to "make it all better."

It's important for Cancers to extend the Provider archetype toward themselves by providing what's of true and lasting

importance to them: self-respect, self-appreciation and self-support. In doing so, they fill themselves up and make themselves even more prepared to provide for others.

Home is another extremely important factor that Cancers' Provider archetype seeks to establish. Cancers need a place they and loved ones can retreat to, and feel safe in; a place that nourishes all who enter. They will devote lots of love, time and energy to making their home cozy and livable; decorating and home improvement are on the top-ten list of fun things for Cancers to do. So, it's likely Cancers will pay great attention to even the littlest details of making their house a home. But Cancers don't try to create a show home. They want a comfort zone. They want a place that is charming, inviting and filled with creature comforts: comfy, well-stuffed furniture, linens and bedding that are soothing to the touch (maybe they are family heirlooms), and a lovely—albeit little—wild garden.

The Way to a Cancer's Heart Is Through the Kitchen

Unquestionably, Cancers' kitchen is not only the heart of their home, it's probably the center of their Universe (unless there's a baby, of course). That's where the Providing can really take place. It's from there that Cancers cook: for themselves, their family, the teenagers down the street who need a "snack," the overworked people at the office who "need a healthy meal every once in a while," and anyone else they see who needs sustenance. It's as if Cancers were born cooking: They just naturally know how to whip up something scrumptious. But nothing too fancy: Cancers' cooking comes in great amounts, and it's the kind of food that soothes the soul and nourishes like only a mama's cooking can. Cancers generally shun the gourmet food that gets divvied out in teeny proportions. They want substance and lots of it.

Some Cancers want to provide a home so badly they'll do anything to do it. I have Cancer clients who work unbelievably long hours, just so they can afford a nice place. Although they're never home, they're comforted by the fact it's there when they're ready.

Cancers' Provider archetype is also intensely driven to provide financial security for themselves and their loved ones. Cancers understand the importance of money, so they don't part with theirs easily. More than any other sign (besides Taurus), Cancers have the ability to get remarkable value out of their dollar to provide for life's needs. Ever concerned about those possible rainy days, Cancers save and stash cash, usually in all kinds of locations—from the few bank accounts they hold, to the handful of twenties stuffed in their sock drawer, to Grandma's antiques they can sell in a pinch if they're really desperate. (Thank God, they're never really desperate, because, in truth, they're too sentimental to sell Grandma's antiques.)

No matter what Cancers' financial status, they always seem to be able to take care of their own needs. If a Cancer is a parent, they care for their children incredibly well. I have seen the children of Cancer single parents, or of Cancer parents of modest means, be better provided for than children of wealthy parents. Cancers just know how to provide, and they do it.

Cancers have to be careful, however, of their sign's tendency to worry about money: It seems no matter how much money Cancers have, they fear going broke. They start to imagine not being able to pay the bills, then not being able to pay the rent, then, they're homeless . . . and it's downhill from there. This is when it's time for Cancers to get honest with themselves: When have they ever been broke? A good percentage of them *never* have been, because they've made it their business not to be, and they're good creators—and providers. The ones who *have* been need to ask themselves if that experience was as terrible as what they're projecting the next one *will* be.

Importantly, Cancers need to know that just because their emotions tend to worry about money, it's not an indicator of their financial reality.

In their fervor to provide for others, there's one thing Cancers have to provide that they might overlook, and that is to provide others opportunities for them to take care of themselves.

Harry, a doting Cancer father, learned this from his daughter. For years (she was twenty-nine!), he insisted on paying her rent, for fear that his daughter couldn't afford it. He just couldn't bear the idea of his child homeless. But upon retiring from work, Harry found his budget no longer allowed for supporting his daughter. Harry spent many sleepless nights worrying that his daughter would be unable to care for herself. Although things were dicey at first, to Harry's amazement, his daughter started to become more ambitious and more involved with work. As a result, she actually received a series of promotions—which included salary increases. It seemed Harry's daughter needed to know she had to take care of herself before she would take the initiative to prosper at work.

The Cancer Gifts: Giving, Nurturing, Making Things Work

One of Cancers' greatest gifts is **Sensitivity.** When Cancers direct their sensitivity inward, they can tap into a deep source of natural knowing about how life works. It's a gateway for Cancers to touch into their feelings, their creativity and their Spirit. This deepens Cancers' self-awareness and gives them reference for what's truly right for them. Sensitivity also contributes to Cancers' incredible instincts giving them that "gut" reaction that helps them to know what to do and what not to do, as well as who and what to trust.

Directed outward, Cancers' sensitivity offers them keen insight into where others are coming from, which deepens their **Compassion.** Cancers have a kindness and a knowing way that comforts and nourishes others. Because they know how painful hurtful remarks and actions can be, their sensitivity also serves as a motivation for them to be harmless in word and deed. Cancers know just how and when to reach out to console another who's hurting, or to do whatever it takes to help someone or something flourish.

Some Cancers use their sensitivity to nourish their family; others use it to become excellent therapists or counselors, knowing just how to advise their clients in the tenderest way. In truth, most Cancers are natural psychologists and can't help but counsel and support others. So even if their interests lie outside of the counseling arena, it's likely Cancers will still be the ones people seek out for help.

Other Cancers use their sensitivity to **Recognize the Potential** inherent in situations. Whereas some signs look for the obvious openings, Cancers can "sense" the opportunities in life that might be quite subtle or hidden. My Cancer client, Leah, uses her sensitivity to find the sales racks at posh department stores. Another Cancer client, Jan, senses the mood of the stock market and usually makes great picks. Yet another, Michael, senses what kind of subtle behaviors casting directors are looking for in the characters he's auditioning to play, and adjusts his performance accordingly.

Cancerian sensitivity can also be a valuable asset in artistic endeavors because Cancers are able to tap into the subtleties that humans respond to. They can either paint things that soothe and nourish (or tickle the fancy), or use their sensitivity to capture the essence of humanity and become gifted actors.

Cancer people's sensitivity gives them a natural **Alliance with**

Women. Even the most masculine Cancer males are able to understand female's concerns and points of view. This makes them incredibly attractive to women. And it also gives them the edge in female-related businesses.

Cancers are also **Psychically Sensitive.** Their wide feelers pick up loads of information from their environment that is invisible or unsaid: others' feelings, thoughts, even the way other people's bodies feel. This psychic sensitivity can make Cancers susceptible to the moods of others. This can help Cancers in their care-giving, but it can also cause Cancers some emotional confusion. For no apparent reason a Cancer can go from being cheery to feeling down. If that happens, it's a good time for a Cancer to check and see if they "took on" an emotion of someone else. If so, a Cancer can resolve to let it go, and return to their inner balance. (A book on psychic self-protection can be a valuable resource for a Cancer.)

Cancers' psychic sensitivity also helps them tune into the natural cycles of life: to know when timing is right for something, when trends are about to change, what the world at large is feeling. It also helps them be uncannily aware of others in their environment. (I tell kids of a Cancer parent to just forget about trying to pull off anything sneaky—their parents have an invisible web that tells them just where and how they are—even if those kids are fifty!)

Importantly, Cancers' psychic gifts allow them to peer into the magical—or spiritual—working behind what "appears" to be real in life, and know the reality of those levels.

In order to use this psychic ability masterfully, most Cancers probably need to learn to distinguish between their own emotional reaction, or projection and something from their intuitive knowing, which is clear information. At first, they can seem the same, however, with practice testing results in the world, Cancers will learn the differences between these different types of impressions. Some Cancers report the tip-off of genuine intuition is the absence of emotion: Projections or reactions (or fears) generally have a feeling connected to them. Intuitive information comes through with neutrality. With awareness, each Cancer can undoubtedly find their reference points.

In short, Cancers' sensitivity is extremely attuned to their inner and outer world, and it gifts them with valuable information and insights. Few other signs have their sensitivity and natural knowing. They have to use the information wisely, though. If Cancers' "feelers" detect that someone is upset, or acting thoughtlessly, they might think it's because of something *they* have done. Cancers might suppose others are upset because they've hurt or angered them.

Cancers' sensitivity takes things very personally—sometimes, too personally. They can interpret that everything that happens around them is directed at, or because of, them, even when it's not. Therefore, it's important that Cancers remember to be objective: Others might just be having a rotten day, and (believe it or not) it has nothing to do with them. (One way to get clear on this is to check it out with the upset party. If the Cancer is the cause, they can make amends. If not, they can go about their merry way free of the concern they might have otherwise carried around for hours or days.)

Tenderness is another tremendous asset Cancers use in many ways almost every day. It allows them to nurture and cherish even the most delicate, precious, elements of life. Whereas other signs might trample over life, not noticing, Cancers are aware and thoughtful, insuring harmlessness. They use this tenderness in practically everything they do, from showing affection to feeding the cat, to negotiating big contracts. As dynamic and courageous as Cancers are, they do what they do with a soft touch.

A word to the wise: This soft touch of Cancers doesn't mean they are softies. There is a great power in Cancers' tenderness, and because it is so effective, they needn't push, shove or hustle.

I saw this quality in action in Cancer "CJ," who is one of the most prestigious Realtors in my city. When I heard of her sales reputation, and of the high-profile clients that fill her Rolodex, I figured she'd be one raw dynamo of a woman. But when I met CJ as I accompanied her and my friends who were looking at some new homes, she was soft-spoken, feminine and kind. What amazed me about CJ was the gentle, abiding way she did her job: She never pushed, never did a "sales job," but rather graciously felt out where my friends were at. She started to intuit what they wanted, even though I thought they were being kind of unclear. After a few showings, CJ said she had a hunch and wondered if my friends minded going off to a completely different area than they had targeted. They hesitantly agreed, and after some minutes we drove up to a most perfect home for my friends! We all gasped at how right it was, on every level. CJ smiled and said that she just follows what her instincts tell her. Then she trusts others will do what's right. I came to see her success was in yielding to what's present, and trusting the rightness of life. That's power.

Like the crab, Cancers are **Tenacious.** Simply put, once they've decided they want or need something or someone, they aren't letting go. Cancers' emotions give them a passionate power that keeps pursuing whatever it is they desire. Cancers know what they want and they will stay focused until they get it. And then, as far as they are concerned, nothing or no one is getting it out of their little claws if they don't want them to.

Cancers' tenaciousness helps keep them on course in life. Long after others lose interest or allow discouragement to stop them in their tracks, Cancers stay **Determined** to get what they want. Cancerian Energy is a force to be reckoned with. This isn't always something they broadcast, however. Cancers can sometimes make it seem as if they're giving up on something, when actually they're just lying in wait until they spot the next opportunity to seize what they're after. Many times, a Cancer will seem as if they're working in a direction other than the one they really desire, but that's not the case. Cancers know how to circle toward something, and come at it from an angle others wouldn't have suspected.

Cancers' tenacity also has a quality of **Resourcefulness.** They know how to make the most of what they've got in order to build even more. Cancers can wring every drop out of a resource or circumstance, using it to its fullest capacity, or even using it for a purpose it wasn't designed to do. They can also apply their resourcefulness to how to get what they want. Whereas others look for obvious opportunities, Cancers recognize the subtle pathways and out-of-the-way openings that can be taken toward a goal. Even when the odds are against Cancers, they surprise everyone (including themselves) by finding a way to make things happen.

Cancers use their tenacity to grow spiritually by staying aligned with their inner core, no matter what is going on around them. By tenaciously holding to those emotions, thoughts and actions that serve them, they can more readily recognize and release those that don't.

That's the challenge of Cancers' tenacity: knowing when they need to hang in there, versus understanding when something isn't working out because it's not fated to. That can be hard to figure out. One key is if someone tells a Cancer they don't want to be with them they're probably telling the truth. This might sound obvious to other signs, but Cancers' tenacity many times causes them to believe that if they just hang in there a little more, the love they know is possible will rekindle. Or Cancers can hang on out of sentimentality or from lack—not knowing where to get security next. Those are times when Cancers have to tenaciously hold on to their own Self, their core, their Spirit, and let the other go.

The Cancer Fears: Mortified of Being Shell-less

Cancers' most primal **fear is of being unable to care for themselves or loved ones properly.** The thought of not being able to put food on the table or pay the rent is enough to keep Cancers up all night worrying, but it also makes them get up in the morning to go do something about it. This fear motivates Cancers to get busy working to ensure there will be plenty of cash so they will never, ever be homeless.

Fear of being emotionally hurt is one of Cancers' major bugaboos. They really hate it. Even though Cancer is truly a strong sign, many don't think they are strong enough to endure a hurt. There is some part of their nature that feels like it will just dissolve into a million tiny pieces, if hurt. Or, Cancers fear the pain will be so intense, they couldn't endure it. (Exception: parenting. Cancers will endure any pain, humiliation or hurt if it's part of taking care of their child.)

Cancers' fear of hurt can be immobilizing, and prevent them from expressing who they really are. Or they can become reluctant to go after what they want, if they think someone might respond in a way they find uncomfortable. Cancers might shrink away from asking for a date, or put off asking for the promotion they deserve, or hold back from letting those around them know how really fun and special they are. Cancer's dynamism might be stuffed down or turned off, so no one can say or do something in response that could hurt them. But, in doing so, they might be keeping something hidden that others could love.

Cancers can also become secretive, thinking the more shrouded they and their plans are, the safer they will be. This can intensify into a fear of being exposed simply for who they are and what they feel. There is absolutely nothing wrong with either of those, but Cancers can come to believe there is. Or they might become jealous, thinking if others know their plans, they'll try to steal them away.

Because of these fears, Cancers might be tempted to wall themselves off from others, thinking that will protect them. But, actually, it works against them. Shutting themselves off from others means they're shutting themselves off from the multitude of ways the Universe can give to them through others. When Cancers don't allow others in, they are robbing themselves of receiving the riches those others have to offer. And it makes it harder for people to give them what they want and need because Cancers might be keeping their needs and desires a secret from others.

Cancers also want circumstances to be just right before they make their move. But, in life, circumstances are rarely perfectly right. Instead, Cancers are learning to create the safety inside themselves so the world can do whatever it does, and they can still go after what they want, no matter what the atmosphere. Waiting for the circumstances to be just right, or fearing hurt because they're not, can keep Cancers from doing those things that could be part of their highest destiny.

Cancer in Relationships: "To Have and to Hold . . . *Tightly*"

Cancers adore intimacy, seek love, and are most tender and caring to friends and loves. They will sweetly touch and nurture you, and want to know everything about you: how your day went, who said what to whom and how they said it, and what your current troubles might be. They lend an attentive ear to all, and ask questions hoping they might assist you in fixing anything that is "off" with you. Then they'll make you laugh with their quirky, goofy humor. Who wouldn't want a Cancer around?

But, sometimes, Cancers feel like their loved ones don't want them around. Cancers can "clam up" and won't tell those close to them what's wrong. Or they will seem needy and clingy, trying to get reassurance. It's at those times Cancers are learning more about taking care of themselves. If you find yourself in that type of situation with a Cancer, you don't need to rescue them and convince them they are valuable to you. But you might remind them you love them and appreciate them.

Sometimes, Cancers just get crabby. Usually, it's when they are stressed out or feeling hurt. If your Cancer is being crabby toward you, you might want to bring it to their attention. They might not even realize they're acting that way. Tell them it hurts (if it does). They'll defend their position for a minute, but their compassion for your feelings will encourage them to alter theirs. It might also help them get to the bottom of why they are crabby in the first place, which usually has nothing to do with you.

Because Cancers live the archetype of the Nurturer-Child, they can create that dynamic in their relationships. It's healthy for the Cancer to be able to be both the Nurturer and the Child—to give and receive nurturing and guidance. It's important that Cancers watch so they don't get polarized on one end, either the Nurturer or the Child end. That can turn even the most romantic partnerships into parent-child dynamics; and, ultimately, that won't work.

If you are trying to woo a Cancer, do those things that make them feel safe and protected, even nurtured. Dinner is always a wonderful place to start: cook for your Cancer. They'll love it, and probably return the favor a hundred times over. Ask questions about their family of origin, paying special attention to "Who's Mom?" questions. And if there's anything you can see that you can fix around the Cancer's house, do it! They'll be putty in your hands.

If the Cancer you're dating happens to be raising children, you need to know that is truly their first job, and they will put their children's needs in front of yours. It's the ideal scene that you love the Cancer's children, because that will seal the deal with the Cancer. But sometimes personalities clash. If you don't mesh with a Cancer's kids, it makes it very difficult for the Cancer to consider you permanent. What could impress a Cancer in that situation is if you handle differences with maturity and love. They may see you have something valuable to bring to their family.

If you are getting serious about a Cancer, it's imperative to talk about the issue of kids: Do you want them? What are you willing to go through to have them? I've seen many couples with at least one Cancer partner have problems over children more than any other subject. (Well, how to spend money is a very close second.) You may as well bring that issue up and work it out before marriage—or any kind of partnership.

If you're trying to catch the eye of a female Cancer, show her you are sensitive to her feelings. She craves being deeply understood and cared for, and appreciates anyone who will extend themselves to do so. But in order for her to be attracted, she also needs to see a little "can-do" or take-charge ability. She's looking for security and wants a partner who can be counted on to keep her safe and provided for—especially materially. But don't overdo it to the point of seeming like a brute: She disapproves of thoughtless or dominating behavior. She's looking for a long-term partner; so show her how life with you would be comfortable and safe, and how she'd be better off with you than anyone else. Talk about what kind of home you'd share, maybe how it would be decorated. But, mainly, bring up the kids. Make sure you match intentions there. If you do, that's it; she'll be in hook, line and sinker.

If you're trying to catch the eye of a male Cancer, nurture him! He's attracted to someone who extends tender consideration toward him. He wants to be treated with special concern and doted on, wherein he knows he's particularly cared for. Show him ways you can provide for him. This might be through emotional support, creating a cozy home and family life, or even through your financial means. If the Cancer male you've got your sights on is more the Parent type, he's searching for someone he can take care of. Your vulnerability might be more enticing to him than anything else. Either type—Parent type or Child type—finds curvaceous bodies most attractive—especially ones with full bosoms. So if you've got it, flaunt it (but not so much that he has to deal with competition from other men). Because Cancer men are emotional, your intended Cancer is seeking to connect in an emotional way. He's interested in what he feels from you—so show him through your eyes and heart that you're there with him.

The Last Word on Cancer

Cancer is about giving, nurturing, providing and sensitive caring. When Cancers learn to provide those things to themselves at the same level as they give them to others, they are on the fast track to being uplifted and self-fulfilled.

Chapter 5

Leo

(July 23–August 22)

Leo is the quality in you that is dramatic and regal, seeks to create extravaganzas, and enjoys entertaining and ruling others. It's also the part of you that's learning that the power of your love is more effective than the love of power.

Ya gotta love Leos. No, really, you have to love them or they'll go away. The good news is, it's easy to love Leos.

Leos have tremendous charisma and courage that they use to entertain—and rule—a crowd. Leos are much like royalty at heart. They sense there is something special and magnificent about themselves, and they express it through their dignified manner and their stand-up leadership. Everything Leos do has a trademark of style: from their exuberant behavior to their ability to make life around them sizzle with excitement.

Leos naturally seek and exude power. They enjoy using it to promote themselves, and to bring their many creative visions into reality. Wanting to always be the "best," Leos will do whatever it takes to ensure they come out on top of matters and they have an impressive array of talents to support that. Leos not only come up with creative ideas, they also possess the organizational skills and the social magnetism to make those ideas happen. Leos lavish their legendary generosity and loyalty on those they love and respect. That, combined with their big-hearted nature and their flair for fun makes others want to be a part of Leos' success.

The Leo Mission: Learning the Power of Love

All of us are learning what Leos are born to discover: The power of love is greater than the love of power—as well as how to love one's self without needing love from others. As Leos express themselves authentically through the direction of their heart, the courage and the Divine Essence of who they truly are naturally shines through.

Leos' resolute will and sizable ego give them the confidence to go after what they want in life. Their challenge is to teach their ego and will to serve their heart, so they are guided by the wisdom of their Higher Nature, which loves. When Leos allow their open heart to lead the way, the power of the Sun shines through them, and their brilliance, dignity and foresight lets them move mountains.

The Leo Challenge: Let the Heart, Not the Ego, Be the Source

One way Leos learn that it's much wiser to use the power of love is by getting burned from indulging the willfulness of their powerful egos. Leos' egos are their greatest challenge and most powerful teachers. They are so grand that, if Leos let them run rampant, they might confuse their ego's will with God's will. When Leos allow one of their best assets, their confidence, to turn into arrogance, they become convinced that their own wants and desires are more important than anyone else's. Then, they turn from being beloved leaders to barking dictators. In doing so, Leos may get to the destination they envision, but it won't have Leos' signature of fun and the support of others to make it all the more worthwhile. In fact, when Leos push through their demanding egos, it leaves others fuming and resenting their overbearing control.

Not only that, but when Leos use their determination to will their personal desires into manifestation, they might disregard correcting feedback and end up creating something they wish they hadn't.

Sometimes, Leos' overbearing arrogance results in (gasp!) humiliation. Leos can become driven and self-important, and believe that there is nothing they can't do. Although this can be a positive affirmation, if it comes from a place of superiority or entitlement—wherein Leos believe they are so special that they could never be denied what they want—they are likely to be in for a rude awakening. If Leos don't get what they want, they can be stunned and shocked.

If, instead, Leos use their wills (and egos) to carry out the promptings of their majestic hearts, they operate from a source that is so dynamically wise and charismatic it compels others to willingly assist them. Then, Leos end up creating results that are a blessing for them and everyone around them. When Leos let their heart be their powerful guide, they intend to do what's the highest good for all concerned. That leads Leos to accomplish feats more magnificent and important and fun than anything their egos could have imagined.

Simply put, love is the foundation of Leos' true power. When they choose to be loving, rather than willful, Leos become truly great. They will need no applause (although they'll get that, and the support of others as well), because they'll have a deep inner satisfaction that comes from expressing their Divine Essence.

This love, by the way, is found differently by every Leo. Some just feel the magnificence of their hearts and go from there. Others open to the powerful energies of their hearts as a result of positive experiences with loving children, animals or Nature itself. Leos can even connect with the power of their hearts' energy by envisioning someone or something that they deeply love, and letting that energy fill them up. However they find it, it's important that Leos tap into the energy of their hearts, for it is the wisest and most compelling asset they possess.

The Leo Key: There Is Power in Humility

One powerful strategy (though it's one that Leos resist) for Leos to use so they are both powerful and loving is this: Bring a dollop of humility to everything they do. Humility helps keep Leos open and grateful, and prevents their egos from getting overblown. When Leos are humble, they can still be awed by who they are and what they do. (After all, that's their birthright.) But humility gives the credit to a higher source. Some Leos do this by saying or thinking something like, *The universe did great things through me today!*

Regal Leo, Royal LION

Leo's astrological symbol is the Lion because lions reflect their power and big-hearted nature. Just as the lion is considered the king of beasts, Leos' nature gives them strength and a dignified regal presence that translates into leadership and magnificence.

In the jungle, lions have little to fear. And Leos can be grander than their fears, stepping beyond "I can'ts" to "I cans." The natural courage and pride of the Leo nature ensures that they will take risks in life to create something worthy. Lions have the air of calm self-satisfaction; they know they're great. Leos give off a similar feeling that they are something special, indeed.

Leos' lion-like nature ensures that they walk, act and love in a way that conveys honor and pride. Leos even often look like a lion with their mane of hair, which they proudly coif, and sometimes augment with hats, jewelry or whatever suits their fancy.

Just as lions are loyal and protective of their own, Leos are unswervingly loyal to and protective of their loved ones. When Leos are happy, they purr. They say sweetly admiring things to those around them, and are grateful and gracious to those who give to them. But if Leos are angry, look out! Just as a lion roars when bothered, Leos roar when their powerful will is being thwarted. And if Leos' pride gets hurt—which can happen fairly easily no matter how dynamic they are—they will retreat into their den to lick their wounds.

There's a difference between male and female Leos that's exemplified when studying the animal kingdom. It's the female lion who does most of the work for the pride, while male lions guard the territory with their gigantic presence. Female Leos tend to put much more pressure on themselves to accomplish things than male Leos do. Female Leos often want so badly to exceed others' expectations, they will not only fulfill their promises, but do much more than they commit to. Male Leos, on the other hand, are quite satisfied with the contributions they make, and rarely feel like they have to overexert themselves to measure up. Both gender Leos, however, are masters at "selling" what they've done. They know how to build up and show off whatever efforts they've made.

Full of FIRE, the Power of the Sun

Leo is a Fire Sign, which makes them highly inspired and motivated to live life to the fullest. Leos are irrepressible: If something or someone captures their fancy, their enthusiasm catches fire and they're off to make it happen. Leos' expression of Fire is primarily directed toward creating. Just as a little spark can turn into a gigantic bonfire, so can Leos build magnificent creations from their littlest ideas.

Leos' Fire energy gives them confidence—they don't take time to reflect or worry about possible failure, rather, they believe in themselves and the goodness of the universe, and trust they are going in the right direction. There is fearlessness with this: Leos have a willingness to risk wholeheartedly pursuing whatever excites them.

Leos' expansive personal power has a need to consume anything that interests them: They are 100 percent present and involved with whatever they deem worthy. Leos ride the powerful energy of their passions, and plow full steam ahead, barely noticing obstacles (let alone warning signs), confident they will get to their goal. There's no stopping a Leo once they've locked their sights onto a target.

As Willful as a Lion

Leo is one of the four Fixed Signs. (Taurus, Scorpio and Aquarius are the others.) Being a Fixed Sign means Leos are driven to become fully engaged and deeply established with whomever and whatever they choose to involve themselves. And Leos do just that: If they love someone, they love them all the way; if they want to achieve something, they harness all their power and go after it. Fixed energy is willful, strong and structure-oriented. This gives Leos incredible personal strength and resolve. And it makes Leos dependable—they stick around to see matters through. This loyalty prompts Leos to stay true to their word: If they say they'll do something, they'll do it.

The unique Leonian expression of Fixed energy is demonstrated through their powerful use of creative will. Fixed energy helps Leos to harness their intuitive and creative gifts, and gives them a stick-to-it-iveness that allows their intentions to become manifest. Fixed energy also gives Leos a strong capacity for loyalty. They aren't easily seduced from their integrity's sense of what's right. Instead, Leos use their discipline and far-sighted vision of what's truly important, and that sees them through.

Leos' Fixed energy makes them determined. They figure that if something is worth wanting, it's worth committing to. They stick to their plans to achieve it. Leos use their determination to keep up their confidence, as well as their style, and absolutely refuse to get petty or whiny when the going gets tough. They treat obstacles like mere annoyances, because (wink, wink) Leos know the Universe is on their side, and they'll end up getting what they want.

The challenge of being a Fixed Sign for Leos, however, is recognizing when to pull their intentions off something and move on. Fixed Signs commit fully and completely—sometimes, to the point of getting stuck. Leos need to occasionally check in to review what they are committed to. At times they may discover they are committed to what they think they should do, rather than what's really working for them. Although Leos may sometimes believe that letting go or wanting out of a commitment is a sign of weakness, sometimes it's a sign of wisdom and real strength.

Everything Revolves Around the SUN

Leo is ruled by the Sun, which is one reason Leos think that the world revolves around them. The Sun governs individuality, power, vitality, expression and leadership, and Leos are imbued with all those traits. The Sun gives Leos a brilliant and expansive nature that radiates power and warmth. Just as the Sun brings forth life wherever it shines, Leo's exciting and loving presence makes things happen. The Sun is a Luminary because it generates light, and Leos' sunny disposition and charisma bring light and fun to whatever they involve themselves in. [The Moon is also a Luminary because it reflects light. See chapter 4.]

Leos are one of the strongest signs of the zodiac; they have a physicality that is vivacious and appealing, a resolute will, and their expression is dynamic and entertaining. Indeed, being ruled by the Sun makes them a force to be reckoned with! It's good to be a Leo! (Don't believe it? Ask a Leo.)

Being ruled by the power of the Sun, Leos have a need to feel great energy run through them, and personal power is one way to do that. Each Leo is driven for a different kind of power, but usually they seek the status and influence that power can bring. Whatever kind of power a Leo is attracted to, it's likely they will want a lot of it. And they will do what it takes to get it. Leos will use their determination, their charm and their strategic skills to navigate themselves right to the top. And, because Leos assume they can do the best job anyone can, they are comfortable when they get there.

Leos experience joy and confidence when they are in the limelight, and possess an innate ability to be at the forefront of any situation, whether it's the lead role in a play or the top executive of a corporation. Leos revel in being in the spotlight, and they handle it with finesse. They are generous and dynamic leaders, full of good ideas.

But Leos can take this too far and believe that they *should always* be the center of everyone's universe. When that happens, Leos become self-involved and demanding. The energy of the Sun becomes overwhelming and Leos begin to take energy from others, rather than radiate it toward them.

If Leos think they should always be the center of attention, they risk feeling something is wrong when they're not. They might feel awkward when being just ordinary, thinking they should do something in order to stand out more. Maybe they should—there might be something of substance they want to express, but are holding back. But, if all they want is attention—without really contributing anything—then it may be good for Leos to step out of the spotlight and just carry on being one of the many stars in the sky.

It's important for Leos to know that they are always enough, whether or not they're being noticed. That's why Leos need to keep in touch with their heart in everything they do. Being in touch with their heart keeps Leos connected with their Divine Essence. That keeps Leos clear about the value of who they are, and connects them to their own self-loving presence. From there, Leos' heart gives them instruction about how to lead and express in a way that makes them naturally compelling, as well as generous and thoughtful to others. That's what true royalty is.

Concerning the body, the sign of Leo correlates with the heart. That means that *Love* is Leos' greatest strength and most compelling quality. In truth, love is Leos' elixir of life: Without it, life is one-dimensional and colorless. Leos' heart energy fills them with so much love it cannot be contained. (This is especially true as children—they want to hug and love up every living creature around. That might become socialized to be more discreet, or even forgotten, but it remains Leos' truest nature.)

It also means that love, and matters of love, will be Leos' greatest challenge and their wisest teacher. The more Leos tap into and develop the power of their loving, the more they will discover an inner resource of energy that is constantly replenished, no matter what they do. If Leos underdevelop their heart—or their loving—they might, instead, find themselves depending on the power of their will. That makes Leos effective, but it can wear them down because they are not really in the "flow" as they are when following their heart.

Leo is what's known as a **Social Sign.** This means they identify themselves in relation to others around them. It also means they have a need to feel they are affecting others with their deeds in order to feel fulfilled.

The Leo Archetypes: Watch the Monarch Create to Entertain You

In order to fulfill their destiny of discovering their true majesty, which is of their Spirit, Leos (and those who are Leo-like) will live the archetype of the Royal One, the Potent Creator and the Entertainer. These qualities provide Leos with a glimpse of the true nature of their spiritual being.

The Royal One

Leos embody the archetype of the Royal One because they are, in a word, regal. Leos just know there is something very special about them, and they accept that as a natural fact. Because they honor and respect themselves, they carry an air of nobility, which attracts others to them. Leos' sense of Self is big: They are so satisfied with who they are and what they've been given (no matter what they have, it's the best) that they can't help but overflow and share themselves with all of their kingdom. They generously give of themselves, and make outstanding contributions to whatever they're involved in.

Since Leos are royal, they do what comes naturally: rule. (Just ask a Leo, they will tell you that Leos rule!) **Leos make compelling leaders because they trust in themselves, and trust in their strategic sense of how things should get done.** They follow their own visions and tastes, and, sensing they are superior, have total confidence in doing things their own way. Leos' contagious enthusiasm, as well as their impressive ability to sell their ideas, entices others to rally around to carry out Leos' dictates.

True to their royal nature, Leos are beneficent, even beloved, leaders. They motivate people and inspire loyalty by first recognizing, then bringing out, the best in whatever others have to offer. Leos know how their ego likes to get stroked, so they encourage others and praise their abilities, making sure others feel their contributions are important. (Leos easily praise others because they are secure in the fact that they are great, too.)

Leos' dignified self-respect commands the respect of others, and their integrity makes them worthy of the regard of others. Their regal leadership style makes them comfortable to envision, then carry out, the big dreams. Leos figure, *Why have a little, modest success when you can have a huge, flashing success?* So, they go after the brass ring in whatever area that interests them.

Therefore, Leos assume they should start at the top. Why not? They are royalty, and that's where they belong. Leos use their ability to promote themselves to convince others, including authority figures, to take a chance on them. Usually, they're glad they did. Leos are too proud to fail.

In living up to their regal sense of Self, Leos are usually as good as they say they are. Whatever Leos endeavor, they can do it all. They not only come up with clever ideas, they have natural organizational skills and can intuit how things should come off, step-by-step. On top of that, Leo's charisma attracts others and inspires the dedication necessary to bring their plans to fruition. In fact, Leos are a rare combination of the idea person and the follow-through strategist, making sure that everything is done with incredible style and class.

Along with their visionary intuition, Leos also possess solid common sense. They have a knack for recognizing what will work, and what isn't worth the effort. Although Leos dream big, they are actually realistic about what they will commit to. They don't take stupid chances. So, if someone tells me they're concerned about a Leo getting in over their head in something, usually I counsel that the Leo will pull it off.

Because of this good sense, Leos offer good advice to people. They are not jealous of others' success (very happy with their own, thank you), and generally want others to succeed and have a good life (like they do). They simply have a leader's innate sense of what another is truly capable of. So, if a Leo tells someone that they have a talent that should be developed, or a certain path is a good one to take, they're offering them a vision grounded in their usually highly reliable sensibilities. Conversely, if a Leo tells someone that they are off course, they're probably right.

The problem with Leos' "Royal One" nature comes if they forget that it's their Spirit that's nobility. (Everyone else's Spirit is, as well. Leos are just more in touch with the fact than most.) If a Leo thinks they are the only noble one, they will decide they are more important than everyone else. Should that happen, Leos could get a sense of entitlement, and assume that the world is there to serve them. Instead of being a most loving and fun leader, they become a despot, and consider other members of the human race mere pawns whose only purpose is to serve their bidding. In that mindset, Leos only tolerate circumstances in which they exercise total control, and they put others off by negating the value of their input.

It can be heady for Leos to think they're better than all the rest, but in truth they're missing the mark. If Leos decide that they are more special than anyone else, they will become separated from their heart—their essence—and from others. Instead of authentic expression, Leos will do things to try to demonstrate their superiority, and, eventually, that becomes flat and lonely. Then, because no one else will be as convinced of their specialness as Leos are, they will wonder why they don't get the support and recognition that is rightfully theirs. That's because others are just seeing Leos' ego and not their True Self.

Jay got taken over by his ego just that way. He was considered a brilliant rising star when, at only twenty-nine years old, he got the job of head writer for a popular sitcom on CBS. (Leos ascend fast in their careers.) Up to that point, Jay had been one in a group of writers who created scripts by working together as a team. But when Jay got promoted, he assumed he was far better than the other writers in his group. He discounted everyone else's suggestions, instead, bragged about how clever his own ideas were. Rather than considering the feedback from his writing team that many of his ideas needed improvement, Jay just figured, "What do they know? I'm a head writer!" and rallied to push his ideas through. Unfortunately, Jay's sitcom got cancelled after one season, and Jay was out of a job—and out of touch with the writers who had once supported him. When we spoke some months after this happened, Jay confided in me that what he missed the most was the camaraderie of this writing team. He realized how, in thinking he was better than they, he actually mistreated the people who could have helped him succeed.

Having to be superior or special can limit Leos' choices in life. They might decide that the ordinariness of life is beneath them, and shun the simple things that add up to making life rich. Leos can also feel they have to always be special. That can put enormous pressure on their self-image, because there are bound to be times when Leos are as ordinary as the next guy. That's okay. Leos need to know that.

You Can't Lead Unless Someone Is Following

Leos' Royal archetype loves recognition and attention, and they'll do a lot to gain it. Leos want to be special, and feel they are special, but they might not really believe it until they see that others think they are. Leos want (some say need) others to admire and respect them and think extra well of them. Leos crave the applause, the adulation and the material symbols that say, "You're something marvelous," and they will do plenty to deserve it. Leos don't want just one or two people to admire them—they want *everyone* to.

Because of that, flattery will get you everywhere with a Leo. Leos love compliments and acknowledgment. Actually, any type of positive attention is appreciated by Leos. They swell up inside, happy that they've been noticed for the goodness that they embody. And Leos freely give out flattery—they know how good it makes them feel, and they're willing to lift others the same way.

Sometimes, Leos will elicit flattery. More than any other sign, Leos know how to ask for acknowledgment when they want it. They might say something like, "Didn't I do a great job?" And, because they did, others will say, "Yes! You did!" But the irony is that Leos might not take that compliment in, or even believe it, because they know they set it up. Leos will still do it, but they won't be lifted by it. Why not just let it in? A compliment is a compliment, no matter how it comes about.

Although Leos want recognition from everyone, they are particularly inclined to crave it from their father. (This is especially true of Leo females.) Fathers are a potent symbol to Leos—perhaps father symbolizes God, or the world itself to them. If a Leo was lucky enough to have a supportive father, they probably have an inner security and confidence that knows there's nothing they can't do.

But many Leos have a destiny to *not* feel recognized by their dads. The reason for this is that Leos are learning to recognize themselves. If they can do that, even when the all-important father doesn't seem to, they establish and anchor an ability to recognize themselves, no matter what the world thinks of them. When Leos finally recognize and accept that God loves them, even if others don't seem to, it's powerful.

Leos' need for recognition can bring out their best when they use it wisely. One way Leos do that is by letting their need for recognition serve as a motivator to move them past any fears or doubts that would keep them from expressing themselves or taking a risk. Imagining they'll get the reward of praise and applause when they accomplish something can ignite Leos' courageous excitement and spark them into doing whatever needs to be done. Wanting to be recognized as someone who's honorable also prompts a Leo to live with integrity. Their need for recognition certainly keeps Leos from laziness or sloth, because there's no acknowledgment in that.

But if Leos think they have to have recognition to be valuable or loved, they will do all sorts of things that might not be really right for them. They might get a prestigious, but empty degree in college; or stick with a high-status, but unfulfilling job; or agree to burdensome projects, just so someone will think they're good or important. Needless to say, looking for recognition from the world cannot only be tiresome, it can also keep Leos distracted from the truly joyful things in life.

The truth is, Leos are really seeking recognition from themselves. When they realize they are enough, whether or not the world thinks so, Leos find peace and contentment.

Pride is another motivating aspect of Leos' Royal One archetype. Pride serves Leos by keeping them respectful of the Spirit of their essence. It prompts Leos to stay committed to making the most of themselves, and guides them to make dignified decisions.

But pride can also be a booby trap for Leos. If directed toward supporting their ego's image of who they should be, pride can throw Leos off course, making them unwilling to receive correcting feedback, or to realize they're out-and-out wrong. Pride can also keep Leos from risking learning something new, for fear they won't be the best. Leos' pride can lead them to believe that, if they're not the best, they're nothing. Of course, that's not true. But I've seen many a Leo step away from a promising endeavor for fear they won't win the gold.

Vanity is also a facet of Leos' regal archetype. Recognizing their inner and outer beauty is the way Leos find gratitude for how God made them. Dressing themselves up to look spectacular is one way Leos celebrate their love of all things theatrical. It's fun for them.

But vanity can cause Leos to go astray, if they get fixated on making—or thinking—their image perfect. Vanity will distract Leos from the inner beauty that is their true source of Light and loving. There is nothing wrong with having all those pictures of themselves and gigantic mirrors in their house, and preening to make themselves as gorgeous as possible. Leos just need to make sure they look beyond their glamorous image to their magnificent soul.

Because Leos' Royal One archetype recognizes how much they have been given, Leos always feel they have enough to give away. Hence, Leos are generous in heart and materiality. They will bestow onto others bountiful gifts of encouragement and appreciation, not to mention presents galore. (Indeed, one of Leo's favorite activities is selecting and presenting lavish gifts, as if to say, "I love you so much, I want *you* to have the best I can give.") Never ever wanting to seem stingy (lowly behavior unfitting for royalty) Leos may tend to over-give for their resources. But they never begrudge a dwindled bank balance when they see the look of appreciation in their receiver's eyes. Indeed, being loved is more important than a bank balance any day.

But Leos need to watch the trap of extending generosity as a means of deserving love, or feeding their image. Sometimes (okay, many times), Leos feel like they have to give in order to be loved. They will devote hours and hours of their time supporting others in the hope that they will be recognized as the great person they are. If they give in order to receive, Leos are setting themselves up for disappointment—not to mention feeling wiped out and used—because others might not appreciate them the way they want. Many a Leo has told me they feel overburdened by the demands others put on them, when, in fact, it's the Leos who are putting the demands on themselves.

If Leos are overcommitted, it's likely their ego is looking for strokes. That's their time to recall their own inner worthiness, and let someone else take over some of the tasks for a change. The same goes for material giving: There's no doubt Leos are generous and have great taste. But if they spend just to impress others, they are selling out. Instead of a valuable gift from their heart, Leos are actually gifting their ego's image. It won't be the same, somehow.

The Potent Creator

Leos embody the Potent Creator archetype as they have an intense need to express themselves through creative endeavors. Creative expression is Leos' ultimate passion. Art, entertaining, design, dance—all are exciting to Leos, and it's likely they will take a shot at most (or all) of them, at one time or another throughout their life.

Being creative is a spiritual experience for Leos. As they let themselves discover the creativity that flows through them, Leos connect with the creative impulse of the Divine One. Because of this, Leos are pretty much driven to create. Perhaps it's their willingness to do it, or it's that they're naturally gifted; whatever the reason, Leos generally excel at whatever creative project they undertake.

There are lots of avenues in which Leos will express their Potent Creator, and a quality of potency of creation shows up in whatever they do. That stems from Leos' intense enthusiasm to become fully enmeshed in whatever they choose to do. Leos are able to clearly define and envision what they desire. That clear intention can move mountains in making things happen. They won't take "no" for an answer when trying to make something happen. Instead, they will tirelessly do whatever it takes to make their desires manifest. Although Leos would love instant results, they are completely capable of exercising patience and endurance, never giving up until they get what they want.

There is usually an element of drama to what Leos create: They have a flair for bringing powerful and moving images to life. Leos love intense colors, striking design and art that makes a definite statement. They adore anything lavish because it reminds them of royalty. Leos want their home and their wardrobe to reflect their uniqueness, and they shun anything that looks ordinary. They want flair, quality, dynamism and strong self-definition in whatever they do, because that's a true reflection of their nature. It's the act of creating, as well as the outcome, that Leos yearn for. It gushes out of them.

Leos will bring drama to whatever they do—including their emotional expressions. This can be fun and expansive for Leos, and, when well directed, positive for others. However, sometimes Leos' flair for drama can result in them over-amplifying their emotions to the point of letting their feelings take over. For example, instead of addressing those they feel have wronged them, Leos might roar and yell and let the whole neighborhood in on their upset. That's okay, as long as the Leos accept what they're doing. Because Leos enjoy a healthy blast of emotions, it can actually make them feel closer to the people that they exchange them with—especially if those people meet them with the same emotional intensity. It is those times when the drama runs Leos, or takes over their better judgment, that they need to learn to exercise self-control. Sometimes, an ordinary, "I'm a bit hurt" will suffice.

Many Leos express their Potent Creator through parenthood. Children are likely to be a very significant avenue of Leo's expression. Although Cancers have the reputation for being the doting parents, Leos can dote as much, if not more. They are the proud parent who circulates pictures of their kids around dinner parties for all to admire. Leos' children are their *creations,* and they are proud as can be of what they've created. (Note: Some Leo fathers act distracted and disinterested in their children while at home with them. But out in the world they brag about who did what, and how cute they were when they did it, and how impressed everyone was, just as if they were following their every step. Go figure.)

Because Leos consider that their children are as special as they are, they applaud their every move and encourage them to be the best they can be. Leos can be challenged, however, when their children start to develop individualities of their own and don't necessarily want to follow Leos' ideas of who they should be. It's then Leos have to give their creations wings and let them fly.

Many Leos choose careers that involve or cater to children. Leos themselves are childlike (because they're fun-loving) and they know what kids are about. Leos can be attracted to education, art or counseling children as a way of doing something that's not only creative, but fun for them as well.

Leos might express their Potent Creator archetype through business. Few are as creative in business as Leos are. (Both male and female Leos are very savvy.) When their Creator energy is directed toward commerce, Leos know how to build an empire. Their organizational skills grasp how to set a strong foundation, and their ability to market makes Leos' product fly. No matter what they have to offer, Leos know how to make it sizzle and entice others to want what they've got.

Their gregarious and affable nature is well suited for marketing and sales, but Leos' aspirations are generally set on running things. Leos' urge to move to the top and take things over is a natural asset in the business world. And, because they know how to encourage people and bring out their best, Leos have the ability to collect a top-notch staff of loyal coworkers for a support team. Although

Leos are well suited for any business, they are especially good at ones that involve entertainment or luxury, image, kids or sports.

The challenge of being such a Potent Creator shows up when Leos step away from the wise counsel of their heart and let their will and ego lead the way. Leos' attunement to the Highest Good gives way to a controlling, demanding, willful act of making things happen perfectly, according to their egos' vision. Their loving heart turns hard and joyless because they feel like they are carrying the weight of the world. And they are.

When Leos sacrifice their loving, they sacrifice the assistance of the universal flow, and they end up with only what their energy alone can muster. They might get the end product they envision, but it will lack their signature magic.

My Leo client, Berti, a wedding planner, tells me she has to watch for this all the time in herself. She says that, if she is too determined to have the weddings come off in the absolutely perfect way she envisions, she is invariably furious and exhausted by the end of the day. That's because, no matter how meticulously she has planned, there is invariably something—or someone—that doesn't cooperate. When things start to veer off course, Berti says she knows she has a choice: Either she can push and force and try to will things to go according to her plans, or she can use her graciousness and humor to make what seems like a snafu become a part of the beauty of the ceremony. Of course, the latter strategy works better. And, Berti confides, maintaining her flexibility, rather than using her control, results in her looking better and more composed at the end of the day. That's a great payoff for a Leo.

The Entertainer

Leos demonstrate the archetype of the Entertainer because they can't help but be one. Not only do they have an irrepressible urge to express themselves, they also adore an audience. Considering themselves shining stars, Leos want to be watched, applauded and egged on. They will do whatever it takes to get an interested response from their onlookers. They will present themselves as funny, witty, silly, dramatic, mad—or will provide any other kind of performance that gets the attention. This attention and applause feeds Leos' energy, and they can go on forever if they're being noticed or appreciated. The saying, "All the world's a stage," encapsulates Leos' point of view, and they make darn sure they use this world, their stage, to the fullest. Whatever Leos do, they do with an eye to their audience, making sure it's well pleased. Indeed, if Leos don't have an audience, things might not seem so interesting or compelling to Leo.

Many Leos make their living as some form of entertainer: be it an actor (every Leo is an actor, some just get paid for it), a singer, a musician, a writer, a dancer or an artist. All are great career choices for them. If they don't do it professionally, they might do it for a hobby. They'll love it, and, more than likely, they'll be good at it.

But Leos don't have to be a literal performance artist to be an entertainer—they can just be themselves and that's entertaining enough. Leos' vivacious energy makes them the one who tells the joke, makes up a story (they naturally embellish everything, just to make it more interesting), or behaves in such a dramatic way that people stop, watch and listen.

Remember: Leos don't have to be entertaining in order to be loved. They need to watch they don't fall into the trap of thinking that they have to have a satisfied audience in order to be worthy. That could put pressure on them to be someone they think others want them to be. They risk getting caught playing a role, instead of being who they authentically are. Acting in an inauthentic way throws Leos out of their heart, their power source, and they start missing the purpose of being a Leo. If Leos let their entertaining-to-please-and-be-loved go too far, they might get so used to acting that they forget who they truly are. That would be a shame.

Entertaining others is icing on the cake for Leos, not the meat and potatoes of their worthiness. Leos' egos love the applause. Their Spirit loves the authentic expression. They choose, at every moment, which master they follow.

My Leo client, Joey, was the kind of guy that everyone (including me) liked right away. However, as I looked over his astrological chart, it became apparent that he thought he had to be liked, loved and fun, in order for anyone to want to appreciate or include him. When I pointed this out to Joey, he agreed and told me he goes so far as to hide his true feelings—including his sadness and grief over his father's death—because he thought that would be unappealing to others. As a result of our session, Joey resolved to experiment with being more authentic in his expression of what was—and was not—true to him. To his surprise, people not only still loved and adored him, they began to take him more seriously. Turns out, he began to express a depth and profoundness (which was always part of his nature) that others found truly wise and motivating. Instead of playing to an audience, Joey's natural expression created one, because others wanted to know what this cool guy had to say.

But Leos do have an entertaining spirit, and they are happiest when they let it soar. Sometimes, a Leo client will tell me they dream of doing something in the spotlight, but they shy away from it thinking it's too ego-y of them, or they're not worthy. To that, I say, "That dream is your soul's urge to express, and as a Leo it's your job to let it loose."

The Leo Gifts: Heart and Soul

Courage is one of Leo's greatest blessings. The word courage comes from the Old French word *corage* which means "heart and spirit." Leos are loaded with both. Their enormous heart and brilliant Spirit incite them to respond with an enthusiastic "yes!" to life's abundant offerings. Never wanting life to be ordinary (never, ever!) Leos take the risks to achieve greatness and they succeed more times than not. (Whenever I meet with anyone who's celebrated at the top of their profession, they invariably have a strong Leo influence in their astrological charts. It just makes them strive to succeed and be noticed for their success.)

Leos' courageousness doesn't prevent them from feeling fear. It just prompts them to want something more. So, even if a Leo is scared or intimidated, courage will move them past that toward their goal.

There is nothing halfway about Leos. They jump into whatever interests them with both feet. They laugh out loud, proudly announce what they're thinking, and valiantly defend their honor and the honor of others. And, while others are still considering whether or not something should be done, Leos are already out the door making it happen. Leos know how to live: They make things fun and exciting—with them there is never a dull moment.

By far, the greatest way Leos demonstrate their courage is by fearlessly, passionately, loving. They have the courage to risk their heart because love is the core of their being and it's what they're truly after. The truth is, when Leos open their heart, the brilliance of the Sun comes right through them, and their charisma and joy and light just bowl people over. Life awakens around Leos in amazing ways, because the love is so potent.

Courage also enters into Leos' willingness to stand up and make a show of themselves. This takes guts, because leaders risk criticism and negativity (which hurts Leos). But Leos would rather others challenge them than not notice them. Don't get me wrong: Leos fear failure like everyone else. But they don't let that inhibit them, because their fear of being too ordinary is stronger.

In short, Leos *do.* They don't think about it, ponder it, evaluate the list of pros and cons, or wait until someone asks them: They just get up and make it happen. Leos' courage gives them a confidence that they can succeed. Importantly, Leos trust in themselves. They have faith that they have what it takes to get the job done. Courage gives Leos honor. They are willing to do the noble thing, even if it's hard or overwhelming.

Leos' courage also gives them the gift of making the most of life. Instead of waiting for opportunities, Leos create them for themselves. And, if life hands them lemons, they make gourmet lemonade.

Leos are also endowed with the gift of **Strength.** Leos' strength is a rich inner resource which they can rely on in order to accomplish whatever they set out to do. This is a strength of loving, a strength of will and a strength of resolve. Leos have an unusually strong inner constitution that allows them to remain steady and focused no matter what is going on around them. Their inner power can withstand all kinds of flak, and it resists the world's temptations that could drag them off course.

Indeed, Leos' strength makes them one of the most **Powerful** signs of the zodiac. They're charged, therefore, to use that strength in a way that uplifts them and others, and to avoid using it to dominate or repress others.

On top of all that, Leos are **Fun!** They figure if something isn't going to be fun, they're not going to waste their important Self's time. I call my Leo friends "camp directors," because, not only do they think up fun stuff to do and execute all the arrangements, they call up and tell me how much fun we're going to have when we do it. Then, they make sure they're as entertaining as possible, so we do have the good time they promised. It's fun to have a Leo friend.

Leos also have the gift of **Presence**—a way of moving through life that has the kind of drama and dignity that turns heads, commands respect and makes others want to know them. This presence is intended because they feel a calling to conduct themselves in a way that befits their self-image that they are head and shoulders above others. Leos have an eye for the best and the coolest, and they're determined that that's what they'll have.

Leos have a knack for doing things in a **Classy and Stylish** way. There's just something about them that knows how to "do it right." Not only is there elegance and stateliness in their movements, Leos refuse any behavior that is beneath their dignity. Wanting to be grand, never trivial or small, Leos choose the magnanimous way. They give the best of themselves and shun actions that would make them or others seem petty. So even if Leos do feel low—or hurt or jealous—they are sure to keep their heads high, never snivel and do their best to be civil. (But if they're mad, they'll blow. There's nothing petty about their anger.)

Leos' class and style translate into their creations as well. They know how to put things together in an outstanding way that says, "Look over here!" Their great taste ensures, however, that things will be well appointed and appropriate, even if they are a bit over the top.

Because Leos are so aware of image, and so good at creating one, they need to be sure that they are not confusing haughty self-indulgence with class and style. Leos want to be the best, but that should be the best they can be, not a measurement of being better than others. If Leos think they should be better than others, they put themselves in a very insecure position. They start comparing themselves to others, and it's very likely someone will have—or be—something better than they. Leos can then lose their center because their attention is on their and others' presentation, and that separates Leos from expressing their authenticity (which is their power).

Image is fine when Leos know that's all it is. But, when they start to believe they have to live up to that image, Leos are selling their genuine Self very short. Who Leos are in their heart is so much grander than any false image they could concoct for themselves.

The Leo Fears: Adore Me, See Me, Do What I Want

Being loved and admired is so central to Leos' identity, one of their greatest **fears is being overlooked or dismissed**—in other words, not being loved. Leos' lower Self can think that, if they're not loved by others, they're just a nobody. This fear can propel Leo to doing all sorts of pleasing things for others, driven by a need to receive their approval. Leos will end up needy and at the mercy of others, instead of fulfilling their Leo birthright of fullness and self-direction. The thought of being lonely or living without the appreciation of others can be dreadful, indeed, to a Leo.

If Leo seeks to overcome the fear that they aren't lovable (instead of being run by it), they can learn some of their most important lessons. When Leos discover what it means to truly love themselves (as opposed to being fascinated with their image), whether or not others love them, they gain their greatest liberation. Leos will realize that, although they prefer to have love in their lives, they don't need it in order to stay alive or be worthy. In learning to love themselves, Leos awaken to the fact that they needn't be anything other than who they genuinely are or do anything that is not authentic for them. When Leos learn to love themselves for themselves, their love is so great, it overflows, and they naturally feel the connections to others that they crave.

Leos can mistakenly believe they have to be super-special in order to matter. Because of that, they can fear they are somehow not enough. Even if they are greatly accomplished, or entertaining, Leos can always wonder if it was good enough or if they measured up. This can get them to do things they don't really need to do, just because they're trying to deserve the respect and value of others.

It helps when Leos set out to be the best they can be, and dismiss their urge to compare themselves and try to be better than all others. When Leos simply resolve to express in their most authentic and honest way, they might discover they are more centered and happy than ever.

Believe it or not, one of Leos' greatest **fears is that the universe will not provide them with what they should, or want to, have (thinking they are both the same)**. If Leos fear the universe will shortchange them (by somehow overlooking how special they are), they might go against the flow of life. They will manipulate, demand and try to dominate the will of others in an attempt to force an outcome they want. Although Leos might seem quite pompous as they're doing all this, underneath they are being run by fear.

So it's advisable for Leos to develop trust—in the universe, or God, or the goodness of life, or whatever helps them have faith that what is given to them is truly what's best for them. And that what is theirs is theirs, and they will not be shortchanged. One way Leos can do that is by fully appreciating everything they have been given and approaching life with humility.

Leo in Relationships: "Love Me . . . or Just Love Me"

Leos' need for love is high on the list of what drives them. They desire love of all sorts—romantic, family, friendship—all make a Leo's heart sing. Leos know they give love to get love, and so they give it with gusto. Nothing pleases Leos more than to embrace their beloveds, to surround themselves with those whose hearts are open to them, to give and receive the warmth of love's glow.

Because Leos are so giving of their hearts, it can hurt them if others are not. If they feel they are unloved, or not adored, it can stun them. Leos don't understand because they've tried so hard and given so much. Those are the times to remember that loving themselves is the key for them.

Because Leos love so strongly, and believe so much in themselves, they will sometimes try to "make" someone love them by using the sheer intensity of their brilliant heart to break down an intended's indifference and woo them into relationship. Sometimes, this works wonders. There's nothing like being in the spotlight of a Leo's love. But, other times, a Leo's love can make them blind to the fact that someone doesn't really want to be with them: They feel if they love someone enough, they'll come around. But this isn't always the case. As determined as Leos are to win their chosen's heart, sometimes it's not for the best. Then, Leos need to remember how many other potential admirers there are in the world, and go out and find them.

In truth, Leos are choosy about who they bring close to them, and, of their many admirers, they select people who will entertain them, encourage their creativity, equal their high standards, and be as loyal as they are.

Although Leos adore relationships of all kinds, it's romantic relationships that are Leos' specialty. Of all signs, Leos make the best suitors. Courtship itself is its own extravaganza: Leos dote, they call, they plan great dates—not to mention shower thoughtful presents regularly. Courtship brings out all things Leo: wooing, display of fabulousness, declaring the specialness of the love, tingly romance, fun activities and adoration.

Leos are generous lovers. They give of themselves wholly and freely, sharing all that they are and all that they have. And Leos want that in return. Love is a big to-do, not to be put aside for after business. Leos want it all, all the time. They are also big on loyalty in love and demand that in return. They value their heart, and those who give theirs to them. Leos loathe mistreatment of love, because love is the most valuable commodity.

Keep in mind that Leos rule. They expect that life should go their way, and they control what they can to make it so. So, if Leos are partnered with another leader personality, there can be a clash of wills. Someone's gotta give in, and Leos find that difficult. If a Leo's partner is as dominant as they are, it might work best to delineate each partner's area of control, so Leo maintains an air of self-respect that they're not being dominated. And don't take it personally if a Leo tries to encroach on your area of power to give you direction. It's just their nature to show they love you by managing and advising you.

And forget about being jealous. Your Leo partner is loyal to you, and that's that. They expect you to be secure enough in yourself that you don't doubt yourself. They are going to "work the room" and be all shiny, making sure they win other people's—including the opposite sex's—attention and approval. It's a need. They want to show off and be loved no matter what, and using their sex appeal is one of many assets they capitalize on. Leos want you to sit back and enjoy their show, proud that you are the one they chose.

Sex and sex appeal are very important to Leos. They are very up front about their sexuality, but rarely seduce or act coy. Rather, Leos will show off their sexual prowess like they show off everything else. Leos' appetite for sex is strong. The Fire element in them makes them passionate and playful, anxious to please and be pleased. When you're with a Leo, you're in for a show, in the most exciting sense of the word.

Leos want a partner that can equal their power, and they are attracted to others who think well of themselves. Because love is such a big deal for Leos, they expect a lot—and they give a lot. They can be what's called "high maintenance." Never take a Leo for granted, or assume they know you love them just because you told them a week ago. They want a steady stream of attention, special treatment and declarations of love. They give it back as well, so you will be on the receiving end of a lot of goodies if a Leo loves you. A Leo won't play games with you, either. If they're interested in you they will let you know. If you're not the one for them, they have the class to let you know that, too. But they'll adore you for asking.

If you are interested in a Leo, you'd better make yourself spiffy and interesting. Dress well when courting a Leo—either male or female. Show them you think so much of them that you are willing to pull out all the stops. Make them aware they are the most important thing in your life, and you value and admire them. They'll purr at your efforts and open their magnificent hearts. And they'll give you that kind of attention back a hundredfold.

If you are trying to catch a female Leo's heart, you will need to be strong within yourself. A Leo doesn't respect someone she can boss around (although she'll try), and she has a need to look up to and admire her partner. Remember, she's a queen, and will settle for nothing short of royalty as her consort. But you do get a lot of mileage out of flattery, doting attention and glorious acts of romance. (Never, ever seem like you're patronizing; and, for God's sake, don't be needy.) She loves a show, and appreciates it if you put one on for her.

You needn't be the type that captures the attention of everyone in the room, however. She'll take care of that. If you do need to be the center of attention, you'd better be willing to share the spotlight with her. If the two of you end up competing, she will resent you.

If you are looking to catch the eye of a Leo male, dress upscale, smile beautifully, and carry yourself with an air of self-respecting honor. Sounds like he wants royalty? He does. Leo men are looking for the queen who can support the kingdom. He wants a companion who lives up to his image of grandness—one that he (and others) can respect and admire. If you win the heart of a Leo, he'll put you on a pedestal and love showing you off. And he'll show *you* the Moon. This man knows how to sweep you off your feet by showing you the best time, and best loving, you've ever had.

Big hint: Leo men want to be respected and admired. He does not want to be criticized, controlled, corrected or in anyway managed. You win his heart by making a big deal of all he's done well and right. Shower him with sincere compliments, and he'll be putty in your hands. And be affectionate and attentive: Leo wants to know he's number one and cared for above all else. He'll do the same for you.

A Leo man wants a partner who can equal his power, but not one who tries to compete with him. After all, he's the one who should be getting the attention. Flattery works very well on Leo men, but it needs to be realistic because he resents a phony. If he's interested in you, he will stop at nothing to woo you. If he's not going to great lengths to get your attention, chances are he's not really interested. If he is he'll let you know through the intensity of his attention, gifts and smile, all of which say, "You are magnificent!"

The Last Word on Leo

For Leos, love is the key to every door. And the most important love is the love of Self.

Chapter 6

Virgo

(August 23–September 22)

Virgo is the quality in you that is analytical and industrious, seeks to bring order and healing, and enjoys helping others. It's also the part of you that's learning that everything is already perfect.

You won't find dirty dishes, or disorganized closets in a Virgo's house. Not a messy desk either—at least not for long. If you like order, you'll love your Virgo friends.

Virgo, along with being one of the most intelligent signs, is also one of the most industrious and organized signs of the zodiac. **They have an incredibly refined consciousness that seeks perfect order, and likes to create perfect order.**

Virgos use their gifts of analysis and critical thinking to understand even the subtlest nuances of whatever interests them. Their drive toward excellence and high standards inspires them to achieve their absolute best in everything they do, and makes them an invaluable asset to whomever they're supporting. Virgos especially enjoy using their powers of discernment to distinguish what's good and useful from what's not useful and can be thrown out. That leads to Virgo bringing greater health and maximum efficiency to any situation they're involved in, and they do so tirelessly.

Virgos are truly servers at heart. Nothing makes them happier than making a valuable contribution. Service purifies Virgos. When they're willing to do whatever is for the highest good of all concerned, they tap into the Divine Flow, which helps them to effortlessly provide what's needed. In doing so, Virgos have an almost magical ability to uplift and heal—and to experience heartfelt fulfillment that's beyond compare.

The Virgo Mission: Learning That, Oh Yes, It Is Perfect

All of us are learning what Virgos are born to discover: Perfection is always present and all we have to do is recognize it. Virgos' awakening comes when they direct their considerable intelligence to noticing the perfection of the *process* of life—to accept that no matter what is going on, it is *exactly* as it should be. Sure, life is messy, and often seems to come up short. But there's a higher purpose to what and how things happen.

As Virgos train their consciousness to cooperate with and embrace what's present (rather than criticize or complain about it), they become awestruck by the universe's uncanny intelligence and fine work. From there, Virgos can appreciate how everything happens for just the right reasons, and trust that they don't have to improve upon a thing. With that attitude, Virgos are better poised to do what's truly effective in each moment, and to bring Light and healing service to whatever they're involved in. Something about Virgos' destiny will almost invariably involve both their service skills and their ability to discern.

The Virgo Challenge: Seeing What's Wrong to Discover What's Right

Surprisingly, Virgos can learn to recognize the perfection in the natural unfoldment of matters by getting stuck in the confines of their perfectionism, and its cousin, faultfinding criticism. When Virgos expect life, themselves and others to measure up to their own (impossibly high) standards of perfection, they set themselves up for disappointment and feelings of inadequacy because life rarely reflects their expectations. Virgos can make matters worse for themselves by using their powers of analysis to look for what's wrong in any situation (instead of acknowledging what's right, and working from there), and becoming hypercritical of themselves in particular and life in general. These tendencies make life difficult and defeating for Virgos, but they are Virgos' most powerful teachers.

The Virgo Key: Going for Excellence Is Perfect

The secret to Virgos' happiness is to learn to exchange their drive for *perfectionism* for the healthier tactic of the search for *excellence.* **Perfectionism focuses on what's *wrong.* Excellence focuses on what's *right,* and lifts Virgos' awareness to the goodness of who they are and what's happening around them.** When Virgos look for and notice what's excellent—about themselves, others or the world—it automatically brings out their Higher Nature.

The same trick goes for Virgos' faultfinding criticism: It does a Virgo wonders if they learn to replace their strategy of faultfinding *criticism* (which is full of judgments of right and wrong, good and bad) with *evaluation,* which is only information and is free of judgment. When Virgos use their clever minds to evaluate, they can recognize the useful from the un-useful, and make decisions that support and serve them. As Virgos learn to go for excellence, and evaluate along the way, they bring out their attunement to, as well as their cooperation with, the Divine Flow.

The Purity and Innocence of the VIRGIN, Not the Naïveté

Virgo's astrological symbol is the Virgin—a maiden who's sorting the wheat from the chaff after the year's harvest. This symbolizes Virgos' use of discernment to clarify what has value and should be capitalized upon, and separate it from what isn't necessary and should be released. Virgos sort out the wheat from the chaff by developing those qualities that exemplify their truest nature (which is love) and letting go of anything that does not.

Virgos separate the wheat from the chaff of their consciousness by learning to hold to those thoughts and ideas that uplift them and to release the thoughts that don't. When Virgos forgive judgments, dismiss negative criticisms, and learn to focus on what's good and right, they purify their mind and keep it open to higher knowledge. Virgos separate the wheat from the chaff of their actions by clarifying what has true usefulness versus what is simply a distracting activity. For example, it's great to be an energetic worker. But it's also great to know when to call it quits and go out and have some fun.

Virgos are Virgin-like in that they have a natural inclination toward purity. They are attracted to the most refined, untainted, uncomplicated qualities in others and in things, and they shun the overexpressed or overdone.

Virgos demonstrate the Virgin quality in the many ways they seek to purify themselves. They purify their bodies by maintaining a healthy diet. They purify their minds by using their intelligence to choose thoughts that uplift them and release negative judgments that keep them down. Virgos purify their emotions by extending tenderness toward themselves and remembering they are already perfect enough.

Virgos also love to purify situations by finding the best and most useful strategies for handling them, and banishing activities that aren't effective. No matter where they are, Virgos' eagle eye quickly assesses what can be done to make things operate even better. This is a valuable asset, but it can also be a source of frustration. Usually life will not take on the perfect order Virgos envision it should have; rather, life has its own wacky perfection. It works better for Virgos to keep their purifying intentions on what they can control: the strategies *they're* taking. In doing so, Virgos can remain more neutral about how the world does what it does.

Virgos' Virgin quality gives them a gift of *innocence*. Innocence helps

Virgos to experience life in an open and curious way. Instead of having preconceived notions about how things should be, or judging how things are, innocence doesn't assume a thing—it just experiences. When they're connected to their innocence Virgos can recognize the amazing magic of life, and the ways things work out with remarkable intelligence. They also can see through false images of matters and people in order to recognize their pure essence.

Note that Virgo's symbol is involved with harvest time. This means Virgos are harvesting in this lifetime much of what they have put into motion in the past (whether past years or past lifetimes), so they might find they have gifts and opportunities coming to them that they cultivated previously.

Really Down to EARTH

Virgo is an Earth Sign, which means they are practical and grounded. Virgos have a firm grip on how this world works, and know what steps to take to make things happen. (This is so obvious to them that they can't believe it when others don't see it.) Virgo's unique expression of the Earth element is their ability to *apply* their ideas in practical ways. They combine their keen intellect with an Earthy "This can be done!" attitude, and set out to bring the highest efficiency to whatever they choose to be involved with.

Virgos' Earthiness makes them extremely industrious. They are happiest when busy and productive. Laziness has no appeal whatsoever to Virgos, nor do lazy people. Virgos' energy enjoys doing projects, accomplishing goals and always having something to produce.

Virgos' Earthiness also makes them reasonable and realistic about life. They don't waste time being distracted with daydreams or fantasies (except for fantasizing that things should be more perfect). Instead, Virgos live life by doing. They roll up their sleeves and deal with what needs to be done. Virgos' Earth influence enables them to be energetic and efficient workers—they're enlivened when being of service, and they relish getting the job done. Virgos are constantly on the lookout for a helpful act they can do with gusto and correctness. No one's as happy as a Virgo doing good service.

Virgos Go with the Flow

Virgo is one of the four Mutable Signs. (Gemini, Sagittarius and Pisces are the others.) Mutability gives Virgo the inclination to change and to flow with whatever their circumstances dictate. Virgos adapt and fit in. **The unique Virgo expression of Mutability is their ability to adjust their actions to whatever's needed in order to be effective and useful.** Mutability keeps Virgos moving. It helps them avoid getting stuck in a rut by giving them an ability to try various approaches to life, along with a willing interest to try new and improved ways of doing things. Mutability keeps Virgos searching for new understanding and methods that might improve life.

The challenge of being a Mutable Sign is knowing when to flow and adjust, and when to hold their ground. Virgos can so readily adjust to what's needed—to help others, for example—they might forget to check in with themselves to see what *they* need. If so, they will feel resentful that they're the ones who are making all the adjustments, while others are sticking to what they want. It works best if Virgos use the flexibility of their mutable nature to attune to and flow with what's present, while making time to tend to the basics of caring for themselves.

Virgo is what's known as a **Social Sign.** This means they identify with themselves in the context of those around them. Because of this, it's important they feel as if they are impacting or serving at least a few others in order to feel fulfilled.

MERCURY's Mental Magnificence

The sign Virgo is ruled by the planet Mercury. (Gemini is also ruled by Mercury, but expresses it completely differently in that sign.) Mercury is the planet that governs the mind and its activities: thoughts, ideas, concepts, the ability to communicate and the need to understand matters. Mercury's strong influence gives Virgos a pronounced mental inclination (okay, they're smart), and an ability to quickly shift their focus from one subject to another without missing a beat. Mercury expressed through Earth sign Virgo gives it a tilt toward practical thinking; a shrewd intelligence that has a penchant for the analytical. Virgos' able and quick minds sort, categorize and prioritize everything in sight, evaluating how things can be used to produce results.

Virgos put their ideas to immediate use and see their benefits impacting everyday situations. Virgos want to learn and teach things that are real and useful. They dismiss ideas that are too abstract or too ambitious as not worth considering, if they can't make them work right now. Virgos love to sort out the chaos in life and come up with ideas that offer some kind of meaningful order. Virgos' minds also can't help but improve upon things: They quickly analyze how something is working, and spot ways it can be changed so things work better.

Virgos' key question is, "How can I use what I know to make things better?" Their inclination to seek order allows them to bring maximum efficiency to whatever they're dealing with, making them invaluable assets to whomever they're supporting.

Mercury makes Virgos quick: They can learn faster, and do more in a day than most others can do in a week. They need to keep that in mind when they're judging the apparent slowness of other people's process.

(Recently, astrologers have considered Virgo to be ruled by the asteroid Chiron. Chiron repesents a wounded healer, which reflects Virgos' penchant for healing. The jury is still out on this, though. For our purposes, seeing the Mercury influence in Virgo is fine. In fact, it's perfect!)

The Virgo Archetypes: Helping, Healing, Holding for Essence

In order to learn about the presence of Perfection, Virgos (and those who are Virgo-like) will embody the archetypes of the Server, the Healer and the Purist.

The Server

Virgos display the archetype of the Server because service is Virgos' most essential urge, the core of their Spirit's expression. Virgos just love giving of themselves! In doing so, they access an inner power and insightfulness that enlivens and lifts them. Virgos have a unique willingness to do whatever it takes to assist others. That willingness taps them into the flow of the Divine. When there, Virgos are downright awesome: super clear, organized to a T and tirelessly motivated because love of service is their fuel. In fact, Virgos express love by being helpful.

This need to be of service is one of Virgos' main drives. They want to be contributors in life, and they will actively search for opportunities to do so. Virgos' energy and heart expand when they give of themselves, and they enjoy having something worthwhile to do.

Service gives Virgos a sense of place in life, and that's important. Their urge for order assesses who's supposed to do what. When Virgos see there is something they can or should do, they understand where they belong in the scheme of things. Knowing that, Virgos feel secure. As long as they know there is something of value that they can contribute, Virgos feel important. Hence, no matter what they accomplish, they are always ready for the next thing, because they want to keep their place.

Although Virgos are sure to get the big job done (on time and perfectly), their greatest joy comes from making sure that even the tiniest details are executed with precision. Indeed, Virgos definitely subscribe to the idea that "God is in the details."

Virgos' love of service makes them industrious workers. They work hard at everything—even their play. Virgo energy likes to "get something done," and they try to be productive in each and every activity. Virgos' love of service also can easily translate to their loving their job. Their profession can be so important to them that it can be the key to their self-identity, or the reason for their existence. It's not, of course; finding and expressing their Spirit is. But Virgos' work can be a useful avenue through which they discover themselves and tap into the greatness of who they are.

Because Virgos identify so closely with their work, they risk confusing their personal adequacy with doing a good job. These two aren't related, and Virgos should make it their business to know that. Sometimes, Virgos will be absolutely brilliant and effective at what they do, and other times they'll be a flop. (Ugh! They hate that!) But they are just as valuable either way. If Virgos don't understand that, they should find a way to. One way to do that is to tap into their spiritual essence. It will remind them that they are valuable just because they're here. **Improving things is not the rent Virgos pay—it's only a pastime while they do what they came here to do: discover God.**

Virgos' nature is so empowered by work and a job well done that they have to be vigilant to avoid becoming a workaholic. It's one thing to be good at work. It's another to avoid all other activities life offers (including awkward situations) by working. Work is one way Virgos can express their gifts and their Spirit. But there are many other avenues for that as well—like relationships, recreation, even hobbies. And Virgos need to be sure they treat themselves to the fun of life, as well as the work of life.

Because Virgos' work is so important to them, they should put a lot of thought into the career they choose. Professions that provide a necessary service to others are always recommended. The healing arts, teaching or counseling are naturals for Virgos. But their practicality also makes them very savvy and motivated in business. Virgos could excel at everything from accounting to running a business, especially one that has a service orientation. Even creative Virgos will direct their eye for precision toward making even the subtlest aspects of their art importantly defined.

But the key to Virgos' happiness is not having the perfect job. Rather, Virgos can use any job to tap into the perfect state of service. When Virgos work with an attitude that it is their service—not their outcome—that is their highest expression, they can find fulfillment in any act.

Remember, however, the most important service Virgos are to do this lifetime is service to their *Self.* In truth, Virgos are learning to serve the Spirit of who they are. They do that by using their powers of discernment to discover the actions, thoughts and emotions that support and empower them. As Virgos discern more of those, and release what keeps them contracted or negative, they serve their truest essence.

It is imperative that Virgos take the time to keep themselves healthy, relaxed and replenished. Taking care of themselves fills Virgos up, and then gives them an overflow of energy from which to give. That translates into the incredible joy of service Virgos are intended to have.

However, many Virgos think, *First, I'll fix the entire world; then, I'll tend to myself.* They might put off taking care of themselves until everything around them is handled and orderly. But, let's face it: that rarely happens. There is always something—or someone—that could use Virgo's fixing or help.

If Virgos make service to others a priority over service to their Self, they're off course. One sign that they are not taking care of themselves is feeling overburdened. They can agree to too much and become overwhelmed by what they expect of themselves. If their work or service to others seems a joyless schlep, or if they're angrily thinking, *I'm the only one who's really doing any work around this place!*—it's a red flag that their approach is off. There's an air about Virgos when this happens that broadcasts, "I've had it with you people!" and those around them have an energy about them that moans, "*Now* what?" That's when Virgo school is in session!

When Virgos are resenting that they are doing all the work because others aren't doing their fair share, *they* might have something to do with it. Virgos should check to see if, through their being so efficient, they have "trained" those around them to expect Virgo to do all the work. Many times, the Virgo "I'll do everything!" approach teaches others that, well, the Virgos will do everything and no one else need exert themselves. Virgos need to recognize that, by doing only their portion, they serve others by empowering them to do theirs.

Part of doing service or a job well is knowing when to ask for help. Sometimes, in Virgos' need to supply perfect service, they are convinced that they should be able to do everything—and they feel ashamed when they can't. That's needless, but perfectionism is ruthless that way. Instead of appropriately asking for help the minute things get tough, Virgos might doggedly hang in there until they finally feel utterly exhausted and angry. Then, it occurs to them that they need help. But instead of asking for it, Virgos can tend to demand it of others, because Virgos look at others in the same overdemanding way they view themselves.

Of course, this is off-putting to others, and they might not respond the way Virgos want. Virgos can then become even more resentful and angry, because they project that others never support them. But, in truth, Virgos are promoting the whole dynamic by not supporting themselves in the first place. Part of supporting themselves is knowing their limits, and asking for help from a balanced place before they've reached them.

When Virgos make themselves and their health a priority, they are serving the God within. In making themselves job number one, Virgos fill up. They can then tend to the needs of the world with the gusto, the joy and the signature gratitude that they get to be of service in the first place. That is Virgos' essence, and it is how they were meant to be.

When Virgos find they are acting like the driving taskmaster, it's probably because they have let their perfectionism sneak in. They work harder than anyone else because they imagine that they (and others) are not doing things well enough. But Virgos need to remember that they are the ones who are laying those standards onto themselves. No one else burdens Virgos the way they can burden themselves. They tell themselves, *If I just try a little harder, I can get this just perfect!* Occasionally, this is true. But they needn't push, exhaust themselves, or drive themselves and others crazy trying to reach that perfection. In truth, they are shoving it away. This is not a way to serve.

Joan claimed she was going to quit her job at a news station because she just couldn't handle it anymore. When I asked her what she couldn't handle, she said, "It's just too much pressure!" I asked, "Are you understaffed?" "No." "Are you getting bad reviews?" "Of course not!" "What," I finally said, "can't you handle?" Joan said, "There's always new news and I always have to be on top of it!" When I reminded her that her Virgo need to be perfect (versus excellent) might be at play, she calmed down. "Yeah," she said, "I'm doing a good job, and I guess I just want the world to stop so I can feel done!"

It's times like that when Virgos need to just do what's in front of them in the moment, and not let themselves get overwhelmed with what they might have to do later.

Virgos need to remember that they are going for excellence—not perfection—in what they do and who they are. Their awakening comes from recognizing that the process is always perfect and so is the outcome, even if it's vastly different from what they expected. That's part of life's mystery and intelligence. Keeping their heart awake and humor active can help Virgos put life into perspective and keep their service joyful.

The Healer

Virgos will also exemplify the archetype of the Healer. They possess a natural healing energy along with an intense motivation to fix what's wrong—with people or situations. If ever there's a problem, Virgos are there; ready, willing and able to make matters better. Virgos have a Healer's consciousness: They know just what's needed, and they have a capacity to provide remedies and support to whatever has gone off balance or off track. They'll heal by finding ways to bring better order and alignment around them. More than anything, Virgos love bringing vitality and efficiency to whatever they are interested in.

This healing ability can take countless forms, but medicine (especially the natural approach) or counseling are very likely outlets. Even if a Virgo is not a professional Healer, it's likely they'll have extensive knowledge of herbs, wise diet choices or self-help strategies that make them their own Healer, and the one people call if they need healing advice (which they delight in giving).

Virgos' Healer consciousness makes them gifted diagnosticians. If something is off, they know it, and they know where to look to find out just what it is. Even the trickiest problems are no match for Virgos' insight—they can narrow their focus down to the tiniest aspect of a problem and discover the source of the malfunctioning. (I want my doctor *and* my car mechanic to be Virgos!)

In truth, Virgos need to watch how they use this gift because, sometimes, in their enthusiasm to discover what's wrong, they might overlook everything that's working well. It is possible that things can be working perfectly, even if some of their parts seem not to be. That old adage, "Don't fix it if it ain't broke," might help Virgos remember to keep looking at the bigger picture.

If Virgos find that they're feeling frustrated because things aren't working well, it's time to shift their focus. They need to challenge themselves to see what might, in fact, be working right. Sometimes, a situation is about something other than what Virgos think it is. It works better if they use their considerable intelligence to find out where the blessings are. That's the method of a true Healer.

Along with being good at diagnosing problems, Virgos are also good at finding remedies for problems. Usually, they are elegantly simple. Virgos have a way of breaking things down to the essence of what's needed, and coming up with reasonable, easy-to-do solutions.

Virgos' Healer archetype gives them an intuitive understanding of nature. Whereas others need instruction about the workings of the Earth, Virgos have always just understood it. This natural understanding not only gives them a deep appreciation for nature, it allows them to work in beautiful harmony with it. Virgos are frequently lovers of plants or the Earth itself, and enjoy professions that help nature thrive. Botany, gardening, landscape design and veterinary medicine may all be rewarding careers.

Understanding nature can lead to Virgo understanding natural healing. They are witch-like (in the best connotation, which is wise-like)—they know how to use what exists naturally in this world to heal the world. They do this instinctively, and without a lot of fanfare. Virgos rarely take all the credit for the useful things they do. They understand that somehow Spirit works through them.

The challenge of Virgos' Healer archetype is thinking that they have to heal everything around them. They might be driven to relentlessly point out (even if they're not asked) what people are doing that creates dis-ease or trouble. Although they consider this a valuable service, others might see it as being critical, and resent Virgos' interference. Virgos tend to be shocked and surprised about this, thinking, *Who wouldn't want my advice?* But not everyone wants to improve their lives, or even if they do, they may not want to do it Virgos' way.

What works better is to teach health by demonstrating it. When others witness Virgos taking good care of themselves physically, emotionally and mentally, they can learn from that behavior what's right for them. People learn according to their own perfect timetables. There's no need for Virgo to push them into anything, even if Virgo does think it's for their own good. If someone's not ready for something, even the clearest advice won't help.

Then, there are those times when Virgos will want to help others so sincerely, they will become overly responsible and try to do the healing for them. Forgetting that others are ultimately in charge of healing themselves, Virgos will try to heal them with their own energy, or through their own effort. Because Virgos possess healing energy, this could work. But they could end up exhausted, drained or sick themselves. That's because Virgos can deplete their own energy to heal the problem, rather than letting the Divine One's inexhaustible supply of energy flow through them and do the healing.

A good way for Virgo to remember to let the Divine One do the healing is by setting their intention for the Highest Good of all concerned to happen through them. That allows Virgos to become neutral because they've set the responsibility for healing square where it belongs: between the one who needs healing and God. Virgos' job is to simply be the powerful conduit through which healing energy can flow.

In Virgos' urge to heal and bring perfect order back to life, it is important that they remember this critical point: There is already perfect order. Because Virgos see what needs to be done to improve things, they assume that: (a) they're absolutely right, and (b) everyone should listen to their advice.

But that's not the way it works, is it? What Virgos need to understand is that people have the perfect right to make their own mistakes and learn from them; and Virgos themselves are learning that it simply might take longer than they think it should. Instead of offering wise counsel, Virgos might think they have to insistently push their ideas on others so they finally "get it." (Virgos are great eye-rollers, impatient with the seeming ineptitude of others.) When Virgos think it's their job to fix anything but their own consciousness, they're off course.

The truth is, the universe is unfolding just the way it should. If Virgos seek perfection according to their own expectations, they might be overlooking the real perfection that's already taking place. Many times chaotic or inefficient situations are the ideal forum for those involved to learn something they wouldn't learn any other way. Virgos' drive to make things "better" is tricky, and needs to be wisely directed.

Rodney, a Virgo bus driver, learned this from the elementary-school kids he drives back and forth to school. He told me he was at wit's end the first few weeks of the new school year because the kids kept changing from the seats he assigned to them (in well thought-out alphabetical order, of course), to sitting in other seats with their friends. No matter how much Rodney protested, the kids just kept moving. It finally dawned on him that the children had their own order of how they wanted to sit. When he learned their order, he was able to keep track of them as well as if they had remained in the seats he'd assigned.

Importantly, if Virgos decide they need to make situations better because they judge them as "wrong," they are off-course. Judgments throw Virgos out of acceptance, as well as separate them from their heart and the Divine Flow, which is their higher intelligence and power source. Then, Virgos will try to use their will and energy to force things, coming from the ego importance that they know what's best for everyone.

One way Virgos know they're doing that is if they're crabby, complaining, frustrated and *intolerant*. That's a sure sign they think something or someone is acting "wrong" (including themselves), or that they are projecting that others aren't measuring up, and that gets them down. When Virgos are like that, it's a signal that they're operating from their lower nature.

When that happens, it helps if Virgos remember their job is to bring excellence, not perfection, to what they do. That puts them back in touch with their sole responsibility: their own consciousness and intentions. As they look with neutrality—or, better yet, with love—at what they and others are doing, Virgos step up to their higher frequency that knows just how to have an appropriate and positive effect on whatever they're engaged in.

The Purist

When Virgos are demonstrating the archetype of the Purist, they have a quality of refinement and virtue in everything they do and possess. Virgos recognize the essential perfection in people and things, and tap into the intrinsic power that lies in their simplicity. This eye for purity results in Virgos' ability to get to the heart of matters quickly, because their clarity pierces through false images or confusing distractions. This allows them to make valuable contributions, because they know just where to put their efforts to transform and enhance whatever is necessary.

This purity gives Virgos a style of behaving that has an innocence and simplicity to it. They have gentleness about them, and a soft touch. And they strive for excellence with an intention of being of service, rather than of being aggrandized. Virgos love recognition as much as anyone, but find it distasteful to use that as their motivator. Instead, Virgos use the desire to demonstrate pure quality, efficiency and intelligence in what they do, recognizing the excellence that moves through them.

Virgos' Purist archetype gives them a taste for things subtle and simple, never flashy or gaudy. They enjoy the finest quality in whatever they possess—not because of the status these things represent, but because Virgos thoroughly enjoy the essential perfection of them. It pleases them to witness something functioning at the highest efficiency, while having a subtle presentation (like Virgos themselves). Virgos love quality workmanship, tasteful minimalism, clean lines and an everything-has-a-function quality in their possessions.

Virgos also want literal purity. They'll banish anything messy, dirty or toxic in their environment! They want the best in foods and are the first ones to shop at the organic grocers because, more than any other sign, Virgos understand that we are what we eat. Virgos are picky about their diet, not because they are hedonistic and demand great taste, but because they don't want to violate their systems with chemicals or bad foods. Even the rare Virgos who aren't health-conscious are still very discerning, usually swinging toward the gourmet. (Even Virgo junk-food junkies are particular about the junk food they select.)

Virgos' purity essence can even result in making them hypersensitive to things the rest of the world doesn't even realize exist. A Virgo might be the first one to start coughing if there's a pollutant in the air, or feel squeamish if something is cooked just a tad off. Other people can think that Virgos are just complainers, but, in truth, Virgos' sensitivity can react if things aren't entirely pure. (However, many hypochondriacs are born under the sign of Virgo. They might not truly be reacting, but they *feel* like they're reacting, to germs and toxins. That's a Virgo trait—hypochondria or not.) Virgos can also have sensitive reactions to "emotional impurity." For example, Virgos can also get squeamish if someone's "story" is not 100 percent true.

Virgos' purity theme can be reinforced by the fact that the part of the body ruled by the sign of Virgo is one that absorbs and cleans: the intestines and the elimination system. First, that's a message to Virgos to take their fiber. Second, it's a representation that Virgos purify by absorbing what's useful, and letting all else go.

Virgos tend to be pure in personal presentation. Personal hygiene is extremely important to them (and they deeply wish it were more important to others). They are always showered and groomed, their haircut is perfect and fingernails are attended to. Virgos dress tastefully, choose natural fabrics (that breathe, of course) and make sure everything fits just right. (You won't catch a Virgo with an inappropriate hemline or exposing an unfit body part.)

And (this is a big one) Virgos are neatniks. Their purity craves order and cleanliness in every nook and cranny of their surroundings, and they'll make achieving this job number one. No messy piles, overstuffed closets or senseless knick-knacks can exist in their orbit. The motto, "A place for everything and everything in its place," is Virgos' prime directive. (It would be a fairly safe bet that the people who started those stores that sell all things organizational were Virgos.)

No place is too small or insignificant for Virgos' organizing zeal. Everything from their desk drawers, their kitchen cabinets, their undies (which they probably iron), to last decade's tax records are properly arranged and shelved. It is likely to be the little things Virgos most enjoy organizing. They can remain composed if they come home to a hole in their ceiling, but they'll blow if someone puts a pan on the wrong hook. Orderliness refreshes and calms Virgos; disorder can make them nervous. This can make Virgos anxious around kids. Some Virgos opt not to have kids because of the mess they cause. Others temporarily suspend their neatness until the kids are ready to clean up after themselves.

Another important thing to Virgos: NO BACTERIA! Virgos know that what you can't see *can* hurt you, and they are sure to disinfect everything in sight. Virgos scrub themselves like surgeons, shower frequently (tending to notify others when they need to), and invest heavily in disinfectants for every surface of their house. This urge reflects their psychological and spiritual need for getting rid of anything that's not pure. (Felix of *The Odd Couple* is an exaggerated stereotype of a Virgo.)

Purity, however, does not mean being perfect, and Virgos need to really grasp that. They are already perfect in essence, and that's what they need to know. Virgos' Purist archetype helps them to do that by prompting them to purify their own nature, and, in doing so, to become more in touch with the Divine. Purity helps Virgos give up or renounce those things that limit them or separate them from their True Selves, like addictions (Virgos' main ones are criticizing and systematizing), bad habits, judgments, pettiness and self-doubt. The spiritual expression of Virgos is to discern and develop their true essence, and step away from their lower expressions.

The challenge of Virgos' Purist archetype is accepting that our world is, in fact, messy—at least by Virgos' standards—on every level. If they devote all their time and creativity trying to exact order, or to clean and disinfect, Virgos might miss the more important things that are going on—like loving relationships. It's a good idea for Virgos to frequently check to make sure they are not using cleaning as a distraction from getting involved in uncontrollable, but growth-rendering, situations.

Sometimes, the most seemingly impure situations are the ones with the greatest promise of Light (or goodness). If Virgos use their remarkable consciousness to seek out the Light in every circumstance—no matter how muddy it might appear—they are using their gift in its highest form. Everything is perfect. The more Virgos look to see how that's true, the more they will see that *is* true.

The Virgo Gifts: Doing—and Doing the Right Thing

One of Virgos' greatest assets is their **Industriousness.** They are highly motivated to get things done, and done well. Instead of sitting around waiting for others to direct them to do a job, Virgos initiate ways to make themselves productive. Even young Virgos will busy themselves with helpful tasks or ingenious creative projects, ably focusing themselves to completion. (You can raise your Virgo child's self-esteem by asking them to do things they can do well, and sincerely prizing their accomplishment.) Virgos love being busy, so they are the first to spot what's needed. It satisfies them to be worn out by a job well done, finally relaxing as they happily survey all they have accomplished.

This industriousness translates into doing well in the world. Virgos' intelligence combined with their hard work allows them to excel in their profession. But it's not always necessary for them to climb to the very top. Virgos don't work for power or glory; they work to be recognized as very good. That's the highest compliment a Virgo can hear. Many Virgos don't need to be the boss because they see value in supporting excellence in others. Those Virgos enjoy being an indispensable right-hand person, and do it with almost machine-like precision and loving gusto. Virgos are honored to take care of all the details that support the work they value.

But Virgos aren't only industrious at work. They are industrious at anything they find worthy of their time and attention. This can translate to being an industrious lover, parent or friend, making sure they cover all the bases, doing what they expect a person should do.

Actually, taken to extremes, this industriousness can lead Virgos to try to become a "superperson," working diligently at their job, then coming home to prepare a healthy meal, reading to the kids (because they think they need to be better educated), cleaning the whole house—and, in between all of that, doing some volunteer work and taking a self-improvement class. Other signs can be exhausted by Virgos' schedule, but the Virgo need to be productive spurs them on.

Industriousness should satisfy and refresh Virgos, not exhaust or deplete them. If it does drag Virgos down, there's a chance they have self-worth confused with being productive, which is off course. What Virgos are really here to accomplish is attunement to their Spirit. Working wisely can awaken Virgos to that, but overworking can distract them from it altogether. Keep in mind that very few people at their deathbeds wish they would have cleaned out their closets more often or worked late more nights. Usually, they regret not connecting more deeply with others. Virgos should not let themselves get so focused on getting things done that they forget the most meaningful expression of their nature, which is loving.

Virgos do themselves a favor by releasing expectations of others to be as industrious as they are. They simply are not, or they express their industriousness differently than Virgos do. Those born under the sign of Virgo are uniquely motivated to work. Other signs are motivated to do other things, like have fun, be creative, or just sit and contemplate. And that's okay. Virgos need to keep in mind that they work because they love to, and others needn't measure up to their standards to be worthwhile. They, like Virgos, are worthwhile just because they are.

Another of Virgos' gifts is their power of **Analysis.** They have an uncanny ability to break things down to their essential truths. Virgo's consciousness seeks to identify the bottom line of matters, deftly sorting truth from falseness, importance from insignificance. Analysis helps Virgos create a mental system that brings order to their life and everything in it.

Even the tiniest of details are significant to Virgos, and they notice the subtleties of facts. Their consciousness serves as both microscope and projector. They can scrutinize the largest matter to the point of probing its tiniest molecule, or amplify the smallest particle into its greater significance. This kind of intelligence pierces into the core of life and brings Virgos incredible understanding of whatever interests them. They can familiarize themselves with every facet of a subject and understand the basis for how everything works.

Analysis is not only a gift, but also a lifestyle for Virgos. They are never *not* analyzing. Although it can often help them to better understand life, at other times it can drive them (and others) crazy. If Virgos don't direct their analytical skills toward finding the goodness that's present, they might overanalyze what doesn't work, and forget to find what does.

This overanalyzing can be applied to themselves and others. That stifles Virgos' spontaneity and ability to be present, because they get lost in thinking, thinking, thinking. Instead of doing what is useful, which is another of Virgos' gifts, they get distracted trying to intellectually figure things out, without truly being involved in what's going on.

Virgos need to watch the tendency to get so caught up in analysis that they miss the forest for the trees. They love narrowing their focus down to the tiniest detail. But, if it gets caught there, they might forget there is a whole big world and higher purpose going on, and that the detail is just a miniscule part of it. **Virgos must remember to use their gifted minds to consider how things fit into the big picture.**

Although this analytical quality is really useful to Virgos' understanding this world, it is actually given to them so they can examine what they are allowing into their consciousness. As Virgos grow spiritually, it takes more discernment to differentiate the Light from Darkness. Sometimes, negativity parades itself as something helpful or positive. Virgos' analysis allows them to check things out to determine whether something lifts and expands them, or if it blocks them.

For example, one thing Virgos need to analyze is whether they're helping from an ego position to make things perfect for them, or to do what's best for everyone involved. Virgos also can use their analyzing to assess what blessings are present in what seems like a difficult or dark situation. When Virgos use their powers of analysis to locate the good that is always present, they are making the utmost of their gift.

Virgos love to **Categorize** all sorts of things. They do this with objects, ideas and people. With objects, Virgos enjoy deciding what goes with what, and where they should go. With ideas, they deftly move them into usable chunks, finding how one idea relates to another. With people, Virgos decide where they are in reference to themselves: Are they smarter, faster, richer? Maybe they think someone is above them. Maybe they're below them. Virgos also like to "type" people: "Intellectual," "Dope," "Do-Gooder," "Scorpio." However they do it, they have to be careful not to be so sure they've got people "pegged" that they miss who they really are. And Virgos always need to remember to give people room to change.

Critical Thinking is an important aspect of Virgos' analysis. Because they naturally sort out the good from the bad, Virgos pride themselves on identifying what problems exist. This makes them gifted troubleshooters because they love zeroing in on what that nasty problem is, and getting rid of it.

This critical thinking helps raise Virgos' consciousness by helping them sort out positive expression from negative. And it helps them spot where healing or redemption is needed in order to bring people or situations back on course.

It is Virgos' job to direct their analysis and critical thinking toward not only identifying the problems, but also toward finding solutions, or opportunities for expansion. If they don't, they might become obsessively focused only on the problems. Then, they become just plain critical, which is a Virgo trap.

If Virgos use their considerable intelligence just to discover what (they think) is wrong with a situation, they can become quite negative. They will turn into complainers and fault-finders, and that's disheartening and hurtful to all concerned, especially them. Virgos might tell themselves they're just telling it like it is and that everything is all wrong, but that is rarely the truth. The truth is that possibilities exist everywhere, but Virgos' negative approach has blinded them to those. Virgos' cynicism has trapped them into believing the goodness is all gone.

One signpost that Virgos have become merely critical is their becoming picky and hard on everyone around them. That means they have gotten stuck in negative thinking. It can also be pointing to the fact they have given up on lifting themselves, and, instead, they are starting to work on others as avoidance. But that won't work because, eventually, they have to deal with themselves.

The fact is, most Virgos are by far their own worst critics. And they are ruthless about it. Nothing escapes their critical self-judgment: They can do a project 99.99 percent perfectly, but fault themselves for that .01 percent they missed, then torture themselves about it. This self-criticism creates deep-seated feelings of inadequacy for Virgos. (When they combine this with perfectionism, they're sunk.) No matter what, they just don't feel that they are good enough, and they judge that there is always something they should have been, done, said, felt, (fill in the blank) better. When in the hole of self-criticism, it is hard for Virgos to feel joy—even for a job well done (their elixir) because they refuse to acknowledge they're okay.

Virgos know this about themselves. They have already analyzed that others aren't as exacting toward themselves, but think they are powerless to do anything about their own constant self-criticism. But there are things Virgos can do, if only they let themselves choose to. Being self-critical, or just plain critical, is another indicator that school is in session for Virgos. By learning how to step out of the critical loop just one more time than they step into it, Virgos learn to strengthen and direct their consciousness toward what's uplifting. Indeed, criticism is a signal Virgos are in negativity. That's it. At any single moment Virgos can shift into positivity.

One way Virgos can do that is to be more intellectually honest with themselves. Are they paying as much attention to what's right as what they think is wrong? By making it a practice to follow a self-critical remark with a self-appreciating remark, Virgos can begin to develop more positive awareness and self-talk. They could even go one step further and say, "I forgive myself for judging myself for (whatever the issue)," after they have criticized.

Another tool that works to shift from criticism is Virgos' gift of **Evaluation.** Criticism has a negative judgment or charge to it. Evaluation, however, does not. Evaluation provides the same function as criticism, looking at what works and what does not, but, instead, it holds neutrality. The pain Virgos feel while being self-critical is their signal to shift into self-evaluation. Then they are giving themselves a chance to gain without pain.

But, sometimes, Virgos just like to point out what's wrong. It can actually be a fun game to them. Some Virgos even consider it "their job" to find what's wrong. (It's not.) Instead of "Where's Waldo?" it's "Where's Wrong-o?" So if a Virgo finds they have some complaints, it helps to find a neutral party (even a pet) and tell them all about it. Sometimes, it feels great just to get them out. But they should then ask themselves what's right, or what can be useful about what they consider wrong, so they turn their consciousness back to a positive charge.

Virgos' **Attunement to Excellence** is also a rare gift. Virgos have an urge to make the absolute most out of themselves and their environment. When they are on the positive side of their excellence drive (the negative side is perfectionism), they work joyfully and tirelessly toward getting every last piece of whatever they're involved in just right. Virgos' excellence has an intelligence, in that they have an innate sense about how to do things well. Even if some Virgos don't have the highest IQs, they are still somehow smart about things.

This drive to excellence can be directed into the service Virgos do for others, and they do it to the last drop. If a sick friend asks them to pick up a prescription, they'll gladly do it, plus they'll get them some fresh juice, then tidy up their kitchen. If Virgos are in charge of a project at work, they will make sure it's done on time, covering all the bases, including a well-edited report about it at the end. Virgos love doing, getting all the details to be just right, so the whole is made up of perfect parts. The act of executing this kind of excellence thrills Virgos, and they have an almost spooky endurance to work 'til it's done.

This excellence is given so Virgos bring out the best of their nature. Instead of considering their issues or faults as just something they and everyone have to deal with, Virgos set out to improve their expression so they can demonstrate their personal best. But Virgos need to remember they aren't supposed to criticize themselves if they don't demonstrate their vision of excellence. They are learning like everyone else.

Mistakes are invaluable for finding out what doesn't work—which is actually a huge step forward. Virgos benefit by accepting that they make mistakes and can learn from them. High standards give Virgos something to aim for. They will get there as they learn to do things. It's a process, and no one—even Virgos—is expected to do everything perfectly the first time.

Virgos do well to make sure they don't let their need for excellence in all they do stop them from taking risks and trying new things. Although Virgos love nothing more than doing something with competency, that could keep them stuck. They might hesitate to take on new endeavors for fear they won't be good at them and will look incompetent. This can keep Virgos locked into jobs they've grown out of, stuck in limiting routines in life, or inhibit them from getting to know people they're interested in. It's important that Virgos let themselves learn; that keeps their intelligence stimulated. Incompetence or mediocrity are not crimes, nor do they make Virgos unlovable. Virgos' challenge is learning to trust themselves and their potential.

Virgos are also amazingly **Thorough.** Once they are on to a worthwhile project, they do it, and do it well, from beginning to end. Virgos want to make sure there is nothing they have missed, overlooked or left out of their awareness in getting something done just right.

Sometimes, Virgos can take this too far and get a little too thorough. Knowing when something is good enough is as important as covering each and every base. So tidying up a sick friend's kitchen to help out is great service. But going on to clean and reorganize the rest of their home, including the garage and attic, might be overkill.

Virgos are also driven to **Create Order.** Their first love is bringing order out of apparent chaos. It is so very satisfying for Virgos. There are hundreds of ways Virgos create order every day. Cleaning things, strategizing how things should be done and helping others solve their problems are some of the ways Virgos help make life more orderly.

But there's a higher order that Virgos are looking to access, and that is the order of the Universal Flow. As they direct their attention toward seeking the good or the God in things, they begin to recognize that life has its own perfectly orchestrated order, which happens on its own, without humans needing to direct it or interfere with it. Virgos become "blissed out" by the unspeakable beauty with which life unfolds. Importantly, they come to recognize that chaos, the nemesis of their perfectionistic lower Self, has its own place in the order of things (as Pisces people often try to tell them), and they learn to trust and relax when the inevitable hitch comes into their plans.

The Virgo Fears: Imperfection—The (Gasp!) Fatal Flaw

Deep down, Virgos **fear being imperfect, and, therefore, unlovable.** Virgos have a type of inadequacy that they have to deal with. No matter what they accomplish, or what they achieve, they can still feel they are somehow not enough, somehow flawed. This is truly painful for Virgos because they try so hard. It can drive them to unnecessary lengths in an attempt to finally feel adequate.

This fear of being deemed inadequate can cause Virgos to dread receiving any kind of correcting feedback—not to mention out-and-out criticism—from others, thinking it's a strike against who they are, instead of being an indicator of something they are doing. They mistakenly conclude that if others think they are doing something wrong, they have no value. (This might be merely a reflection of their own judgments that other people's value is based on effectiveness.) This fear can cripple Virgos by convincing them they better not take risks or step into the limelight, in case they might be exposed as inept. While it seems like a curse, it is actually another one of Virgos' greatest teachers.

A painful feeling of inadequacy is actually an invitation for Virgos to learn that they are valuable no matter what. Instead of trying to reach perfection, it is their job to finally realize that who they are in all their competency, as well as all their shortcomings, is totally acceptable. As Virgos learn to accept this about themselves, they begin to accept it about everything and everyone else in life. They awaken to the unconditional love and perfection of all that is, which is what they are truly seeking. That opens the door of Virgos' heartfelt alliance with the universal flow, which is their birthright.

Virgos can also **fear chaos,** thinking it might be the death of us all. Order is what Virgos seek, but it's also what they depend on. They are secure when matters are familiar or going as planned. This is okay if order is simply their preference. But if Virgos are dependent on order so they can feel safe, life becomes threatening because chaos is part of the Divine Flow.

If Virgos don't trust their core Self, as well as the innate goodness of life, they can fear that chaos will rob them of what they have built. They might also fear chaos will drive them insane—not true clinical insanity, but the "I can't deal with all this overwhelming stimulation" kind of distress.

The need for order is really the root of Virgos' control need. They think they can control themselves and life when it is patterned or predicable. But control attempts to limit matters, and Virgos are greater than that. Rather than attempting to control all matters, Virgos are actually learning to take dominion over themselves. That means they more successfully exercise choice over what they allow in their consciousness and what they let go on by. In fact, it is when Virgos accept the unknowable—and uncontrollable—that they avoid "insanity" by growing into a greater consciousness that more readily aligns with the grandness of God. Chaos teaches Virgos to trust and to align with what *is.*

Virgo in Relationships: "Loving Is Fixing"

Virgos are very gentle and giving in relationships. They appreciate the love and attention they get from others, and are anxious to reciprocate. Virgos express their need to be necessary by looking for things they can do to help and they show love by willingly giving advice, doing favors, as well as whatever else they think will support their loved ones and friends. Even if they are critical (and they are), Virgos are not trying to discourage. Rather, they think they are offering valuable ways for the other person to improve.

The vulnerability of Virgos is their fear that they are inadequate. They sometimes underestimate their intrinsic value in relationships, so they can choose relationships where their main role is helper. If they take this too far, they may end up trying to heal a "lost lamb" instead of choosing to be with a person who is an equal companion.

It is important for Virgos to understand that they are lovable—warts and all. Sometimes, being unconditionally loved helps them realize that. But many Virgos push that kind of love away. The old Groucho Marx joke, "I don't want to belong to a club that would have me as a member," points to this tendency in Virgo.

Many times, Virgos wonder what's wrong with the person who shows them attention. Help them overcome that by showing them what's right about you. Not in a bragging way, but in a friendly, confident way. They'll come around.

Remember, Virgos are about work. So, you want to date a Virgo? Make it a work date! Do something where one or both of you can get something accomplished. Believe me, productivity is an aphrodisiac for Virgo. Then, afterward, off to the health-food restaurant for a low-fat, romantic dinner with your Virgo. They'll love you for it.

The sign Virgo has the reputation of being prudish, or not very interested in sex. That's true of only a small percentage of them. But Virgos do need a sense of purity about their sexuality. For some that means feeling pure love and affection (rather than lust) for their lovers. For other Virgos, purity means their courtship is conducted in a certain tasteful way. Almost all Virgos like the kind of purity where in everyone gets srubbed up first.

If you are trying to catch the eye of a female Virgo, display your intelligence and ability to get things done. Virgo females are impressed by people who give of themselves, as well as ones who demonstrate competency. And never, ever make uncouth or directly sexual remarks. Yuck! A Virgo woman can be vivaciously sexual, but that's not what she wants as the basis of her relationships, and she rarely responds to anyone who attempts to elicit her animal attractions. What she wants is someone who's bright, refined and classy (but not so self-involved that they spend too much of their income on image). In a perfect world, that's someone she can share her work with. Very important: Be and smell clean!

If you are trying to catch the eye of a male Virgo, let him know how very bright you are, dress appropriately (sexy clothing can embarrass him), and smell fresh—like you've just showered. (Forget heavy perfumes—artificial, and he might be allergic.)

Virgo males have a kind of shyness to them, and they aren't that sure they are desirable. They are incredibly flattered when they discover someone likes them, but then they wonder why. What's wrong with the admirer? If you can show your appreciation to your Virgo male in specific ways ("I admire the way you conduct your business"), and avoid over-the-top flattery ("You are the best dancer in the world!"), you'll win his trust that you do, indeed, find him worthwhile.

But, oh my God, he's picky! He's got a certain set of criteria he's looking for. One Virgo male told me, "First I look to see if she has good teeth." (He has great teeth.) Another Virgo male told me, "She has to have exquisite posture." (He had poor posture.) So, don't get discouraged if at first a Virgo male ignores you—he might just be looking through his list of must-haves and must-have-nots. You can break through that with your wit, clarity and ability to lend a hand with his very important projects.

The Last Word on Virgo

What Virgo offers is the opportunity to see the perfection in the process of life, and to recognize that going for excellence is the perfect strategy for living a fulfilling life.

Chapter 7

Libra

(September 23–October 22)

Libra is the quality in you that's gracious and artistic, seeks to create harmony and balance, and enjoys relationships. It's also the part of you that's learning that the peace and partnership you seek is always within you.

To be, or not to be? To be! . . . No, not to be! . . . Wait, it's to be. . . . Or maybe it's not to be. . . . Hang on . . .

When it comes to decisions, Libras are built for elegance, not for speed. That's because Libras enjoy the process of evaluating: considering the pros and cons of a subject in order to identify the purest truth or the absolute best way to proceed. No matter what they're involved in, Libras will strive to create an atmosphere of harmony and balance—sometimes even going to extremes to accomplish it.

Libras have a remarkably developed sense of balance. They are acutely aware of even the subtlest dynamics of how people and things relate. This love of balance allows Libras to bring every situation to its most elegant alliance, and gives them the ability to create refinement and harmony in all that they do—be it art, relationships or their work.

Libras' natural graciousness and charm put people at ease, and their diplomacy and intelligence serves to uphold human values and ethics. In fact, Libras are peacemakers at heart; they seek justice in all matters, and strive to uphold what's fair. In the process, Libras will weigh all the factors, look at all the angles, consider all the implications—and, then, they will consider it some more.

The Libra Mission: Learning Universal Harmony Through Peace Within Themselves

All of us are learning what Libras are born to discover: The highest form of peace is Inner Peace—a state of being wherein they are able to stay aligned and balanced within themselves, no matter what is going on around them. By choosing to stay peaceful within, Libras are more neutral and objective about matters of the world. That poises them to contribute to every situation in a most impartial and effective way. When holding to their inner peace, Libras act as tuning forks that help their environment come into greater balance as a result of their harmonious presence.

The Libra Challenge: Finding Peace in the Midst of Conflict

Sometimes Libras learn peace by experiencing just the opposite: conflict. Libra energy finds conflict uncomfortable (at best), downright unbearable (most of the time), and even frightening (at worst). Most Libras also believe that they are obligated to resolve conflicts—even if they are not one of the parties involved. Although they do whatever they can to avoid it, conflict is Libras' greatest challenge and most powerful teacher. In fact, conflict teaches Libras that the harmony they seek is within them.

Libras are not only sensitive to conflict, they can also be very bothered when matters are unjust, unfair or just plain out of alignment. They can work tirelessly to resolve whatever they find to be "off balance," only to discover there is something—or someone—else out of whack. Many Libras even hold off being happy or content until everything is peaceful in the world around them. But that means they're waiting a mighty long time, because the world rarely reflects the kind of perfect harmony that Libras envision.

The Libra Key: Inner Peace Is Always a Choice

If, instead, Libras tap into an inner peace, striving to remain balanced and neutral within themselves regardless of whether or not the world seems fair or peaceful, they realize the secret of peace: It is always present in their consciousness, if they choose to find it.

It is also likely that Libras will learn about the relationship with their True Selves through conflicts in their personal relationships. Libras might cater to, negotiate or downright give in to others in an attempt to establish the harmony they crave. But, as others go about doing what they do (including doing what they need to do for themselves), imbalances and differences can emerge that disappoint Libras' ideals about how their relationships should go. That's a setup for Libra. Instead of trying to come into perfect harmony with another human being, Libras are learning to establish harmony within themselves. Ultimately, then, the harmony they yearn for is in the relationship between them, their Higher Self and God.

When they are in a cooperative, attuned alliance with who they are, Libras connect with a higher essence of their own nature, which gives them immense satisfaction and contentment. Standing on this solid foundation within, others needn't do or be anything different in order for Libras to maintain balance within themselves.

Libras can, however, learn a lot about achieving a good relationship with themselves via their relationships with others. As Libras recognize that all of their relationships reflect some aspect of their relationship with themselves, they can determine which strategies are helpful and should be developed, and which are alienating and should be released.

Weighing the Options with the Libra SCALES

Libra's astrological symbol is a set of balancing Scales, often held by a blindfolded woman. Scales denote Libras' style of weighing and evaluating, whether it is points of view, choices or strategies. This is their way of deciphering what is truly just and balanced. When evaluating what's right, Libras have the ability (some say need) to consider all facts, possibilities and aspects, looking for the truest and best conclusion. The blindfold also comes into the symbolism, depicting Libras' need to determine pure fairness or justice without being swayed by outside prejudices.

It is important to note that Libra is the only sign of the zodiac not symbolized by a living thing, but by inanimate scales. That reflects Libras' need for pure objectivity. They want to be absolutely fair and just, and they don't want human emotions, needs or weaknesses to distort their assessment of truth.

Libras seek "rightness" above all else. It's not perfectionism (as it is with Virgo or Capricorn), or an ideal world (as with Aquarius); rather, Libras seek an overall moral or elegant balance, and intelligence in the world. They want things to be fair, equal and harmonious.

However, Libras do understand that "rightness" can vary according to circumstances. Although they strive to be objective, they know that things don't happen in a vacuum—we are all being affected by countless influences all the time. So part of Libras' consideration about whether or not something is just or right includes what kinds of influences were present. For example, they might consider a thief who steals to support an impoverished family less an offender than a thief who steals to support a drug habit. (Even upon reading this, I bet the Libras started weighing and arguing the different points of view.)

Libras understand that truth and "rightness" can vary greatly according to a person's unique perspective. As much as they love the truth, they understand that everyone has his or her own valid *version* of the truth, according to that person. Because of that, Libras tend to be quite fair and just in dealing with conflicts.

Libras use their weighing ability as their method of making the best decisions possible. Indeed, they consider any decision "wrong" if it wasn't the absolute best one. The downside is that this weighing can go on and on . . . and on and on and on. Libras don't want to miss considering any point. One minute, one decision appears to be the best; the next, another one does. This is how their mind works. So, sometimes, this weighing matters to make the best choice catches Libras in indecisiveness. This can be exasperating (especially if everyone's hungry, and Libra is trying to decide between pizza and Chinese food).

Although Libras love peace, they also have a gift of argument, and some Libras exercise it all the time. If someone says black, they will say white, just because they think white also needs to be considered. This can be infuriating to others because they think Libras are being contrary. They're not. Libras just need to see all perspectives, and their personality wants others to do the same.

"Yes, but . . ." is one of Libras' key phrases. They will hear a valid point of view from someone and say, "Yes, but have you considered . . ." and then go on to raise the point not yet covered.

A key for others in dealing with Libras is to understand this need to consider all sides of a decision. If you want to cut the session short, agree with them. Then they'll start arguing with themselves and you can go on your merry way.

AIRy, Airy, Not Contrary

Libra is an Air Sign. (Aquarius and Gemini are the other two.) Being an Air Sign means Libras are most comfortable with the thinking function (as opposed to being emotional or doing practical tasks). Libras strive to objectively understand and assess matters, and come to conclusions that are fair and logical.

The unique Libran expression of the Air element is their ability to mentally grasp relationships, seeing how one thing influences another and finding the ways in which the various factors can be balanced. Libras have a keen sensitivity to how people interact with one another, especially sensing when there's balance and harmony, and when there is not. They also notice and evaluate how things relate to each other and to their environment. Indeed, nothing stands alone in Libras' perceptions; there is always something that will be in some juxtaposition to it.

Libras' Air quality leads them by inspiring them with concepts and ideals about what is possible, especially within the realm of creating peace and harmony. Libras intuit how things can be brought into greater alignment. These ideas, in turn, govern their actions.

Although Libras have deep emotions, they choose to subjugate them to the clarity of their mind. Libras don't care for intense emotional scenes and prefer to have a demeanor of composed refinement. Same goes for Libras' "gut" instincts: They consider them, but their ideas about what's right weigh more heavily.

Being an Air Sign makes Librans social and communicative, with an ability to breezily detach from one situation and flow on to the next. But when matters aren't breezy, when they are heavy or intense, Libra may step away to get some "breathing room." While they're gone, Libras might be thinking things over, or perhaps talking the situation over with friends. Then, when they get the objective perspective they need, Libras will return, ready to talk things out.

Because Libras' Air quality holds such high idealism about people and life, Libras risk being disappointed if everything doesn't measure up to their visions of what's possible. Or Libras can be surprised to find that the process of bringing their visions into form is much more arduous than they had hoped.

Libras are gracious and elegant, but all too often life is not. The practical reality of reaching a goal can tend to be more laborious or even distasteful than Libras' lofty sensibilities want to tolerate. Achieving a desired goal might necessitate that matters be thrown off balance, or that Libras have to deal with other people's agendas and conflicts. That's when Libras need to be able to be at peace within themselves, so they don't let the harsh world stop them in their tracks.

The CARDINAL Quality of Libra: Dynamically Initiating Relationships

Libra is a Cardinal Sign (Aries, Cancer and Capricorn are the other three). Cardinal energy makes Libras dynamic, with a charge to initiate things and forge ahead in new directions. Libras' particular expression of Cardinal energy is the way they initiate relationships: Libras know just how to strike up a relationship and then keep it blossoming. It's exciting for Libras to make contact with others. They are not only sure to introduce themselves, they also make introductions to everyone around, hoping to find ways people can successfully interact.

Importantly, although Libras want fairness and justice for all involved in their interactions, their Cardinal energy gives them a distinct desire to get what *they* want personally. Libras' sense of fair play, however, prefers that everyone would agree with what they want, and consider it just.

Libras also demonstrate Cardinal energy by taking the initiative to correct imbalanced situations. They will point out where things are unfair, speak up when they think something has been handled thoughtlessly and stand up for the underdog (or help him stand up for himself).

However, Cardinal energy has a tendency to get bored easily. So, ironically, when matters are harmonious, Libras might stir things up. To rationalize their action, they will tell themselves that matters could be even "more fair" or "better balanced." After Libras have managed to bring up the contentious issues, they can then go back to their favorite activity: making the peace.

Libra is what's known as a **Social Sign,** which means that they identify with themselves in the context of those around them. Because of this, it's important for Libras to feel as if they are impacting or serving at least a few others in order to feel fulfilled.

The Love and Beauty—or Love *of* Beauty—of VENUS

Libra is ruled by Venus, the planet of love and beauty, and Libras specialize in both. Libras have an intense drive to be loved. Depending on the individual Libra, this might be the love of many, or just a few, or one special someone. But it is that I/Thou (me and you) relationship that Libras need, because they use it to reflect back to them who they are. No Libra exists in a vacuum. By experiencing themselves in relation to another, they learn more about their being-ness, as well as what they're really made of. So Libras will actively reach out to find the "other," searching for the highest expression of the I/Thou, which is love. In addition to love relationships, Libras enjoy all sorts of *partnerships,* and devote time and energy to making theirs work.

Libras live for love. They adore courtship, but crave and enjoy all other forms of relationships as well. Indeed, they will seek relationships in everything they do. Relating is the elixir of life for Libras, and Venus supplies them with everything they need to attract others: She imbues Libras with charm, a dazzling smile, an ability to say just the right thing, and the openness that gives a green light to those who are interested.

It's not only Libras' own relationships that interest them—they want to know what is going on between everyone else as well. They have a natural understanding of human nature, and they are always interested in learning more. It's not that they're snoops or gossips, they just enjoy exploring the ins and outs of others' relationship dynamics. This can go on for hours, with Libras wanting to know even the tiniest details of how their friends and acquaintances interact. "Exactly how did they say they need a change in their lives? What will that do to their work situation? How will that affect their children?" Because of this consuming fascination with people, psychology, sociology and anthropology are sure to interest Libras because they never tire of learning about social order.

Venus also imbues Libras with a love and appreciation—as well as a talent—for beauty. Whereas Taurus (which is also ruled by Venus) loves comfy, sensual beauty, Venus gives Libras excellent taste for refined, design-oriented beauty. Libras search for beauty in all things. Actually, the first thing a Libra notices about any thing or any person is whether or not they have beauty. It's so integral to them, that Libras' careers could be directly related to beauty. Art, music, design, architecture, cosmetology—even plastic surgery—anything, really, that involves beauty or beautiful things, can be very fulfilling careers for Libras.

The Libra Archetypes: Evaluating the Beauty of Peace

In order for Libras (and people who are Libra-like) to fulfill their power—and destiny—of understanding the true meaning of peace and higher relationships, they will embody the archetype of the Peacemaker, the Beautifier and the Evaluator.

The Peacemaker

Libras embody the archetype of Peacemaker by naturally and fluidly doing whatever they can to bring people (or things) in their environment into peace and harmony. Their keen sense of fairness is constantly attuned to what is going on, and immediately recognizes if something is off balance.

When matters are off balance, Libras instinctively say or do what may remedy matters. They know just how to soothe angry tempers, or how to smile and tell a joke to cheer someone up, or emphasize a point that others are missing. In seconds flat, Libras will stand up for an underdog, but, in the interest of fairness, they will also point out how those in control are doing a good job. (Some Libras do this inside themselves without saying a word. Others stand up and openly fight for justice.) Libras' idealism envisions how things could best be handled in order to create a world that's a win/win for everyone, including them.

Simply put, Libras have an aversion to disharmony and injustice. It is painful for them to witness maltreatment, disrespect or domination in any form. When they do, they will put their Libran gifts into action and try to bring matters into a greater harmony. Libras' Peacemaker archetype considers balancing their environment job number one, and they will relentlessly work at it.

Whereas disharmony bugs every Libra, each one has a different way of dealing with it. Some Libras gently retreat into their own inner state of harmony, and stay there, hoping others will work out their differences. Other Libras take actions to stop or remedy the disharmonious situations. Wherever on that spectrum Libra is, not a day goes by that they don't somehow use their gifts to make matters more *fair.*

Most Libras are natural-born diplomats. They have a gift for saying things that aren't directly confrontational, but still pack the wallop of truth. Libras disarm people with their charm, yet gain their respect with their intelligence and ability to cut to the heart of the matter. Libras' psychological insights help them intuit what makes people tick, what their strengths are, where their weaknesses lie—and what they are really after.

Libras also have a sixth sense about how far they can take a person, always careful not to upset them or take them over the edge (unlike Scorpios, who are intent on taking people over the edge). On that rare occasion when Libras do push someone too far, they have a marvelous ability to verbally backtrack over any insults in an attempt to smooth things over. ("Did I say that you're annoying everyone in the office? What I meant to say was that, at times, others don't understand why you do what you do.")

Libras' peacemaking skills provide understanding into what motivates others, and how they can package an idea so that others will think they are getting what they want.

Mediation and negotiation are natural acts for Libras. Because their consciousness can step into another person's point of view, Libras can readily understand the inherent value and truth that opposing forces possess. Their objectivity helps override any emotional reactivity that might sway objective truths, so they deftly stick to the facts.

As mediators, Libras are able to bring out the essence of what people really want and need, and cannily present ideas in ways even opponents can understand. Even where there's conflict, Libras are able to notice something that the warring parties have in common or agree upon, and they can help build peace from there. As negotiators, Libras will use their consensus-building ability to find where the give and take can be.

Any profession where Libras can serve as mediators, negotiators or diplomats could be truly fulfilling for them. Working in the legal profession (they are excellent judges), serving as agents, being involved in conflict mediation, and any kind of refereeing are wise choices.

At the heart of Libras' diplomacy, mediating and negotiating is their urge to make—and keep—the peace. But they need to remember that the peace they seek is peace within themselves.

Libras are discovering that step one of finding that inner peace involves coming into alignment with whatever is happening. When Libras take an accepting stance of, *Yep, this is happening,* over a disruptive stance of, *This can't be happening, it shouldn't be happening, I won't let it happen!* they are able to be more neutral. Neutrality helps Libras' objective intelligence shine through, so they can be clear and calm about what the best approach to every situation would be.

However, in Libras' process of evaluating right from wrong, they might think they are obligated to take a stand *for* or *against* something, or even think "againstness" is a proper way to initiate change for something better. But it's not. Directing their energies against something actually fills Libras with a negative charge. It traps their focus on what they think is wrong, and that separates Libras from the wisdom their core peace offers.

Peace is the absence of "againstness." When Libras release any stance of "againstness," they position themselves to receive the wisdom of their higher awareness.

Back in the early 1980s, I counseled a Libra woman who was a vice president of the Fortune 500 corporation she was suing for sexual discrimination. She had an excellent case: Her boss would call her "bimbo" and regularly make unwanted advances in plain view of other executives. Typical of a strong Libra woman, she wasn't so much hurt by her boss's actions as outraged by them. When she came to see me, she had a lot of "againstness" toward not only her boss, but also corporate life and men in general, and it was wearing her out. She was losing her stamina, not to mention her Libran balance.

I offered her the idea of holding peace within herself as she moved through the process of seeking justice, reminding her she didn't need to be "against" anything in order to bring it to the light of resolution. We discussed that she just needed to present the facts and let them speak for themselves. She caught on to that idea right away. Although it was a lengthy court case, she was able to stride through it, keeping herself balanced and neutral. While she knew the behavior of her boss was wrong, she understood she didn't need to go "against" him emotionally—and she was able to see more clearly that he did not represent all men, so she was able to relax. In the end, she won a fantastic settlement and invested it in her own now-flourishing PR firm.

While Libras are campaigning for peace, they might believe that everyone should get along—whether they want to or not. But there are bound to be times when others do not want Libras' peacemaking services or Libras' idea of peace. So Libras need to be comfortable within themselves while conflict is happening. Sometimes conflict is the only way people (and they) can learn. Conflict also has a highly creative quality to it and loads of power. If Libras fear occasional conflict, they might strike up a peace at any cost, but not be peaceful within themselves, which is their real purpose. To be at peace whether there's a love fest or a fight present is Libras' key to Higher Consciousness. Then they are truly powerful.

An interesting point: Many famous military leaders are Libras. They are demonstrating their commitment to peace by being willing to fight for it and the way of life they choose as best. And some of the most successful peacemakers are Libras, who know what it takes to bring contentious factions into agreement.

One of Libras' primary life challenges is finding a way to get what they want while maintaining peace and harmony with those around them. (They are no mousy doormats.) True to Libran nature, they can swing from "giving in" and keeping the peace by pleasing others, to being quite opportunistic, slipping through the door and getting what they want while others are looking the other way.

A common Libran misunderstanding is that they should attempt to keep the peace, even at the expense of their own needs. Because they want harmony above all else, Libras might go along with what would make others happy, even if that means sacrificing what's important to them personally. Sometimes, it may be a wise choice for Libras to sacrifice their personal preferences to keep the peace. After all, harmonious relationships are the bedrock of their happiness. However, Libras have to be really honest with themselves about this, or else they will deflect themselves from what's right for them.

It helps if Libras intend to be as fair to themselves as they are to others. A good way Libras can determine if they're better off sacrificing what they want (to keep the peace) versus taking a stand to get their way (and possibly ruffling some feathers), is to check inwardly to see which decision leaves them the most balanced inside. If Libras give in to others but feel crummy about themselves or their life circumstances, chances are they are being unfair to themselves. If so, then they have stepped out of alignment with their most important relationship: the one with their Self.

A red flag that Libras are out of alignment with their power is thinking they have to hide the truth or even fib in order to keep the peace. Some Libras don't truly give in to keep the peace; they just disguise their true feelings and preferences. They might act like they're going along with something, while all the while they have another, hidden, agenda.

Peace is attuning to that safe place within one's Self, and being okay with honestly and directly stating wants and needs—no matter how judgmental or disappointed Libras fear others might become.

Another aspect of Libras' peacemaking gifts involves their ability to consider and validate other people's points of view. Libras not only can see where others are coming from, they also understand why others believe or act as they do. This is a tremendous asset in creating good relationships.

But Libras need to consider and validate themselves as much as they consider others. The challenge is that Libran energy never wants to be seen as motivated out of self-interest. So Libras risk overvalidating others, while undervalidating themselves. Or Libras might be so taken with the validity of another's argument for something, they'll go along with it without even considering if it's true for them.

For example, while Rachel, a dynamic Libra who owned her own ad agency in Chicago, was dating Dan, a freelance writer, he expressed a deep longing to move to the mountains of Colorado and live a simpler life. Rachel understood his desire because city life was getting more hectic all the time. So when they married, Rachel and Dan moved to a small mountain community. But Rachel became increasingly restless and unhappy. Finally, she recognized the problem: She never asked herself if *she* wanted to move to the mountains. Instead, she was just going along with Dan's dream. When Rachel realized that she had to consider her own preferences as much as Dan's, she recognized that Dan and she had to find a way to work out their living needs as a couple. They did so, in perfect Libra fashion: For part of the year they live in Chicago, and the rest of the year they live in the mountains. And both parties love it.

Sometimes, Libras might feel they have to justify what they want as somehow fair and right for everyone else involved, too. So, when Libras say, "I bet you would love going to the movies," it's really their way of saying, "I want to go to the movies."

The other side of the Libra coin is that, when they know exactly what they want—and have a determined intention to achieve it (but still don't want to risk any unpleasantness, competition or confrontation that might come from them going directly for it)—Libras might become somewhat opportunistic. Instead of overtly acknowledging their ambitions, Libras will hide or disguise their motives, and act like they are just there to support what everyone else wants. But, in truth, they are just waiting to spot an opening to get what they want.

While there's nothing inherently wrong with that approach, it is the deception that takes Libra off target. If Libras can present it outwardly to others for what it is—waiting for an opportunity— they can feel it is fair, and being fair is the root of their self-esteem. If they can't find a way to make this approach fair, they're better off just standing up and asking for what they want, whether people like it or not.

The Beautifier

Libras demonstrate the archetype of the Beautifier in their ability to bring beauty and harmony to everything they do. Librans are downright driven to make things look good. They have an incredible eye for design and color, shape and balance. Libras love beauty—indeed, gazing upon it can connect them with their Higher Self. They search for, and demonstrate, beauty on every level.

There is something beautiful about each Libra. This can be good looks, and often is. They usually dress well, too. Libras gravitate toward colors that compliment them, and they know just how to put together an outfit for a most pleasing effect (but never gaudy or over-the-top). Libras are sure to add those special touches, too, like a gorgeous scarf or fantastic tie. That bumps up their appearance even more. And the Libran sensibility knows how to accentuate the positive, so to speak, and they dress to cleverly distract from any flaws.

A big part of Libras' beauty is their poise. They have a way of holding themselves and moving in a way that is fluid and elegant. Even if they are upset or hurried, Libras will carry themselves with an air of balance and equilibrium. Because of this natural grace, even if Libras are just wearing jeans and T-shirts, they look refined and put together.

But deeper and more important than physical beauty, Libras carry a *vibration* of beauty. That is the beauty of Spirit coming right through them. As it does, their very presence clears the air, heightens the sensibilities, and helps others awaken and take notice of the beauty that's all around. The more Libras tap into their inner harmony, the more they are able to align with this frequency of beauty that everyone around them can benefit from.

Libras' personal spaces also have elegance, class and beauty. Libras have a flair for decorating and specialize in vistas that flow and relate. Even if their style is eclectic, Libras have a knack for putting things together in a way that makes everything look its best. Libras are big on flowers and *objets d'art* that add that perfect touch to the overall design. It's important that Librans include art in their personal space because it uplifts them so. And color—Libras know their colors. I have Libra friends who have picked paint colors that, at first, their painters refused to put on the wall, fearing they'd be dreadful. But—*voilà!*—they were *fabulous!*

Because Libras' sense of beauty is tied up with balance, they find anything unbalanced hard to tolerate. They just have to straighten crooked pictures, move a vase a few inches so it figures more perfectly on the shelf, even mentally rearrange an awkward room so they can feel at peace.

Libras are eager to assist others in establishing beauty. They will thoughtfully offer advice (they'll probably wait to be asked, even though they've been thinking about it constantly) on how others could enhance the beauty of their personal presentation or environment. If anyone needs either beauty or decorating tips, ask a Libra.

Libras usually also have a musical gift of some sort. Perhaps they sing or play an instrument, possibly both. The Libran gift of *Harmony* gives them a natural affinity with all aspects of music. They understand rhythm (Libras are good at math, the basis of rhythm), and they have an ear that knows what's in tune and what is not (painfully so). Even if Libras haven't developed their own musical skill, it is still a very important part of their lives. Music lifts Libra's energies and helps them align with their Higher Nature. A career in any aspect of music could be a good one for Libras.

It's important that Libras remember that it is that "frequency" of inner, spiritual beauty that they truly seek. Otherwise, they can be driven to distraction by the physical beauty that is—or is not—around them. Some Libras become so involved with their appearance, or the appearance of their surroundings, that they become obsessed with the *image* of beauty instead of the more powerful *essence* of beauty. That's a shame, because it restricts their otherwise expansive awareness that true beauty is a reflection of the Divine.

Other signs are not nearly as interested in beauty as Libras are, so they don't care if things are unkempt, mismatched or unsightly. If Libras *need* to be surrounded by beauty in order to be happy, rather than simply *prefer* it, they risk being irked much of the time because, let's face it, aspects of this world can be downright ugly. I recommend to my Libra clients that they create as appealing an environment as they can. But when that's not possible, Libras can't afford to let that pull them out of balance. It is a wise Libra who remembers that beauty is always present in their Spirit, even when they can't find it in the world.

The Evaluator

Libra lives the archetype of the Evaluator by striving to impartially determine what's right, fair and true, from what's wrong, unfair or false. The Libran scales are always at work attempting to sort out and determine the best possible way things can interact. Libras collect input from as many perspectives as they can, then they weigh them over and over to see the pros and cons of each side. This process can take quite a long time because Libras' minds Ping-Pong from one point to the next. Then they make their decision—about anything—based on their much-considered assessment of what's best.

What is most important to Libras is being able to *justify* their decision as the ultimate truth. Whereas some signs may just *feel* something is right, and others simply *want* something to be right, Libras work hard to mentally evaluate all kinds of factors to come to a *practical reason* for their ideas to be right. They will do their best to suspend their own needs or emotions from their evaluative process because they don't want the truth to be colored by anything but the facts. When Libra's Evaluator—finally!—determines what's right, that's it. Others can argue, fight or cry about their decision, and, although they will feel compassion for them, Libras will feel obligated to stick to it because they've worked hard to make the fairest choice for all concerned. Libras don't want to be lured off course.

Now, prepare yourself for a shock. Believe it or not, there are times when Libras' evaluations draw the wrong conclusions. I know that's hard to believe, since they have such a sincere commitment to locating the ultimately fair truth. But I have seen Libras determine a point of view is the correct one, then argue it in the face of raw facts that prove it's wrong. Even if life is demonstrating over and over that Libras' strategy is off course, Libras can come up with an endless loop of "Yes, buts," "Okay, onlys," and "That won't work becauses" 'til the cows come home.

In this way, Libras use their considerable intelligence to support their limitations to an astounding degree. If someone offers a solution, a Libra will find a reason it won't work. Another solution is offered, but, "No that won't work either." That kind of thinking results in Libras staying stuck in frustrating or dysfunctional situations, thinking that there's no right choice but the one they're making. Meanwhile, others are steaming with frustration, because their Libra friend is complaining about life not working, but won't change their approach.

Eventually, however, most Libras do use their Cardinal energy to move themselves out of a tough situation. Their Cardinal energy prevents them from being victims.

This Evaluator archetype can really tie Libras up when they believe there is only one *best* decision, and to make any one but that would be a terrible mistake. Whereas other signs just jump into decisions and learn from the results, Libras don't want to learn from mistakes, because they don't want to make any. This is paralyzing. Libras become frozen with indecisiveness, one of the main challenges of their sign.

Indecisiveness happens when Libras' evaluative process can't come to a clear conclusion; their facile mind moves in a constant loop of the pros and cons, searching for the one perfect solution. They keep bouncing back and forth from one decision to the next, thinking that sooner or later they'll realize what the best choice is. But since all of the options have positives—and negatives—one decision appears as good (or bad) as the other. To make matters worse, Libras have a fear that, if they make the wrong choice, they'll be stuck with something that's not their best opportunity or highest destiny.

Meanwhile, others are waiting to marry them or not, move to another city with them or not, or simply go to dinner with them or not, and Libras are struggling between yes and no, stay or go.

When this happens, it's likely Libras' highest choice is 50/50. Libras' lesson is to *decide*. Pick one option and just *do it*. Commit to it. When Libras do so, that decision does, indeed, become the

best possible choice they could make.

That's why the Libra Evaluator archetype is attracted to indisputable subjects, like science and math. In those disciplines, either something works or it does not. Indeed, Libras would love it if everything were that clearly ordered. I have one Libra friend who is gifted in many creative ways. But, when she talks about the beauty of math and its clarity of truth, she lights up as if she's talking about God.

This Evaluator archetype plays out in relationships, as Libras are continually considering the "fair play" of the dynamics of everyone they're involved with. Libras will attempt to find a way each person can get their needs met, yet still keep the highest harmony for the whole group. This could be with a group of two (Libra and one person), or a huge group of people, like a country.

Whereas others might be focused only on themselves, Libras' focus is on others, with a desire to make all things fair. It's not that they're overtly controlling (like Leo), or that they like to see what they can get people to do (like Scorpio), it's more that Libras act as a guide to make sure everyone is considered. (They do become controlling, however, when they insist that all involved do things in their so-called peaceful way.)

Libras are especially clear in their evaluative practices when matters don't involve them. When considering the issues of others, Libras' impartiality makes them clear and decisive, and their judgment or assessment of matters is guaranteed to be unprejudiced and fair. Libras' remedies or suggestions for others will have a "take everyone's concerns into account" quality to them, so all parties involved have something they can benefit from. Indeed, they provide excellent counsel.

But Libras' evaluations can get a little cloudy if *they* are involved in the matter they are assessing. Although Libras strive to be impartial and fair, they still have themselves to consider, and they have strong preferences that need to be satisfied. To be sure, evaluating what is the right thing to do when they are part of the equation is one of Libras' biggest challenges. They can make some errors in their approach to resolving this particular issue.

One big error is Libras' evaluating selfishness as a bad thing. Because Libras don't want to seem unfair (have their motives interpreted as selfish), they might decide against themselves in important matters. For example, they might put off asking for money to go to college because they recognize someone else in their family might need that money for something *that person* wants to do. That's okay, as long as Libras feel balanced inside about their decision. But, when Libras end up feeling resentful that others are doing what they want while they're making sacrifices, that might be Libras' signal they need to start doing more of what they want.

Let's face it, sometimes, everyone needs to be selfish. Not in a self-absorbed, Lower-Self way, but in a Higher-Self way where we make choices that support our growth and development. And that's whether others are inconvenienced by it or not.

One of the favorite pastimes of Libras' Evaluator is eliciting other people's opinions. Libras like to know what other people would do if they were in Libras' shoes. They use these ideas as a sounding board to help them evaluate and choose their best course of action. When trying to decide on a subject, Libras might call everyone they know and ask their advice. Funny thing is, Libras rarely actually *take* the advice. Rather, Libras use it to strengthen their own position. This is in matters great and small.

For example, Jerry and Ashley frequently go out to dinner. Jerry loves Chinese food. Nevertheless, he'll ask Ashley, "Where do you want to go to dinner?" She'll say, "Let's try that new Thai place." He'll say, "Don't you think Chinese would be better?" She'll say, "Do you want Chinese?" (She knows he does—he always does!) He'll say, "I do if you do." Jerry probably kind of wanted Chinese food, but wasn't sure until he heard what Ashley wanted. When he compared the various choices, he knew his was the right one.

Then there are times when Libras become so sure of their assessment of matters that they become downright righteous. They can be so intensely justified that their opinion is the correct one that they judge anyone who acts otherwise. They will decide anyone who behaves in the ways they prescribe as morally and ethically incorrect is a downright bad human being who needs to be convicted. When they take this position of absolute moral superiority, Libras sacrifice their valuable neutrality and risk making big mistakes about people. In this case, they lose the essence of their Evaluator and become the Judger.

It's best if Libras hold off righteousness by remembering that it's okay for differences in points of view to remain just that—differences. Libras don't need to convince anyone of the validity of their point of view but themselves.

Libras' Evaluator serves them spiritually by giving them the ability to look deeply into what's going on to find the course of action that carries the most light—or love, or goodness. In doing so, Libras can exemplify that "the right way" is what's for the highest good of all concerned.

The Libra Gifts: The World's Greatest Balancing Act

One of Libras' most useful gifts is their **Social Skills.** No other sign has quite the ability to attract others, charm others and disarm others (although Leo can be a close runner-up). They do this with natural grace and ease. Indeed, Libras' key phrase might be, "I like you, do you like me?" because they truly appreciate people, and want to be appreciated in return.

No matter whom Libras are with, they know how to fit in. Not because they are chameleonlike (like Pisces), but, rather, because they know how to deftly attune to the social mores and fluidly do what is considered acceptable. Libras are comfortable attracting attention to themselves, and they hold the spotlight in a poised and eloquent way. At the same time, Libras are eager to hear from others and pass the attention and conversation around, asking about everyone's views, making sure all are included. They enjoy the light fun of complimenting and flirting with others—with members of both genders, not in a sexual way, but in a "Let's like each other" way. (President Clinton, a Libra Rising, was known to flirt with females and males alike.) But they also crave in-depth conversations of profound or controversial subjects.

Sometimes Libras' social skills extend to the animal kingdom. They can be extremely interested in, and good at, forming relationships with animals, and devote their skill to building valued alliances there.

Libras' social skills reach beyond seeking popularity. They have an aptitude for understanding the underlying dynamics of human interactions, and they have insights into how to help make the world a better place. Libras have a deep respect for their fellow humans and strive to act in the most ethical of ways. They also have a desire to assist others in doing the same. In that way, Libras might devote their time to addressing moral or social problems. But this doesn't mean they have to be a people-person. Some Libras assist humanity, but aren't very social at all. In fact there are two types of Libra: the social ones and the loners.

The social Libras overtly use their social skills by devoting the lion's share of their energy to their relationships. They make relationships the focus of their lives, spending their time and resources connecting with others. They adore talking one-on-one with others (bigger groups are okay, too, but the one-on-one is most powerful for them) about whatever common interests they can identify. Libras will be the ones that call around their circle of friends, making sure everyone knows what everyone else is up to. Indeed, they love to be loved, and they give and receive it with equal enthusiasm.

Social Libras need to remember to enjoy the very important time for themselves. If they don't establish a good relationship with themselves, they can become overly dependent on being satisfied by others. Libras will think they *need* people, instead of simply preferring their company. When that happens, they go from social to needy. Overly social Libras will make sure that they are around someone—anyone, no matter who they are—just to avoid being lonely. Obviously, this can prompt them to stay in relationships that aren't healthy or even interesting, just because they're better than nothing.

When Libras find they are looking for love of others to fill some emptiness inside themselves, Libra school is in session. That's the time when they need to remember that the relationship with their Self and the Divine One is what their highest destiny calls for. That's a good signal to set out to deepen it; and, it is guaranteed they will be satisfied, empowered and happy that they did. They might even discover that others find them more attractive when they aren't feeling as if the Libras need them.

This drive to be in relationships can bring out the best in Libras: It keeps them open, engaging and attentive to others. But, if Libras believe that everyone should like them in order for them to be valid, they risk becoming a pleaser, and directing their creative energy into making other people like them, instead of being true to their essence and fulfilling their destiny.

So Libras need to ask themselves periodically if they are doing what rings true to their Spirit, or merely what they think others think they should do.

Some Libras are loners or have a loner side to them. That's because, although their sign is one of the most relationship-oriented, it's really the relationship with themselves they're after. These kinds of Libras find that too much social interaction distracts them from what's really interesting to them—and are even bored by most people. So these Libras prefer the company of themselves and maybe just a few others. It's not that they are unfriendly; it's likely they are as gracious as can be with those they come into contact with. They just aren't that interested in getting terribly involved. That's great. It's important that all Libras do what they need to keep their inner balance and peace.

Whether social or loners, most Libras nevertheless will learn their life's lessons through their relationships with others. That means that some important relationships in their life will necessarily be challenging. Those are the situations where Libras gain the Libran wisdom: that they only need to find balance and harmony within themselves to be at peace. Usually the relationships that seem most problematic are with the ones closest to Libras. This could be a parent, a spouse, a lover or the people Libras work with.

Sometimes, Libras will create problems in relationships by having excessively high standards or expectations of them. They will demand their relationships be close to ideal before they are satisfied. Libras might want every interchange between themselves and others to be perfectly balanced and loving the way they envision it all the time. And, when they are not, Libras feel disappointment. This strategy will cause Libras pain, because it is putting their demand for balance outside, rather than inside, themselves. It's not likely the world will live up to Libras' expectations, or provide them everything they need. And it shouldn't, because, as Libras learn to remain in harmony with themselves, it's more likely they will be attracted to healthy relationships with others.

This is not to suggest that Libras should stay in bad relationships and just keep a good perspective. They should not. But some relationships they just can't walk out of. If a relationship is difficult, it is likely the Libra is the one who has to find a way to make it work. Making sure they have a good relationship with themselves is one great way to start.

Libras are also blessed with **Intelligence.** Although all signs possess intelligence, Libras have a kind of Renaissance intelligence in that their interests embrace many different disciplines or media. Libras have an insightfulness that gives them a unique grasp of things, and that is always a bit beyond the way the mainstream of humanity understands things. That is partially due to Libras' ability to be objective, but it's also attributable to their ability to recognize relationships between matters that might be very subtle, but are nonetheless extremely important.

Astrologers used to say that Libra women think like men. (It was considered a compliment.) That meant that Libra women, as well as Libra men, were able to approach matters in an objective, nonemotional way, letting the facts speak for themselves. Librans have a certain practicality to making things function well—be it a formula, an engine or a design for a building—and Libras of both genders just know how to do it.

I do find a high percentage of Libra females tell me they prefer the company of men to women. Some attribute this to feeling awkward with what's traditionally considered many females' emotionally based exchanges. This preference of male company isn't a seductive or queen-bee thing, it's about camaraderie—Libras tend to find more in common with males' interests or points of view. Maybe that will change as the coming generations give both sexes a broader choice of interests.

Libras contribute. They don't withhold their thoughts or insights from others, or consider themselves the prima donnas of knowledge. Rather, they enjoy exchanging information with others, trading what they've learned. Libras understand that by sharing with others they don't lose anything; they know they gain valuable information from others' experiences.

And Libras possess the gift of **Grace.** This expresses itself in many forms. Libras possess a certain graciousness: a cool and refined—yet concerned and kind—respect of others, which gives them an air of gentility and civility. That draws others to them and puts them at ease. Libras easily give of themselves in order to make others comfortable in their presence. Physically, there is an **Elegance and Decorum** about Libra that is naturally pleasing to the eye. Whatever their social status, Libras behave in a way that stands head and shoulders above the rest. This isn't because Libras put on airs, because they do not. Rather, Libras have a sense that each movement can be one of style. They can make going to the refrigerator to get a jar of mayo look like a choreographed act. They're not showing off, they are just beautifully measured. Libras are never too loud or too invisible.

Libras' grace extends to others by their intention to preserve the peaceful balance of a situation, and refrain from being disruptively pushy or demanding—or needy. Libras will present their requests gently and judiciously, making it clear they are equally concerned about everyone else's needs or views, as well as their own. Libras have a way of offering their ideas so others see themselves reflected in Libras' remarks, and feel an alliance with them, perhaps causing them to see that what Libras are saying is right.

Instead of seeking ego gratification for having their ideas selected, Libras build consensus, and give credit to others for their contributions and insights. Although they might be feeling impatient (they are a Cardinal Sign, and inside they might be impatient as can be), Libras behave in a way that yields to other people's process, so everyone can carry on together. This makes Libras outstanding partners, valued friends and a joy to work with.

There is another kind of grace Libras might possess, especially if they are spiritually oriented. That is the out-and-out grace of asking for and allowing spiritual help. Of course, spiritual help is available to each sign equally. However, the basis of the grace Libras receive comes from their willingness to ask God for assistance, and consider God as their Partner. That keeps Libras open to, and available for, spiritual help. (Spirit doesn't inflict it; waits to be asked.) As Libras let go of any conditions that they might hold between themselves and God, they are able to recognize and receive more and more grace.

More than anything, Libras are influenced by their **Awareness of Balance**. They notice the balance of all sorts of forms: inner balance, social balance, artistic balance, human-spirit balance. Libras have an innate mechanism that detects where things and matters are on a continuum—or a seesaw—in or out of "alignment." Depending on other aspects of their chart, some Libras are satisfied with just observing the state of balance. Others reflexively work to bring things closer to the middle, or to a state of balance. That middle, or balance, isn't an apathetic or mediocre middle; rather, it's the poised center that allows for creative swings in either direction.

Interestingly, Libras learn about balance by going to extremes. This happens in little and big ways. In little ways, Libras might do something like eat loads of chocolate for six months, then quit cold turkey for another six months, to make up for their indulgences. In bigger ways, Libras might remain quiet or contemplative for a period of time, then call everyone they know and socialize like mad for a similar period of time. This isn't a calculated or even a conscious thing; it's just their inner nature establishing an ultimate balance. The older Libras get, the shorter the swings of extremes become, so they live closer to their central balance most of the time.

The challenge of this drive for balance is remembering that the world has its own balance, but that it might look terribly imbalanced to Libras. Libras can wonder about whether God exists because they see that things are so painful or unfair so much of the time. Libras might take it as a personal mission to try to force balance in those circumstances around them. Sometimes, they'll be successful, but, many times, they won't. That's when the lesson for Libras comes up: Libras' real mission is maintaining an inner balance, no matter how nutty things are around or outside them.

I have one client with a particularly difficult life. She tells me, "I just figure that's how life is, and I do my best to be the best person I can be within my circumstances." In keeping this kind of balance, she is a port in the storm for many people around her.

Some Libras don't want to "throw themselves out of balance" by overexerting themselves, so they don't. In any way. They don't want to exercise too much (or at all), work too hard, or disturb themselves by cleaning house on their day off. Libras can have a lazy streak that says, "I don't want to bother, so I won't." And there's no need to, as long as they are happy about their decisions (and can convince those around them to be happy with their decisions as well).

But there is an aspect of Libra that can work against them, which sometimes parades as laziness. Libras can elect to not fully invest themselves in something—or hold themselves back from doing their best—and tell themselves it's because they "feel lazy." That's not the true reason, though. The deeper truth is Libras might not feel their best is going to be good enough, so why try at all? Or, if they know they're only giving 80 percent of themselves, they won't be disappointed if they fail, because, well, they didn't do their absolute best. In those cases, it might behoove Libra to move off their balanced comfort zone and see what they truly have in them. They might be thrilled with the results of going 100 percent.

The Libra Fears: Don't Make Me Sing Solo

Libras' need for relationships can translate to a **fear of being alone.** Because they find meaning and identity through the I/Thou relationship, Libras can fear that if no one is there, they'll be of no consequence, or die of loneliness. Of course, this doesn't make practical sense, but fears rarely do. If Libras find that they're hanging on to others as a way of keeping themselves from being lonely, it helps if they remember that their highest Libran intention is to connect with a relationship between themselves and God. The more Libras put energy into that, the less fear of anything—including loneliness—they'll have.

Libras can also **fear not being liked.** Not being liked can be really painful for Libras because they try so hard to be nice and fair. This fear of not being liked can be rooted in a belief that if they are not liked, something is wrong with them. Instead of having confidence in their expression, Libras might look to others to see if they are doing or saying something "right." They fear that if they do it "wrong," they'll be judged or dismissed. This can tempt Libras to not be honest about what they think or feel because they're afraid of alienating someone.

Or Libras can fear that if they are not liked they might not be included. That's the worst! Libras hate to be left out. In any way. They hate to be left out of a conversation, left out of a planning session, left out of a group they want to belong to. Libras try hard to include others, and find it extremely disappointing and heartbreaking if others leave them out. They want to know they're part of the equation, at least in some way.

Libra in Relationships: "Can't We All Just Get Along?"

With all this talk about how relationship-oriented Libras are, one would think they would be masters at relating to others. But, of course, Libras have relationship issues just like the rest of the signs of the zodiac. The difference is, they might be much more interested in their relationships and relationship problems than others are.

Libras want to be in alliances with others that have a quality of intellectual exchange. They shun overtly sexual "Hey baby" come ons, preferring good conversation where both parties are truly heard. Libras' love of beauty gives an edge to the better-looking people in the room, but, in the interest of fairness, they'll consider anyone who makes an interesting pitch.

Libras are strong, but their strength comes in a yielding way. They want their significant others to have confidence in their perspective, because that gives Libras something reliable to bounce their evaluative thinking against. If you are someone who finds indecisive people annoying, avoid Libras, because that's what they do. One minute you're going to a movie, then you're staying home, then you're going to a movie. Then, it's *which* movie?

Libras can certainly be indecisive, and demand the right to be. But they hate it in their partners. They want to be with someone who takes a stand and lives it. That doesn't mean they won't argue with you—they will. Libras argue over everything, but they don't know or admit that they do. They think they're offering a series of opinions that need consideration.

If you are trying to catch the eye of a female Libra, it's a good idea to get yourself as beautifully groomed as you can. Get a good haircut, wear nice clothes, including shoes, and show that you have some appreciation for aesthetics.

Even if you're not so hot in the appearance department, you can capture a Libra's attention by showing her you have good taste. My client, Georgia, thought Bill had no chance for even a date until she noticed his outstanding cashmere jacket. That opened the door for him to show her how interesting he was, and they've been together ever since. But looks don't seal the deal; they're just the preliminary consideration. In order to win a female Libra's heart, you will have to demonstrate a goodness and ethical straightness that she can admire. Taking her to beautiful or artistic places will be appreciated, but that's not enough. She also wants to know that the two of you work well as a team. Demonstrate how being with you enhances her life and makes things more interesting. If she begins to show any indecisiveness about being with you, give her space. She hates being ignored, and she'll call you right back.

If you're trying to catch the eye of a male Libra, make sure you look good. Dress fashionably—nothing too loud or sexy, but elegant and with good fit. Smile and approach him with something interesting that shows how the two of you have common interests. He's looking for a companion who he can do everything with, so it's important that he sees your similarities. However, one thing Libra does not want to do together is process emotions. Libra men are put off by shows of intense—or even frequent—emotions, preferring more of an objective approach to life. This is true of his courtship style as well—he'll be as charming as can be, albeit a bit detached. So, let him know you care for him, but no hints of neediness or inappropriate displays of passion.

It's likely that you'll be the decision-maker of the couple, but you'll need to do it in a way your Libra thinks is fair and thoughtful of his preferences. You'll have to be very patient with him—it's likely he will change his mind a few times about whether or not he wants to make a commitment to you. He takes his decisions very seriously and doesn't want to screw things up. (Hint: Give him LOTS of space when he's indecisive. He'll miss you and want you back.)

The Last Word on Libra

Libras are looking for peace and balance. They will find those qualities in the world only if they find them in themselves.

Chapter 8

Scorpio

(October 23–November 22)

Scorpio is the quality in you that's intense and insightful, seeks to solve mysteries, and enjoys wielding power to control matters in order to develop their potential. It's also the part of you that's learning to transform what seems negative, in yourself and in the world, into something positive and useful.

Sex. Sex. Sex. That's all people think about when they hear "Scorpio." Or Power. Power. Power. And it's true. But there's more!

Scorpio is by far one of the most complex and intense signs of the zodiac. They possess deep emotions, powerful desires, probing and analyzing minds, and, yes, highly developed sexualities. They have an affinity for power: They know how to channel it to wield influence and control over whatever they are involved in. They especially enjoy moving people and resources into actions that are somehow transformative.

Although Scorpios are quite mysterious and private about themselves, they are masters at exposing the mysteries or hidden aspects of whatever or whomever they're interested in. At heart, Scorpios are problem-solvers: They love to use their penetrating intelligence to discover what's not working as well as it could, then use their strategic skills to make things better.

The Scorpio Mission: Learning to Transform Negative to Positive Through Loving

All of us are learning what Scorpios are born to discover: By tapping into their Higher Nature, they can transform anything that seems negative, both in themselves and in the world, into something positive and useful.

Scorpios' greatest tool for transformation is love. When they use the wisdom of their hearts to guide their intense emotions and perceptive minds, they can tap into a metaphysical force that allows them to be alchemists of Light. When that happens, Scorpios can go about their business of bringing matters that are hidden, judged or misused out into the open, and act as agents for healing and positive progress.

The Scorpio Challenge: Finding the Positive *in* the Negative

Because Scorpios are so powerful, they are constantly faced with challenges as to how to use power beneficially. Always, Scorpios have to choose between using their power to bring positivity and expansion to themselves and others, versus using their power to create difficulties or destruction. Scorpios can be so keenly aware of their negative possibilities that they can sometimes wonder if they are darker—even more evil—than others. The truth is, this awareness of good versus evil, or dark versus light, is Scorpios' greatest teacher.

As Scorpios choose to direct their power for constructive outcomes, they strengthen their foothold in their Higher Nature. They empower themselves by learning that *they* have dominion over their Lower Nature's urge to use manipulation, gossip or the undermining of other people's wills to get what they want, and thereby steer themselves away from the negative ramifications that can happen as a result. When Scorpios, instead, harness their personal power to act through their higher qualities of loving and positive resourcefulness, they can make a beneficial impact that astounds even them.

In seeking to express what's positive, even when there's negativity present, Scorpios not only align themselves with their remarkably expansive inner power, they actually gain greater power, because the "force" is with them, so to speak.

Of course, in learning how to transform what seems to be negative into something that's positive and useful, there are bound to be times when Scorpios get caught in the negativity. When that happens, they can become so focused on problems—either actual or potential—that they can think problems are all that exists. They become cynical and brooding, believing that life is not going well at all. In those instances, Scorpios are learning to employ their greatest resource: an ability to create transformation. When they remember they can change *anything* within themselves into something useful, Scorpios can rise to great heights from the most terrible-seeming situations.

The Scorpio Key: Intention Toward the Highest Good of All

One of the key tools Scorpios can use to help guide them in using their power for positive expression is the intention to do what's for the highest good of all concerned. **When Scorpios have everyone's benefit (including their own) as their intention, they become most ingenious and clever at helping matters transform in a positive, even magical, fashion.** When Scorpios' intentions are high, they are, too, and that opens them to insights and forces that seem to be beyond their personal abilities. They then serve as conduits for the higher works of the Light. Remarkable things can happen as a result of Scorpios' presence. The more they practice being a conduit of Light, the more they learn to anchor that approach as their primary life strategy.

One of the easiest ways Scorpios can lift themselves out of their emotional and mental darkness of "all that's wrong" is by applying their creativity to see how a matter can transform into something beneficial, to themselves and others. When Scorpios use their insightful thinking to look from the problem to the solution, and focus on what can be gained or used from any situation—no matter how lousy or terrible it seems—they are able to make the most of it.

Sting Like a SCORPION or Fly Like an EAGLE

Because of the complexity of Scorpio, there are two distinct symbols that represent the very different ways in which Scorpios manifest their sign. Each Scorpio chooses which symbol to express. Most express both.

The most traditional symbol of Scorpio is the Scorpion. Like a scorpion, Scorpios will fiercely defend their (extremely defined) boundaries and preferences, refusing to suffer any fools who might inflict upon them. I call Scorpio the "Don't mess with me sign," because Scorpios are the first to defend their position and eager to retaliate a slight. Just as a scorpion uses a deadly stinger to defend itself, Scorpios can apply their "deadly sting" to those who threaten them.

This "sting" might come in the form of Scorpios' saying something cutting that is right on target, and especially painful to—or about—another. Or they could sting by betraying someone or using them as merely a means to get what they want. Scorpios could sting someone just by giving them *that* stare that says, "You're in trouble." (No other sign can give that stare as well as Scorpio.)

Scorpios can get hurt fairly easily. When they do, their temper gets triggered, and they sting. However, Scorpios should be careful with that because what goes around comes around, and they can end up stinging—or hurting—themselves. This could be regretting what they've done, or setting something in motion that creates problems they have to deal with down the line. (Scorpios should make a mental note: "Do not sting self.")

Scorpio's other symbol is the Eagle. That's because, like an eagle, Scorpios can fly high and gain altitude over the limitations of their lower nature or ego desires. In doing so, they can relinquish their personal needs and desires in order to do whatever it takes to contribute to situations in a way that is for the Highest Good of everyone involved. When Scorpios are expressing the eagle aspect, they are able to look at things in a penetrating yet objective manner, and neutrally understand the deep implications of what is really going on.

The eagle energy enables Scorpios to step away from negative impulses, and, instead, choose the positive. Scorpios will then behave in a way that demonstrates wisdom and power beyond what their personal will or talents are capable of. As a result, they can ignite their own and others' spirits in a way that is utterly transformational. When they do this, Scorpios can seem like magicians.

(Many Scorpios tend to sit with their feet tucked under them. That's the perch of the eagle. And many Scorpios actually look like eagles!)

Not Just Any WATER; *Deep* Water

Scorpio is one of the three Water Signs (Cancer and Pisces are the other two), which means they are most comfortable with—or driven by—the emotional side of their nature. The unique Scorpio expression of the Water element is the remarkable depth to which they feel things, as well as their ability to use emotional energy as an avenue of transformation—one of the key qualities of their sign. Importantly, it's Scorpios' emotional desires that motivate them. They know exactly what they want and how to use the power of their emotions to propel them to take the necessary actions and risks to achieve their objectives.

Scorpios have a deep sensitivity to their own and others' feelings, as well as very adept "feelers," which provide them information about what's going on around them, even if it's very subtle. If someone is trying to mask or hide something, they can forget about it because Scorpios will sense it.

Scorpios' Watery emotions also lead to one of their greatest assets—but what they work like mad to hide: their vulnerability. Although Scorpio is one of the strongest signs of the zodiac, underneath it all they are quite vulnerable and gentle. Scorpios want very much to be liked and loved, and they dread being hurt. In truth, it's Scorpios' vulnerability that opens them to what they really want in life: love and transformational power.

Being a Water Sign means that Scorpios are challenged to use their powerful emotional energy in a way that expands and benefits them and others. Included in that is learning how to use their intention to shift emotional energy away from negative expressions that can potentially hurt them and others, and toward positive expressions that can heal and uplift. In either application, Scorpios' power is awesome.

So as part of Scorpios' schooling, they are given the entire gamut of emotions to experience, deal with and find some benefit from. It's likely they will experience tender love, seething resentments, uplifting joys, intense hatred, warm compassion, jealous rage, and everything in between. All that might happen over a span of their lifetime . . . or over a single weekend!

Not that Scorpios would *show* these feelings outright. Scorpios don't want the world to know how they feel (except perhaps when they're mad), because that would expose them, and they don't want that. Scorpios generally put on a cool, almost mysterious exterior, even if they're exploding inside. But just because they can mask their feelings doesn't mean Scorpios are not dealing with them. Try as they may, Scorpios eventually realize they can't squelch their uncomfortable emotions, or resolve them simply by wishing they weren't there. Emotions are part of life and they won't just go away for Scorpios—or anyone.

In fact, emotions are essential energies that Scorpios are learning to harness and use for directing themselves into positive action. For example, Scorpios might use the power of hatred to eventually fuel deep forgiveness, or learn to use the emptiness of grief to be filled with compassion. The jealousy that most Scorpios feel (intensely) could be harnessed into courageous motivation. Scorpios can transform the negative energies of envy or jealousy into a positive resolve to develop and create in themselves what they see in others.

When Scorpios transform their emotional energy from the contraction of negativity into the expansion of positivity, they are able to take what would cripple most people and instead use it to propel themselves to great personal heights. This is an awesome thing to see in Scorpios, and a great gift. So Scorpios needn't fear or judge their passions—they are available as sheer power for them. Scorpios' life circumstances will teach them (over and over again) how to use the power of emotions for the best possible result.

Scorpios' rich emotional nature also creates a space for deep intimacy with others. Scorpios want to completely connect with those (few) who interest them, and sharing all emotions is one way to do that. Scorpios' interest in others spans way beyond their likes and dislikes, their humor or their accomplishments. Scorpios' passions want to investigate every nook and cranny of another, including their deepest, darkest fears. And, in truth, that's what it takes for Scorpios to feel intimate.

Because Scorpios experience so much within themselves, they have extensive inner references that provide them with penetrating insight about what's going on with others. Scorpios' delving deeply and honestly into their own life issues and challenges builds a reservoir of understanding about the psychology and motivations of others. Scorpios offer excellent counsel to others because no matter what someone tells them about themselves, Scorpios have probably felt or experienced something similar at one time or another. Most times Scorpios know another person's problems long before they are disclosed.

The FIXED Quality of Scorpio: Stabilizing Themselves

Scorpio is one of the four Fixed Signs (Taurus, Leo and Aquarius are the other three), which gives them strength, determination and a tendency to become fully enmeshed in whatever they are involved in. Being a Fixed Sign means Scorpios crave stability and constancy, as well as a bit of structure in their lives. Inherent in this is one of the paradoxes of Scorpios' nature: Although their Fixed energy prompts them to stabilize and establish, their sign is also uniquely charged with a drive to transform matters. Even though Scorpios want stability, they almost can't help but stir things up wherever they go.

One way Scorpios might try to satisfy both urges is by attempting to control and create changes for others, while remaining constant and unchanged themselves. They might figure that, as long as they are measuring out or directing how matters are unfolding, they will maintain some of the stability and predictability they desire. So Scorpios will do and say things to get others to do what they want, hoping to nudge matters in the direction they think is best. Some people might call that manipulation, but, when Scorpios do it, they wouldn't call it that—even though that's exactly what it is.

What Scorpios think is "best" depends on their level of evolution. Some Scorpios want what's best for them, even if it's at the expense of others. Other Scorpios want what's best for everyone involved, and sacrifice their own preferences in order to make that happen. Most are somewhere in between.

One of the things Scorpios like to control is how other people live their lives. Scorpios have clear notions of what people are capable of, and they set out to help them realize those capabilities—whether others want that kind of help or not.

But if others try directing Scorpios (even in a direction they want to go) or prompting them to step out of their comfort zone, Scorpios' Fixed energy does not appreciate it one little bit. They want to move and grow and change when they're good and ready, and they don't want anyone pressuring them, or revealing anything to them to force that. As much as Scorpios feel compelled (feel it is their mission, actually) to encourage others to transform, they resist letting anyone—or anything—try to make *them* budge an inch. Many times, Scorpios' battle cry is, "I will not change!" and they will set their intentions to be just the way they are. The world can just deal with it.

My Scorpio client, Doyle, was a family practice physician who was involved in a highly dysfunctional partnership. There was constant bickering and backbiting among him and the other physicians in his practice. Because Doyle would come home every night furious and edgy, it was difficult for him to interact peaceably with his wife and three children. His wife pleaded with him to quit the practice and join another that could better support him. But he would not, and he told her not to interfere in his business.

Finally, his wife couldn't take it anymore, and she divorced him. Only a few months after the divorce, Doyle decided to quit the partnership, because now it was *his* choice. Finally, getting free of the tension at work, he calmed down and was able to be more loving in his personal life. But it was too late; his ex-wife had already moved on.

More than any other sign, Scorpio can cut off its nose to spite its face (or sting itself to death when feeling backed into a corner). Therefore, Scorpios need to practice their own transformational vigor on themselves. Even if it seems like they are changing just to please another, change still might be the most powerful act they can commit. It might also be their wisest choice.

Although Scorpios might be adept at using their Fixed energy to remain constant by directing the world around them, it's usually not their highest choice. Instead, it's more efficient for Scorpios to go to the heart of their Fixed energy by developing *inner stability,* so they can stand safe and steady inside themselves while the world does what it does. That way, Scorpios don't expend their energies on matters that aren't truly their concern, and they learn to control and stabilize what really counts: their own energy and consciousness. That keeps Scorpios the clearest and the highest, because their efforts are directed toward what they are truly in charge of, which is, of course, their internal world.

Scorpio is what's known as a **Transpersonal Sign,** which means it's concerned with the greater social order. This gives Scorpios the wiring—and the need—to involve themselves in matters that include or affect many people. This doesn't mean that Scorpios necessarily want to be personally involved with all these people (they are very private and picky about who they surround themselves with), just that some aspect of their life needs to impact on or contribute to many others. If it doesn't, Scorpios might feel somehow underutilized, even worthless.

Of course, not every Scorpio's destiny overtly involves super amounts of power or influence. Some make their transpersonal impact by being loving in everything they do. Although they might never know the direct results of their actions, they are sure to have a ripple effect throughout the world.

More Depth for Scorpio: Ruled by PLUTO, King of the Underworld

The sign Scorpio is ruled by the planet Pluto. Pluto governs things that are super-powerful, yet somehow hidden or mysterious. Included in this category are desires, sexuality, the flow of money, political power, fuel sources and spiritual resurrection. Pluto also rules the underworld, or the aspect of humanity and life that most people find distasteful—or don't want to deal with—like criminals, terrorists and death. Scorpios will find some or all of these topics interesting; and might even select a career that involves them.

Pluto gives Scorpios an ability to read between the lines, seeking answers to mysteries, wanting to get involved with those things that have layers of power and truths that beg revealing.

Pluto also governs regeneration: the act of dying and being reborn into something renewed. It correlates with the *phoenix*—a bird that falls from the sky, crashes into a fire and burns, then gloriously rises up out of the ashes in a transformed state. And, in many ways, Scorpios are much like phoenixes. There is something about both their nature and their destiny that leads Scorpios through episodes wherein they have to completely give up and give over; indeed, let something "die." This can be a most difficult or painful process, but it's crucial to their transformations to experience and express their inherent greater personal power.

Although Scorpios' Fixed energy prompts them to hang on to what they have established in life, their greatest empowerment actually comes from the Pluto/regeneration aspect of releasing their grip on matters and giving them up to a higher source. It is after Scorpios fully let go, surrender, perhaps even feel there is nothing left, that magic happens: Scorpios rise out of the ashes and regenerate themselves, capturing stronger, more useful and profound powers and energies. They go on to flourish, perhaps in a completely different direction, or with a completely different attitude.

The Scorpio Archetypes: Sleuthing for Control or the Power to Change

In order to learn about transforming negativity into something positive, Scorpios (and those who are Scorpio-like) will embrace the archetype of the Detective, the Controller, the Power Broker and the Transformer.

The Detective

Scorpios demonstrate the archetype of the Detective because they are irresistibly drawn to investigating and solving the mysteries of life. Their penetrating consciousness dives deep into whatever they are involved with; they have an instinct and a need to get to the very bottom of things. Scorpios quickly penetrate past pleasant appearances, as well as others' defenses or cover-ups, and perceive what is really going on.

One Scorpio described her ability to intuit the existence of hidden things and problems by likening them to glowing fingerprint dust. She said her attention just sweeps a room and whatever is "off" glows out at her. Scorpios are constantly looking to find what's hidden, and what, in their opinion, needs to be exposed.

Scorpios' Detective energy possesses an outstanding gift for probing and analyzing. No detail is too obscure for Scorpios' attentive inspection; sometimes, the subtlest clues can lead them to their greatest insights. It's pure joy for Scorpios to slice things apart, break things down, and put every aspect of what interests them under the microscope in an attempt to understand what's going on. And they are relentless about it: They don't reserve their penetrating analysis for one or two areas of their lives; they approach everything they do with the same Detective's intensity and curiosity.

Taken too far, this can drive Scorpios and others crazy. They can over-analyze themselves, their problems, or the problems of the world to the point of obsession. They will keep going over and over something searching for the solution or insight that relieves their upset. But obsessiveness blocks Scorpios' creative thinking, and gets them nowhere. If Scorpios find they are obsessing, it might be because their approach is off.

When obsessing, Scorpios should revert to one of their most effective strategies: letting go. (That's the very last thing they will want to do when they're obsessive, but it would serve them to try it anyway.) When Scorpios take their attention away from something, it interrupts their pattern of thinking. That allows some time and space between them and the issue. Then, Scorpios will be able to "fly above it," and see it from a much clearer perspective than the one that their analyzing microscope-mind might offer. This strategy will also prove to be a relief for others, because when Scorpios are obsessing, they are not very present—or loving. Indeed, obsessing can make them irritable.

Nothing, but nothing, piques Scorpios' interest like "forbidden territory." Matters that are off limits are precisely the ones that they want to explore. Scorpios are compelled to discover exactly what is hidden, why it's hidden, and what will happen when they expose it so it's not hidden anymore. They are compelled in this way with both people and things.

If someone has a secret, Scorpios will do their Detective work to get it out of them. If someone indicates some part of them has never been explored or touched upon, Scorpios want to be the very first to do so. And, if someone tells Scorpio that, to them, something is taboo, well, Scorpio will be just that much more motivated to confront them with it. Scorpios want to break new ground. Not in the Explorer sense (like a Sagittarius), but in a penetrating sense—they want to poke through and expose what no one else has yet.

Scorpios play the Detective in their relationships by constantly seeking to reveal what truly motivates those around them. Scorpios' first concerns are what others want with them and whether or not they are loyal and can be trusted (Scorpios put them through tests to figure that out.) After that has been established, Scorpios' probing shifts to discovering what makes a person tick, what kind of power they have and, most interestingly, what their problems are.

Scorpios' fascination with—as well as their sixth sense about—

human psychology gives them uncanny insights into the authenticity of people. They size up a person to assess how congruent they are with themselves, where their strengths are, and how their weaknesses manifest. This makes Scorpios gifted psychologists or psychiatrists, profilers or detectives. But it also makes them savvy in marketing, politics or drama—anything, actually, that benefits from understanding the human psyche.

Because of Scorpios' insight, they need to exercise integrity and patience. They quickly recognize where others' weaknesses are, and can be tempted to take advantage of them by manipulating or playing on them. Or Scorpios can push to expose other people's issues to try to prompt them into dealing with them before they are ready to do so. But in doing so, Scorpios might end up confusing, annoying or even diverting others from their own progress with this prodding.

It's likely Scorpios will use their Detective quality as a defense mechanism to expose others before others can expose them. Scorpios are secretive by nature, and don't like others to know anything more about them than they want them to. (But they sure do know lots of other people's secrets.) Scorpios can get enormous amounts of information out of others, while disclosing nothing about themselves.

Scorpios have a knack for sidling up to someone and asking, "What's wrong?" with such a knowing look that the other person figures the cat's already out of the bag, so they may as well own up to the problem. In truth, the Scorpio didn't really know anything was wrong and was just fishing.

Or Scorpios can play the Detective by positioning themselves in what seems like a plain old fact-gathering pose. I have a Scorpio client who serves on the board of directors of a major corporation. She has confided in me that she learns how fellow members will be voting on various decisions by presenting herself as a neutral party. She'll say something like, "I can see you all have some pretty strong differences in opinion, so why doesn't everyone present their point of view while I mediate?" In doing so, she gathers valuable information about where others stand without divulging her thoughts at all.

The Detective factor also displays itself in Scorpios' hunting down the key elements of what makes matters run. Their intensity ensures that they will go deeper than anyone else has the mind or inclination to in order to solve the mystery. Long after others have given up, Scorpios are still thinking, still searching, still following up on clues—and enjoying every minute of it.

In organizations, Scorpios' Detective skills are invaluable. They can ferret out how the resources are flowing, and where the problems are. They spot where there are jam-ups and overruns, but they will look much deeper than that. Scorpios want to make sure that everyone involved is fully accountable, and playing for the same team. If someone has a hidden agenda, is being dishonest, or just not up to snuff, Scorpios will recognize it and bring it out into the open. Except, of course, when this applies to them. They'll keep all of their agendas and strategies hidden, even as they expose everyone else's.

Scorpios' Detective archetype supports their spiritual growth by prompting them to solve the greatest mystery of all: the meaning of life. They are drawn to subjects that offer insights about the mysteries of our existence, as well as ways to pierce through the illusions of this world into the truer realities. Scorpios' Detective insight also helps them discern between that which is truly uplifting (or prompted by the Light) versus that which is negative (or involving the dark). Scorpios' Detective keeps them ever seeking to reveal greater truths.

The Controller

Scorpios demonstrate the archetype of the Controller insofar as they want to feel that they are the masters of their universe. One of the ways they do that is by having power and, to them, power is control. And the more control they have, the more power they feel.

Exactly what Scorpios seek to control depends on individual consciousness. They could seek to control themselves, their loved ones, or the world at large. Whatever it is, Scorpios' need to control is at the root of much of what they do.

Since people are part of their universe, Scorpios consider them fair game for controlling and directing. Scorpios find the power that comes from controlling others heady and exciting: They enjoy the feeling of getting someone to give something valuable up to them. It's not so much about what they get (like Taurus), it's more about the influence they've exerted. Scorpios love knowing they can get others to do their bidding.

Scorpios control so they can feel safe. As long as they are directing and overseeing matters, they feel there's less chance something could sneak up and surprise them, or threaten what they've got.

Scorpios want to control others so they can keep *them* safe, as well. Scorpios see as plain as day how others create problems for themselves through their decisions and actions. And Scorpios feel compelled to do something about it. Their urge is to jump in and explain to others where they're getting themselves in trouble, and try to steer them in another direction. If that means they have to exert control over them and demand they take another course, well, so be it.

But, of course, other people want—and need—to do what they think is best. They might consider Scorpios' dire predictions as Scorpio just being negative or worrisome. It might be better if Scorpios first ask others if they want their feedback. If they do, Scorpios can freely give the benefit of their awareness. If they don't, Scorpios can still hold a positive focus of others having the wisdom to make the most of whatever happens. Who knows, they might be making the best possible choice for who they are and what they need to learn, no matter what Scorpio thinks they may need.

Scorpios are learning to replace their need to control others with respect for other people's wisdom and right to make their own choices.

But this can be challenging for Scorpios—especially with people they dearly love, like their kids. Scorpios love their children passionately, and want to control them so they can protect them from all painful and bad things. However, this control can become overbearing. Scorpios can fear that anything their children want to do is fraught with danger. (When Scorpios are fearful, they interpret things with a negative slant.) They need to recognize that children (and other loved ones) have to learn from their own experiences, even painful ones.

What might work best is for Scorpios to present their concerns about what their loved ones are doing and explore the many possible outcomes they may be creating. There might be negative ramifications, and there might be positive ones. So, for example, when Scorpios help their children look at the many possibilities of their actions and decisions, they teach them how to look ahead and be responsible for their creations. That way Scorpios aren't controlling or limiting their children's learning by dictating their decisions; rather, they are teaching them true intelligence and successful techniques for living.

Scorpios' drive to control can also come from their urge to protect the world from bad or un-useful things. They can set their sights on social change, and do whatever it takes to bring their visions of a better world into reality. If the basis of their actions comes from doing the highest good for all concerned, Scorpios can be unbelievably gifted leaders—indeed, carrying out things that are far greater than what even they thought they could manage.

But if Scorpios try to control the world from an intention of imposing their personal agendas onto others, they might forfeit their ability to tap into higher wisdom—or their connection with the "force," so to speak. Instead of being instruments of good, Scorpios might just become dictatorial and oppressive in their strategies.

Scorpios also like to control how justice or fairness come to a situation. If someone does wrong, Scorpios want to exact judgment, so they know they've done wrong and atone for the errors. This can quickly turn into revenge, which the Scorpio nature is prone to. Revenge is very seductive to Scorpios, and they love to see it in action. Scorpios can wait for long periods of time in patient anticipation of that perfect moment (they know that moment will come) when they can exact revenge toward someone who's done them wrong. Scorpios' error lies in thinking that it's their job to bring about revenge. They can exact it brilliantly, but it carries negativity with it, and so might not be their highest choice. Revenge might set a whole new set of problems into motion that might, in fact, backfire on them. So it's usually Scorpios' best choice to leave revenge to God, instead, directing their power and creativity to healing and moving on.

Scorpios use control because, when they see what's possible in a situation, they are driven to make it so. They will appoint themselves the arbiters of good, and assume they know what would be best for everyone else. Or some Scorpios don't so much care about what's best for everyone else, they just want to make sure they get what they think is right for them.

Although it can seem like power, control is actually a powerful addiction; one can never seem to get enough. And, as with all signs, control asserts itself from Scorpios' Lower Nature. Feeling the need to control comes from a lack of faith that the Universe will provide Scorpios with what they want, so they set out to make it happen themselves. The power that comes from controlling is incredibly seductive to Scorpios. So herein lies one of Scorpios' lessons: They can control, they like to control, so why is it usually best to *not* control?

Control blocks Spiritual Grace. While Scorpios are managing and pulling strings, they could be getting in the way of a greater spiritual action taking place. They might not think they are worthy of spiritual action, but they are. The universe has an intelligence that is far beyond anyone's comprehension. When Scorpios release control, they might find that things work out in a way that is far better than even their own grandest vision. Sometimes, Scorpios can align more with grace by just resetting their intentions. When Scorpios resolve to let go of control and, instead, cooperate with how matters are unfolding, they are more prone to recognize the perfection of what is already naturally taking place.

The best use of Scorpios' drive to control is channeling it to control themselves. Not the kind of control that comes from self-suppression, self-denial or withholding. Rather, Scorpios benefit from using control to *guide themselves* toward choosing to develop things that support their Higher Nature—like expressing love, compassion, forgiveness and service—and step away from doing things in response to their Lower Nature—like succumbing to anger, revenge, lust or greed. For example, Scorpios might control their Lower Nature's urge to retaliate a hurt by rerouting their focus toward activities that support them. Or they might control a desire to foster resentment by forgiving their *judgments* and moving on. Scorpios could control the urge to act on their distracting sexual fantasies or fixations; instead, directing their sexuality toward other forms of creativity, in ways that enliven Scorpios.

The Power Broker

Power is related to control, but it is not the same thing. Scorpios are inclined to embody the archetype of the Power Broker because they possess, understand and enjoy power. They are driven to impact matters, and power allows them to do so. Indeed, power is one of life's great elixirs for Scorpios, and they are attracted to people and situations that can help them gain it. Scorpios understand the flow of power, instantly spotting who has it and who doesn't—and they know how to get power from those who have it. They are also brilliant at bringing power out in people and places where it is undeveloped or lying dormant. Scorpios are rarely overt about this, however. They yield their considerable power in a stealthy manner: Without drawing attention to themselves, Scorpios will effectively and relentlessly go after what (or who) they want, perhaps disclosing their intentions to others after they get what they were after.

Depending on the rest of Scorpios' charts, the kind of power (or powerful impact) they seek can be in the social, political, financial, sexual or spiritual realms. It is likely they will focus only on a few of these forms of power, but, in truth, all forms of power entice and fascinate Scorpios.

Some Scorpios seek social power in that they enjoy directing what goes on with those around them. Whereas most signs figure people are going to do what they want, Scorpios recognize that people can be influenced and managed. Their strategic gifts give them a blueprint of what they would like to happen, and their desire for the power of control prompts them to steer people to behave in the way Scorpios envision. Scorpios' insight into other people's psychology lets them know what buttons to push to motivate others to do what they want. This makes Scorpios excellent managers or directors, because they can see what others are capable of and they know just how to bring it out in them.

Whereas some people love status (Leos and Capricorns especially), social-power-seeking Scorpios love the *power* status can bring. They are more interested in influence than in glamour; so, many times, Scorpios will stand outside the spotlight. Being the powerful one behind the scenes also offers Scorpios more secrecy and privacy in carrying out their plans. They don't mind if someone else serves as the figurehead, as long as it's understood that Scorpios have the real power.

Scorpios can also be attracted to political power because of the immense influence that it can bring them. Their need to contribute to the world as a whole, along with their strategic savvy, equips them to handle even the most daunting political climates. Because Scorpios grasp the big picture, they aren't intimidated when dealing with vast amounts of people, resources or assets. In fact, Scorpios are enlivened by the possibility of what they can affect.

Scorpios are brilliant at group dynamics, and can be irreplaceable assets to whatever situation they are involved in. But if the point arises when their strategic vision turns into control for personal gain, it can backfire on Scorpios. They risk becoming utterly exhausted while trying to pull strings and manipulate others to go in the direction they dictate.

There are other problems inherent in trying to run the universe. For one thing, Scorpios are probably not the only ones in a group who are vying for power or control. There is bound to be someone else who wants to direct things or has a vision that differs from theirs. (A Capricorn? A Leo? An Aries? Another Scorpio?) This could lead to power struggles, wherein Scorpios' creative energy gets sidetracked while they are attempting to defend their turf. It's important for Scorpios to stand up for what is theirs, but protecting what's theirs is different from controlling everyone else.

Competing for power can be exciting for Scorpios because it keeps them on their toes. But it can also bring out the worst of their nature. They can become scheming, oppressive and undermining. Rather than tapping other people's resources to develop the best they have to offer, Scorpios will instead attempt to squelch the power of others, and suppress their expression and input. Then, instead of being valued as brilliant strategic leaders, Scorpios will get a reputation of being tyrants.

If Scorpios find they are, indeed, trying to maintain power by oppressing others, it might be a signal they are being run by their fearful lower nature. Some Scorpios choose to live life that way; but, it's grueling, and keeps joy at bay. It works better if Scorpios set their intention to bring out their own personal best. Then, their incredible power and assets will naturally pull Scorpios above the crowd. When Scorpios are being the best they can be, and seeking to assist others in bringing out their best, they are most charismatic and magnetic. People want to be around them because of their compelling presence. Then, Scorpios' strategic abilities can be positively directed into growth and forward-moving goals.

Financial power is also enticing for many Scorpios. They understand that money yields tremendous power, and so they seek to possess or control a lot of it. It's not so much that Scorpios love the stuff that money can bring (like Taurus), or need a batch of it in the bank for security (like Cancer)—those are both important considerations for Scorpios, but not what drives them. It is really the potential for influence and change that makes money attractive to Scorpios. They recognize that money makes things happen, and they want to use money to do what they think is best.

Scorpios are also drawn by the mystery of money: They love to locate it, study it, move it and, importantly, draw it to themselves through investing, inheriting, or any other way that makes it available to them. It's not only Scorpios' own money they find fascinating; in fact, it is *other people's money* or resources that compel them the most. Scorpios want to know what others are doing with their money, how much they have, how they earned it. This interest can easily be parlayed into a fruitful career—many Scorpios are responsible for handling other people's money and resources. They know how to make the most of other people's money and can gain financially by doing so. (In fact, Scorpios tend to attract other people's money to them, including inheriting more than others.)

I advise Scorpios to educate themselves in finances no matter what their lifestyle or career, for a couple of reasons. One is that Scorpios are naturally good with money, and it's likely they will make their own best financial advisors. The other is that it's very important that Scorpios feel fiscally potent. If Scorpios do not feel fiscally strong, there can be problems. They can develop a tendency toward greed and become fearful they might not be getting their share. Then, they can desire more money, but not be discerning about how they get it. Or Scorpios might think the only way to get money is by connecting to those who do have money. They will involve themselves in relationships not out of affection, but out of desire for another's money. But this is tough on Scorpios' self-image, and is usually a betrayal of themselves and the other person.

Another danger of Scorpios' not developing their own financial power is becoming frustrated at not having the opportunities money can bring, and becoming jealous or resentful toward others who do. If Scorpios are having problems with money, they can even lose interest in sex. Feeling financially impotent can lead to Scorpios' feeling sexually undesirable, and prompt them to withdraw from lovemaking. But it works better for Scorpios to continue on with their sexual activity, because that can serve to stir up their creative juices. Scorpios have an interesting sex/money alliance: The more they have of one, the more they can have of another.

Sex is another power Scorpios enjoy wielding. Although some other signs are as sexual as Scorpio, no other sign knows how to *use* sexual energy for power like they do. Scorpios instinctively know how sexual energy can make people think and do things. Scorpios have an allure, a certain sensuality that attracts people, making them desire Scorpios. Scorpios know how to use their eyes, body and aura to draw others in. Usually, this is conscious, but, for many Scorpios, it is instinctual, and they are surprised when others respond to them in sexual ways.

Some Scorpios find sexual power their number-one motivator—so much so that many of their life's decisions will be swayed by whether or not sex will be involved. For them, sex is the high point, the meaning of it all—no power is greater. Scorpios love the heightened state that comes from engaging sexually; they love the pleasure, the power and the attention of sexual exchanges.

Other Scorpios enjoy the power that comes from the *allure* or anticipation of sex. Thinking about sex, wooing, fantasizing, exchanging sexual innuendos can build a powerful energy that these Scorpios can crave. Actually, a good percentage of Scorpios I've counseled tend to be the latter: They love the power of the build-up to sex more than the actual act itself! (Taurus, their opposite sign, loves the actual sensuality of sex.)

Some types of Scorpios combine their sexuality with their drive for control and use their sexuality to have power over people. One way they do that is by seduction. They could use their sexuality to manipulate others, getting them to compromise their will or integrity. But sometimes seductiveness backfires on Scorpios: Those they're attempting to seduce can view them with suspicion and back away. Or members of the same gender will be angered by Scorpios' using sex to get their way. That might be okay with Scorpios because it denotes they have power. But it causes separation.

Sometimes, Scorpios use sexual power as leverage to get others to do their bidding. For example, they might begin a relationship by being very generous and open with their sexuality. In a way, they'll give a "taste" of the exquisiteness of their sexuality. But then Scorpios might withhold their sexual energy unless others do what Scorpios want them to. Instead of being truly available sexually, Scorpios might use it as a bargaining chip. Of course, if someone wants to relate to Scorpios that way, it's his or her choice. But, in truth, it eventually becomes frustrating, even demeaning, for their partner, who often will just leave.

Scorpios are likely better off allowing themselves to express their sexuality in its genuine form: When they don't combine it with power or control, their sexuality has an allure all its own. Others will always find Scorpios irresistible and charismatic. Their very presence yields an influence so enticing, there's no need for them to manipulate.

Some Scorpios allow the power of their sexual drive to control them. Issues of sex might dictate their decisions, and that can limit Scorpios, even get them trapped. Sex might prompt Scorpios to stay in relationships that don't serve them, or hold them in relationships that are just about sex. Scorpios' sexual intentions override their ability to recognize the other things of value a person has to offer.

Actually, the sign of Scorpio rules sex, and that means that *Sexuality* is, indeed, one of Scorpios' greatest gifts, as well as significant areas of learning. As Scorpios learn to take dominion over their powerful sexual drive, they channel their creative energies into wherever *they* choose. Scorpios can be marvelously expanded and uplifted by their sexual energies, and use them to express themselves creatively or to propel themselves into all kinds of valuable experiences.

However, many Scorpios have some sort of karma—or life lesson—regarding sex. Sometimes, this involves needing to learn to positively direct sexual desires. Other times, sex or sexual power has been used against Scorpios, or they have been sexually abused in some way. When this happens to Scorpios, it can result in very deep mistrust of sex or anger about it.

If Scorpios have suffered from some difficult sexual experiences, they might feel quite powerless in regard to sex and be quite driven to avoid sexual experiences. Their decisions might be dictated by a need to keep sex, or vulnerabilities that come from sex, far away. That's a shame because Scorpios can benefit immensely from healthy sexuality.

So it's important that Scorpios strive to heal whatever hurts they have about sexuality. Although it might be difficult, healing of sexual issues might just be Scorpios' greatest acts of empowerment. By finding ways to come to terms and forgiving whatever has happened to them—and also forgiving their feelings about it—Scorpios are able to free up tremendous amounts of energy, personal power and wisdom. Many of the leading emotional-trauma therapists have dominant Scorpios in their charts and have used their experiences of sexual abuse to find redemption in themselves, as well as the power to heal others.

The Transformer

Scorpios will display the Transformer archetype by becoming an agent for change and revolution in everything—and everyone—around them. They are compelled by the process of people and things *becoming:* Nothing is more interesting or worthwhile than watching something—or someone—transmute into something different, and, hopefully, better than it was before. In keeping with Scorpios' phoenix nature they understand that some things must die or become completely altered in the process of bringing out new potential, new life.

In fact, Scorpios' very presence stirs things up. It's almost as if any underlying problems, unused resources, mysteries or hidden agendas become revealed the instant Scorpios put their attention on a situation. But identifying problems is just the prelude to Scorpios' true gift. They combine their creativity with their strategic gifts to come up with viable solutions to alter matters—either to fix them, or to make them function even better.

Scorpios portray the Transformer by supporting others in shedding any illusions, false identities or limitations that keep them from recognizing their Spirit, so they can go on to express more of who they truly are. Scorpios have an eagle eye for untapped abilities and gifts in people, and they also recognize how others miss making the most of them. Because of this, Scorpios can be incredible, no-nonsense teachers, coaches or mentors by providing others with specific strategies for developing their natural assets.

Scorpios also love to portray the Transformer by prompting people one more step beyond where they feel comfortable. Scorpios usually sense when others can go—or do or be or change—just a notch further, and they enjoy being the one that nudges them over the line. However, Scorpios can become so determined to see someone change in a way they desire that their prodding can actually trigger an unnecessary crisis in that person.

It is important for Scorpios to remember it is their most powerful resource—their *Loving*—that acts as the strongest instrument of transformation. Instead of awakening others with their intellectual insights—or their emotional penetrations—Scorpios' loving is a non-inflictive, yet extraordinarily powerful, energy of healing and wisdom that supports others, so they can transform themselves in their own good time. This loving is steadfast and enduring, and it stays in place no matter what.

The power of Scorpios' love brings a sort of magic, a transformation of even the darkest of matters so something can be redeemed and brought to light. It can assist both Scorpios themselves, as well as others, in transcending life's most difficult, even horrendous situations. Indeed, even if Scorpios don't logically know what to do about something, their loving energy brings a force that opens doors for the best solutions.

One way Scorpios let their loving direct things is by offering their understanding to another. For example, they might listen to their fears or problems without judgment. By coming to terms with their own life's issues, Scorpios have developed quite a lot of compassion and wisdom about how darkness operates. Someone might reveal their worst actions, their greatest regrets, their most hideous secrets to Scorpios, and, understanding what it was like when they were in a similar situation, Scorpios just hold that person with love. When Scorpios treat others with compassion, they demonstrate how others can express compassion toward themselves. That encourages the act of greatest transformation of all: self-forgiveness and acceptance. That changes everything for the better.

Many times, Scorpios will help others transform by using humor. Even in life's darkest moments, they can find what's funny. By making people laugh, Scorpios help release tension, clear the air and offer a respite from the pain.

Scorpios will also work to transform matters by confronting those around them with their observations about the emotions and issues that they think others need to get in touch with and deal with, so they can transform themselves into something greater. Instead of accepting the defenses or masks of others, Scorpios' yearning for intimacy wants to get to the depths of another. In fact, Scorpios often try to help others transform their weaknesses into greater strengths by touching on others' pain, denial or blind spots.

For example, if a Scorpio did not point out to a friend that she thinks her lover is a user, or her oldest child needs counseling, or her unresolved issues with her alcoholic father are driving her to behave in a self-defeating way, the Scorpio would consider it tantamount to withholding valuable information that could lead to transforming the friend's situation for the better.

Of course, Scorpios' insight isn't always welcome. The reason people have masks or engage in denial is that they don't want to look at the truth—or have it revealed by anyone else. When Scorpios present their observations (which might, by the way, be incorrect), they may be forcing others to confront something they are either unwilling, or unable, to deal with. So before Scorpios throw up an unresolved issue they see in another, they should ask themselves what their intention for doing it is. If Scorpios are doing it out of love, they can ask their heart to give them the wisdom to know what's the best way—if any—to proceed. But if Scorpios are just trying to gain the upper hand or retaliate for someone's hurting them, they should remember how their Scorpio sting backfires.

Scorpios embody the Transformer in any organization or social situation by seeking to make the most of what's possible. It's not that Scorpios seek perfect order (like Virgo); rather, their ambitions lie in developing the maximum potential of any resources they, or others, possess. Just as Scorpio Ted Turner used the once-modest medium of cable television to transform the importance of television news, Scorpio energy recognizes what big things can grow from small seeds. Scorpios' Transpersonal energy envisions great potentials and their strategic gifts know how to turn those potentials into reality.

Scorpios do some of their best transformational work by helping others during critical emotional times. The Scorpio nature is attracted to the intense dramas of life, and is ready, willing and able to accompany and assist others as they explore their deepest feelings and issues. **When others are at their worst, Scorpios are at their best. They are unafraid of crisis; indeed, the phoenix energy in them trusts that, through personal darkness, will come healing and redemption.**

Scorpios are most insightful and strong companions to others as they make their passage through the inevitable painful periods of transition. Birth, death, critical illness and surgery, divorce and financial transitions are all situations Scorpios find honor in assisting others through. Because of this, Scorpios are most capable counselors, therapists, chaplains, hospice workers, attorneys, probation officers, surgeons, or providers of any other service that involves them with others' deep transformational processes—the ones wherein the people involved will never be the same.

Death itself fascinates Scorpios. They understand it to be the ultimate in transformation. It's likely Scorpios come to terms with death—their own or others—early in life. This might be because an aspect of their personal life's challenges involved death. Or it might simply be that death is an important symbol for them. By considering death, Scorpios are prompted to live a meaningful life, and discard any issues that would prevent them from being fully alive.

Because Scorpios crave transformation and regeneration, and death of circumstances prompts that, they are sometimes willing to risk something dying or ending rather than allowing it to carry on stagnantly. Scorpio energy hates a situation that seems unresolved or compromises them. So instead of just living with it, Scorpios will push it to the limits, knowing there's a possibility they might lose it altogether.

My Scorpio client, a writer named Marina, did just that. She felt her publisher was treating her unfairly by keeping her dangling about a project. She couldn't take the not knowing if they would use her or not. So she called up to confront them and force them to make a decision, knowing full well they might fire her. She pushed them into making a choice, and they chose to cut the project and let her go. She later told me she preferred losing her job to living with the uncertainty.

Sometimes, Scorpios would rather die than change; other times, they would rather die than not change. What's important is that they control the matter.

Scorpios' Transformer energy is attracted to areas of darkness because they offer the greatest opportunity, as well as the greatest need, for their transformative gifts. But Scorpios need to take care not to let themselves get caught in darkness. If Scorpios believe that darkness is all there is, they forfeit their transformative gifts and just hang out in frustration over what's wrong. If, instead, Scorpios set their intentions to extract whatever good is possible from a situation, they become true alchemists.

The Scorpio Gifts: Getting to the Depths

One of Scorpios' greatest gifts is their **Willingness to Go Deep** into matters that interest them. Instead of fearing the unknown or uncharted waters, Scorpios are irresistibly attracted to them. Their emotional and mental strength enables them to navigate situations that others would find downright overwhelming. They do whatever it takes—even if it's extremely precarious or daunting—to expose whatever is hidden or misused, in order to execute necessary change. Whereas others might fear or mistrust deep involvement, Scorpios feel that's the only way to go.

Scorpios **Go Deep Personally** by being intensely in touch with their own emotions and intentions. They are profoundly aware of all of their feelings, from the most pleasurable to the most painful. Scorpios accept the fact that pain is part of life, and they don't deny when they are troubled. That's because Scorpios can capture energy and power from even the most uncomfortable or painful emotions.

In fact, part of being a Scorpio involves going through at least one period of prolonged personal darkness, during which life seems excruciatingly difficult, meaningless or both. Anguish or depression stay with them long after others think they should get over it, whatever "it" is. Others will suggest Scorpios just snap out of it, or start to think positive thoughts. Really, Scorpios just want to kill them when they say this because, if they could change their mood by thinking positively, they would have done it long ago.

This long trip through personal darkness is an important passage to personal and spiritual awakening. Scorpios feel as if something inside of them is dying—and it is. It's their Ego Self, which is the part of them that keeps them separate from their greater connectedness with themselves, others and God. There's a slow wearing down during this process, and Scorpios give up a lot of what they thought they should be and what they should have. Some Scorpios even imagine or contemplate suicide at this point. I find that when a Scorpio reaches a point of considering death, it is actually the dark before the dawn, and the phoenix energy is at play. What they are really saying is, "I'll let any of my considerations, defenses or demands die so that I can be reborn."

Then, the awakening happens. Scorpios come out of the dark and the dust and into the light of who they truly are, and they realize the profound expansiveness of their essence. In doing so, Scorpios come to know what has true value for them in this lifetime. Life takes on a much more profound meaning, happiness returns, and they're grateful to be alive. Usually, it's love of some sort that brings them out of the darkness. And that is Scorpios' lesson: Loving is the greatest transformer of all.

This personal depth translates into Scorpios' ability to become **Deeply Intimate** with others. Social niceties are fine, but, in order for Scorpios to feel a true connection, they want to get to another's soul. Scorpios are comfortable committing to long-term relationships that endure through all of life's challenges. Superficiality holds no appeal for them. If Scorpios are in, they are in through thick and thin.

Scorpios also **Go Deep Intellectually.** The obvious holds no allure for Scorpios because there's nothing to ferret out or expose. Instead, Scorpios are attracted to complex or hidden matters, wherein they can exercise their powers of analysis and problem solving. Scorpios direct an incredible focus on a subject to derive the subtlest of its truths. Where others might acknowledge that life has mysteries, then move on (like Gemini), Scorpios aren't satisfied until they've solved whatever mysteries or problems they notice.

This depth brings a **Thoroughness** to Scorpios' thought process, and they rarely jump to conclusions. Rather, Scorpios take the time to study matters. Scorpio students are the ones who study, study, study, then study some more. They want to be totally prepared.

One of Scorpios' tools for going deep intellectually is their **Suspicion.** It assumes that matters are not as they appear, that there is something more to almost every situation. Because of that, Scorpios are alert to the hidden meanings and implications of things they become aware of. They ask questions others wouldn't even consider, and they are careful to check the validity of answers. Scorpios do this with all their faculties: Their mind analyzes, their feelings sense, their body feels "right"—or it doesn't. Beyond that, Scorpios have an uncanny intuition. Whichever of their sensors sends up a red flag, Scorpios are sure to follow the lead to get to the truth of the matter.

Scorpios are not about to be anyone's sucker, and their suspicion helps them steer clear of much of the deception of the world. But they have to be wise in using it. If Scorpios are suspicious that things might not be as good or as right as they appear, it's also important to suspect that things or people might be better or more perfect than they appear. That way, Scorpios keep themselves attuned to the whole truth, including the goodness of a situation.

Scorpios are also suspicious of correcting feedback. They think others are just unclear, or worse, trying to throw them off the right trail.

But it might behoove Scorpios to consider the feedback. Scorpios have a powerful nature, and their self-reliance can convince them that they're right even when they're wrong. (They will generally err on the side of suspicion.) Reflection and the intellectual honesty entailed by seeing all sides of a story help them stay clear.

Scorpios' suspicion can also serve as a tool for discovering more of their spirituality, by prompting them to look beyond the false images or façades of life into what's really happening. Scorpios sense the great intelligence and the serendipity of life, and want to know who's pulling the big strings. That leads them to investigate the Divine, and it works. Scorpios' suspicion also keeps them alert to the subtle ways negativity can infiltrate situations, and helps guard against their being blindsided by negative energies.

Scorpios' willingness to go deep is a spiritual gift, insofar as, no matter what they understand or how profoundly they experience their spirituality, they are eager to penetrate even more deeply. Put another way, their ability to go deep can translate to their ability to go higher.

Scorpios also have the gift of **Wit**: a kind of overall "knowing" about what's going on around them and how to use it to their advancement. Scorpios not only quickly size up a situation or person, they also have instincts for knowing how to work a situation to get the results they want. (And they do know what they want.)

The Scorpionic kind of wit sometimes comes from a culmination of all of their assets: intellectual insight, emotional awareness, intuition and strategic savvy, all of which translates to Scorpios just *knowing*. Scorpios' Detective qualities sniff out the hidden implications and intentions of others. Their constant watchfulness, probing and analyzing collect infinite amounts of information that leads to Scorpios' knowing. Scorpios' developed emotional "IQ" understands the nature of others—regardless of whether or not they reveal it—and helps them to know just what to do.

But there are other times when Scorpios just have a spontaneous "a-ha!" about matters, where their intuition just tells them what's real, what's at stake, and what's the best way to handle a situation. It all comes clear in an instant. Scorpios just know, and they know that they know. Scorpios can look at a person and know more about them than they know about themselves, or they can have a vision of where matters are likely to go. And they know all of this without any conscious effort.

Scorpios' wit also expresses through their ability to **Fascinate and**

Entertain others with their insights. They are the first to notice incongruities, insincerities, and especially ironies, and they can deliver their observations with sharply cutting clarity—oftentimes humorously. Sarcasm is Scorpios' humor of choice because they enjoy the stinging darkness and intelligence of it. And no one is better at it (though Capricorns are a close second). With just a few choice words, Scorpios can cut cleverly to expose the foibles of any person, place or thing.

Of course, Scorpios will use their razor-sharp wit to defend themselves, too. Anyone who challenges Scorpio had better be ready for a verbal comeback that could very possibly set them reeling. Sometimes, Scorpios can say the most stinging thing with such smoothness, it takes the recipient of the remark some time to realize they've been sliced open. Then there are occasions when Scorpios are not so subtle. Sometimes, they will simply explain to others what they're doing to annoy them. Other times, Scorpios just lose their cool and get mean. (Yes, Scorpios get mean.) If Scorpios are hurt, or if someone thwarts their plans, the barbed and poison Scorpion tail of their wit lashes out and puts the offender in his place.

Scorpios' gift of wit is designed to awaken them to spiritual understandings. It helps them to recognize truths (or realities) that transcend what their mind (or emotions) understand. Scorpios intuitively grasp life's larger meaning, the abiding power that we all live by, even if we can't prove it with our five senses. By using their wit, Scorpios tap into Universal Wisdom and are able to assess what works to expand their consciousness, then choose to do whatever that is. It also guides Scorpios to recognize what contracts their consciousness, or separates them from the Divine. Scorpios' wit gives them the good sense to step away from whatever that is.

Scorpios have the **Confidence** in themselves to rely on what they know or sense. Whereas other signs might look around to validate whether or not their feelings or ideas are accurate, Scorpios just trust their knowing. They generally feel no need to bounce opinions off of others, because, in truth, they figured out long ago that they understood more than most others. Scorpios also have the chutzpah to act on their instincts: They are willing to bet on their doing the right thing in the right way. Scorpios believe they know what's best in a situation, and they do it—in addition to trying to get others to do what Scorpio thinks is right. It is very rare that Scorpios stop to reflect about whether or not they're right. They just know they are.

Scorpios are **Resourceful.** If one angle doesn't work, they will try another, then another—until they find what does. Indeed, Scorpios love the challenge of conquering problems and people who at first don't yield to their control. Scorpios use their wit to discover and access whatever assets are available to help them achieve their objectives. They research, reassess and ponder as many strategies as they can try to create an opening, or opportunity, for their success. And Scorpios are **Relentless**: They simply refuse to give up until they have accomplished what they set out to do.

Scorpios also possess **Magnetism,** an alluring attractiveness that draws others to them. Part of that comes from Scorpios' confidence and self-reliance. Their personal power and sex appeal makes them compelling. Another factor of Scorpios' magnetism is their mysteriousness—something powerful, yet hidden, that entices others. People want to find out what's under Scorpios' smoky exterior. Scorpios' magnetism is hard to define—even Scorpios might not know how it works, but it's there.

Scorpios also have the gift of **Strength** in many forms. The Scorpio Spirit has an indomitable quality that allows them to persevere through even the most extreme challenges. Indeed, true to Scorpios' phoenix nature, they can even crash and burn, then resurrect themselves and flourish again.

Scorpios' karma, or the choices they make, can sometimes lead them to overwhelmingly difficult situations. But, instead of collapsing, indomitable Scorpios rise to the challenge. They become fully present and alive, even if they are in excruciating pain. It is as if the power of the difficulty ignites an equally powerful strength in Scorpios. Sometimes, this is a willfulness, wherein Scorpios refuse to be overcome. Other times, it's a passion that will not be stamped out. Scorpios have a spiritual power that goes beyond the body or the mind, demonstrating time and again that who they truly are cannot be destroyed.

Scorpios' strength also helps them outlast any opposition or challenge that they might face in life. Instead of giving up easily, they endure to the end, even if they have to cross the finish line on their elbows and knees.

Scorpios possess strength in their **Convictions.** There is nothing wishy-washy about them: They pick an opinion, an attitude, and they stick with it. Others can argue, rant and rave, but Scorpios will hold tight to what they have assessed as right. Scorpios needn't have a majority vote to know they're right: They have their own vote, and that's enough. Scorpios can't be seduced or swayed away from their principles, regardless of the consequences, because, no matter what happens, it can't be worse than their betraying their inner knowing. (They can, however, pretend they are changing their position for strategic purposes.)

Because of the strength of Scorpios' convictions and intentions, they are comfortable with **Commitment.** Nothing, but nothing, can lure Scorpios off course concerning what—or who—they have set their sights on. They make their choice and they stick with it.

It's a good idea for Scorpios to periodically evaluate what they are committing to. If they're committed to being committed, they might believe changing their mind betrays some sort of weakness. That could get them stuck. Sometimes, Scorpios' greatest strength involves using their wit to let go of commitments or positions that no longer serve them, so something new can be created.

The Scorpio Fears: Losing Power? Scorpio, We Have a Problem!

Scorpios **fear not being potent,** or being unable to make their desired impact on a situation. They want to think they can manage the world around them; in doing so, they feel safe and valuable.

Usually, Scorpios fear being impotent in almost any area of their lives; but, depending on their charts, there can be certain places where this fear is magnified.

Some Scorpios fear seeming to be impotent because they don't have enough knowledge. These Scorpios hate nothing more than to be exposed as someone who isn't in the know, someone who doesn't have the right answers. These Scorpios can compensate for this by going to great lengths to study and research matters, so they feel they are fully prepared with the power of knowledge.

Other Scorpios fear being impotent in managing their own emotions. They don't want to seem vulnerable or weak, thinking that could open them to some sort of humiliation or annihilation. These Scorpios can be overly cautious emotionally, trusting very few with their truest feelings.

Still other Scorpios fear impotency in their livelihood. They fear that if they are exposed as not really up to the job, they will lose it, and be out of financial resources. Or they fear they won't have the power to effect the kind of control or impact they desire in their profession, and be left behind as others succeed.

Many Scorpios fear loss of sexual potency. They figure that if they don't have the power to allure or seduce, they can't have as great an impact on others, or as much value as a human being. Sexual prowess and potency are so integral to the identities of these Scorpios, they can find it crushing to get older, for example, and lose their appeal. The opportunity in this, of course, is for Scorpios to find other ways of being with others and connecting that don't involve sexuality.

At the root of all these fears of impotency lies a belief that they need to control and manage in order to be safe. If Scorpios are willing to face those fears, and risk not being potent, they might discover they are more potent than ever. By relinquishing personal potency, Scorpios are more in a position to channel spiritual power, which is more wise and powerful than anything their personalities could concoct.

Scorpio energy can also **fear annihilation.** As interested in other people's crises as Scorpios are, and as courageous as they can be in resolving others' crises, Scorpios can still fear that somehow a crisis can take them out, or at least profoundly compromise them. Scorpios are extremely aware of the dangers of life, and don't want to fall prey to any of them. Life appears to be full of booby traps or land mines, and Scorpios are careful as can be to avoid getting hurt.

It's not just physical annihilation Scorpios fear, it's also annihilation of their dignity. Scorpios would prefer if others admired or loved them, but the least they expect is respect. Scorpios want to be taken seriously and treated honorably. Even if others fear Scorpios, they respect them. When Scorpios are respected, they feel they have power and some control, and that keeps them feeling safe.

Scorpios also **fear being humiliated.** If someone behaves in a way that threatens Scorpios' poise, embarrasses them, or humiliates them in any way, that's it. They are cut out of Scorpios' life completely. However, Scorpios can many times use humiliation to tap into a deeper sense of what is, in fact, good about them. If Scorpios' image or dignity is bruised, they might be forced to reach deeper to find that part of themselves that is much grander.

Scorpios **fear being exposed.** That could be because they might think their power and influence come from keeping their strategies secret. Or it might come from thinking that, if others truly knew them and their intentions, they wouldn't love them. Many Scorpios overcome this fear by discussing their dark side and getting the exposing over with. In doing so, they take back any power they might have been giving others, as well as realize that what they think is so dark about them isn't so bad after all.

Scorpio in Relationships: "You're *Intense,* Baby!"

In relationships, Scorpios are all or nothing. Because they become deeply committed and involved with loved ones, it's likely they will select only a handful of loved ones that they'll devote their time and energy to.

Therefore, Scorpios are extremely discerning and careful about whom they will surround themselves with. Before they allow someone close to them, Scorpios will test them to evaluate whether or not they are worthwhile. First, Scorpios will test someone to see if they're safe and trustworthy. Then they will test to see what their intentions are. Scorpios are not about to permit someone into their sphere who could jeopardize them.

But what attracts Scorpios about others is their depth and personal power. They will look to see the depth others are able to go to—with themselves, as well as with Scorpio. If people are superficial, or skim along a surface image of "goodness," chances are Scorpios won't be interested in them. Scorpios are drawn to others who can match their intensity and connect with them emotionally. They want to surround themselves with others who will go the entire emotional distance with them; otherwise, Scorpios cannot truly respect and trust them.

Scorpios want to be fascinated and compelled by another, and they want someone whose mystique continues to unfold and thrill them. Most people don't pass Scorpios' test: Either the Scorpios don't trust them, or they just don't have the power to draw the Scorpios in.

If Scorpios do decide someone is worthwhile, they will invest a tremendous amount of energy and caring. They will be quite affectionate, intensely loyal and protective. Scorpios will want to know everything about who the person is and what makes them tick. (If your Scorpio partner stops paying attention to you, perhaps even taking you for granted, something is wrong. Check to see if you're living "under their thumb" in some way, or have ceased to be mysterious or compelling, or if you've given your Scorpio complete control of you. If so, you might try doing something utterly surprising, or something that sends a signal that Scorpio isn't fully controlling you. You'll have that Scorpio's attention back in no time.)

The key to keeping Scorpios' interest is ensuring emotional passion between the two of you. Scorpios want to exchange energy with those they love; they want to feel there's something potent going on. Loving, probing, compelling, enticing, even fighting, are all ways in which Scorpios feel connected. But, during these exchanges of passions, do not humiliate them. Remember, that is a crime they're likely never to forgive.

Keep a certain kind of mystery about you. (Your Scorpio partner will be sure to do the same.) I'm not talking about skirting issues, or playing games that prevent intimacy. They hate that, don't respect it, and will step away. For that matter, you had better be honest with them, 100 percent of the time. If a Scorpio catches you in a lie, you've had it. There is no trusting you after that. Mystery means letting Scorpio know there is something else about you they can get to know—some new territory they have yet to discover. They love nothing more than to think they elicited something in you that no other person ever has.

Scorpios will get completely under your skin. Indeed, once you are in an intimate relationship with one, it's likely you will never fully be free of their influence. I know countless people who, long after their relationships with a Scorpio have ended, still considered what their Scorpio ex-partner or ex-friend would think of their actions. Scorpios' power over another can extend through time and space. But this is not a two-way street. If Scorpios decide they are finished with a relationship, that's it. They will cut someone out of their life completely and fully, and intend never, ever to open up to them again.

If you are trying to catch a female Scorpio's eye, you've got to have power. Depending on the Scorpio, she'll expect her partner to have enough sexual power to allure her, or enough personal power to compel her, or enough financial power to make her feel secure, or enough intellectual power to keep her fascinated. She loves subtlety, so don't come on too overtly; let yourself kind of seep into her. She'll want to know more and more. Remember that Scorpio is a Water Sign. That means she's primarily emotional, so connect with her through feelings. Even though she's one of the strongest signs of the zodiac, she's actually quite vulnerable, and treasures a partner who treats her with tenderness and loads of consideration.

Demonstrate your depth to her: Let her know she's dealing with someone who can handle her emotions. Do not lie. And do not look at other women within a 100-mile radius of her. She'll feel jealous. But worse, she might be humiliated. That will be it for you. (Note: Female Scorpios have a weakness for good-looking men, especially the first time around in marriage. If a guy's handsome, she might suspend all other partner qualifications and grab him.)

If you're trying to catch the eye of a Scorpio male, do it ever so subtly. Entice him with your sexuality, but don't be too overt. Let him know there's something about you no one has ever had the wit to understand or tap into. Present yourself with depth and mystery. Let him know there is a lot to you that could fascinate him; that he'd feel lucky to discover. Don't make it too easy for him, but spare him the games. He's very sensitive and wants to know he can trust you the whole way. Being a Water Sign, he wants to connect emotionally. Let him know you would treat him with loving-kindness. But also let him know you are strong within yourself and can't be conquered. He'll take that as a personal challenge. Don't lie, and don't give him any sense that you disrespect him. Flirting with other men, even through body language or subtle innuendos, turns him off. He wants to know you'd be as loyal to him as he would be to you. Really, he's looking for a woman that compels him with the strength of her softness.

The Last Word on Scorpio

Scorpios are learning transformation through loving. The deeper they go into the depths of darkness and yet still somehow love, the higher they will go into the Light.

Chapter 9

Sagittarius

(November 23–December 22)

Sagittarius is the quality in you that's gregarious and philosophical, seeks to make life one big adventure, and enjoys the freedom to roam and explore. It's also the part of you that's learning that the Good—or the God—is inside of you.

Sagittarians are just amazing. Like the Archer that is an aspect of their symbol, they have an uncanny ability to keep their eye on the target, w-a-a-a-y off in the distance. Of course, they have to be careful that they don't trip over what's right in front of them while focusing on that distant mark. But, knowing Sagittarius, they would just get up, dust themselves off, and gallop off again on their very merry way.

Sagittarians are the most high-aiming, gregarious and optimistic signs of the zodiac. Being philosophers at heart, they seek higher wisdom and meaningful knowledge, and they adore inspiring others through all they have learned. Sagittarians are extremely confident in themselves, and enjoy the thrill of taking risks and pushing themselves to their limits to discover what they are truly capable of. No matter what a Sagittarian endeavors, they do it with gusto. They know they will surely grow and benefit from whatever they undertake.

Nothing satisfies the Sagittarian nature more than the challenge and excitement of exploring uncharted territory. As they immerse themselves in the wonder of new ideas, places or situations, their Spirit awakens and they tap into their own expansiveness, and that of the world.

The Sagittarius Mission: Learning That Good—and God—Are Alive and Well in Everything

All of us are learning what Sagittarians are born to discover: The Good—or the God—is always present, both in this world and inside of themselves. Sagittarians are naturally inspired, and there is something within them that feels quite magnificent. Whereas their fellow Fire Sign, Leo, feels like royalty, Sagittarians feel royally appointed; some call it ordained. They sense they are an important part of a greater order, and feel called by something larger than themselves to do lofty work. That feeling comes from sensing the expansiveness of their Spirit, which gives Sagittarians faith in themselves and in life. They trust that good things will happen to them, which prompts them to take risks that others would shrink from.

Some Sagittarians express their sense of ordination by becoming involved with their church or spiritual group. Others find their worship in other ways, such as communing with the great outdoors. Whatever path calls them, it is important for Sagittarius to intend to tap into their Divinity in whatever activities they pursue. As they do that, they serve as a beacon of Light, fun and encouragement for everyone they come into contact with.

The Sagittarius Challenge: Finding Meaning in Apparently Meaningless Times

Sometimes, Sagittarians learn to recognize the Good—or the God—within themselves and life by going through periods when they believe they have no meaning or faith, or when life seems excruciatingly ordinary. Sagittarians become disillusioned, even disoriented, because everything they've built in life hinges on their having some higher purpose to fulfill or profound meaning to discover. Although this dip into grayness rarely occurs, it's probably the absolute worst thing that could happen to Sagittarius. They might think that, without faith and meaning, there's no reason for their being. And that's crushing to them: Why go on?

The Sagittarius Key: Digging Deeper to Go Higher

But, in truth, it is during those very times—when Sagittarians don't have meaning, or hope, or something (or someone) to look up to—that life is providing them with an opportunity to dig deeper to discover a whole new level of meaning and purpose. When Sagittarians' ideals are suspended, or their sense of right and wrong becomes disjointed, or they're not sure what the heck's going on, they can more easily release the dogmas, expectations and rules they have been living by, which might not be serving them. When Sagittarians lose meaning, they become more vulnerable. This helps them open up to even greater, more essential truths and values they might otherwise have overlooked. Sagittarians are also learning to realize that, although their minds and their egos might occasionally not know what's true (or who is running the show), they have an Inner Spirit that does.

Although these times of meaninglessness can be quite disheartening, they actually offer Sagittarians a unique meaning all their own. So Sagittarians needn't rush through them and try to quickly reinvent meaning if they don't have it. There can be something illuminating about living meaninglessly for a while. They can begin to appreciate the simplest, most ordinary aspects of themselves and life, and that might eventually lead to the greatest illumination of all.

HORSE-ing Around—but with a Higher Purpose

The symbol for Sagittarius is the Centaur: a creature that is half human, half horse, and is drawing a bow, aiming an arrow toward the heavens. This symbolizes the dual levels of the Sagittarian nature. The centaur is human from head to pelvis, signifying that Sagittarians have all the human abilities and consciousness intact. The human drawing a bow upward symbolizes Sagittarians' tendency to aim their consciousness high in life, toward something that uplifts and brings meaning. For most Sagittarians, this upliftment is some sort of philosophy or spirituality.

The horse body of the centaur symbolizes Sagittarians' connection to both the wisdom and the pleasures of this world. Although Sagittarians are most inspired, they are also hedonistic and intend to fully partake of this world while they reach for something higher. Sagittarians don't deny themselves anything; rather, they include all they desire and everything they do into their spirituality and philosophies. They have the ability to blend higher thought into everyday life experiences.

As a reflection of their centaur symbol, many Sagittarians have a somewhat horsey look. They have long, thin faces and horse-like features, including big, ear-to-ear grins. Sagittarians also tend to hold their heads up high and to nod in a big way, just as a horse does. And because the sign Sagittarius rules the hips and thighs, they seem to swing their hips and stretch their long (great) legs, as they walk; sometimes, looking like a horse getting ready to canter.

Consumed by the FIRE of Enthusiasm

Sagittarius is one of the three Fire Signs (Aries and Leo are the other two), which imbues them with enthusiasm and courage, and the need to keep growing. Fire gives Sagittarians inspiration and confidence to go after what they want in life, and they love to let their interests consume them. Once Sagittarians want something, that's it: Their inner Fire burns for it, they set their intentions to satisfy their passion, and no obstacle can stand in their way.

The unique Sagittarian expression of Fire energy comes through their intellectual zeal and their expansive, optimistic thinking. Fire gives

Sagittarians a blazing urge to discover life's meaning and fills them with inspiration. Just as a huge bonfire can come from a little spark, so can Sagittarians cultivate lofty thoughts and ideals from the tiniest sparks of knowledge. Sagittarians feel they can do just about anything, and their Fire gives them the confidence to try. However, just as a fire can die down if it's not being fed, Sagittarians' enthusiasm can die down if their passions—or interests—aren't being fed, or when they've had their fill of a subject or a person.

Sagittarians passionately follow the promptings of their hearts, striving to live a life that demonstrates the higher principles they aspire to. The outstanding thing about Sagittarius is that they will withstand any circumstances, no matter how challenging, as long as they think they're learning something. So, when the going gets rough, Sagittarians keep focusing on the fact that they are learning something—even if they don't yet know what that something is. For Sagittarians, life is for discovery and for satisfying their passion to explore, learn and grow.

Sagittarians' Fiery intellect provides tremendous communication skills. Few signs can hold an audience's attention and seem as fascinating or knowledgeable as they. Sagittarians want to make their imprint on others and they desire to inspire, to lead and to teach, as well as entertain. Good news: They've got the wit, humor and eloquence to do so.

Sagittarians' Fiery intellect also sparks them to be outspoken. They feel obligated and compelled to speak their truth freely and openly, and do so with great honesty and gusto. If Sagittarians think something is right, they'll say so, and they will present their reasons why. If Sagittarians think something is wrong, they'll say that, too. They step past any fears of upsetting others, because they value truth more than they value making others feel comfortable. Sagittarians believe it's a high calling to be forthright. And they enjoy shaking people up, and out, of their comfort zones.

Sagittarians' unabashed frankness can sometimes shock others. They may be so open and honest that others can be taken aback. Sometimes, that's because others just aren't used to people being as honest as Sagittarians. Other times, Sagittarians will shock others by saying what they think *in that moment,* without any editing. As a result, Sagittarians can put their foot in their mouth, or insult someone without the slightest intention of doing so. Putting "their foot in their mouth" is something Sagittarians are famous for and have to accept about themselves. Sometimes, they'll just say the wrong thing, in others' estimation, but they can't live in fear of doing that because they need to speak freely.

Fire also gives Sagittarians strong "gut" intuitions. They recognize very quickly what's right for them and then they're instantly off to make it happen. Sagittarians are faster than most signs, which gives them a jump on any competition in life. But being Fiery can also make Sagittarians very impatient. Life and people might not move as quickly as Sagittarians want them to, and that can frustrate them. If Sagittarians remember that patience allows time for Spirit to work its magic in life, it will help them cooperate with life's timing of unfoldment.

The MUTABLE Quality of Sagittarius: Flexible Philosophies

Sagittarius is one of the four Mutable Signs. (Gemini, Virgo and Pisces are the other three.) Mutability gives Sagittarians flexibility, and the ability to adjust their sights and behaviors to what's present and needed in every situation. Mutability allows Sagittarians to be changeable, and it also gives them a need for change. Sagittarians will get antsy, or downright rebellious, in overly structured situations. Instead, they prefer to be able to take a variety of approaches in whatever they seek and do.

The unique Sagittarian expression of Mutable energy is their ability to be fluid and flexible in their philosophies. Sagittarius is a particularly intellectual sign, and Sagittarians will devote their considerable intelligence to seeking ultimate truths. Sagittarians use their mutability to keep gathering knowledge and experiences that continually illuminate them ever further. So instead of settling on one idea or angle of philosophy, they will keep learning and searching for what's next. Sagittarians' Mutability also helps them extrapolate greater understandings from a little knowledge so they are able to gestalt the grander implications that just a little piece of information offers.

Mutability allows Sagittarians to change their mind about things. One day, they might fully believe something is right or true. The next day, they can be on to something else, dismissing the truths they've spouted before. In that way, Sagittarians keep themselves open and learning, ready to be illuminated by their next adventure.

A Heart as Big as JUPITER

The planet Jupiter rules Sagittarius. Jupiter is the largest planet in the solar system, and that reflects Sagittarians' expansive nature. Sagittarians seek to "live large" by creating a life of significance, and demonstrating the grandness of their essence. They keep their focus on the big picture, and the ultimate goals of life, refusing to become pinned down (or bored) by the inconsequential small stuff.

Sagittarians' expansive nature seeks big experiences. They figure, if a little of something is good, why not have *a lot* to make it great? The saying, "Eat, drink and be merry," describes the typical Sagittarian approach to life. And they figure they're worth the absolute best. More than any other sign, Sagittarius has the capacity for *more*. Whereas other signs might feel unworthy of too much money, too much love, too much self-esteem or too much fun, Sagittarians expect it and accept it. This isn't a materialistic attitude; rather, it is one based on their fondness for sensuous pleasures: They figure it's their job to fully indulge in what's provided in life for enjoyment, and they do their best to get the job done.

Sagittarians' expansive nature prompts them to aim high in life. Not in a way where they work hard trying to measure up to what others deem important (like Capricorn); but, rather, in a way where they aim for high volume and high excitement.

The challenge of having Jupiter's utterly expansive nature is letting it go too far, so it becomes excessive. It is the job of Sagittarians to discern what truly expands their Inner Spirit versus what inflates their ego. Too much of even a good thing can cause Sagittarians to veer off course from their true values and the meaning of life. The excessive side of their nature convinces Sagittarians that they shouldn't deny themselves anything, even if they don't have the resources—or the ability—to handle it. This can give Sagittarians a taste for manic energies: Instead of living life at a healthy pace, they might think going to extremes is more exciting, even if it burns them out in the process. But Sagittarians don't anticipate they'll burn out: They think they can go on forever.

I have counseled countless Sagittarians who are surprised to learn from life that they can't spend as much money as they want, or eat as much food as they desire, or get involved with each and every person or situation they're attracted to, without receiving some occasional (or not-so-occasional) negative consequences. They thought they were free to do whatever they wanted and were going to get away with things that others can't. So Sagittarians need to remember that it is Inner Expansion—the expansion into their Divine Nature—that is infinite. Outer expansion has its limits, and, when those are exceeded, there is a price to pay.

Jupiter's influence also gifts Sagittarians with a jovial and gregarious nature. Devotion to finding the deep meaning of life doesn't translate into somberness—just the opposite, in fact. Sagittarians are in an almost continual state of expansion into all life has to offer. They will create a festive atmosphere wherever they go. Sagittarians are the first to throw their heads back and laugh at a joke (theirs or someone else's), and look for the fun that can be had. Although life has profound meaning, Sagittarians don't want to take it too seriously. Besides, they expect that at least part of life's meaning is found in fun and excitement. So, they set out to make it so. If Sagittarians are in a situation where they can't find fun, or make it happen, they'll move on.

Jupiter's largesse also makes Sagittarians feel very grand and overflowing with the bounty of life. Because of that, Sagittarians are magnanimous and generous, and give freely of themselves. Why not? They only live once (in this body). Sagittarians abhor pettiness (penny-pinching really irks them) and insist on philanthropy in whatever medium they are giving from. Sagittarians are generous financially because they enjoy living the good life and want to help others live it, too. Besides, they believe there's always more where that came from.

By far, Sagittarians' greatest generosity is when they give of their Spirit. Sagittarians will willingly share who they are and what they're about with whomever they come across. Sagittarians are generous with sharing their knowledge and their viewpoints, and they are generous in their interest in others, which encourages others to express themselves.

Sagittarians are also generous with their compliments. They will throw out comments like, "Hey! You're looking great today!" with an intention of bringing some joy to others, even if it's for just that moment. And when they decide to flatter, they do so in a big, big way.

In truth, Sagittarians' feelings of inherent good fortune are accurate. Jupiter is associated with good luck, and Sagittarians do have it. Perhaps they create their own fortune by using their optimism to make the most of their situations. Or maybe Sagittarians are optimistic because good things happen to them. Either way, they tend to attract positive experiences, and they live by the philosophy that life is to be lived with gusto and passion.

But Sagittarians need to watch becoming so dependent on their good luck that they gamble what is truly important to them. Jupiter can fill Sagittarians with a cockiness that can convince them that they are invincible. They can be so sure they're going to luck out that they risk something—or someone—really important, disregarding any thoughts that they might lose. It's a marvelous trait to think the glass is always full. But it might not always be full of what Sagittarians envision. There is great wisdom in expecting the best outcomes, but there's also great wisdom in exercising temperance, or even saying "no" to some of their desires. (Sorry about that, Sag.)

Jupiter rules subjects and activities that lead to higher thinking such as philosophy, religion, spirituality, law and foreign affairs. This gives Sagittarians a penchant for such subjects, and it's likely they will either choose a career in one of these fields, or at least study these subjects as an avocation.

Many Sagittarians express their Jupiterian-influenced Energy by possessing remarkable faith. This can be faith in God, faith in life, faith in nature, or faith in their Higher Nature. They need to believe in something greater than themselves; something that's good, something that redeems. Sagittarians thrive on faith because they need to feel there is Ultimate Good running the show. Whatever Sagittarians find faith in serves as the bedrock of their reality.

What with Jupiter's inspiration toward all things philosophical, and being a confident and enthusiastic Fire Sign to boot, Sagittarians can get so excited about what they think and believe that they become downright righteous. Depending on how they use this powerful stance, it can either expand or contract Sagittarians. When used expansively, Sagittarians' righteousness inspires them to "do the right thing," or behave in a way that displays dignity and virtue. This gives Sagittarians something to aim for, a code to live by. They love the idea of living a valiant life, and of choosing to let the light of who they are triumph over any darkness, whether in the circumstances that arise in their life or inherent in their nature.

When Sagittarians are inspired to act on the righteousness of their higher principles, they can be the most courageous heroes. They can pull off things that others think impossible, just because their intention is clear and their Jupiterian aim is high.

But there's a kind of *self*-righteousness that can get Sagittarians in trouble. Their self-confidence and intellectual acumen can combine to convince them that they are smarter, wiser, holier, more moral, or in some way more evolved, than all the rest. Because of that, Sagittarians are sure they are more right about matters than anyone else. They can build a case *for* themselves and *against* others with such ease, they will fail to notice that they've neglected to consider all the facts. When this happens, Sagittarians become intolerant toward anyone who thinks differently than they, deciding that person is just stupid.

Sagittarians can then become Crusaders (another aspect of Jupiter), believing they need to "shed the Light" for all to see, dismissing the possibility they might be off course, either in what's right for others, or even for themselves.

One way Sagittarians can recognize that they are expressing the self-righteousness of the Crusader is if they are appointing themselves to make judgment calls about other people's lives, even if they are not invited to do so. Sagittarians might go beyond judging inside of their consciousness (which we all do all the time), into announcing their judgments, as if these pronouncements were truth itself being proclaimed from the heavens. (Jupiter, after all, was the king of the gods.) In the process of judging good from bad, right from wrong, the wisdom of the Sagittarian heart is drowned out, even shut down. Crusading turns the heroism of Sagittarians' nature into fanaticism. They can devote their power to trying to force their ideals onto others, thinking they are Divinely charged to save them.

If Sagittarians realize they have become self-righteous (or someone has told them that they have), they can easily turn it into virtuous righteousness. One of the quickest ways to accomplish this is to remember to take themselves less seriously. Laughing at themselves can be Sagittarians' best medicine and greatest awakener. Then, they can remember to reopen to the wonder of life's mystery. When Sagittarians step out of thinking they "know" what's right, they might become open to even greater understanding. Another good way for Sagittarians to shift out of self-righteousness is to reconnect with their curiosity. They can ask themselves if there is another truth they might be able to recognize. When Sagittarians make room for the mystery of the power of the real truth, they won't have to work so hard to defend it. It will defend itself.

The Sagittarian Archetypes: I Think, Therefore I Roam

As Sagittarians (and those who are Sagittarian-like) live their mission of discovering the Good—or the God—within themselves, they'll embody the archetypes of the Philosopher, the Adventurer and the Free Spirit.

The Philosopher

Sagittarians display the archetype of the Philosopher because they are, basically, philosophical. Sagittarians approach life with an eye to discovering the meaning of it all. They have a uniquely expansive consciousness, which looks beyond the everyday ordinariness of living, and seeks to find clues about the deeper implications of their existence. Whereas other signs are content to make a living, have a family and accept life as it appears, Sagittarians intuitively feel their life is more important than that: They think it is about learning deeper truths and attaining realizations that, ultimately, will free them.

In order to be truly happy, Sagittarians need to feel as if they are immersing themselves in experiences and subjects that give them, and perhaps others, wisdom and insights and a sense of connecting to something grander than ordinary life.

As Philosophers, Sagittarians enjoy bringing insight to themselves and others by interpreting life in an upbeat way. They like putting a positive spin on things, and seek to find the Good in all they find. Sagittarians are geniuses at shifting perspective for the better. If someone says it's a lousy day because it's overcast and raining, Sagittarians will point out how the landscape is getting nourished and the atmosphere is kind of cozy. I have one client whose sister felt exasperated by her young child's prolonged fits of anger. My client said that, to him, the tantrums sounded like a symphony. (He lived far away.)

The Sagittarian Philosopher takes the broad perspective on life, focuses on the overall meaning of it, and generally refuses to let the little concerns or setbacks of life get them down. No matter what happens, they will use their philosophy that, "This (whatever 'this' is) isn't so big in the scheme of things," and will do their best to work around any troubles. Indeed, more than any others, Sagittarians have the ability to make any situation a positive, worthwhile one. Perhaps that's why they seem so lucky—they are continually finding ways to use everything to their advantage.

Because Sagittarians intuit the grandness of their nature, they can think that means they are supposed to do something really important in this lifetime. This can be a great motivator. It inspires Sagittarians to develop themselves to be the best "them" they can be. But if Sagittarians feel they should do something important in a worldly sense in order for their lives to have meaning, it can become a trap. Sagittarians can be unsatisfied with what their destiny truly calls them to do because they decide it isn't enough. In truth, being loving, and discovering ever more deeply the nature of their Spirit, are probably the grandest acts of Sagittarians' destiny. Everything else is just filler.

In embodying the Philosopher archetype, Sagittarians will gather their wisdom by embracing the roles of both *seeker* and *teacher.* As they learn, they teach and as they teach, they learn. Both sides of this equation are of equal importance in the development and expression of Sagittarians' Philosopher archetype. Even though Sagittarians were born naturally wise about life, the seeker aspect of their Philosopher is hungry to learn even more. Sagittarians begin searching for understanding at a very early age. They crave higher knowledge like the air itself. Indeed, Sagittarians live life from a basic set of questions: "Why am I here?" and "How can I make the most of my life?"

The search for the answers to these questions is the elixir of life for Sagittarians and they are thrilled by the anticipation of coming across the knowledge that will ultimately illuminate them. So, they will explore countless avenues of interest, enthusiastically hoping—expecting even—that doing so will bring them insights that reveal to them the meaning of life.

If Sagittarians overdevelop the seeker aspect of their Philosopher nature, they will risk discounting their own wisdom, and project that others have the wisdom they don't. Instead of building a meaningful moral/philosophical/intellectual compass of their own, Sagittarians might look to others for direction and meaning. They could try to live up to the ideals of a righteous life of others, without checking out for themselves whether or not others' truth works for them.

Sagittarians could even go so far as to put those they consider wise ones up on a pedestal, and expect them to live a flawless life, perfectly demonstrating the wisdom they profess. But it's not anyone's job to behave in the way Sagittarians idealize. No matter how wise another person may be, they are bound to do something that eventually disappoints Sagittarius, because no one in a physical body does everything perfectly all the time. Should Sagittarians see their "guru" has feet of clay, instead of simply dismantling their pedestal, they might dismiss all the wisdom they've been given—even if it has been very useful.

Sagittarians' best strategy as a seeker is to "check things out" to see if the information is right and awakening for them. They do best to take what wisdom is offered, and leave their "teacher" to live the life and karma they need to. A teacher is not a model of perfection; a teacher is, at best, a short cut to excellence. Sagittarians are blessed when they can learn something from someone. A teacher can awaken a Sagittarian, regardless of whether or not their behavior is what the Sagittarius expects it should be.

The teacher aspect of Sagittarians' Philosopher archetype expresses itself through their passion for expounding upon the truths they have collected. As much as Sagittarians love the search for meaning, they adore presenting what they have learned to others, hoping it will uplift them as well. Sagittarians are enthusiastic and generous when teaching, and are anxious to instruct. They are ready, willing and able to take the center stage, and let others know about what they have learned so far. The teacher aspect of Sagittarians' Philosopher is an incredible inspirer. This makes them natural motivational speakers—either professionally or just in their everyday chats.

For Sagittarians, everything has meaning, and they translate that meaning into whatever they talk about. Their enthusiasm for inspiring others gives Sagittarians the ability to make any subject—even an otherwise dry one—utterly fascinating. Sagittarians know how to add zing to their topic with side stories, humor and bits about why their subject is important. Few signs have the eloquence, the enthusiasm or the clarity to make even the most difficult issues understandable. That captures their audience and gives them an incentive to learn.

Sagittarians step into the teacher role very easily. Whereas some signs believe they have to have full mastery of a subject before even considering teaching, Sagittarians can learn just a little about something and turn right around and begin to teach it. Sometimes, that's due to their ability to extrapolate an overall understanding of a subject from learning just a little piece of it. Other times, it comes from Sagittarians' ability to come off as knowledgeable and poignant, even when others in the room might actually know more than they do. Indeed, a little information can go a long way with Sagittarians.

Because Sagittarians are so eager to share their philosophy, they might go from teaching to *preaching.* For them, it's a good idea to check to make sure their audience wants to hear all they've got to say. I asked my Sagittarian hair stylist, a really bright and interesting gal, what advice she'd give her fellow Sagittarians. She said, "I'd tell them to look into the eyes of the people they're talking to. If they glaze over, it means you've started to preach, and they've tuned you out." Then she laughed her big Sagittarian laugh, as if to say, "I'm speaking from experience."

If Sagittarians go overboard on the teacher side of their Philosopher archetype, they start thinking that they have got things all figured out and become know-it-alls. Sagittarians can become intolerant of other people's wisdom, and, instead, appoint themselves the wise one—even the guru—who is called to enlighten everyone around them. Sometimes, it is true that Sagittarians are the most thoughtful or experienced ones in the room, and others can benefit from their knowledge. But, other times, Sagittarians can underestimate the wisdom of those around them, dismissing them because they think they're not as evolved as they are.

This is a Sagittarian pitfall that shuts them off from being open to learning new things, and prevents them from benefiting from the value others offer. The Universe teaches Sagittarians through those who cross their paths. If Sagittarians think people in their world can't teach them anything, they might be missing the next piece of their enlightenment puzzle. If Sagittarians realize they are doing this, they would do well to flip back into the seeker mode. Sagittarians can do this by using their curiosity to see what others can teach them, or at least to go into neutral with an acceptance of others' paths. That will keep Sagittarians clear, as well as charged up and interested in life, just as they should be.

As Sagittarians exercise the teacher/seeker aspect of their inner Philosopher, they are likely to explore countless areas of interest during this lifetime. In doing so, they will be sure to develop a life philosophy that is right for them. There is one philosophy, however, that lies at the core of Sagittarian's essence: They should be free to do what they want when they want, and they should also be free to come up with their own ideas about life. Sagittarians will strive to live from this basic premise in everything they do.

Religion and spirituality are natural avenues of interest for the Sagittarian Philosopher. Sagittarians are curious about discovering the truths these paths offer, and enjoy finding out what their fellow thinkers have discovered about the meaning of life. Some Sagittarians find their answers in one religion, then set out to live its teachings to the fullest extent. Other Sagittarians pick and choose truths from various religions or philosophies, then combine them into their own unique philosophy of life. This search for truth is a lifelong process for Sagittarians. No matter how much insight they gain, they are always inspired to learn more.

Remember: Although Sagittarians genuinely seek the ultimate truth, their joy actually comes from the *process* of discovering it. It is as if they are among the Knights of the Round Table searching for the Holy Grail. Do they want to find it? Sure. But the search is where the joy lies.

Sagittarians might also love exploring the moral and ethical principles of life. They enjoy evaluating what's good or redeeming from what's bad or unrighteous. This doesn't come from a need to control others, or set strict rules that others should live by. (The thought that one person should dictate another's behavior turns them off.) Rather, it comes from

Sagittarians' natural idealism about the ways in which humankind (and they) can lift themselves up to something great or Divine. It fascinates Sagittarians to think things over in order to assess the best answer to life's moral and ethical questions. It is one of their ways of connecting with their Spirit and accessing God. Because of these interests, Sagittarians can find fulfillment and success in the career of law (they love arguing the ethical merits of what's right), teaching (higher education is an especially great forum for Sagittarians' expansive thinking), as well as any profession that calls for them to express their ideas. Many Sagittarians are found in the writing and publishing field. However, they might decide to go straight for the essence of their Sagittarian interests and choose a career in theology, the ministry or philosophy itself.

Sagittarians' Philosopher enjoys a good debate among fellow knowledgeable people. They like to exercise their persuasive skills, and they enjoy batting around ideas and viewpoints. If things get too settled, Sagittarians will stir up a controversy by egging someone on, trying to get a rise out of them. Of course, they love to score points and win by "being right." But even in the (rare) event they discover they are not right, their good-hearted nature feels better for the experience. Never a grudge held.

The interesting thing about their Philosopher archetype is that Sagittarians don't feel the need to stick to one philosophy or ideal. They adopt a philosophy that works for them at any given time. For example, during certain periods of Sagittarians' lives, they may be quite liberal in their beliefs and use certain reasons to defend their view. Then they might go through a conservative stage and wholeheartedly argue the exact same reasons to support their opposite view. The truth, for Sagittarians, is the truth of the moment.

Because of this, Sagittarians might fear they would be considered hypocrites. Or others, who prefer them to be more consistent, may consider Sagittarians to be hypocritical. It's important to understand that inconsistency based on flexibility and open-mindedness does not make anyone a hypocrite. Sagittarians' Mutability allows them to change their perspective and align themselves with a philosophy or truth that seems correct for whatever situation they are dealing with. That can make Sagittarians seem inconsistent outwardly, but in their own experience, they are being very consistent because they are being true to themselves.

There are other times when Sagittarians' expansive mind might intuit the truth of lofty possibilities and knowingly profess them. Yet their behaviors might fall short of demonstrating them. That's because part of Sagittarius has great wisdom, but other parts aren't as developed or as capable (yet) of living up to the higher principles they understand to be right. Again, that doesn't mean Sagittarians are hypocrites, just that they are *still learning* how to embody the ideals they aspire to.

The Sagittarians who understand and accept this about themselves are the happiest, because they allow themselves to laugh about the errors they make, knowing it doesn't make them less worthy or less Divine. These Sagittarians give themselves a great breadth of behaviors and usually extend the same tolerance to others.

The Sagittarians who try to behave as piously as they idealize they should are much harder on themselves, and many times more rigid about the lives they lead. They believe that, if they aspire to something, they should be able to demonstrate it—and they judge themselves when they can't. Because they are trying so desperately to live up to an ideal of perfection, they might demand that others do the same, which the others might not care to do. This leads to unnecessary disappointment in Self or others. That's a shame, because the Sagittarian nature is at its best when aspiring for the good of all. **It is important for every Sagittarian to remember it's the *inspiration toward* their ideals, not the perfection of them, that creates their joy.**

Actually, Sagittarians are so inspired and optimistic about life, it's hard for them to believe or accept when they—or others—are not. If they come across anyone who is hurt, depressed or simply just blasé about life—or even when they themselves are—they might feel compelled to lift that person out of the funk, urging a positive approach to matters.

Sometimes, Sagittarians' inner wisdom knows just what to say to spark new life in someone who has lost his or her way. Other times, Sagittarians' desire to lift others might come across as their wanting others to "just get over" their feelings. And Sagittarians actually might be wanting that.

In keeping their vision of the grand scheme of things, Sagittarians can sometimes overlook the importance of experiences of the present moment. For example, I have one client whose Sagittarian son told her, "Accidents are part of life; you just have to get over it!" when she expressed her pain over her husband's car accident. He's right: In the big picture, we're all likely to take some falls. It is part of life. But her grief is as vital to her experience as other, happier feelings. It would have been more effective for her son to extend his understanding toward her, knowing grief is as valid an expression as any other, then gently express his point of view. But Sagittarians are not noted for subtlety.

Being sensitive to feelings—theirs and those of others—is one of Sagittarians' greatest challenges. Their positive philosophy might consider feelings of hurt, anger, sadness, rejection, and especially hopelessness as unnecessary negativities, even self-indulgent or annoying. So they might try to rush themselves and others out of those kinds of feelings and into ones that are more expansive and happy, before they are truly resolved. This denies the importance of the learning that comes from these feelings and sells short the transformation they offer.

It helps to remember that many signs, including Sagittarius, occasionally need to plunge into darkness and perhaps stay there for a while, in order to ultimately tap into their Light. By understanding that the process of dealing with one's own negativity might be an avenue toward redemption, Sagittarians' Philosopher can better recognize the value and the Light that's offered during difficult times. In doing so, not only will they be more tolerant and accepting of other people's ways of dealing with life, but also of their own dark hours. That prepares Sagittarians to be truly wise, supportive and helpful in the way that others need them to be.

Sharon, who's a Sagittarius with a successful counseling practice, once told me she sometimes wants to scream when her clients come in week after week with the same dark feelings or issues. Fortunately, she understands that that's her Sagittarian nature. Sharon shifts out of her impatience with what she thinks is her patients' wallowing by moving into her curiosity about what she calls "those souls' (apparently very) challenging journeys." When she remembers they might be receiving meaning from their experience, she taps back into her wisdom, not to mention her patience.

By keeping their focus on the importance of the grand scheme of things, Sagittarians keep from worrying about much of the "small stuff" of life. They dismiss petty hurts and slights, not letting them get in the way of enjoying life. Sagittarians will overlook many things that members of other signs would really object to, because they figure it's not worth the bother or the bad feelings. Really, Sagittarians tolerate a lot from others and expect that tolerance in return—even though some of the other signs are not as thick-skinned or carefree as Sag. Even so, "Live and let live" is another Sagittarian credo.

The Adventurer

Sagittarians embrace the archetype of the Adventurer because they love—indeed, need—the excitement of exploring unknown territory of some sort. Sagittarians thrive on navigating new waters, and it thrills them completely to do something, or be somewhere, no one has ever gone before. Sagittarians' Adventurer seeks experiences that challenge their wits, as well as their physical skills. They want to test and develop what they are made of. Stable, predictable situations offer no attraction to them and can actually be stifling. Instead, Sagittarians prefer experiences that involve a gamble, a promise of new experience, even an element of danger. It's then that they feel fully alive, using everything they have to overcome a worthy challenge.

A good adventure is a spiritual experience for Sagittarians: They tap into a magnificence within themselves that goes beyond their ordinary faculties, into something quite expansive and universally connected. In many ways, Sagittarians try to make all of life one long adventure.

The "great outdoors" is the Sagittarian Adventurer's true home. When they step into the expansive vistas of Nature, their awareness itself expands, and they can better access their Spirit. Their perspective on life grows even grander, and they realize all is well and as it should be. Because of Nature's constantly changing scenery, there's always something new for Sagittarian Adventurers to experience and conquer when outdoors. That both excites and refreshes them.

So it's likely Sagittarians will be drawn to activities that involve being outside, be it through high-energy sports or frequent strolls along a nature trail. Even if Sagittarians are strictly city people, they need the outside to refresh themselves and keep their perspective about things.

Sagittarians are also likely to be physically adventurous. Depending on other aspects and elements in their chart, this can mean anything from being fast drivers to indulging in extreme skiing on some remote avalanche-prone mountain. Sagittarians enjoy doing daring things and taking risks. They love the feeling of adrenaline running through their veins, the thrill of doing something that takes loads of concentration and skill. Sagittarians will continually challenge themselves to see what else they are capable of. They enjoy depending on their faith in themselves. Being on the edge makes Sagittarians live in the moment, and that's an awesome feeling for them. Indeed, it can connect them with the Divine.

Travel is another type of adventure Sagittarians are likely to hunger for. They consider themselves "citizens of the world," and do their best to get to as many spots in the world as they can. At a moment's notice, Sagittarians' bags are packed, and they are ready to go. No other sign racks up as many frequent-flyer miles as they (Gemini is a close second), or devotes as much of their time or financial resources to travel. It's a high priority for Sagittarians—they need to "get out of Dodge" regularly to refresh and renew their Spirit.

Although all kinds of travel interests Sagittarians, they are most attracted to exotic locations and experiences that differ radically from what they are used to. Sagittarians want to learn something from the places and the people they encounter, and to be transformed in a way that makes them better human beings. So, instead of seeking those all-the-comforts-of-home accommodations (as Cancer and Taurus does), Sagittarians are more likely to want to "go native," because they want to fully immerse themselves in the experiences that other lands and cultures have to offer.

So when Sagittarians are in Rome, they do as the Romans do, so to speak. They'll quickly adopt the lifestyle of the city or culture they are visiting and blend right in. In no time, Sagittarians are "regulars" down at the local hangout, schmoozing for hours with the natives as if they lived there their whole lives. Sagittarians are rarely strangers in strange lands.

Sagittarians' gift of gab helps them communicate, regardless of whether or not they know the language. But, usually, they will know the language, or some derivative of it. Sagittarians' worldliness gives them a penchant for foreign languages, enabling them to pick them up easily, if not become fluent in them. Actually, Sagittarians could make a satisfying career of either speaking a foreign language or dealing in the goods of foreign lands.

If Sagittarians' budget or lifestyle doesn't allow for the physical travel they desire, they can always travel in their minds. Along with studying foreign languages, Sagittarians might study foreign culture, art and religions—all without leaving home. The root of Sagittarians' need to travel is to get a fresh perspective on life, and expand from seeing things they are not accustomed to. If Sagittarians can't get on a jet to do that, they can challenge themselves to do it in other ways. There might be a good reason their destiny keeps them from going elsewhere. Sagittarians' consciousness might benefit more by exploring their local surroundings with the same curious openness and fascination they would employ in exploring an exotic country.

Sports can be adventurous for Sagittarians because they not only challenge them to be the best they can be, they are also fun and involve the camaraderie that Sagittarians enjoy as well. When playing a sport, Sagittarians' Fire energy intends to win, and they are fearless competitors. But the minute the game is over, Sagittarians are the first to extend their hands, win or lose, and express appreciation for their opponent. All of life is a game to Sagittarians, and sports are no different. Sagittarians make it their business to be good sports, because it's all part of life's grand adventure.

Sagittarians are also intellectually adventurous. Their mind seeks to grapple with ideas and thoughts that expand their awareness. They love to make their mind reach to grasp something great. Sagittarians enjoy considering new territories of ideas, perhaps realizing something no other as yet has. They seek out subjects and people that can challenge them, and point them into directions that hold wonder and mystery. Most Sagittarians have stepped away from, even if only for a short while, the accepted views, beliefs or religion of their family and culture, in order to see if a greater truth existed.

Perhaps Sagittarians' most rewarding adventure of all is staking new claims in their Inner Territory. They can do this by pursuing spiritual paths that open up the vistas of their consciousness. Whereas some signs don't want their thoughts expanded or their reality to be challenged, Sagittarians crave it. They instinctively sense there are places they could go in consciousness that are radically different from what this world offers. Sagittarians will explore meditations, ancient rituals or spiritual teachings that can open doors to the vaster mysteries of life.

Because adventure is so important to Sagittarians, they are greatly challenged during those times when their lives seem void of adventure, and, instead, too familiar and boring. Sagittarians can begin lusting after another life—the one that they think they "should" be living, feeling discontent with the one they have created. That might be Sagittarians' signal they have gotten stuck, and need to let go of some of their attachments so they can move on. But, most times, Sagittarians' lives are just as they should be, and need to be. Their discontent simply signals that they need an attitude shift. They can ask themselves if they have been holding themselves away—or perhaps above—what and who their lives involve, so they are not fully present. If so, school is in session for Sagittarius.

One of the greatest lessons of Sagittarius is discovering that their truest adventure comes from being completely present with what is. After all, it is the experience of being fully present that makes adventure so satisfying for them. When life seems too ordinary, it's probably because they are not fully participating, and that makes them lose touch with their essence. **Sagittarians can expand inwardly by bringing the consciousness of adventure to whatever they are doing, and bringing everything they are into their current experience. In short, they expand by becoming more involved with what's *now*.**

In doing so, Sagittarians can tap back into the magnificent Spirit of who they are, no matter what's going on around them. By Sagittarians' intending to bring their Spirit to what they do each moment, they might tap into such a fantastic place within themselves, their outer adventures pale in comparison.

The Free Spirit

Sagittarians personify the archetype of the Free Spirit because, more than any other sign of the zodiac, they are one. (Aquarians are also Free Spirits, but, sometimes, their commitments to their ideas hold them back.) Sagittarians have the innate expectation—actually, the feeling of entitlement—that they should be free to do whatever they want, whenever they want. Sagittarians assume that God wants them to explore whatever interests them, or they wouldn't have those interests to begin with. Sagittarians figure as long as they are not hurting anyone (and they rarely intend to), they are free to go and do whatever they are called to.

This Free Spirit archetype makes Sagittarians incredibly spontaneous and willing to try anything new and adventurous. It keeps them young at heart and ensures they will live exciting lives. Sagittarians want, even demand, to keep their options open in life, so they can be off to do what they please, when they please. If they want to go to Tibet, there should be no reason not to. If they want to quit their job and study ceramics, Sagittarians figure they should be able to do that as well.

Sagittarians give themselves complete inner permission to live the life that calls them. Where some signs try to measure up to other people's expectations or needs, Sagittarians want to live a life that is directed by them.

Therefore Sagittarians consider rules—even laws—as mere guidelines or suggestions. They don't think they necessarily apply to them, unless they see value in them for themselves. So, whereas Sagittarians will accept that others need to drive the speed limit, they feel free to travel at the speed they decide is best for them. (They also believe they are able to handle fast driving better than anyone else.) Some think Sagittarians are incorrigible. Sagittarians just figure they are expressing their freedom to be themselves.

So it works best if Sagittarians create a lifestyle that gives them the freedom to be mobile in both thought and action. They might even do this by resisting or leaving situations that burden them with the responsibility of commitments and timetables, even if they offer worldly success. Having freedom to roam is more important than anything else to Sagittarians.

In truth, the high form of being a Free Spirit is being free from needing conditions to be a certain way in order to feel happy or satisfied. So no matter what is going on around them, Sagittarians are learning to remain free inside themselves by being in touch with their essence or Divinity. Sagittarians remain joyous by accepting life, seeing the Good in it, no matter what its circumstances. That's what they are really after. All the outer exploring Sagittarians will do is what they do while they're learning inner freedom.

If Sagittarians are not in touch with their Inner Freedom, they can easily feel trapped during those inevitable times in life when they can't do exactly as they like. When Sagittarians' commitments dictate they do certain things at certain times, they can project that their style is being cramped, or that they are being kept from a higher destiny they are really supposed to follow. Sometimes, that's true—Sagittarians may need to sacrifice it all to pursue their dream. But, usually, Sagittarians' feelings of being trapped are rooted in an error in their perspective. They might be looking to outer freedom as a condition to feel free, instead of remembering that freedom is a state of consciousness.

During those times when Sagittarians feel trapped, they can challenge themselves to find the liberation within themselves. They can align with their inner vastness and freedom to choose a positive attitude as they deal with their seemingly limited situation. That will teach Sagittarians more about the true essence of freedom: It is always available inside themselves.

My Sagittarian client, Reverend Donald, confided to me that, although he loved the inspirational aspects of his ministry, he was feeling quite confined by the politics and personality clashes that came with being the head of a church. He was seriously considering leaving his ministry to become a fly-fishing instructor when I posed to him the Sagittarian challenge: Could he expand himself inwardly, even as it seemed his church's demands were contracting and confining him? Two years later, I received a beautiful letter from him, in which he expressed how much he had learned from expanding inwardly. He realized that no matter where he was, there was always going to be some sort of challenge, so he resolved that he could always enjoy himself by keeping free and open inside himself. His ministry, by the way, was flourishing.

Sagittarians' Free Spirit archetype also displays itself through their need to freely express their thoughts or ideals. They want to be able to speak their truth. Sagittarians are suspicious of, and suffocated by, situations or groups that demand everyone think alike. Even if they agree with them, Sagittarians still reserve the right to change their minds, or at least entertain other ideas. And their outspoken nature demands freedom of expression and the right to be heard, even if it bugs other people.

If Sagittarians do find themselves in a stuffy situation, their Free Spirits feel elected to "wake things up," and do or say something that gets a rise or creates a controversy. That's okay with Sagittarians. Their Free Spirit wants to spark the freedom in others, even if it has to start a fight to do so.

Hope is an integral aspect of Sagittarians' Free Spirit. They need to feel there is a great future ahead, something to look forward to. Depending on their charts, this great future can mean fun after dinner or enlightenment by the end of their life. (For most Sags it's probably both.) When Sagittarians have hope, they can endure even the toughest situations because they remain focused on how good it's going to be later. Even if Sagittarians are temporarily defeated by something, their hope redeems their optimistic disposition, and makes them stand up and try again.

During those rare times when Sagittarians don't have hope, school is in session. They are learning the value of reaching deeper than hope—which looks to the future—to letting themselves become completely immersed in the *now,* even if it's a painful now.

Hope can be a great motivator for Sagittarians, but it can also be an incredible addiction. They can get so focused on what *might* happen that they forget to be fully present with what *is happening.* So if Sagittarians use times of no hope as opportunities to learn to be more attuned to the present moment, something quite remarkable and worthwhile might happen: They might realize the "now" just ain't that bad.

Moreover, the power of the present can awaken Sagittarians to what sages have been saying for centuries: Now is all there is. When Sagittarians grasp that, they make the most of it. In doing that, they truly become free.

It's likely the Free Spirit in Sagittarians loves the Free Spirit in animals. Sagittarians share an affinity with members of the animal kingdom: Something in them (perhaps their inner centaur) connects deeply with them, and they make Sagittarians feel alive. Animals open Sagittarians' hearts, because Sagittarians sense the purity of their nature, and that helps Sagittarians align with the purity of their own. Although Sagittarians tend to be keen on all animals, they usually feel a special affinity toward horses. Maybe because of their grandness or their unique kind of intelligence, Sagittarians can see something within horses that soothes and inspires them. Sagittarians also favor dogs, which offer camaraderie by being Sag's buddy.

The Sagittarius Gifts: Loving Life and Telling the World

One of Sagittarians' greatest gifts is their ability to **Communicate.** They love to talk, express, expound. And they do, more than any other sign (except for Gemini, who can out-talk even them). Sagittarius' communication gifts differ from all other signs' in that they intend to inspire or teach—or at least entertain—with whatever they say and do. Sagittarians want their conversations and actions to have meaning, or to leave others with something better than they had before being with them.

Actually, Sagittarians can be so enthusiastic, so inspired by whatever they are talking about, they can become downright evangelistic. The more they talk about something, the more excited about it they get. This prepares Sagittarians beautifully for professions in which they have to convince people of things, because they do it every day, anyway.

This often translates into the Sagittarian gift of **Salesmanship.** They have the ability to get so excited about their point of view, and so eloquent in delineating why they are right, others can't help but at least consider—if not swallow, hook, line and sinker—whatever Sagittarians are promoting. Selling is fun for Sagittarians. They love the energy of hope and possibility that comes from looking at something from the best possible angle. So they can sell themselves, their ideas or a product with equal enthusiasm.

Sagittarians are also exciting **Storytellers.** Their love of entertaining, combined with their urge to make a major point, motivates them to describe life in a way that fascinates, as well as teaches. Sagittarians can make taking the dog in for a haircut sound like the most profound or funny experience in the world. Part of that comes from Sagittarians' mastery of the art of embellishment. They don't mind a little exaggeration here, a larger-than-life size story there, to add spice and interest to what they are saying. Exaggeration makes ordinary things extraordinary, and that's what Sagittarians are after. (Some signs, especially Earth Signs, are quite literal and want the raw facts, without the embellishment or exaggeration. To Sagittarius, this equals boring.)

Joie de Vivre (literally, joy of living) is probably Sagittarius' greatest gift. They are happy to be alive. Sagittarians have a sunny, good-natured disposition that intends to enjoy life to the max. Their optimism seeks what's good about the people they are with and the situations they find themselves in, even if it takes a little effort to do so. Because of that, Sagittarians whistle along happily, while others moan and complain about their lot in life. Sagittarians figure, "Why be glum? There's so much to be happy about!" and make it their business to wring the most out of what they are given.

And Sagittarians like being themselves. Even though they have issues and challenges (as we all do), all things considered, they are grateful to be who they are. Sagittarians notice that they have got a lot going for themselves: They recognize their intelligence, they appreciate their broad philosophy and they respect that they try to make decisions for the Highest Good of all. Sagittarians' appreciation of who they are supports their self-esteem and self-respect, and that spills over into an appreciation for others.

This joie de vivre gives Sagittarians a "Why worry?" attitude. Because they insist on staying positive, they can lift their focus off what isn't working and keep it on what is—or what might be. Sagittarians figure life is for living, so why waste time focusing on problems when there are good things to think about? This can make them seem carefree, and much of the time they are. When Sagittarians do have concerns, they try to get "bigger" than them. They want to keep their attitude high and expansive.

Usually, this works great for Sagittarians. But if it gets to the point where they are denying what's bothering them, rather than keeping a positive attitude, Sagittarians might be setting themselves up for a fall. And they might be acting irresponsibly. Sometimes, life insists Sagittarians deal with things that are unpleasant. If they try to ignore those things, they aren't really being positive, just out of touch.

It works well if Sagittarians apply their positive attitude toward their concerns and seek to find what they can learn from them. Then Sagittarians can participate fully in life's challenges, while keeping worry at bay.

Sagittarians also have great **Senses of Humor.** Part of their joie de vivre comes from seeing the humor in themselves and in the world around them. Sagittarians never, ever want to take things so seriously that they can't have a good laugh at whatever's happening. Sagittarians love jokes. They're sure to share the ones they know, and, if someone else offers one, they'll stop everything to enjoy it. And the Sagittarian laugh is contagious. It's a generous belly laugh that reflects all the joy within them. Others can't help but join in.

Playtime is a big factor in Sagittarians' joie de vivre. They might work hard, but Sagittarians' play is what's important. Whereas some signs put off fun until everything else is handled, Sagittarians make it a priority. Play refreshes Sagittarians, expands them and connects them with their Spirit. So, Sagittarians understand play shouldn't be denied, and they love being childlike and silly, letting it all hang out. Sometimes, playtime involves some pretty sophisticated recreation, complete with equipment, toys, etc. But, other times, it's just an impromptu laughing spell, where Sagittarians realize how funny everything is and help others do the same.

Sagittarians are also gifted with **Insight.** They have the kind of consciousness that has "realizations" about things, wherein they instantaneously become aware of truths. This is an almost breathtaking occurrence, because knowledge comes over Sagittarians so fast, and their perceptions shift so rapidly, they are almost bowled over by the speed of it. Sagittarians can be illuminated and forever changed within seconds.

This kind of intuitive insight doesn't come from piercing analysis (like Scorpio) or methodically evaluating the facts (like Virgo and Libra); but, rather, it comes from a ready openness to the truth, which seems to come to Sagittarians all at once. In an instant, they get the entire picture in all its fullness. That's a thrill for Sagittarians. It doesn't happen all the time, but, when it does, they trust it.

Of course, there are other times when Sagittarians build up to their insights by learning all they can about a subject. But instead of just accumulating facts, Sagittarians' minds search for their implications, their overall meaning, looking to find an angle that has never been thought of before. Instead of getting caught in the details, Sagittarians keep their perceptions wide. That enables them to recognize correlations and "if/thens" that others have missed.

Sagittarians can be insightful about their loved ones, their careers and world events, as well as the overriding meaning of existence.

Sometimes, they amaze even themselves with what they know and understand.

The only drawback to this is that what can seem to be an insight to Sagittarius might just be them jumping to conclusions. Sagittarians are used to fast knowing, and trust it and like it when it happens. But, sometimes, they need to take time and gather the facts in order to have true knowledge. But because Sagittarians' minds are so quick, they could become restless with this process and resist looking fully into matters. They might become mentally impatient and start assuming things, not wanting to bother with getting the facts. Then they'll take a little information and jump to a conclusion that seems right, but, in truth, they've missed a critical piece of information. Or when others try to explain something to Sagittarians, they might say, "Yeah! I've got it," when actually their minds are kind of blank.

This can obviously lead Sagittarians astray, because they can act on ideas they think are right before they've thought them through. Others can find this frustrating because Sagittarians can be so sure they are right about something, even when they are presented with facts to the contrary.

So it is important that Sagittarians learn to differentiate between times when their insights are clear versus times when they are making assumptions. Some Sagittarians say they can tell the difference by the way they feel: If they are pushing, defending or impatient at all, chances are they're being mentally impatient. When there is an "Oh, yeah," like a lightbulb going off in their heads, they're having a true insight.

The Sagittarius Fears: Get Me Out of This Box!

Sagittarians **fear anything that might confine or trap them, or in any way limit their freedom or choices.** Because of Sagittarians' need to be free to explore, they can feel hemmed in at even the slightest hint of not being able to move.

This fear of confinement can be quite literal—they can feel extremely uncomfortable in small or stuffy places, and need to break out, move around and get some air.

Sagittarians can also fear the confinement that comes from being in boring—or rigid—situations. Because they thrive on excitement and adventure, Sagittarians can feel trapped or suffocated when they have to do the same familiar thing day in and day out, or if they have little room to express their own style, and continually have to do things a certain, prescribed way. Those kinds of circumstances can make Sagittarians feel like running, screaming, for the hills. And, many times, they do!

So it's best when Sagittarians can create lives where they have a lot of freedom to do what they want. But life isn't always like that, is it? There are bound to be cycles where life offers them just ordinary, humdrum circumstances. If Sagittarians find they are dealing with a confining situation that they can't get out of, they can find inner excitement by looking to their attitude, instead of to their circumstances, to expand them. If Sagittarians could manage to find something interesting or adventurous in how they go about their ordinary situations, they might discover a whole new, meaningful layer to themselves, as well as their circumstances.

Sagittarians can also **fear being confined in situations that are stifling intellectually**—where there's nothing to learn, or where they are stuck around others whose thinking seems petty or shallow. They can fear that they are wasting their time—not growing—because they are not stimulated. If Sagittarians can't leave that situation, they can try leaving their judgments of it. They can challenge themselves to learn something—anything—from what and who is around them. They might receive the greatest illuminations from the most ordinary folks.

But, usually, Sagittarians' fear of confinement is rooted in a **fear of loss of freedom**: They don't want anyone or anything to limit their choices or their ability to act on them. Sagittarians are most at peace when they know they have options, when they know they can bug out if something—or someone—starts to get stale or ordinary, or no longer holds their interest.

But this can lead to an overdependence on outer freedom in order to feel free inside, and that's missing the point of being Sagittarius. In truth, Sagittarians are learning to be vastly free inside, no matter what they are—or are not—doing. That is illumination. That is liberation.

Although Sagittarians might consider keeping their options open to be mandatory to their well-being, others might interpret this as their bolting, or escaping when things get too real or too heavy. And Sagittarians might be doing so. They tell themselves it's because the situation is getting too confining, and they need to get some space. But what might be happening is that they are being challenged to grow in a way that they don't want—or don't feel in control of—and resist by leaving. Sometimes, life wants to teach Sagittarians something very valuable through uncomfortable situations, and it really pays off if they can hang in there long enough to be transformed by what's going on—even if it seems really ordinary.

This fear of confinement can make commitment—to people and/or situations—tough for Sagittarians. On the one hand, they recognize the need to commit themselves, so they can reach more meaningful levels of their relationships, career, etc. But on the other hand, Sagittarians fear those very commitments might clip their wings, or even keep them from their higher destiny. Sagittarians always need a way out. Commitments can limit, if not completely deny, that.

Sagittarians can try to avoid commitments altogether and live life completely without them. For some Sagittarians, this is a most satisfying lifestyle because, in truth, they are committed to their freedom. That way, they can travel when they want to, date who they want to, and quit their jobs at a moment's notice to sail around the world.

Other Sagittarians try committing halfway. They allow themselves to be involved until something else, perhaps better, shows up. This can work okay, but, eventually, there's bound to be someone or something that protests and puts pressure on them to either commit fully or leave.

Sagittarians might try facing their fear of confinement and commit themselves wholly. In order to do this, they will have to see great meaning and valor in the act of commitment itself—as well as in what or to whom they are committing. Because commitment does limit Sagittarians' choices, they need to frame it so that there's value in making the one choice they have decided upon, and exploring it to its fullest. That way, Sagittarians can seek the wonder and adventure in the committed situation that they otherwise would be seeking elsewhere. Because commitment gives Sagittarians an ability to go to greater depths and experience greater insight, they can trust that the sacrifices they need to make to honor their commitments will be worth the payoff of the expansive understandings they are gaining through them.

It helps if Sagittarians see the heroism involved in making commitments. When Sagittarians recognize that commitments challenge them to greatness because they have to say "no" to some things, they can start to understand the process—and value—of inner freedom, rather than merely remaining addicted to outer freedom.

Sagittarius in Relationships: "Love Is S-o-o-o . . . Philosophical!"

Sagittarians want relationships that keep them on their toes, and challenge them to keep learning, seeking and growing. They aren't looking for someone they can curl up and watch TV with: They want someone who will offer them excitement, intellectual and physical stimulation, and, importantly, someone who gives them plenty of room to roam. Sagittarians enjoy a trusted "sidekick," a buddy who they can speak freely and openly with, who's ready at a moment's notice to embark on some adventure.

More than anything, Sagittarians seek someone they can respect and admire. They are bored by those who go along with the status quo or show no signs of independent thinking. They also don't respect others who kowtow or act subservient to them—they enjoy some feistiness. Sagittarians aspire to live up to high ideals and want someone who does the same.

You can bring out the best in your Sagittarius by taking them on a trip, even if it's a weekend jaunt to the next county. Remember, Sagittarians are thrill-seekers. They want everything in life, including their relationships, to be exciting. So surprise them with new places to explore, new ideas to talk about and new ways to show affection.

When Sagittarians are in love, they get completely consumed. They'll swoon, they'll profess their love, and they'll treat their beloved as the god or goddess Sagittarius sees them as. And, they love to romance like they do everything else in life: big! They're the ones who hire planes to write, "I love you" in the sky, or propose on mountaintops. They need someone who's going to go along with this. If you're the type who asks, "How much did you pay for that plane?" or often says, "I've got work to do," you might be cramping their style and blowing out their flame of passion. Here's what *not* to do: complain, find fault or insist that every negative feeling has to be worked through. Sagittarians just don't see the need for all of that, and consider it negative and completely unappealing. They also detest a liar. So if a Sag catches you in even a little white one, you'll fall from grace in their eyes. They'll never look at you the same, somehow. So, be honest. It's more compelling, and Sagittarius can surely handle it.

If you're trying to catch the eye of a female Sagittarius, let her see that you are living up to some meaningful inspirations. She wants to know that you're trying to make something outstanding of your life. Talk to her about your philosophy: what you think is going on, what you consider your purpose to be, what you've learned about life, what you still want to learn. And be sure to ask her about her philosophy: What does she think? Why does she think that?

A Sagittarian woman is attracted to a partner who is confident in himself, because she is confident in herself. She wants an equal with whom she can explore life's adventures. And she needs a tremendous amount of freedom. Any signs of someone wanting to control, dominate or get her to "settle down," and she'll be out of there. Instead, give her lots of room to move, respect her ideas and she'll be your (very sexy) buddy.

In fact, Sagittarian women have a tomboy quality that allows them to act like one of the guys, yet still remain quite feminine. Men don't have to walk on eggshells around their Sagittarian female friends, worrying that they might hurt their feelings or offend their sensitivities. Sagittarian women are tough and funny, and want a man to be himself; they can take care of themselves.

If you're trying to catch the eye of a male Sagittarius, wear a skirt (he's attracted to legs) and let your sex appeal shine. (But be natural. He doesn't like too much primping and fuss.) Most important, let him see you know who you are. A Sagittarian man is very attracted to beauty (okay, he has a roving eye), but that's not what wins his heart. (Although he will go for a good flirt—anytime anywhere—it's sport to him; makes him feel good and makes her feel good. End of story.) He's after someone he can respect and put on a pedestal. He wants a partner who matches his aspiration to become a thoughtful, interesting, principled person of consequence. So, find ways to demonstrate your moral, ethical or spiritual principles, so he can see you're the real thing.

And if you like the outdoors, or sports, let him know. He loves nothing more than a partner he can take on an adventure without having to worry about whether or not she's having a good time or can handle the terrain.

The Last Word on Sagittarius

If there is one word that describes and defines Sagittarius, it is *expansive.* The real secret, though, is that the greatest expansion is inward.

Chapter 10

Capricorn

(December 22/23–January 20)

Capricorn is the quality in you that is ambitious and responsible, seeks to build something of importance, and enjoys setting and accomplishing major goals. It's also the part of you that's learning to discover the essence of Inner Authority and Self-Mastery.

Look up at the mountain. Way up. See that tiny speck moving at the very top? That's a Capricorn just having fun. For Capricorns, having fun can be working hard to reach the top—whether it's the peak of the mountain or the pinnacle of success in anything they undertake.

That's because Capricorns are by far one of the most ambitious and capable signs of the zodiac. They continually challenge themselves to develop into someone significant and to build something substantial out of their lives. In fact, Capricorns are goal-seekers (and goal-reachers) at heart. They have clear intentions about what they wish to achieve and high standards for how they go about achieving it. Fortunately for the rest of us, much of what Capricorns wish to achieve involves making a difference in this world.

Capricorns are just loaded with skills that help them accomplish their considerable goals: They possess keen foresight that recognizes opportunities, self-discipline that allows them to stay focused and adhere to their well-laid plans, and strategic savvy that knows the best and most efficient ways to get things done. The truth about Capricorns is there is very little they can't accomplish because they enjoy accomplishing.

The Capricorn Mission: Learning Freedom Through Self-Discipline

All of us are learning what Capricorns are born to discover: By developing the disciplines of Inner Authority and Self-Mastery, we become freer to express our Higher Nature.

When Capricorns honor the promptings of their Inner Authority, as opposed to looking to the world for validation, they direct their considerable gifts toward accomplishing things that have tremendous meaning and satisfaction *for them*. They discover the joy that comes from respecting and honoring their own references for what's important, and they reap the rewards that come from living in a way that is purposeful and worthwhile to their Spirit. In doing so, Capricorns not only become people they themselves deeply admire, others are inspired by them and learn from their example.

Capricorns discover the true meaning of Self-Mastery as they use their powerful intentions to take dominion over their inner universe, rather than trying to control the outer universe. In other words, Capricorns are learning that the most important control they have is in guiding their own consciousness. Instead of allowing the circumstances of the world to dictate how they act, think or feel, Capricorns are learning to choose for themselves how they act, think or feel—regardless of what is happening around them. A far cry from self-denial, Self-Mastery is self-empowerment and self-direction.

As Capricorns use their powerful intentions to release negative, defeating emotions and attitudes in exchange for uplifting ones, they set the stage for their innate wisdom and grand nature to make a positive impact on whatever they're involved in. Then Capricorns create a life of true significance—to themselves, as well as others.

The Capricorn Challenge: Seeking Their Rewards from the World

If Capricorns don't take the time to determine what is of true and lasting value to them, they can be seduced by the world's definition of importance and success. In doing so, they believe they are important only if the world thinks they are, so they try to gain validation and recognition from others. The need for recognition is Capricorns' greatest challenge and most powerful teacher.

Instead of building a life according to their inner direction, Capricorns can spend their valuable time—even a lifetime—living up to the expectations of this world in order to receive the acknowledgment they actually can only receive from within themselves. Capricorns could do all the "right things" with all the "right people" to become quite successful and respected, but end up feeling somehow disappointed by it all.

Sooner or later, most Capricorns who seek worldly success as their only means of validation discover that the rewards that come from that strategy are frequently hollow and unsatisfying. That's because they are living according to the standards and expectations of someone other than themselves.

That kind of disappointment can lead Capricorns to their higher purpose. Instead of looking to the authority of the world for direction, they turn to the authority inside—an authority we all have—and begin to ask themselves what they would value doing. They then demonstrate Self-Mastery by doing whatever it takes to make those dreams a reality. That brings the true rewards of life.

The Capricorn Key: Accepting *Self*-Authority

Self-Acknowledgment is the secret to every Capricorn's success and happiness. When they can respect and validate themselves, Capricorns are much less likely to knock themselves out trying to get recognition from others. When satisfied with their own contributions, Capricorns can use their discipline to pursue what they deem important, instead of using their discipline to withstand the grueling demands of meeting others' expectations. In that way, Capricorns live a life that is truly successful, because they live the life they love.

Surefooted as a MOUNTAIN GOAT, Climbing to the Top

The astrological symbol for Capricorn is the Mountain Goat, and in many ways Capricorns behave like one. Mountain goats are able to navigate rough terrain, stepping over rocks and thorny bushes to climb ever higher up the mountain. Capricorns must climb over the rocky, thorny obstacles of life's conditions in order to get ever higher in both their accomplishments and their consciousness. Indeed, as Capricorns keep their vision focused on the peak of the mountain, either in a worldly or a spiritual sense, their many assets will get them there.

Rock Solid as the EARTH, Taking Nothing for "Granite"

Capricorn is one of the three Earth Signs. (Taurus and Virgo are the other two.) Being an Earth Sign makes Capricorns practical and productive, and they greatly enjoy being useful. Capricorns have an appreciation for this physical world, as well as an innate knowledge about how to operate here.

The unique Capricorn expression of the Earth element is the combination of their ability and commitment to use everything within their orbit to its fullest capacity, in order to build considerable structures of success.

Capricorns are the last Earth Sign of the zodiac, which means they are learning how to apply their practical skills to contribute to a greater social order. Capricorns want to contribute something concrete that can make the world a better place. They recognize that money, prestige and success not only can be gained, but also further leveraged to become useful in even greater ways to benefit humanity.

Earth energy also gives Capricorns a relentlessness: They have the stamina, as well as the know-how, to work endlessly toward a dream, and stop at nothing until they achieve it. Although the purpose of Capricorns' lives is Inner Mastery, it's quite likely they will utilize their Earthy practicality to achieve outer mastery and become quite skilled at whatever interests them.

The Earthiness of Capricorns concerns itself with tangible reality. Capricorns take a very pragmatic approach in realizing their visions, always looking to evaluate whether or not something works. If it does, fine, Capricorns will build on it. If it doesn't, Capricorns figure why bother? and change course. To Capricorns, something is right, or it is not. If it's not wholly true, it's false. They don't tolerate fuzzy thinking or gray areas—their consciousness follows a very clear, thin line. Either they—or others—are on or off. Black or white. There's little deviation. Capricorns look for results, not idealized concepts.

The Capricorn expression of Earth also translates to a taste for the finer things in life. Capricorns appreciate the effort and craftsmanship that goes into creating well-made, well-designed objects or art. Anyone who appreciates the finest Oriental rugs understands Capricorns' eye for subtlety, complexity, texture, design and refinement. Capricorns recognize that the imperfections in an Oriental rug add to the beauty of it. That's a metaphor for their understanding of how the imperfections of humanity add to the beauty of our nature.

Beauty lifts and soothes Capricorns' sensibilities. They are especially attracted to the kind of beauty that needs to be understood and explored in order to be appreciated. And Capricorns adore quality. Because of that, they will choose to possess a few fine items over possessing many average-quality items. If they aren't treasures, Capricorns usually aren't that interested.

The CARDINAL Quality of Capricorn: Dynamically Initiating Structures of Success

Capricorn is a Cardinal Sign (Aries, Cancer and Libra are the other three), which makes them active people and dynamic initiators. Capricorns' Cardinal energy enjoys coming up with new directions and projects, and working to get them going and off the ground.

Capricorns' unique expression of the Cardinal energy is their urge to initiate structures and systems that they and others can build upon. Capricorns are the most disciplined of all the Cardinal Signs, and that allows them to envision, then purposefully work to successfully carry out, ideas and strategies that can have considerable impact.

Because Capricorn is the final Cardinal Sign, they might be particularly interested in initiating things that involve social structures, or systems that can affect groups, if not nations, of people.

Capricorns' Cardinal need for action seeks adventure in both the country and the city, because they like what each has to offer. Many Capricorns love the ruggedness of the outdoors, and enjoy the challenge and grittiness of surviving under the severest of conditions. But they also adore the elegance and sophistication of the city, and donning their best clothing to partake in all the finery and culture it offers. Indeed, Capricorns like to feel they are getting the most out of wherever they are.

Capricorn is a **Transpersonal Sign,** which means a significant part of their identity comes from their place in a greater social order. This give Capricorns a need to somehow impact a greater whole, like a group or community, in order to feel satisfied. Some Capricorns have outgoing personalities that make a social impact by getting involved with friends and organizations. Other Capricorns are quite introverted or shy, but nevertheless feel a calling to contribute to humanity. They might choose a career in which they can stay behind the scenes, yet still do work that involves or affects many others.

Whether Capricorns are outgoing or shy, they need to have a core group of trusted friends, as well as an avenue whereby they can contribute to humanity as a whole in some way.

Living Up to SATURN's High Standards

Capricorn is ruled by the planet Saturn. Saturn is associated with structure (including time), authority, accountability, mastery and perfection, and it lends Capricorns a disposition for using those things to attain greater self-knowledge.

Saturn is the planet that delivers life's greatest challenges, yet also offers the endurance and resourcefulness to overcome them. That's Capricorns in a nutshell: They are somehow greatly challenged in this lifetime and must meet those challenges by being patient, and cooperating with time's measured unfoldment of their destinies. But Capricorns also have the wherewithal to eventually succeed, by keeping their sights clear, using their innate authority and wisdom, enduring, and overcoming their obstacles with ultimate success.

Structure—of all sorts, including plans and rules—appeals to Capricorns. They understand that structure serves as a building block from which things can be constructed and achieved. Capricorns use many forms of structure as footholds to bring ideas into actual form.

Capricorns even love actual structural forms. They have an appreciation for Nature's structures (such as mountains and geological formations), as well as smart and efficient human-made structures (such as architectural wonders and well-created infrastructures). Actually, the part of the body that is "ruled" by Capricorn is its structure: the skeleton. Sometimes, that translates to Capricorns having an interest in finding ways to use their bodies' structure to maximum efficiency. It can also translate to Capricorns having sensitivity in their backs, knees and teeth, and having to focus on caring for them.

Those who have careers that involve structures—like builders, geologists, architects, city planners and chiropractors—usually have a strong Capricorn influence in their charts.

Capricorns also appreciate organizational structures. They understand that people have to work together to create a well-functioning society, so they respect the way organizations prescribe specific tasks and duties to people in order to accomplish meaningful things. Careers in any sort of organizational support can be quite satisfying to Capricorns, from middle management to CEO.

Like it or not, time is another structure Capricorns will work with. Many Capricorns have a destiny where time is a distinct factor—success, acknowledgment, even love, can seem to come later to them than they do to others. This may be true, or it can simply *feel* that way to Capricorn. Either way, Capricorns have the endurance to work through time to eventually accomplish a goal.

Saturn is the planet of wisdom and sobriety, and Capricorns have both qualities in their nature. There is something very "old and wise" about them—perhaps they are, indeed, "old souls." The irony is that the younger Capricorns are, the older they feel. This is probably due to the fact that Capricorns feel extremely responsible, starting at a very early age. So responsible, in fact, that their lives can seem "heavy" and they can transfer that feeling into their personality: Capricorns sense they have some burden to carry, so they had better act serious. Some Capricorns are emotionally stoic by nature, others think they have to become stoic to reflect their responsibility and concern.

If Capricorns take their burdensome feelings too far, they risk becoming weighted down by life. Then they become morose, approaching life like it's a tough mission—something they need to endure, rather than enjoy. You can recognize that kind of Capricorn because they tend to give long, plaintive sighs, as if to say, "I'm tired" (which they are, carrying a burden like that all the time).

If Capricorns overdevelop the sober side of Saturn, they can become pessimistic and worrisome. They can focus only on what doesn't (or won't) work, and forget to look at what does (or can) work. Many times, Capricorns don't consider themselves pessimistic, merely realistic. That's true when they use their ability to consider problem-solving a creative act. But if they get negative to the point of projecting that nothing will ever work out, pessimism has taken over.

The same thing goes for worry. Capricorns can worry about anything and everything, but, usually, they worry that they are not measuring up or not carrying their load. Capricorns will worry about others as well: that they can't take care of themselves, can't take care of the world, or can't take care of Capricorn. (This can start for Capricorns with worrying about their parents' ability to care for them.)

Capricorns' pessimism and worry are red flags that they have lost sight of their faith and trust in the perfect support of the universe. Pessimism and worry indicate that Capricorns are assuming that they are running the show (the Capricorn form of arrogance), or that they are the only ones capable of doing anything of consequence or support—which they fear they might not be up to.

In fact, the Divine One is running the show, and has things handled, just the way they should be. Capricorns might not like how things are going, and may try to use their creativity and power to alter them, but they are still included in the workings of a higher plan. Even if Capricorns do not believe in God, they still need to find something they can trust in, or else life will seem perpetually threatening and chaotic.

When Capricorns are pessimistic or worried, it helps if they try giving those concerns up (to God, if they are so inclined) and experimenting with seeing if things don't actually work out just fine. This can be a stretch for that practical Capricorn nature—they might be thinking, *Oh, come on! That's just irresponsible baloney!* But (surprise, all you Capricorns!) it will work anyway. A huge piece of the spiritual challenge for Capricorns is relinquishing their illusion of control. Life will attempt to teach that lesson to Capricorns over and over again. They may as well learn it early on and enjoy the benefits they'll get from realizing there is a magnificent order that's already taking place and that it will continue—with or without Capricorns' agreement or willing participation.

Eric, a Capricorn who's built a successful real-estate business, told me he handles times of worry or pessimism by reminding himself that life is cyclical. If and when things are in a slump, he looks at it like a temporary experience. Instead of fretting and worrying about how bad things are, he starts getting prepared for when things start to pick up. That way, Eric is ready to take advantage of the opportunities that will be offered when the cycle starts to move in a positive direction. That's one smart way of using the Capricorn self-confidence, as well as the Capricorn industriousness.

Saturn's influence can also prompt Capricorns to mistakenly believe that happiness and joy should be held at bay until they accomplish something worthy. This approach not only limits their enjoyment of life, it can actually lead to feelings of depression. By not appreciating the little wins of daily living, Capricorns can feel discouraged and worn down by the grind of everyday life. They think their existence lacks meaningful accomplishment.

It works better for Capricorns to use their powerful intentions to set out to enjoy themselves wherever they are in the scheme of things. In doing so, they not only make whatever they're doing at the moment more interesting, they also bring out their sense of humor, which makes matters more fun for everyone.

Interestingly, the older Capricorns get, the younger they seem to act. That's either because they recognize they're not as responsible (especially for others) as they thought they were, or they realize they are capable of handling their responsibilities, so they don't seem so burdensome. That helps Capricorns lighten up considerably. So by middle age, Capricorns usually become much more content, if not truly happy, and begin to demonstrate the playfulness they might have shunned in their youth. By the time Capricorns reach their senior years, they can get downright giddy!

Saturn also makes Capricorns cautious. Capricorns make it a habit to really check things out before jumping into them. Capricorns refuse to get suckered into something that doesn't have lasting value, or a strong foundation in practical reality.

This cautiousness translates to Capricorns being somewhat careful—even awkward or shy—about opening up and revealing themselves. What others see at first is definitely not all Capricorns are about. Capricorns need to be drawn out and encouraged to express themselves. And they appreciate it when others do draw them out. If others take the time to get to know them, they will not only see how thoughtful and truly caring Capricorns are, they'll also be treated to their fantastic (dry) sense of humor. Capricorns are definitely worth the time and extra effort it takes to get to know them.

Capricorns are also cautious about trusting—anyone or anything. They don't want to be duped or made a fool of, so they'll do their best to sniff out any falseness inherent in a person or situation. Because of that, Capricorns are most astute detectives and readily expose lies (which they loathe), conspiracy (which they suspect), or the insincerity of those around them (which they just plain don't like).

But, sometimes, Capricorns can take this too far, chronically suspecting something is amiss even when it's not. If Capricorns find they are getting too caught up in negative suspicions—even conspiracy theories—they can try exercising intellectual honesty and look at what might be good or right about the picture. If nothing else, that will present Capricorns with other things to consider. It could even give them a reprieve from their fears. Better yet, it might even show Capricorns that everything is, indeed, okay.

Saturn also elicits a challenge for Capricorns to achieve mastery and perfection in almost everything they tackle. It instills in them the vision of the excellence that's possible, as well as granting them the disposition to attempt to achieve that perfection. Being "kind of" good at something generally isn't enough for a Capricorn. Rather, Saturn gives them the need and the expectation to be truly proficient. Capricorns can use this as a powerful motivator: They will take whatever steps are necessary, including relentless practice, to push past their shortcomings and truly master whatever interests them. Usually, Capricorns achieve this mastery through a methodical approach. They will take each step toward the goal slowly and seriously, making sure each stage of what they do is done just right. Capricorns know that a truly strong structure is built from the quality of its constituent parts.

Inherent in this Saturnian urge for excellence is one of Capricorns' challenges: They can have such visions of perfection, and hold such high standards for mastery and accomplishment for themselves, that they can believe that they must be most excellent—indeed, perfect—at whatever they do in order for it to even count. Capricorns build on these aspirations. However, once they do achieve something, they are keenly aware of what else there is to accomplish, so they are never done.

This pressure for excellence can actually lead to dreadful feelings of inadequacy—even shame—for Capricorns. If they use their high standards as measures of who they should be, rather than standards of what to aspire to, Capricorns can judge themselves as not being good enough. If Capricorns feel inadequate, it's likely they are demanding something of themselves beyond what is really called for.

It is very important that Capricorns recognize that their need to accomplish goals and be the best is a preference they hold for themselves, a goal they can aim for, not a prerequisite for their adequacy or worthiness. It's what Capricorns develop within their character as they act to achieve their goals that counts, not the perfection of the achievement itself.

On the other side of the coin, Capricorns' ability to get close to mastery and perfection gives them a remarkable competency to accomplish what few others can, or will. Sometimes, in recognizing that, Capricorns can develop a smug sense of superiority. Instead of feeling inadequate, some Capricorns look around and realize they are far more talented and capable than the rest of "these incompetent Joes and Janes." As one Capricorn told me, "My competence astounds even me!" She confessed it's hard at times to remain humble when she realizes how much better she does things, as compared to others.

Although their smug superiority can even develop into haughty arrogance, Capricorns generally won't "trumpet" their gifts of competency and effectiveness (as the Fire Signs love to do). Rather, they'll simply broadcast a sniffing, "Oh, please," and "If you want to know how to do this right, notice how I do it!" kind of vibe. Instead of shamelessly self-promoting (as Leos might), Capricorns will patiently wait for others to (finally) recognize how perfectly skilled they have been all along.

The rub is that inferiority and superiority are cut from the same cloth, one that is used to separate oneself from others. Both points of view are false. (Of course, given the choice, I'd pick superiority over inferiority—it's closer to the truth and feels way better.) However, both are defense mechanisms that keep Capricorns from the meaningful connectedness of truly sharing with others and allowing them to know them. So, neither really serve Capricorns. What works better for Capricorns is to acknowledge what their contributions are, as well as to value the contributions of others.

Because Saturn provides Capricorns with strong ambitions, as well as challenging obstacles to achieving those ambitions, Capricorns can feel frustrated if they compare what life demands of them to what life demands from others. It can seem like others have things handed to them, or success is easier for others than it is for Capricorns. Capricorns can feel jealous of other people's lot in life, projecting that they are getting the short end of the stick, even though they are more worthy.

In some ways, Capricorns *are* more challenged than others. Part of their lesson is about overcoming obstacles in order to achieve mastery. So, obstacles are part of Capricorns' learning process. But, other times, Capricorns make things harder for themselves by having an overly critical attitude toward themselves and their accomplishments. Capricorns can expect way too much of themselves and feel devastated when they fall short of those demanding self-imposed requirements. Of course, it seems like others have an easier life; they are easier on themselves and don't flog themselves for not measuring up. In that sense, maybe life is easier for others.

The Capricorn Archetypes: Planning How to Build the Obstacles to Climb Over

As Capricorns (and those who are Capricorn-like) fulfill their destinies of discovering the meaning of Inner Authority and Self-Mastery, they'll embody the archetypes of the Climber, the Builder, the Strategist and the Father.

The Climber

Capricorns will express the archetype of the Climber because of their strong need to climb—and get to the top of—something. Some Capricorns literally love to climb, enlivened by each step upward they take, thrilled to reach the peak. There is tremendous satisfaction in surveying the world below and all the terrain they have covered. This can be a metaphor for Capricorns' lives.

Capricorns' Climber prompts them to aim high and expect the best from themselves, and their performance. It helps them to become well accomplished and to distinguish themselves in any endeavor. No matter what they devote their lives to, Capricorns' Climber will help them excel, if not end up right at the top. Although they can ascend to respectable success in any profession, many Capricorns are attracted to positions of status and power. Professions in business, medicine and politics may be good forums for them to achieve that.

Capricorns' Climber archetype is mostly driven by a need for recognition. Capricorns desperately want to be considered important. They crave being admired and respected by others, and they will work hard to deserve it. This drive for recognition can inspire Capricorns to accomplish mighty feats. They will devote tremendous energy and commitment to seeing their goals through by anticipating the honor they will receive as a result of it.

Because they desire status as well as recognition, many Capricorns set their sights on achieving something high profile or prestigious. They want the respect and admiration that comes with high positions. For example, they might work tirelessly to climb to the highest levels of a corporation or become the top in their field. Or Capricorns might attain a goal that others merely dream about, like sailing around the world or moving to a foreign country to help set up medical aid.

Sometimes, Capricorns' Climber archetype seeks recognition through attaining the material symbols of status, so they work hard to make the value of their assets and bank accounts climb. (For many Capricorns, that value climbs to astronomical numbers.) Capricorns can set out to make a lot of money, not only for what it can buy them, but also for the power and status they understand it brings. Or Capricorns will build a magnificent home that they enjoy as part of the satisfaction of their success, or marry someone who's prestigious. Capricorns might even collect rare and desirable items, things that "those in the know" would admire and respect them for attaining.

Although Capricorns adore validation and recognition from almost anyone, they're really after recognition from authority figures, or those whom they hold in high esteem. Capricorns think that when they gain the recognition of those whose accomplishments they admire, they've done the best that's possible.

Usually, the first authority figure Capricorns seek recognition from is their father. Fathers can represent the world to Capricorns, and they look to their fathers to see if they measure up. If Capricorns are lucky, they will have dads who are wise and loving, and willing to help them along. But many Capricorns' karma—or lesson—is to *not* have dads who act as the approving mentor.

This can be crushing to Capricorns' self-esteem. They might believe that if their own father doesn't think they are important or capable, who in the world will? That's when school's in session for Capricorn. Not having a supportive authority figure—be it a father, a boss or even a coach—to guide them makes Capricorns reach inside themselves for the guidance and acknowledgment they crave. It's a set-up to help Capricorns learn their lesson of establishing Inner Authority and Self-Validation, and let go of trying to get recognition from the world. After all, the world's approval isn't what they are truly after. The validation Capricorns are after is their own.

Sometimes, Capricorns' need to be validated by authority figures is a metaphor for their wanting to be recognized by God as a worthy being. Capricorns might consider God as the Ultimate Father Figure, and they want to do well in God's eyes. The saying, "This is my child with whom I'm well pleased," inspires Capricorns to be great. As long as they do those things that make them feel worthy of that statement, Capricorns will be satisfied—whether or not they get recognition from others.

This drive for recognition can bring out the best in Capricorns, but it can also be their Achilles' heel. Capricorns can desire recognition so profoundly that they can be intensely frustrated if they don't get it. They can think that all they have done—and been—is ignored or undervalued, even been a waste of time, if others don't recognize them for the effort they extended. This frustration can prompt Capricorns to try even harder, to the point of exhaustion, attempting to finally get recognized; or it can make them feel like they should just give it all up.

As part of their life's lessons, most Capricorns will go through at least a few periods when they do not receive the recognition they feel they deserve. That's because Capricorns are learning to recognize and validate the value of what they do within themselves.

I've counseled countless Capricorns who devoted great portions of their lives to building successes in areas their father or other important authority figure admired, only to realize they didn't particularly value what they'd created. They reached the top only to wonder why they wasted all that time on something that is of no consequence to them.

Capricorns generally demonstrate their Climber archetype by climbing "the ladder of success" to achieve positions of respect and accomplishment—in whatever their field of endeavor might be. Capricorns will use their considerable ambitions and talents to seek the highest position, from which they can initiate policy and manage or direct the show.

Whereas other Leader Signs might expect instant success (like Aries and Leo), Capricorns will "pay their dues" and work hard to justify their countless promotions. But Capricorns are not truly satisfied until they climb into the director's chair. That's where they truly shine.

Many Climber Capricorns consider leadership their highest form of creativity, and leadership comes quite easily to them. These Capricorns are confident in positions of responsibility and leadership because they trust themselves, and believe their judgments can bring any project to success. Very early in life, Climber Capricorns recognize they have as great leadership skills and organizational skills as anyone, and they are eager to demonstrate these abilities to others.

Capricorns' Climber places high value on authority figures and positions of authority because that's what they themselves aspire to. Capricorns are impressed with others' accomplishments and respectful of their positions, if they are competent. (Incompetence in others, especially authority figures, stirs Capricorns' wrath.)

Respected authority figures are the people Capricorns want to be with. Although they can be shy while relating to their peers, Capricorns enjoy finessing authority figures. It takes Capricorns no time to identify who in the room is important, and they will make it their business to ingratiate themselves accordingly. They will sidle up to others who hold power, schmooze them and help them get what they want—if they help Capricorns get what *they* want. Capricorns love the jockeying for power because it involves them with the people they admire most, and want to be admired by. Capricorns are eager to learn what authority figures know, as well as have doors open for them as a result of their association with them.

Capricorns enjoy having a mentor teaching them the ropes, and they are likely candidates to be selected by one because they are so sincerely dedicated and capable. Having the direction and the approval of someone they admire is a tremendous motivator for Capricorns. They will knock themselves out to gain their approval and show they are worthy of their time and attention.

Inherent in Capricorns' need to climb to high positions is one of their sign's greatest lessons. A major error in Capricorns' thinking is that climbing to an important position is a prerequisite for them to deserve love or be worthy—and that's not the case.

Capricorns are learning that they are completely lovable and worthy just because they are human beings. It's important for them to understand that as a fact. Some Capricorns realize this by finding unconditional love in their lives. When someone else loves them no matter what they do, Capricorns can realize that success or failure doesn't determine a thing about their worth. But regardless of whether or not Capricorns experience that kind of love, they are learning the importance of looking within themselves to find their inherent worthiness.

Sometimes, Capricorns might resist loving involvements until they decide they've accomplished enough to deserve them. The irony is that Capricorns can work so hard and climb so high to deserve the position they think will entitle them to love, that they might neglect existing loving relationships and the people that already truly do love them.

Jack, a high-ranking military officer, recognized this after he retired. He confessed that he spent every waking hour enmeshed in his career, setting and achieving goals in the hope that his accomplishments would make his family proud of him. In looking back over his life, he realized that he was actually cherished by them the whole time.

When Capricorns understand that they are intrinsically worthy and lovable, they will accomplish their great feats out of the fun of self-challenge, not out of a fear of inadequacy. Big difference.

Because Capricorns desire position and prestige, they might become overly invested in attaining, then defending, them—even to the detriment of their mental health. If Capricorns think their worth or the value of life is tied up in their position or status, they can become overprotective of it, for fear that in losing it they lose everything. This can even lead Capricorns to becoming suspicious of other people's intentions, thinking they just want Capricorns for what they take from them. (This projection is sometimes a manifestation of their strategy coming home to roost. They can be guilty of using others to get what they want in life, and think others do the same.) Some do, some don't; but Capricorns can have trouble differentiating because their suspicions can turn into paranoia. An example of this is Capricorn Richard Nixon, whose lists of enemies and suspicion of the press became almost legendary.

Not all Capricorns demonstrate their Climber archetype through ambitious worldly achievements. Some Capricorns climb by developing the best of their own personal qualities, like athleticism or musical talents or intellectual acumen. Other Capricorns climb by living a life of devoted service. Still other Capricorns climb by developing their spirituality. (Capricorns can be worldly and still climb spiritually, by the way.)

What's important to the Climber archetype is moving up toward something that's of value.

However, if Capricorns let their Climber energy go overboard, they can become so focused on their ambitions that they forget to have any fun or sweetness in their lives. Capricorns can get so caught up in what they desire to accomplish (and what they expect others to accomplish), they can forget to relate to themselves and others in a loving or spontaneous way. Instead, Capricorns will become overly matter of fact, assessing value according to how much gets done, rather than to the quality of life.

Needless to say, this makes Capricorns' lives productive, but they might miss out on what it's really about. If Capricorns just identify their worth as coming from achieving things, they might forget their inherent personal value as human beings and beloved ones. This can make them hyper-driven—cold and tough—toward both themselves and others. Capricorns might get the recognition and respect they crave, but the love they thought should be attached can be missing. Some Capricorns have to learn that the hard way.

Sheila was so intent on becoming the top Realtor in her company that she ate, drank and slept real estate. Although her fiancé begged her to do things that they could enjoy together, Sheila devoted all her time to clients. So when it was time to go to the banquet that celebrated her victory as Salesperson of the Year, Sheila went alone. Her fiancé, tired of all work and no play, left her.

Capricorns' Climber archetype is a spiritual gift in that it keeps Capricorns aspiring, climbing toward that spiritual "something" that is greater and more expansive. Capricorns can sense that there is an ultimate good—and a true liberation—available to them, and their Climber archetype propels them to keep stepping over the distracting issues and challenges of their worldly lives to scale the heights of their inner consciousness.

The Builder

Capricorns display the archetype of the Builder because they love the process of *building:* of making a viable, thriving structure out of the sum of its pieces. They especially love the idea of building something magnificent out of the most meager of resources.

Capricorns' Builder has a visionary quality in that it captures the overall possibilities of a project. Capricorns see way beyond the potentials that others recognize, to even greater possibilities; perhaps something that has never been done before. And they have a remarkable ability to manifest whatever they envision. Capricorns feel empowered as they direct each step of a project because they recognize how it will contribute to the whole. Capricorns are deeply satisfied by the creativity, the power and the respect they feel when successfully building something of value. Grand plans don't intimidate Capricorns, either—on the contrary, they excite them.

And Capricorns are capable of planning just how to manifest them. Their organizational skills are legendary. Almost instantly, Capricorns size up how a project needs to be structured to make the most efficient use of time and resources. This is actually an intuitive process for them, but they prefer to think of it as common sense. (That kind of sense may be common for Capricorns, but it's not so common for others.)

Problems and obstacles are no sweat for Capricorns. Being the consummate realist, Capricorns recognize that setbacks are an inevitable part of any project. So they use their powers of discernment to anticipate, and, thereby, swiftly recognize, when something or someone isn't functioning at the highest capacity. **Solving a problem can be creative sport for Capricorns—they enjoy rolling up their sleeves and trying different solutions to make the problem go away. They feel exhilarated by watching something go from dysfunctional to fully functional as a result of their input.**

Because Capricorns are so capable of fixing problems, it can really irk, as well as distract, them if they see a problem go unattended. If they can't do anything to remedy the situation, they are better off shifting their focus to what they can—and do—positively impact. That will keep them from being frustrated and cranky over something that they can't change. In doing so, Capricorns can carry on doing what they do best: using what's at hand to make things even better.

The Strategist

Capricorns embody the archetype of the Strategist by exercising their powerful capacity to use disciplined, structured plans to make things happen. More than any other sign, Capricorn has the willingness to adhere to self-prescribed regimens that take them on a direct path to accomplishing any goal they aspire to. In doing so, they will endure any and every challenge or setback that comes their way, priding themselves on their ability to prevail.

Capricorns' Strategist gives them a penchant for being good and thorough planners. They love to forecast and strategize the specific steps it should take to get something done. Whereas other signs (like the Mutable ones) might enjoy the kind of excitement that comes from "winging it," Capricorns enjoy the excitement and creativity that careful planning gives them.

When in Strategist mode, Capricorns want what they want so sincerely that they make great sacrifices of comfort and fun, reaching into pure willpower and determination to achieve their goal. Indeed, Capricorns' lives can seem like one perpetual boot camp to others. But Capricorns love it. Sticking to a regimen is sheer joy for them. They love facing challenges as a way of defining and developing what they're made of.

This Strategist archetype gives Capricorns the discipline to resist being seduced by personal desires, situations—even people—that can sidetrack them from achieving their ultimate goal. There is a certain kind of ruthlessness to Capricorns' strategy: They know where they are going and they are determined to get right there—no fooling around.

Capricorns' Strategist energy goes for control—either over themselves or the world, or both. Whereas Capricorns' Climber adores the prestige and creativity they get from leading, their Strategist loves the discipline and power. Capricorns know their strategic skills can lead the way to success for themselves and others. And they want to respect themselves, and be respected for their ability to take mastery over themselves and/or the world.

Some Capricorns express their Strategist archetype through determining an ambitious career path and using incredible discipline to achieve it. They will persevere through tremendous rigors and tests of talent, character and patience to prove to themselves and others that they are worthy of the job. These Capricorns also generally delay receiving the rewards of life—love, family or nice things—until after they've achieved their goal. When they finally do, they'll select the best of the best for themselves, nothing less.

Other Capricorns use their Strategist archetype for self-discipline in achieving their personal best. They want and need to know they did the absolute best they could, and that alone satisfies them. Some like participating in strenuous sports that involve control of body, mind and spirit to achieve mastery. Others use their Strategic energy to run their household in a most efficient and supervised manner.

Capricorns' disciplined Strategist energy is also demonstrated in other important ways. Like doing what they say they will do, completing what they begin, sticking to their commitments and showing up on time. For Capricorns, that shows not only honor, but also respect. And they expect that same respect from others. Capricorns won't put up with passive control from others, which being late or not following through on commitments is, from Capricorns' point of view.

The Strategist energy in Capricorns thrives on validation. They want others to validate that their approach to life is a worthy one. It's a way of getting feedback they're on the right track. When others validate

Capricorns, it helps them know they're right in what they're doing, and they should keep going. Without validation, Capricorns can begin to wonder if they're in a vacuum, and not making the positive impact they intend to.

Acknowledgment is also important to the Strategist. When someone understands the value—or the truth—of what they express, Capricorns are encouraged and rewarded, because both they and another benefit from the wisdom shared. The greatest acknowledgment Capricorns can receive is when others act on one of their suggestions, hopefully making their life better as a result.

Because Capricorns love disciplined adherence to productive actions, sometimes they might really need (without even realizing it) a break to relax or have some fun. Sometimes, just the simplest of pleasures—like taking a walk, soaking in a hot tub or getting a massage—can relax and rejuvenate Capricorns, and better prepare them to face the world. Other times, they really need to get away to enjoy themselves. If Capricorns find they continually don't make time to plan some fun for themselves, they might ask someone to arrange it for them. Then, they should let themselves really enjoy. Capricorns can be really fun, and have lots of fun, once they give themselves permission to let go.

Capricorns need to watch that their Saturnian side doesn't prompt them to feel guilty if they are "not getting something done." Capricorns can discount doing those things that nurture them because they consider them self-indulgences, and judge that there is no payoff in such behavior. But, the truth is, Capricorns are a hundred times more effective when they take good care of themselves, nurture themselves and show themselves a good time.

Some Capricorns don't need to be convinced to play. They play with the same ambitious intentions and gusto they do everything else with (like Ellen, a busy chiropractor, who heads for the ski slopes three seconds after she's done working). The motto, "Work hard, play hard," is undoubtedly tattooed on some Capricorn's forehead, somewhere.

Capricorns' Strategic energy derives enjoyment from using focus and discipline, and earns pride from knowing they've done their absolute best. But, if taken too far, Capricorns' strategies can make them incredibly demanding and controlling. They will expect that everyone around them should do things according to the program that they dictate. Capricorns can get so caught up in the "right form" (as they determine it) that they become rigid and inflexible. When Capricorns become so focused on how things "should" be done, they follow the letter of the law instead of the spirit of the law.

Occasionally, adhering to the "right form" can actually get in the way of true progress. Sometimes, that's okay for Capricorns because they believe that, in the long run, adhering to the correct form will net them better results than veering away from it to make short-term adjustments. But it can drive others crazy, especially those who don't value Capricorns' recipe of form or structure. They'll consider Capricorns to be limiting control freaks. Moreover, they can feel like they're in boot camp with a Capricorn as the drill sergeant. Some Capricorns accept that. Others eventually come to decide that an occasional stray from the regimen for the sake of morale or effectiveness is worth it.

Actually, getting caught up in (okay, obsessed with) their "shoulds" of life can be a trap for Capricorns. If they insist that matters should go a certain way—or should be what they desire—Capricorns' emotions can get thrown out of whack, initiating a downward spiral that sinks deeper and deeper into discontentment and feelings of ineffectiveness. If Capricorns could manage to give up the "shoulds" and respect that there might be a higher order in operation (even if they find that hard to believe), they might be able to pick themselves back up and cooperate with what truly needs to be done. Capricorns can become downright illuminated—not to mention liberated—by giving up the very process they thought they needed to succeed.

It's important for self-respect and joy—rather than ruthlessness—to be inherent in Capricorns' discipline and regimen. There is a difference between the kind of self-denial that builds character and the kind of self-denial that represses the Spirit. If Capricorns find they are becoming increasingly more intolerant of themselves and others for petty crimes of indulgence, it might be a signal that they have become too serious or controlling of life. They might want to reroute their discipline so it can help them relinquish their routine, and embrace a lifestyle that lifts and enhances their whole Self.

Life itself should be worth living, regardless of whether or not Capricorn (or anyone) is achieving their goals. Therefore, it's smart for Capricorns to check in from time to time to make sure that their goals and disciplines are enhancing their emotional well-being. Sometimes, the energies of the Capricorn Strategist can get so outcome-oriented that Capricorn can become convinced there is no benefit to expressing—or even having—emotions. Capricorns might even consider emotions to be a sign of weakness or distraction, either in themselves or others.

But that is just not the case. Capricorns' emotions, especially the vulnerable and tender ones, are as important as their other, more practical qualities. Not only can they bring Capricorns joy, they help them to feel connected with others, something their sign needs. Emotions and feelings also allow Capricorns to be aware of the subtle cues life gives them about what's on course versus what's off course. If they dismiss or override feelings—theirs or those of others—Capricorns risk doing things based on their concept of "should," rather than on their attunement with what is of greatest value. Tenderness has tremendous strength to it, and can allow doors to open naturally for Capricorns that they might otherwise break down or destroy—or miss altogether.

It serves Capricorns to remember that people need to feel good about themselves and what they're doing in order to bring out their best. And, believe it or not, that includes Capricorns as well. So it's important for Capricorns to lend emotional, as well as practical, support to whatever—or whomever—they are devoting their strategic skills to. Otherwise, their discipline (of themselves or others) might become severe and demanding, and alienate the very people who could love them or support them in achieving their goals.

One way Capricorns can discern whether their Strategist energy is being used correctly is to assess whether or not they are balanced inside themselves. If Capricorns are out of whack emotionally—feeling frustrated or angry—chances are they are using their Lower Nature to control matters. Capricorns' willfulness, rather than the wisdom of their Higher Nature, might be trying to direct how things go. If that happens, it helps if Capricorns back off just until they feel more in alignment with themselves. That will help them gain perspective on other approaches they can take, as well as help them reconnect with the greatest power within them: their Spirit.

Capricorns' Strategist archetype tends to evaluate others according to how well they discipline themselves. Capricorns have great respect for those who have overcome hardships, or made something out of nothing. But Capricorns can feel contempt for those who either choose an easy path, or let themselves live free of any sort of discipline. *How could they?* they think to themselves, and then dismiss these individuals.

But Capricorns might go farther in life by seeing what they can learn from people who know they are enough *just by being.* They might be able to teach Capricorns some strategies that allow them to enjoy their lives even more than they already do.

Capricorns' Strategic energy can be wisely applied to spiritual growth. Capricorns can tap into incredible expansiveness by using their discipline for stepping away from anything that isn't in alignment with their highest good. Where some signs might fudge their spiritual disciplines—like meditation or prayer—Capricorns can use their Strategist energy to make it a priority to commit to them, whether or not they are in the mood. They know that their discipline leads to inner freedom.

The Father

Capricorns' Father archetype is expressed through their sense of duty and responsibility to lend support to whatever—or whomever—they value. Capricorns feel a deep compassion and caring for others, and would love to see them make the most of their lives. So they do what they can (which is considerable) to help guide them to make the best possible choices. The act of helping others gratifies Capricorns: They enjoy assisting people in developing their abilities and talents, so they are better prepared to make a difference in the world.

Some Capricorns demonstrate the Father archetype by assuming responsibility for the well-being of some greater social order. Just as the father of a family provides the framework of support that enables the family to thrive, Capricorns feel called to provide a structure (or a service) that contributes to, or supports, their community so it can thrive. To accomplish this Capricorns will join, possibly even accept leadership roles in, organizations that are doing something they consider worthwhile. Capricorns will use their Fathering skills to steer and support it, so the greatest number of people can benefit from it.

Because Capricorns have gathered so much wisdom in their own lives, they offer wise counsel to others. Capricorns enjoy helping people gain perspective on their problems by helping them see their bigger picture, as well as ways in which they can reroute their behavior so it becomes more effective.

Usually, Capricorns' Father archetype doesn't express itself in a touchy-feely way. Rather, it's expressed in a way that gives practical, usable direction, such as being honest if they think someone is off track. Capricorns don't indulge people's weaknesses; rather, they pointedly bring up those weaknesses, so others recognize and do something about them. This can make Capricorns seem tough or uncaring, but they're just the opposite: They don't want to see others wasting their potential and will say what they think needs to be said so others wake up.

But there might be times when Capricorns' Father energy does become overly harsh in its delivery of corrective feedback or guidance—to others or themselves. Capricorns can attempt to force a change in behavior, instead of to just guide it. That is rarely met with appreciation, much less gratitude, and it makes people want to avoid Capricorns for fear of their wrath. In truth, that surprises Capricorns because they didn't think they were all that bad. But, yeah, they were kind of rough.

One way Capricorns can determine if they are being a wise "Fatherly advisor" versus a harsh authoritarian is to check what their inner state is while they are giving feedback or direction. If a Capricorn feels at all angry, constricted or frustrated, chances are they will come off as intolerant and controlling. If they hold off just long enough to bring themselves into a place of neutrality and balance, Capricorns will find they are much better positioned to bring the positive influence they envision.

In a way, Capricorns are Fathers to the world. Because of their social concern and wisdom, Capricorns can see what can—or needs to—be done to make the world work better. They see how much better things would be if people would just get out of their petty interests and work as a unit. In some Capricorns, there is a kind of sadness or melancholy when observing the world: They care so much about it, and they see its troubles so clearly. Capricorns believe there's no real need for starvation, poverty or pollution, and they can feel disillusioned that their fellow human beings choose to continue to make the same mistakes that produce these ills.

If Capricorns find they are experiencing sadness or disappointment about the world, it helps for them to shift their perspective by seeing the world more as a place where everyone is learning something they don't know, rather than a place where everyone should already have wisdom. This is a learning planet, and many people are discovering things Capricorns may already understand. Others have to make mistakes, even act badly, in order to find out for themselves how they're going astray. It also helps if Capricorns use their insights to take stock of what is going right and well in the world. That will remind them that, in truth, we are all doing the best we can (even if it isn't perfect).

Some Capricorns' Father energy expresses through their need to care for the environment, to protect it, as well as use its resources wisely. Capricorns cherish and love the Earth. It nourishes them, and they receive peace and calm from interacting with it. So it breaks Capricorns' hearts when they see the Earth being mistreated—even underappreciated—because they are so aware of all the Earth offers. That prompts Capricorns to do whatever they can to help protect the Earth and all its valuable resources.

Capricorns are learning to use their Father archetype to become

Spiritual Fathers to themselves. They are learning to give themselves guidance about what's right for them, and to discipline themselves to grow and develop into people they themselves are proud of being. As they do, they are able to access the guidance of their Inner Spirit, which is constant, wise and caring beyond measure.

The Capricorn Gifts: The Wisdom to Know and the Intention to Do

One of Capricorns' greatest gifts is their **Clear Intention.** Capricorns are incredibly adept at creating, then holding on to, a clear vision of exactly what they want. Nothing, but nothing, can dissuade Capricorns from their goal: They see it, they feel it, and they trust that it's possible.

What's powerful about Capricorns' clear intention is their **Adherence** to it. Capricorns understand the "magic" that happens when they hold both their visions and actions clearly: They notice how circumstances seem to line up to help them achieve what they are after. (Well, in truth, most Capricorns wouldn't call it magic; they'd call it hard work.) Since Capricorns understand there is great power in intention, even when they don't know exactly how to do something, they are sure their intention to succeed will find a way to manifest what they envision. And it does.

What works best is when Capricorns hold a clear intention to do whatever is for the highest good of all concerned. Even though they might not know what the highest good is, their intention to do what's best for everyone keeps them flexible and intuitive, and open to possibilities that might exist beyond their personal visions. Capricorns then can do remarkable work that is so effective, it impresses even them.

Wisdom is another gift of the Capricorn nature. Capricorns are born with a natural knowing about the ways of the world that seems far beyond their years. The outstanding thing about Capricorns' wisdom is that they grasp what has lasting value and what does not. They recognize and comprehend evolved—even ancient—attitudes and ways of thinking. Capricorns are the least likely sign to adopt the latest conceptual fad; rather, they look to what has worked throughout time.

Capricorns demonstrate their wisdom by always keeping their mind on the long-term, big picture. Whereas some signs are focused on what they want for today, Capricorns are aware of how their tomorrows will be affected by their actions of today. So instead of choosing to be instantly gratified, Capricorns' wisdom shows them how putting off an immediate reward might net them a more powerful or beneficial outcome later.

Indeed, Capricorns' wisdom understands the cause-and-effect aspect of life. They are thoughtful about what and how they create: Instead of exhausting all of their resources for a short-term goal, Capricorns look to the long-term effects of what they do and decide to see if it will get them where they ultimately want to go. They are able to see the ramifications of actions. Very rarely do Capricorns express surprise about being in the position they find themselves in, be it good or bad. They know exactly how they got there, and they see how others end up where they are as well.

Capricorns' wisdom knows the world is not just about what they want or do not want; rather, it's about the whole of humanity. They understand there's a "whole" that needs to be considered when they do something—a whole family, a whole community, a whole world or environment. And their wisdom guides them accordingly. Capricorns can adjust what they want or do so it can have as positive an impact as possible on as many as possible. This doesn't mean they sacrifice themselves—they don't. It means they do their best to be as responsible to their community as they can in doing what they want.

Because of Capricorns' wisdom, or perhaps in search of it, they appreciate the elders in their community. Capricorns are attracted to those who have been around for a long time, and set out to learn from them and the wisdom their life has taught them. Even though Capricorns might be the youngest member of a group chronologically, they might be the oldest in consciousness.

Capricorns also have **Social Wisdom** in that they understand people. This isn't necessarily the kind of understanding that knows how to get people to like them (like Libra). It's more a wisdom that can evaluate the sincerity or genuineness of another—whether they are true to themselves (or Capricorn) or not. Capricorns have a very sensitive "B.S. meter" that sees through others' insincerity instantly. They will just dismiss anyone who is insincere, whether they're popular or not. Capricorns don't want to waste their time with someone who won't—or doesn't—take themselves or Capricorn seriously. They don't tolerate such lack of respect.

Capricorns' wisdom seeks those things in life that have depth and meaning. They aren't likely to be carried away with what's fashionable in the moment. Rather, they are attracted to what remains dignified and appreciated over the long haul. Occasionally, this can make Capricorns seem kind of stick-in-the-mud. But, in reality, they are simply choosing to invest their time and energy in activities that can net valuable results for themselves and others.

This wisdom serves Capricorns spiritually by helping them discern what is truly Light, and what is simply glamorous illusion. Their willingness to test results allows them to evaluate what practices lift them, even if the upliftment is subtle. And Capricorns' ability to get outside their own self-involvement allows them to glimpse into the magnificence of God.

Capricorns also have the gift of being **Responsible**; or, put another way, they have the ability to *respond*. Capricorns don't look around for someone else to be accountable for matters, they look to see what their contribution can be and then they jump in.

Capricorns are also **Pragmatic.** They want to use what they know to bring about useful results in the world. Although Capricorns are certainly capable of comprehending abstract concepts and ideals, they are likely to become impatient with them unless they can lead to some sort of useful application. Capricorns are much more attracted to concrete subjects that can help them navigate and use this world to build something worthwhile.

Endurance is a gift that sees Capricorns through to the end. Capricorns have the ability to hang in there—to go the distance, so to speak—in order to achieve what they intend to. Whereas other signs might give a goal one major attempt and then give up if they don't succeed, Capricorns will keep trying, even after a failure or a series of failures. The saying, "If at first you don't succeed, try, try again," describes Capricorns' strategy in attaining their goal.

Commitment figures strongly in Capricorns' ability to endure. While some signs fear committing to their visions because they might be missing out on something better, Capricorns trust that what they have decided upon is worth their full investment. They don't allow themselves to get sidetracked by "maybes" or "ifs"; they know that, if they are going to achieve something, they have to place their whole Self in alignment with it.

So Capricorns endure (stick with to the end) whatever they commit to. Sometimes, that's because they strongly desire the rewards they will receive as a result of fulfilling their commitments. Other times, Capricorns endure even the greatest challenges to their commitments simply because they said they would. Capricorns' word is a binding agreement to them—they don't want to let others down.

But it is important for Capricorns to evaluate if what they're persevering to the end of is really and truly useful to them. Because of their principled adherence to commitments, there might be times when Capricorns get stuck in situations that, in truth, are no longer working for them, or others. There are a few ways to detect this. One of the obvious indicators is if things fall apart. In that case, Capricorns are finally ready to relinquish their commitment, and accept that it's time to stop. But another way Capricorns can recognize that they need to change course is when nothing about the project or commitment lifts them or the others involved. Sometimes, things are just over. There is great wisdom in accepting that and moving on.

Others might think Capricorns' endurance results from their being patient. But, in truth, as a Cardinal Sign, their energy isn't patient at all—in fact, it's *impatient*. Capricorns might appear calm on the outside, but on the inside they are railing and pushing like mad to get what they want to happen. Even so, Capricorns rarely let their impatience compel them to jump off course or give up. Instead, they will stick to their long-term strategies and shift their immediate tactics when needed.

Even though Capricorns have to deal with being impatient, they also recognize the value of **Gradualness.** Life has taught them that some of the best things happen slowly, over time. So, Capricorns are willing to allow for the gradual unfoldment of their desires, knowing that each step is important.

This helps Capricorns spiritually, because, sometimes, spiritual awakening is gradual and subtle. When Capricorns recognize the value of gradualness, they are able to stick with practices (like meditation) that others would lose patience with and quit, even though they are extremely important and effective in the long run—a fact that Capricorns are well aware of.

Capricorns, like the other Earth Signs, also possess extreme **Determination.** They set their sights on something, and then resolutely stick to it. Capricorns' determination musters incredible energy and courage: They see the end result and they use whatever resources are available to get there.

The Capricorn Fears: Call Them Anything but Nowhere Man

More than anything, Capricorns **fear being insignificant.** It's tremendously threatening for them to think that they might not make significant contributions, or be recognized as people of importance. Capricorns might feel that translates into worthlessness, and if they aren't important, then what's their value?

But, like everyone, Capricorns have value in just being. So it can be the most liberating act of Capricorns' lives to face that fear, and accept that they don't need to be as significant as they think they should be. First, that brings a humility that allows Capricorns to become more aligned with God's plan for them, instead of their ego's plan for them. Through being willing to be nothing, Capricorns might allow themselves to pursue a direction that can give them everything they are truly destined for, and even greater than their ego's sense of importance ever could have grasped.

Being willing to be nothing is incredibly freeing for Capricorns. When they allow themselves just to be, they begin to recognize the inherent value of themselves and others. Instead of doing, doing, doing, in order to seek fulfillment, Capricorns might realize fulfillment by just being.

Capricorns can also **fear not being able to build or make a difference in any way.** That can give them a sense of powerlessness—a feeling that their life has no meaning if they can't impact their world in a significant way. Some Capricorns make positive use of this concern by serving others. That's always a wonderful avenue for Capricorns to recognize their effectiveness. But that might not resolve the belief that they have to make an impact on their own in order to be valid. It's important that Capricorns realize they have power just in being alive, and being present. In doing so, they can better tap into their spiritual presence, which carries power in and of itself.

Capricorns can also **fear appearing weak or unprepared to manage in life.** This can prompt them to make the most of themselves and mature quickly so they can rise to whatever life challenges them with. But it can also prompt Capricorns to develop a stoicism—a hardness wherein they don't allow anyone (including themselves) to see their vulnerability or tenderness. Not indulging weakness is helpful. But Capricorns' thinking that vulnerability makes them weak can serve as a detriment. Sometimes, it is vulnerability that allows them to have awakening insights into their truest powers and gifts. It takes great courage to be vulnerable. Nothing weak about it. (Loved ones have been telling them that for years, I bet.)

And Capricorns can **fear losing control**—or losing the sense that they are, indeed, the masters of their universe. This fear can serve Capricorns by prompting them to be vigilant about what's going on, and keep them focused and involved. However, in truth control is an illusion—life has a way of always sneaking in surprises that aren't planned for. And control is an addiction—it starts to take over and, trying to maintain control, sucks up such massive amounts of time, effort and resources that we distract ourselves from the higher choices we could be making. What works better is for Capricorns to control what they can—which is their own attitudes and perceptions. When Capricorns set their intentions on using everything for their upliftment and advancement—and release their worries, fears and egos' demands of having life go a certain way—Capricorns are using control in the highest form possible.

Capricorn in Relationships: "Slowly but Surely"

Capricorns consider their relationships very precious. However, they don't enter them easily: They're careful about getting to know others, and are cautious about opening their hearts, for fear of being too vulnerable. So if you are trying to get to know a Capricorn, take it slow. What they're looking to find out is whether or not you are genuine—with yourself and with them. They loathe phoniness, false admiration and superficiality. They want to make sure you have substance, intelligence and sincerity.

Do what you can to gently draw Capricorns out. At first they might seem standoffish, even arrogant. That might be a cover for their shyness or feelings of awkwardness. They're surprised by someone showing interest in them personally (though they get lots of attention professionally), and are flattered by the attention, if it's sincere. If you can make them laugh all the better.

But once a Capricorn does allow someone in, they are most loyal, funny and supportive companions. They value their friends and beloveds very much, and protect and support their relationships so they grow and develop. Capricorns are sure of what they want, so they have no problem with commitment. They show up even during the hardest of times, remaining a loyal friend year after year.

The crowning jewel of Capricorns is that they are really funny.

Usually, their humor is dry, sometimes even sarcastic, so you have to be listening to them to get it. But it's worth it.

Initially, Capricorns might be attracted to those who seem important or prestigious in some way. They enjoy admiring others' accomplishments and hobnobbing with success. But in truth, Capricorns are more likely to commit to someone who supports—rather than outshines—them in their world endeavors.

I've had more Capricorns—of both genders—tell me they're looking for what used to be considered a traditional wife. They want someone who will be there for them in an emotionally supportive way, someone who is available to help them manage their everyday life, so they can go out and conquer the world. Capricorns figure they have enough ambition and success potential for both themselves and their mate. What they desire is someone who will help them build a personal life and home foundation.

One powerful way to open a Capricorn's heart is through being tender and nurturing. Because they tend to be so hard on themselves, they feel incredible gratitude for those who treat them gently and encourage them to do the same. (But do not patronize—that's an insult.) Although Capricorns are flattered and impressed by glamorous dates, what really touches them is the times when you extend yourself and go out of your way to do something kind for them. Bring a warm meal to them and rub their tight shoulders the night they're working late at the office and they'll melt.

Capricorns will look to the small gestures as clues that you love them: a touch, a smile, a favor that makes life easier for them. Remember, they're masters of subtlety and enjoy quiet adoration and kindnesses above all else. They'll look in your eyes to see if you really love them.

Very important: no game playing. Show your love of your Capricorn by being as honest and straight with them as you can.

Because Capricorn is an Earth Sign, physical touch is extremely important to them. It soothes and nourishes them like nothing else. But they don't like public displays of affection, and they hate when others are affectionate just out of neediness. So wait until you're home alone or in private with them, then let your affections go wild. In private, Capricorn is a very sensual and sexy sign. They love all kinds of physicality, and love and appreciate a partner who's adventurous and available.

If you're trying to win the heart of a Capricorn female, show her what you've accomplished and how you're the person she can count on.

That will open the door to her interests. In truth, though, she needs someone who loves her for herself, perhaps someone who makes her laugh. Some Capricorn females are attracted to partners who are decidedly unambitious, and instead show strong nurturing skills. But she still needs to respect her partner. If they don't live up to their side of the bargain, she will start to resent that she is the only one doing any work, and she'll start to withhold her affection.

Other types of Capricorn women want a partner who's a real dynamo. They're the kind that wants to be with "the one in charge." And she'll support them and do what she can to help them get there.

Sometimes, a Capricorn female is looking for a partner who's an out-and-out father figure. She adores the strength and the support she feels from a strong, wise, and, perhaps much older, companion. By being with someone she looks up to, she feels softer inside. She's relieved to find someone she can count on other than herself. But make sure not to take this to the extreme, so it just turns into a true father-daughter relationship, and the sexuality falls away.

If you're trying to win the heart of a male Capricorn, do your best to gently draw him out. He'll appreciate your concern for him as a person, even if at first he acts indifferent. He does love beauty (indeed, he can be made breathless by it—although he'll be subtle about it, of course), but he's looking for way more than that. He's looking for real substance and sincerity. He wants to know he's got a genuine partner who has her own capacities and thoughts. He wants a partner who respects herself and enjoys being tender. He, too, is looking for a nurturer, someone who adores him, someone with whom he can relax and show his soft side. So you show your soft side first, but don't be needy, overly emotional or clingy. That turns him off. Instead, demonstrate how you can be strong in your loving gentleness.

Sex is important to a Capricorn male. It embarrasses him to be publicly affectionate, and around others he may behave in a downright businesslike manner. But once you're alone, look out. He's ready for anything. Go ahead and make your advances toward him. He'll not only accept them, but also will adore you forever for making them.

The Last Word on Capricorn

Capricorns strive to excel and be at the top. While they can be supremely successful in the world, they gain their greatest satisfaction by mastering themselves.

Chapter 11

Aquarius

(January 21–February 18)

Aquarius is the quality in you that's individualistic and idealistic, seeks to contribute to the progress of humanity, and enjoys doing things in an innovative and clever (even eccentric) way. It's also the part of you that's learning to connect to others through Unconditional Love.

Aquarians love to surf right on the crest of the wave of transformational change. Their brilliant intellects make them extremely interesting, even to the point of eccentricity. In fact, see the girl with the purple hair? Guess what sign she probably is.

Aquarians are true individuals—and they make it their business to be. Refusing to be predictable or pigeonholed, Aquarians shun the normal or conventional ways of doing things, and, instead, use their innovation to do things that have never been tried before. Aquarians are much like scientists at heart: They love experimenting with new ideas, approaches and concepts, just to see what works. They even employ the scientist's objectivity of observing matters through the lens of pure reason and logic, not wanting emotions to shade the truth. But Aquarians rarely present themselves like scientists; rather, they express themselves by dressing and acting in ways that are outstanding, unique and individualistic.

Aquarians are a truly unique combination of the idealist and the pragmatist: They clearly envision idealistic concepts that can make for a better society, yet they also see the eminently practical steps that can make their vision a reality. They consider personal freedom to be of the utmost importance, and the unencumbered expression of one's Self to be the birthright of every human being. (They will rebel against anything—or anyone—that tries to deny that.)

The Aquarius Mission: Learning That Loving Is Truly Universal

All of us are learning what Aquarians are born to discover: Universal Loving is the strongest human connection. Although Universal Love can be described in countless ways, psychologist Carl Rogers described it as "*unconditional positive regard*" for others. When Aquarians tap into their Universal Loving, they recognize the magnificence of their own expression—as well as everyone else's—and they value it as an important part of humanity. In doing so, Aquarians express their Highest Nature, which is heartfelt and expansive, and they recognize their deep connection to the world around them. This leads Aquarians to the freedom they are truly seeking, which is the freedom to purely express their hearts.

As Aquarians align with their immense and powerful loving, they grasp how everyone and everything in this world has a unique preciousness, including them. From there, **Aquarians serve as illuminating visionaries by demonstrating the higher choices and expressions all of humanity might (eventually) aspire to.**

Universal Loving helps Aquarians understand that they are in the right place at the right time, and it shows them just what is needed to make a true difference in the world.

The Aquarius Challenge: Recognizing We *Are* All One (Even If Your Hair Isn't Purple!)

Interestingly, Aquarians can learn Universal Love by overcoming their own feelings of intolerance, as well as their beliefs that they are so different that it makes them separate from others.

Aquarians pride themselves on their open minds and their love of diversity. However, they are also extremely idealistic and have very specific expectations about how humanity can (or should, from their point of view) evolve and develop. If people fail to live up to Aquarians' ideals, by not behaving in the manner that Aquarians envision they should, Aquarians can become deeply disappointed and judgmental. Aquarians will believe that others are falling short, and judge their expression as unevolved or selfish. They'll become disgusted because, well, people aren't trying hard enough. When they do this, Aquarians step out of their Universal Loving and unconditional positive regard for others, and, instead, become intolerant and aloof.

When that happens, Aquarius school is in session. Aquarians are learning to recognize that all people are evolving and expressing themselves according to their own unique destiny. When Aquarians remember to look upon their fellow humans as if they all are doing the best they can (and they are), Aquarians can resume their appreciation for the diverse ways in which people express themselves.

Or Aquarians can feel that their uniqueness is so extreme, it causes them to be out of step with the rest of the world. Instead of finding useful ways to use their individuality to contribute to others, Aquarians can focus on feeling misunderstood, and consider themselves separate from people. They can believe that there is no one who truly understands them, and, more painfully, that there is nowhere on Earth they truly belong.

But they do belong. Learning how to connect, even when they're feeling different, is a big part of the lesson of being an Aquarius. Being out of step teaches Aquarians to remain true to themselves, and honor their own nature as the valid one God intended for them, whether or not the world validates it. Instead of feeling that they don't belong, the challenge for Aquarians is to find ways they can apply or translate their uniqueness to their relationships and circumstances, so that all involved can be enriched.

The Aquarius Key: Using Individuality to Enhance Connecting

Aquarians can develop their individuality, and use it to reach out to participate with the world as a whole. In doing so, they are uplifted, and better able to make the valued contributions they were born to make. One way Aquarians can keep their intolerance in check, as well as maintain their participation in their community, is to keep in mind that they are evolutionary beings. If Aquarians understand that it's their destiny to be at least a little bit, if not light years, ahead of (or just different from) the crowd, they can release their expectations that others should be on their exact same wavelength.

When Aquarians accept that most people won't catch their vision, at least right now, they can keep their focus on what they are truly here to influence: themselves. In truth, Aquarians' only job is to keep themselves growing and moving forward. In realizing that, Aquarians can better respect other individuals' growth and evolution, just as they do their own. That's freedom.

The WATER BEARER for Sustenance and Change

The astrological symbol for Aquarius is the Water Bearer. This is generally depicted as a kneeling woman pouring water out of a jug. The water is intended for the growth of her community's crops. While kneeling, one foot is in the water up to her ankle, and the other foot rests on the ground. This image describes the Aquarian nature in various ways.

The pouring of the water for the crops of the community symbolizes the Aquarian interest in, and intention to, contribute to the sustenance and growth of their community. The foot on the ground symbolizes

Aquarian pragmatism, the need to practically apply their progressive ideas. The foot in the water symbolizes Aquarians' connection to the flow of life. The posture of kneeling symbolizes Aquarians' ability to surrender their personal will to serving the needs of the whole, to doing what is for the Highest Good.

AIR Apparent

Aquarius is one of the three Air Signs (Gemini and Libra are the other two). Being an Air Sign means Aquarians are most comfortable with the thinking function. They will place greatest value on their concepts and ideas, and act on what they think—as opposed to what their feelings suggest, or even what practical concerns might exist. Air gives Aquarians a strong intellectual capacity, with which they can easily jump from one subject or idea to another, yet somehow consider them all together (a sort of encyclopedia of knowledge in their minds). Air also gives Aquarians a love of the conceptual—they use hard-core facts as stepping-stones to the new reality they envision.

The unique Aquarian expression of the Air element expresses itself through idealized concepts. They are most likely to direct their thoughts and considerations toward developing new and innovative ideas, many of which are about subjects or strategies that uplift and evolve them and humanity as a whole. Aquarians have curious and open minds. They will consider almost anything, as long as they can see some degree of logic behind it. Although they respect what has already been established as truth and fact, Aquarians will push to use what's already known to discover something new. They thrive on innovating, or finding fresh twists and truths that can open new worlds of ideas. Always, Aquarians ask, "How can we use what we know to go further?"

Although all the Air Signs possess a certain objectivity that comes from assessing life mentally, the Aquarian form of Air is particularly logical and detached. They enjoy researching whatever—or whoever—interests them in order to find out their essential truths. Aquarians are sure to sift through emotional influences or persuasive arguments that distort what's real (for them), and, instead, let the facts speak for themselves. They trust that pure knowledge in and of itself can be liberating.

There is an uncanny intelligence that goes with Aquarians: There are certain things they just know. They might not even know *how* they know, but they know. This isn't an enthusiastic "I think I get it" (like Sagittarius), or an "I've analyzed it fully" (like Virgo), or an "I've intentionally sized things up" (like Scorpio). It's a complete understanding. Others can see it when they look into Aquarians' eyes, because the Aquarians look right back at them with a cool, confident gaze of knowing.

Many times, Aquarians will signal that they "know" something by raising just one eyebrow. That's their way, subtle as it might be, of calling attention to the fact that they've "got it." Actually, when I talk to Aquarians about this knowing, they nod and use the phrase, "Ninety-nine times out of one hundred, I'm right!"

There are different ways each Aquarian determines "what's logical." Some are the hard-core "Give me the facts, Ma'am," scientific types. They recognize only that which can be tested and proven time and again. Usually, these Aquarians are attracted to careers that involve science or technology. They're inspired to discover more about the workings of the physical Universe. Indeed, just considering the beautiful perfection of the physical laws of the Universe can enlighten these Aquarians.

Then, there is the kind of Aquarian whose logic includes imagination and intuition. They sense that there are greater truths than the provable laws of science provide. They figure science doesn't know everything, and there are things going on here that are logically valid, even if we don't yet understand them. These Aquarians are interested in progressive theories of all sorts, and are fascinated by subjects and possibilities most other people might even consider nonsense. Topics like UFOs, ESP, parallel universes—and, yes, astrology!—appeal to this kind of Aquarian, because they offer conceivable explanations to life's mysteries. (Interestingly, some of the greatest astrologers are Aquarians. And some of the most vehement debunkers of astrology are also Aquarians. Each has their own commitment to—and alliance with—truth, as they know it.)

Most Aquarians will demonstrate a combination of both these traits: Their logic will come from a mix of science or technology, with intuitive thinking, that enables them to understand what's really going on now, as well as what might be possible for the future.

No matter where on the continuum of science versus intuition an Aquarian falls, there is always something a little quirky about how they see life. Always inventive, Aquarians naturally put a new spin on things, and interpret reality a bit differently than the rest of the world does.

Because Aquarians value and benefit from their minds so much, they might dismiss feelings and emotions as a sidetrack from "true knowledge." Aquarians have a tendency to objectify their emotions or try to make some logical sense of them. But since feelings are nonlinear and don't follow any lines of logic at all, they can't be understood through the mind. Instead, emotions and feelings have to be dealt with on their own terms. Some Aquarians do learn the language of their feelings and emotions and are richly rewarded as a result.

Other Aquarians take a different stance and attempt to negate the value—even the existence—of their emotions altogether. These kinds of Aquarians tend to aspire to be like Mr. Spock of *Star Trek* fame, free of the blinding passions of emotion (yet still contributing to others in a useful way, of course). These Aquarians judge their emotions as not being as useful or as evolved as the mind. So they reject them as illogical, useless and potentially harmful, and try to inhibit themselves from experiencing them altogether. Some Aquarians can even consider emotions, and what people do because of their emotions, as the downfall of the human race. (Not to mention fearing that their own vulnerability would be their downfall.) With that attitude, Aquarians can be downright aloof, not to mention completely emotionally unavailable. But this can rob them of what they value and need the most: meaningful connection with other human beings.

Since Aquarians are learning to discover ways to connect with humanity, sooner or later they realize that this usually involves some degree of emotional availability, even if they initially find that somewhat awkward. If Aquarians fail to develop their feelings, they miss out not only on the vast universe of understanding and wisdom that emotions can provide, but also on the rich emotional bonds that connect people and bring about mutual understanding.

So it's smart for Aquarians to learn how to be comfortable with the emotional side of their nature. That way, they can use the valuable information their feelings and emotions give them, along with the empirical facts. When they do that, they can better develop the intelligence of their instincts, and use their emotional IQ along with their cerebral IQ to be even more effective.

The FIXED Quality of Aquarius: The Courage of Their Convictions

Aquarius is one of four Fixed Signs (Taurus, Leo and Scorpio are the other three), which calls them to firmly establish themselves in whatever—or whoever—interests them. Fixed energy is very strong, structured and stable, and resists outside influences that push for change before it is ready.

Fixed energy lends Aquarians incredible strength of dedication to their ideas. They use that strength to stick to their convictions and values, enabling them to do what they think is right for them, even in the face of being misunderstood or even opposed. Aquarians' Fixed energy also gives them the courage and the commitment to be there for their friends and loved ones—even through the most challenging times—as well as to persevere through obstacles and setbacks to get where they're going. Once Aquarians make up their minds to do something, that's it; nothing can steer them off course.

The Aquarian challenge of being a Fixed Sign is that what they might consider to be persistence can actually be stubbornness. Usually, Aquarians express stubbornness through resistance: They put up their shields and don't let anyone—or anything—move them from the ideas they hold to be true. Even though Aquarians think they are just maintaining what's clearly logical, they might be missing huge pieces of the picture.

One way Aquarians can discern if they're being persevering (versus being stubborn) is to check to see if there is any motion toward their intentions. If they are adhering to a vision and moving toward it, chances are they're persevering. But if they are digging in their heels and insisting there's no value to what someone else—or life—is trying to tell them, chances are they're just in stubborn mode.

This creates a catch-22, in that stubbornness can prevent Aquarians from experiencing what they value the most: freedom of expression. Stubbornness can get them stuck in doing things one way—their way—when there are actually countless other choices. Ironically, these otherwise free spirits can become almost militaristic (not a quality they admire) in their attitude that, "*This* is the way things *should* go." That "should" is the killer. It will constrict not only Aquarians, but also those around them, to the limits of what Aquarians think should be happening, instead of connecting to greater possibilities that are available—even if Aquarians don't recognize what those possibilities are at the time. And Aquarian rigidity can suppress other people's expression, a further departure from what Aquarians truly want to do.

If Aquarians discover they're being stubborn (or are caught in a "should," or an "I'm right!" mode), it helps if they employ their scientific curiosity to see if maybe there is another way matters could unfold. Or they could try using their humanitarian respect to see what others have to contribute.

One of the key principles Aquarians are most committed to is freedom. They are most dedicated advocates of their own—and every other person's—right to express themselves as they see fit. This is not just a concept for Aquarians, it is something they will put their bodies on the line for. They will do whatever they can to help create social change. Some Aquarians create or join organizations that bring greater freedoms. Other Aquarians serve by protesting those that suppress freedom. Most Aquarians simply demonstrate their own individuality with such conviction that it inspires others to do the same.

Aquarius is a **Transpersonal Sign,** which means it represents matters that are global and universal, rather than personal. This gives Aquarians a predisposition to concern themselves with matters that extend past their own personality and personal life issues, and to engage in matters that involve many others, even the world as a whole.

Because of this, Aquarians have a kind of impersonal vibe about them: They deeply care about humanity as a whole, but they don't necessarily want to get to know or become personally involved with the person who is right in front of them. Aquarians can view people as "humanity in general," and not want to single them out as important individuals in and of themselves. Actually, Aquarians will tend to feel that way about themselves, as well. They consider their individuality to be extremely important, yet they might not consider themselves—or anyone else—as an *important* individual. Rather, Aquarians usually see everyone as an equal contributor to the whole of humanity.

Many Aquarians demonstrate this kind of Transpersonal concern by devoting their time to helping others live a better life, even if they themselves have to make considerable personal sacrifices to do so. Other Aquarians make their global contribution by being good friends (which, by the way, they truly are), or simply supporting others by sitting quietly in a group, just smiling and enjoying watching humanity be itself.

Some Aquarians don't enjoy actual group settings and find group dynamics really frustrating. They lose patience with people's petty self-involvements, or they get annoyed at the pressures of group politics. Instead, these Aquarians want to do their own thing. But, chances are, their Aquarian nature will still want to contribute to society in some way. They might do this by choosing careers in which they provide a product or service that affects many people, but that don't necessitate getting personally involved with them. Technology is one great field where Aquarius can accomplish this. Aquarians might be the geniuses behind the scenes of a computer company, a radio broadcast or an invention that makes people's lives easier.

Because Aquarius is a Transpersonal Sign, it's advisable for every Aquarian to find some way to contribute to and/or feel connected to their community. Otherwise, they risk feeling disappointed that they are not doing what (or as much as) they should.

The Eccentricity of URANUS

Aquarius is ruled by the planet Uranus. Uranus governs matters and things that have a progressive quality to them: including technology, science and inventions. That gives Aquarians a predisposition to understanding and being interested in such things, and these areas would make good careers for them. Aquarians are not only the first to explore the latest trends, but also the first ones on the block to have the newest thingamajig—and know how to use it.

Uranus is associated with the quality of genius, and many Aquarians are, in fact, geniuses in some way. Even if some Aquarians aren't true geniuses, they'll still dazzle you with their brilliance.

Uranus also rules electricity, and there is something quite electric about Aquarians. They not only spark innovative action into any situation they're involved in, they also possess a magnetism that draws people to them—even if the people can't put their finger on just why they are attracted.

Since Uranus is the planet that rules freedom, it's responsible for Aquarians' tremendous urge to express theirs. But the highest expression of Uranian freedom doesn't lie in Aquarians doing exactly as they please at every moment. Rather, it's a spiritual freedom wherein Aquarians break free from the encumbrances of their limiting Lower Nature in order to make way for the expression of their Higher Self. Uranus gives Aquarians the urge—and the wherewithal—to step away from the binding demands of their control patterns, vanities and emotional issues, so they are free to choose higher actions and qualities: like honesty, loyalty and, especially (what they are truly here to express)—Universal Love.

Uranus also governs the extraordinary and the unusual, and that's exactly what Aquarians seek. They want to be people who make a "statement" or do something—even if it's shocking or eccentric—that expresses that they are unique. They can be so enlivened by the extraordinary that they can consider things that are normal or ordinary to be boring, even worthless.

This devotion to the extraordinary serves Aquarians by keeping them fresh and open to experimenting with life. But, if their love of the extraordinary means they reject the ordinary—in themselves, in their lives or in others—it can trap them. If Aquarians believe they must be different in order to be worthy of being loved, they can worry that if they are ordinary, or considered to be ordinary (complete with human foibles), they might not have anything outstanding or worthwhile to contribute. And that, they fear, would make them unlovable. This can inhibit them from showing their True Self, out of concern that they would be found to be ordinary, just like everyone else. That holding back can prevent Aquarians from experiencing true intimacy.

It is important for Aquarians to realize that others love them for who they are, not for their outrageousness. Sometimes, Aquarians' commitment to being different can cause separation from others, because most people don't understand why they're trying to be so different. Truth be told, Aquarians are the ones who might reject others as too ordinary, and, therefore, boring or mundane. They might be looking for ideal companions—ones who don't truly exist in humanity at this time.

Or some Aquarians may think they have to continually be involved in exciting, new or edgy situations, because life might get ordinary and stifling if they don't. This can keep them attracted to weird or high-drama situations. But, after a while, even weirdness or high drama can become ordinary.

What works best is for Aquarians to make their peace with ordinariness. When they learn to seek (and find) the extraordinary in the ordinary, they can become downright illuminated during life's most mundane tasks. Indeed, a wise man once said, "Ordinariness is a prerequisite to Godliness." Being special or extraordinary is the ego's demand to stand out, and that keeps us from connecting to the Divine. When we understand that Spirit is present in all ways all the time, we recognize the ordinary as extraordinary. That's more than evolutionary; it's revolutionary.

The Aquarius Archetypes: Individually Innovating Ways to Awaken Humanity

In learning to develop and express the highest expression of their unique essence, Aquarians (and those who are Aquarian-like) will fulfill the archetypes of the Individualist, the Innovator, the Awakener and the Humanitarian.

The Individualist

Aquarians display the archetype of the Individualist because there is something truly unique about the way they express themselves and/or live their lives. More than anything, Aquarians consider being true to oneself to be of the utmost importance. They give themselves the freedom to express what is unique about them in order to distinguish themselves from the crowd, and they encourage others to do the same. Aquarians truly enjoy diversity—the many colors, attitudes and expressions that make up the human race.

Interestingly, although Aquarians strive to express themselves as—and be recognized as—outstanding and unique, they don't want to be considered "special" because that implies separation from the whole. Unlike their opposite sign, Leo, which adores being special, Aquarians abhor anyone being singled out—including them—as special, better or more important. It can embarrass Aquarians if they are. Or they might resist acknowledging others because they don't want them to get a "big head." Aquarians deeply believe that everyone has something special about him or her, therefore everyone should be considered of equal importance.

So Aquarians will strive to be outstanding, but not considered better than, or above, others. Though this may sound almost contradictory, it is an important distinction. In this subtlety lies Aquarians' ability to be complete individuals, yet to function remarkably well in a group. They deeply respect the contributions they make to a group—or an institution or a project—and they deeply respect the assets others contribute as well. Aquarians don't need themselves or anyone else to be prima donnas—they like it when everyone does what they can to contribute to the whole. Aquarians receive tremendous joy and satisfaction when working shoulder-to-shoulder along with others to make something happen. Indeed, being a valuable member of a well-functioning group (be it a group of friends, a team, an institution or a government) is the elixir of life for Aquarians.

Part of Aquarians' Individualist archetype expresses itself socially in their resistance to "going along with the crowd" in any way. Doing so can seem like a suffocating trap to them. Whereas many people consider some degree of conformity as the basis of a solid social structure,

Aquarians consider conformity confining and limiting. If everyone is the same, then how can the world progress? Aquarians can even consider conformity dangerous. They are suspicious of people or institutions that set out to dictate the actions and thoughts of others, because Aquarians think that this robs them of their birthright of being free to be themselves.

Another part of Aquarians' individuality comes from their intention to be different: Depending on the rest of their chart, they will find some, or all, areas of their life in which they can do things in their own particular way. Aquarians might dress differently, act in a distinguishing way, or hold beliefs or interests that few others understand. Or they might choose a lifestyle that is right for them, but is nontraditional.

Other aspects of Aquarians' individuality are simply rooted in their nature. They are inherently different from the norm of humanity in some significant way. The saying, "Follow the beat of a different drummer," is absolutely about Aquarius—it's as if they're wired differently than most. From a very early age, Aquarians notice that most of the kids are interested in things, or playing in ways, that are different from their interests or what they want to do. So, whereas the Aquarian intention to express "differently" defines and entertains them, their inherent differences can sometimes make it feel like it's hard to "fit in."

Needless to say, this can make Aquarians' personal-relationship needs challenging to understand. They can deeply desire to belong—to a group or a family or just to one other—yet, at the same time, have an intense need to be independent and free. They value intimacy with others, but they also require the freedom to follow their own path.

This push-pull can confuse Aquarians—and others—about how much they're really willing to get involved. If they get too involved, to the point where they feel they're not expressing their individuality, Aquarians might become rebellious or aloof. They can separate from participating with others as a way of maintaining their individuality. But, if Aquarians don't get involved enough, they can feel lonely and isolated. This ambivalence can make Aquarians hard to read. Others may wonder what's really going on with them—they seem so friendly, but also present an air of impersonal detachment as well. In truth, Aquarians might be trying to figure themselves out.

What Aquarians need to find out for themselves (through experience) is that great freedom can come from being *interdependent*. That means they interact with others through their individuality, and give and receive from others' individuality. In

doing so, they come to understand that what's gained from others is far greater than anything they think they have to give up.

Actually, what Aquarians do have to sacrifice in good relationships are the things that block their true individuality, even when they're alone: things like self-involvement, selfishness and their need to "be right." Those traits can entrap even the freest bird, and Aquarians evolve by releasing them. When Aquarians realize that they don't have to give up who they truly are in order to connect with others, they have discovered the key to their Higher Natures.

Because of Aquarians' determined search for individual expression, they can become quite rebellious if they find they are involved in a circumstance, an institution, or even a relationship that they think is trying to suppress their (or anyone else's) expression. Aquarians just won't tolerate anyone controlling another's expression. They will do whatever they can either to make a personal statement of defiance, or to bring people together to make a social statement of defiance. However they do it, Aquarians will let it be known they don't agree, and they won't participate with control or suppression of any sort.

Although rebellion can be a powerful personal statement, Aquarians have to watch the tendency to use rebelliousness as their basic approach to life. Otherwise, they can spend their time rallying against the "norm" of their community, and being uncooperative with everyone and everything in it. But, in doing so, they might not be giving their community a chance, since they are not noticing what's right or what does work. They might miss a spot where they could, in fact, participate and make a valuable contribution.

If Aquarians are constantly rebellious, it might be a signal that they have identified power in the wrong place. At the core of a rebellious attitude can be the notion that authority is outside them and needs to be rallied against. But, in truth, Aquarians possess their own Inner Authority. Rebelliousness might be a signal that Aquarians are needing to honor this Inner Authority a bit more, and pay a bit less attention to what they think is wrong with other people's expression of their own authority. Rebellious feelings might also be telling Aquarians that there is something they need to be doing themselves that they are not; and that they should use their strength to discover what that is and do it.

However, if in their attempt to express their Inner Authority Aquarians find they have become outwardly dictatorial, they can shift out of that mode by remembering that social order and social change are things that everyone needs to contribute to, not just Aquarians. When they realize that other people's plans and strategies might add to theirs—or be different from, but as valid as, theirs—Aquarians can return to the team strategy that brings out the best in them.

In their zealous search for expressing individuality, it is important for Aquarians to keep in mind that the individuality they are truly seeking is that of expressing their Higher Self. Beyond developing their interesting—albeit zany—personality traits, Aquarians can delve even deeper to cultivate their Divine Individuality. They do that by relinquishing their egos' judgments, "shoulds" and fears (which only serve to confine them and their experiences), and, thereby, liberating themselves from them. When Aquarians give themselves the freedom to align with their Higher Nature, they express universal loving, which is heartfelt and joyous, and they allow themselves to appreciate and feel a connection to all people and things.

The Innovator

Aquarians express the archetype of the Innovator by seeking to change, hopefully for the better, whatever interests them. Their inventive minds specialize in making matters progress and evolve. So, instead of sticking with what already works, Aquarians ask, "How can this be done differently?"

Finding how else something can be done is an act of creativity for Aquarians. They are more visionaries than dreamers in that they have a highly pragmatic intention: They want things to be different, but they also want things to work. The act of trying different strategies is exciting for Aquarians; they don't get discouraged if something doesn't work right away—in fact, they find that interesting, too.

Usually, Aquarians will seek to innovate everything they spend time doing. Instead of adhering to the status quo, Aquarians will always try to stamp things with their own unique style. This doesn't stem from needing change to keep boredom at bay (as it does with Geminis and Sagittarians); rather, it stems from the need for *discovery.*

Aquarians might innovate on the physical level by experimenting with the ways in which the most ordinary routines can be improved. (For example, the people who invent two-in-one products are probably Aquarians. "Why just shampoo hair, when you could condition, even color it at the same time?" is an Aquarian inventive—yet pragmatic—approach to an everyday task.)

This innovation is also directed toward how they express their creativity: Aquarians will try really odd things to come up with unusual results. Many of them love art that borders on the surrealistic, or a style that departs from what most others find beautiful.

Mike is a good example of an Aquarian Innovator. Back in the early 1980s, he trained to be a Pilates instructor. (Pilates is a form of exercise.) But he wasn't completely satisfied with the kind of results he was getting. So he incorporated his training as a dancer to innovate movements that helped sculpt bodies a better way. Then, Mike turned his innovative eye toward the Pilates machines themselves. After tinkering with their original design, he started building machines according to his own vision of what worked best. Now, Mike further demonstrates Aquarian tendencies in the open and inviting way he runs his classes. He moves from one person to the next, savoring and enjoying their uniqueness as he does so. Then, when class is over, he detaches from that group and puts his full attention on the group of individuals in his next class.

The key here is that Aquarius wants to see newness. They are after progress. They don't mind trying something really weird, because that might be the best invention of all.

The Awakener

Aquarians personify the archetype of the Awakener because they serve to shake up—or shift—the status quo of whatever they are involved in. Aquarians can serve as lightning rods for themselves and others, engendering a move past conventional ideas, perceptions and attitudes that may no longer be working, toward ones that do. Aquarians' ruling planet, Uranus, charges them with a progressive consciousness, as well as the ability to help others develop a greater awareness of options, which, in turn, can make them all feel more free.

Sometimes, Aquarians do this intentionally by saying or doing things they know will shake up situations and make people think. Other times, Aquarians do this unintentionally by just being themselves. Somehow, that alone can make waves in the status quo.

The Awakener quality in Aquarians helps them give insightful and objective counsel to others. Aquarians have the ability to almost instantly recognize where and how other people are blocking themselves, or making errors in their approach to matters. (They just "know" this—unlike Scorpios and Virgos, who look for it.) And Aquarians are honest and factual in the delivery of their assessments: They consider it more honorable to tell someone straight out where they could remedy matters, rather than protect the other person's feelings and weaknesses by hiding or softening the truth.

For example, an Aquarian will tell someone, "Your need for acceptance is making you do things that are beneath your dignity." Or, "You are ineffective in the way you're managing this office. People are becoming frustrated by your inconsistent manner." These truths can sting, but they can also help.

Aquarians don't mind shocking others with what they say or think, either. Indeed, they like to express ideas that wake people up and get their attention. Aquarians enjoy being the ones who have different ideas from the rest, and they will display them proudly.

Actually, some Aquarians develop a taste for the reactions they get from shocking others, and use shock value as a main tool to awaken. Some Aquarians also have a taste for the attention they call to themselves as a result of shocking others, so they constantly cook up ways to do it. Other Aquarians aren't comfortable with shocking others, because they don't like the separation that causes. They will strive to present their potentially shocking ideas in a way that's easier for others to hear.

When attempting to awaken the thinking of others, Aquarians often set out to prove that they are right. They not only wish to suggest to others that their point of view has merit, they also set out to demonstrate its ultimate truths.

The challenge of Aquarians' urge to prove they are right is when they feel they *have* to be right. In that situation, they will become so adamant about their position, they might override the validity of other people's points of view, instead, narrowly and stubbornly focusing on their own. This might, indeed, get their point across, but it also might backfire on Aquarius. Instead of awakening others, Aquarians might just exasperate—even alienate—those around them. They might just push the buttons of those who don't agree; whom Aquarians might have swayed, had they taken a gentler approach. Not to mention that Aquarians might forgo learning something from someone else.

What works better is for Aquarians to tell the truth as they know it, allowing the truth to speak for itself. In doing so, if they're right, others will become illuminated in due time. If they are wrong (gasp!), they might have the space to realize it.

By far the most pure and powerful demonstration of Aquarians' Awakener archetype comes from the considerable strength of their loving. When they are in touch with their hearts, their unconditional positive regard for others pours through, and they contribute to life in the most remarkable ways. When Aquarians embrace the energy of their hearts, they are able to drop any preconceived notions about what they "should" do or say in order to awaken others, as well as let go of any concepts of what "should" be happening. Instead, Aquarians extend themselves in any way necessary to support others, no matter where those others are in their own humanity and evolution.

Aquarians' loving has great intelligence and wisdom that transcends even their own conscious understanding, allowing them to be in the right place at the right time, and to say just the right thing that can truly help others free themselves. In short, it's Aquarians' hearts that tell them what to do or say in order to make a difference.

Aquarius Laura is a good example of this. She's a dental hygienist who works in a busy dental office. A true Aquarian, Laura makes it a practice to educate herself about world events. She told me that she goes absolutely nuts inside when she hears her coworkers express what she calls "limited views"—views that are provincial, one-sided or discriminating. Prejudiced comments are particularly difficult for Laura to accept. She told me she's tempted to awaken her coworkers by poking them with her dental tools and shouting, "That's not how it is!" But then she cools off by reminding herself of the Higher Aquarian principle that everyone is entitled to their individual opinion, and it's not her job to make them see the error in their thinking. (But she admits that she sure does *think* it.) Instead, she resets her focus on finding those things that she likes about her coworkers. That appreciation helps those around her to blossom.

The Humanitarian

Aquarians embody the archetype of the Humanitarian when they are truly and deeply concerned about their fellow living creatures. Aquarians readily envision a better society, perhaps one where everyone (and everything) is cared for and treated with fairness and respect. Aquarians have enormous faith in the power, abilities and resiliency of the human race.

Aquarians' Humanitarian archetype expresses itself through their need to do their part to contribute to the upliftment and progress of this world. They especially value actions and ideas that support the well-being of others. And they will rally against those ideas, attitudes and actions that squelch personal expression or freedoms, or that disregard the value of others. Prejudice of any sort inflames Aquarians. It goes against the very fiber of their being because they understand that everyone has inherent value, and inherent divinity.

Many Aquarians demonstrate their Humanitarian archetype through their disposition toward community involvement. They will take up a cause (or a series of causes), and devote their time and efforts to supporting it. Aquarians will organize projects, donate money, protest wrongdoing, or all of the above, in an attempt to do something that will make a difference in this world.

Aquarians actively support causes of all kinds, from preservation of the environment to championing human and/or animal freedoms and rights. These Aquarians love not only the cause itself, but also the camaraderie of others working together as a team to achieve progress.

Aquarians also demonstrate their Humanitarian archetype by doing countless considerate things for those around them. They will extend a kindness toward someone who seems left out, or lend a hand to another in need. (For example, Aquarians usually will lend money to someone who asks, even if there's only a slim chance of being repaid.) This uplifts Aquarians and opens their hearts: Whether a significant effort or only a small gesture, it connects Aquarians to another being in a loving way.

Virtually all Aquarians demonstrate their Humanitarian archeytpe through being terrific friends. Aquarians treasure their friends, support them and are as loyal as can be.

Importantly, the Humanitarian archetype operates in a way that somehow makes the world a gentler place. Aquarians deeply desire to help humanity evolve, and each one finds something they can do to help.

However, there is a way that Aquarians can turn their Humanitarian qualities into sour intolerance. Because Aquarians' idealism professes that everyone should contribute to the greater whole, Aquarians can judge someone as being selfish or narrow-minded if their focus (even rightly) is placed only on themselves and their own concerns. Or if someone likes the world just as it is and doesn't want to bother with changing it, Aquarians can be disappointed, thinking that everyone should be moving forward by considering the welfare of the group.

When displeased, Aquarians can become intolerant, even contemptuous of their fellow human beings. They dismiss the value of what people have done, or are doing, thinking it's insignificant. The expression, "loves humanity, hates people," can describe this Aquarian situation.

Aquarians need to keep in mind that others may not have the Aquarian intention to help humanity develop. Sorry: Not everyone is wired to be globally concerned like Aquarians are. And that's as it should be.

What works better is for Aquarians to develop some sort of perspective vis-à-vis their idealism. One thing that helps is realizing that, even though it might not look like it to them, most people are actually doing the best they can. After all, we humans aren't all going to evolve the same way, or at the same time. We are all individuals that way. Remembering that will help Aquarians extend tolerance even toward one who seems to be the pettiest person.

The Aquarius Gifts: Moving Us—and Themselves—Along

Aquarians bring about change, and they do so in a multitude of ways. For one, they have the gift of **Invention** that gives them a knack for seeing how things can be improved upon. Aquarians have a natural curiosity that likes to tinker with what already exists to see what else can be developed. They love to experiment with people or things in order to come up with something new, never before discovered or recognized.

Many Aquarians express their inventiveness through a keen interest in and affinity for technology, science or engineering—and an utter fascination with the potential those fields offer. Many times, these Aquarians have an exceptional understanding of the logic of technology. They love to poke around and study it to learn even more about how it works, always trying new strategies. Experimenting is an integral part of these Aquarians' process of discovery. So even if their hunches don't work so well, they figure they've learned something anyway. But when things do work, they are extremely gratified.

The current technology that Aquarians are particularly interested in is computers. They just know how computers work. It's almost as if their own minds work like computers, so the computer itself is just a natural extension of their consciousness. You will see Aquarians in every possible career relating to computers, from the research and development of them to the placement of them in the marketplace, and everything in between.

The inventive quality of Aquarians appreciates what has already been discovered, but doesn't stay limited to what's known. Instead, they use that as a springboard to push knowledge and concepts forward to explore where else they can take us.

Some Aquarians are good at inventing systems. Because they have a consciousness that can conceptualize, they can see how something could work, even before it's created. They are able to conceptualize how many parts can integrate and contribute to a working whole.

Some Aquarians are inventive with people, understanding the potential human beings have, and inventing new ways for people to do just about anything they do. Aquarians can be quite insightful psychologists, adept body workers, even innovative teachers and coaches. Many times you'll see these kinds of Aquarians in sales or marketing jobs, because they understand how people think and what people want. Whatever field they choose is sure to have a bottom-line interest in helping humanity evolve.

Aquarius is also the sign correlated with genetic engineering, and Aquarians are at the forefront of that field. The Inventor side of Aquarius doesn't really care much about the ethical or moral side of the creation, rather it focuses on advancing its possibilities into a pragmatic function. However, the Humanitarian aspect of Aquarius is intensely interested in ethics, and you might find Aquarians hashing out the moral and ethical issues of tampering with nature—*from either the pro or the con side.*

Some Aquarians are interested in improving life via chemical inventiveness, like the mad scientist who zealously tries mixing substances just to discover what comes of them. Sometimes, this experimenting pays off with the discovery of ways to enhance matter by altering its basic cell structures and component materials.

Aquarius tries to evolve things. So whereas some people object to, say, chemical tampering because it interferes with Nature's—even God's—plan, certain Aquarians figure it is Nature's (or God's) plan to give us the ability to alter substances around us. For example, some Aquarians believe in genetically altered food as an elegant solution to hunger and starvation. But other Aquarians think that kind of inventing is terrible and dangerous, because it can get out of hand and change things without control. What these Aquarians have in common is an interest in the very same subject, and the social ramifications it presents.

Inventiveness takes place in an Aquarian's everyday expression as well. They will fix a broken vacuum with a little piece of wire, or jimmy together common items to make a useful device, or just fix their hair in an innovative manner.

Aquarians also have **Visionary** gifts. Instead of looking at how things are right now, they project forward to the future implications of the actions of right now. This insight into the future isn't in the psychic sense (necessarily) but in a projective one. They can extrapolate where actions will take us, and whether or not the results of those actions will match the original intentions.

This visionary quality expresses itself through Aquarians by means of their ability to just know—or envision—something, without being able to truly explain *how* they know. Aquarians can just see how things will, or could, be. They even try to put a logical explanation to it, but, in truth, it is intuition.

This visionary quality is an integral part of the Aquarian nature. Their consciousness is adept at conceptualizing things that don't yet exist in reality, though they do exist in potential. It is so easy to hold to their greater visions, it's hard for Aquarians to believe others can't—or don't—do it. They wonder why others are willing to accept things the way they are (i.e., mediocre), rather than striving to bring about something truly great.

One Aquarian told me he sees, "Vast and intricately developed concepts in their most perfect state, but which can't yet happen in this world." That's the thrill, and the frustration, of Aquarians' visions: They can conceptualize and envision something perfectly—but, alas!—it doesn't yet exist. On the upside, it can also be thrilling to experiment to find the ways ideals can be made manifest.

Aquarians' visionary quality calls them down the roads less traveled. Instead of doing what's expected—or accepted—they're drawn to try a new approach. This can be incredibly gratifying for Aquarians for a lot of reasons. First, they are doing something different. Second, they might just learn something no one has discovered. Third, they can use that learning to help others.

But, sometimes, going this route can be hard or lonely for Aquarians. Not everyone will understand or accept what they see. Sometimes, Aquarians can feel like strangers in a strange land. That's the lesson of being an Aquarian: to be willing to try things others don't understand, but still find ways to connect with others nevertheless.

Although Aquarians have a deep faith in humanity and human potential, they also recognize the negative potential of the darker side of human nature, so they also envision how society can become horrible. Aquarians foresee, for example, how, if power gets into the wrong hands, or technology is misused, we not only can lose our personal freedoms, but life could become downright dangerous. Because of that, Aquarians usually consider their escape route—a means by which they can remove themselves from society if it goes bad, and protect the ones they love.

Many Aquarians express their visionary qualities by being able to hold that vision for others. They completely believe in other people's dreams and aspirations, and help them keep looking toward their successful future. If someone tells an Aquarian of a goal or a possible win, that Aquarian will say, "Yes! I see that!" (But only if they do, of course. If they don't see it, they will respectfully stay silent.) In doing so, they assist another's personal progress.

Whatever subjects they're concerned with, the visionary can seek a perfection (or purity) that the rest of us can aspire to live up to.

Some Aquarians express their visionary gift through becoming drawn to ideals or interests that later turn out to be very popular. It isn't (necessarily) that Aquarians try to make these things popular, it's just that their consciousness is attuned to what's coming, and they tend to be attracted to things long before the rest of society is. Some Aquarians do set out to be **Trendsetters.** But, by the time others have caught on to the trend they have set, they're already off to do something new.

One of Aquarians' most relied upon gifts is their ability to be **Objective.** Aquarians value logic and keeping to the facts in everything they do and say. So, although they may feel quite emotional about something, Aquarians will always attempt to stand back and consider what the clear, true objective of a matter is. "Let cooler heads prevail," is the motto of Aquarius. They don't want to be deluded by the passions of the moment; rather, they choose to keep themselves calm so they can do what's right.

Although Aquarians seek to be objective, and enjoy the act of researching matters, they are also quite **Intuitive.** Many times their first instinct about something is entirely correct. But they'll still back it up with facts.

Aquarians' objectivity gives them a **Greater Perspective** on what's happening. Instead of looking at events in a vacuum, Aquarians are able to raise their perspective to see how all parts of a matter will impact the bigger picture.

Aquarians' objectivity comes, in part, from their ability to detach. They can pull themselves away from a situation in order to get a clear, unbiased understanding of it. Instead of letting their personal feelings—or the views or emotions of others—sway their thinking, Aquarians use their minds to collect and evaluate the data. This detachment allows them to look at matters with an overview of all the pieces of the puzzle. They will consider the pros and cons, and then attempt to summarize them to determine the most effective way to approach something.

Sometimes, Aquarians' detachment and objectivity can appear to be aloofness. In their attempt to be objective and factual, Aquarians can seem very cool—even cold—as if they hold themselves above the situation. In truth, they might be very concerned, but, because they don't value emotions as much as logic, they might only display what they think, not what they feel. What might seem like an Aquarian being separate from or unfazed by what's going on can actually be their way of trying to extract themselves from it in order to see what would be the best thing to do.

But some Aquarians are, in fact, aloof and don't want to get involved with the stickiness of the personal or emotional dynamics of those around them. They feel better when they use logic and facts to keep themselves apart from what's going on, which is their strategy for retaining their individual space.

The trouble with this approach, however, is that logic isn't everything; emotions and passions dictate much of what goes on, including people's perceptions of things. Sometimes, it's the very feelings or emotions of a situation that hold or connect to the greatest truth. So Aquarians have to learn to factor in the importance of other people's feelings, as well as their own, when looking for the truth of some matters.

Aquarians use their objectivity to **Study and Analyze** people and situations. Generally speaking, they will give people plenty of room to define and express themselves. But because they have great minds (and minds like to judge), Aquarians can also have a tendency to judge people or matters. Being judgmental is the negative side of Aquarians' intelligence, and it prevents them from gaining the objectivity they value. Instead of approaching people or situations with an open mind (and heart), Aquarians can jump to conclusions about people or situations because they think they've got someone all figured out, or that they know what's best and right—as well as what's wrong. This is one of Aquarians' greatest traps: It not only prevents them from the true understanding they seek, it closes off their connection to Universal Loving. Judging separates us from acceptance, and also closes off our hearts.

If Aquarians realize they are judging, they can shift out of it by using their Humanitarian interest in the unique expression of others. That helps them to stay open to understanding the value of other people. Then, they can use their objectivity to **Evaluate** the efficacy of someone's approach or thoughts. The irony is that Aquarians themselves hate being judged.

Although Aquarians can use these gifts of objectivity and greater perspective in global ways, they also use them to deal with their personal concerns. When a problem or a difference of opinion with others arises, Aquarians will use their objectivity, as well as their detachment, to resolve it.

My Aquarian client, Susan, says that when she has an issue with others, she will first polarize the different points of view in an attempt to better understand what the problem is. She tells me she just sits with it for a while, letting it just be until she can return to a levelheaded approach to the problem. That might take a little time, but it allows her to be objective about, instead of reactive to, the situation. Then, she tries to find a way to blend her individual preferences with what the other person needs, so they can work things out. In doing so, she says she is able to let go of any negative or judgmental emotions she might have had toward their differences, and, instead, just focus on resolving them so she can go back to feeling connected to the other person.

Many times, Aquarians will also use this process to come to accept and forgive things others have done that hurt or disappointed them. They will do their best to stand back and sort things out in an attempt to understand—either the other person's side of the story, or the pragmatic solution, which might be to let it go and just move on. (Before they resort to that, though, Aquarians can stay stubbornly resentful.)

The Aquarius Fears: Not Conformity!

Because Aquarians regard their individuality and independence so highly, they can fear being consumed by something—or someone—that obscures or denies them. They can **fear "not being able to breathe," literally or figuratively.** (That correlates to being an Air Sign.) Aquarians so primally need room to express and experiment, they can feel literally suffocated if matters even appear to not allow that.

Aquarians can **fear getting involved in any type of situation—be it a personal relationship or a community or an institution—that might deny their ability to be true to themselves.** Aquarians need to tap into their individuality at all times. The idea that someone or something—including love—could "take them over" and cause them to lose touch with their Self really scares them.

This can result in their avoiding deep involvement with anyone—or anything—in an attempt to keep their individuality intact. Aquarians can retain an air of impersonalness that keeps them detached from others and from situations. But that strategy might rob them of what they enjoy the most in life: connectedness to others.

In order to quell those fears, Aquarians need to develop a trust in themselves and in their actions. When they know that they won't betray themselves or their self-expression by being involved with others (out of a need to belong, or be liked, for example), they are more likely to let others in. When they have confidence that they will stick to their real values, no matter what others want or expect, Aquarians can become deeply involved and committed without fearing loss of self.

Aquarians can also **fear becoming dependent on anyone—or anything—for their well-being.** There are a couple of reasons for this. One is that Aquarians pride themselves on finding their own way and using their own devices to navigate life, and they derive great satisfaction from this. They want to discover what they're capable of and don't want—or need—anyone's help. To them, such help is interference that might compromise the purity of their own skill.

The other reason is that Aquarians can **fear being abandoned** or let down by whatever—or whoever—they depend on. That causes them tremendous pain. It's crushing when someone—or something—doesn't measure up to their expectations, or leaves them in the lurch. So, instead of allowing themselves to feel the vulnerability of counting on someone—or something—that will ultimately let them down or leave them, some Aquarians would rather just take care of matters themselves.

But this fear can also prevent Aquarius from truly connecting with others. They might hold people at arm's length so they don't get overly enmeshed. What works better is for Aquarians to consider themselves *inter*dependent with others. That way, they see the give-and-take of alliances, but also realize they won't fall apart if someone bugs out.

Believe it or not, Aquarians can also **fear not being individualistic enough.** They can fear they're too boring—or too ordinary—and, therefore, don't have something uniquely worthwhile to contribute to others. They fear they might be "cut out of the tribe" (so to speak), or rejected as unlovable. So, in order to ensure their social value, they seek ways to continually offer something interesting.

But, in truth, Aquarians do not have to be different in order to contribute. Their loving essence is valuable enough. When Aquarians understand the value of their own humanity, they realize the innate contribution that makes to others. Nothing more is required of them. They can then participate with others in a genuine way; sometimes, being quite unique and interesting, and, other times, being quite ordinary—yet just as valuable. That's the freedom of heart Aquarians seek.

Aquarius in Relationships: "Friends First!"

Aquarians value their relationships—especially their friendships—very, very highly. Indeed, they can consider friendships to be their greatest purpose, as well as what produces the greatest meaning in their lives. Friendship is of the highest order of love because, to an Aquarian, it means unconditional love—without expecting anything other than love from them, someone is still willing to get to know Aquarius, and do their best to understand them.

Friendship is so important, in fact, that it is an integral part of Aquarians' love relationships. They usually don't seek highly romanticized, emotional alliances (as the Water Signs do). Rather, they want partners with whom they can be true friends. They want to know they can say or do anything, and still be accepted. And they will extend the same to others.

Aquarians' need for freedom is an important consideration in all of their relationships. Even in the best of relationships, Aquarians still need time and space to themselves. This might mean just some time alone with their thoughts, or lots of time to visit with their other (many) friends or acquaintances.

This need for freedom can create some problems when it comes to intimate relationships. Some Aquarians just find committed and personal involvements awkward and stifling. They don't want to be confined by a commitment to just one person, not because there might be someone better or more interesting (like Sagittarius and Gemini), but because they don't want to relinquish their right to be able to meet and know other people. Aquarians might project that if they commit to another, they will have to follow that person's vision of life, rather than their own.

Sometimes, Aquarians try to resolve their conflict between wanting both intimacy and freedom by being attracted to people who are in some way unavailable. They can fall hard for someone who is emotionally distant, committed to another, or living far away. In doing so, Aquarians can at once have an intimacy interest, yet retain their freedom. But this doesn't really work for the Aquarians, because they wind up being neither involved nor free.

Aquarians need to discover all the ways they can remain true to themselves, while simultaneously being committed to others. When they do, they open the door to the lasting and satisfying relationships they truly yearn for.

Aquarians will be attracted to those they find different—from themselves and from the crowd. They like people who have their own unique vision, and demonstrate allegiance to it. So if you're trying to attract an Aquarian, let your individuality shine, and offer your genuine friendship. That's the quickest way to the Aquarian heart.

What turns Aquarians off is any hint of emotional neediness or possessiveness toward them. That suffocates them. They lose interest in others who have heavy or intense emotions; they just don't want to go there. So if you are someone who likes to delve into deep feelings and share them with a partner who will freely express their emotions, an Aquarius might not be the one for you. They'll seem too detached and unavailable to you.

If you're trying to catch the eye of a female Aquarian, go ahead and let your individuality shine. Not in a full-of-self way (that's a turn-off), but in a manner that shows you're truly comfortable and confident being exactly who you are. Then extend your curiosity to her: Who is she, and what is she about? Take the time to ask her questions that go beyond her flip declarations of who she is, into the ones that ask her, "What more can you tell me about that?"

However, avoid the kind of emotional probing that will attempt to expose something unresolved about her, because that will scare her away. Instead, demonstrate that you want to understand more about who she is as a person. And give her room. She doesn't want a partner who's needy, and she'll run in the other direction at the first hint of controlling behaviors or attitudes. She's a free bird and wants to be held with an open hand. She wants a buddy and an equal, a companion in the truest sense of the word.

If you're trying to catch the eye of a male Aquarian, let him see how unique you are, as well as how genuine. He's looking for someone he can share a true friendship with. So draw him out, find out what really makes him tick. But keep to the facts, because he's uncomfortable with deep emotional scenes. Find out what his visions are, what he'd like to accomplish, how he'd like to see the world work. And let him know your thoughts as well. He's seeking someone who's confident in their own individuality; not someone who's a doormat.

Many times, Aquarian males are drawn to very strong, perhaps flamboyant, partners (like Leos, their opposite sign). Aquarians enjoy other people's ability to express themselves and relate in favorable ways to others. But if they don't find the same pizzazz and attention directed at them as well, they can loose patience with the flamboyant one, or consider them selfish. (Once an Aquarius considers someone selfish, well, that's it.)

Aquarian men love affection in private, but can be embarrassed or uncomfortable with public displays. So when you're out with him, maintain a level of appreciative decorum. But when you're alone, go ahead and show him just how inventive you can be. He'll not only appreciate it, he'll do his best to return it back to you even more.

But, mainly, be this man's friend. Let him know that he is fascinating and special to you, and you will be at his side, no matter what he chooses to do. Remember, though, that you are at his side not out of clinginess, but, rather, idealism: You'll support him in going after his many visions. Finally, be good to his many friends, and he'll treasure your companionship all the more.

The Last Word on Aquarius

Inventive, innovative and (sometimes) eccentric, Aquarians really express their essence when they recognize that they can be independent, yet still connect the whole of humanity through loving.

Chapter 12

Pisces

(February 19–March 20)

Pisces is the quality in you that is imaginative and mystical, seeks to merge and empathize with others, and enjoys rescuing those in need. It's also the part of you that's learning the expansive power of sacred self-sacrifice.

Pisces people are dreamy—in the literal sense: They often live in a world of dreams and work to overlay it upon what the rest of us calls reality. They can seem to know and respond to what you're thinking without even recognizing that's what they're doing. Life is rarely dull around a Pisces, even less dull if you are a Pisces!

Pisces are extremely caring and gentle individuals. They have the ability to expand their personal boundaries in order to empathize with what others are feeling and needing. In fact, Pisces are saviors at heart: Their compassion prompts them to lend a helping hand to those in need, and they willingly make personal sacrifices in order to uplift and heal others. If you want to feel loved, spend time with a Pisces.

Pisces are also vividly imaginative: Their rich fantasy lives help them to imagine visions that uplift them, inspiring Pisces to connect their visions to life's greater possibilities. That, together with their natural intuition, gives Pisces a deeper glimpse into the magical and mystical truths of life.

The Pisces Mission: Gaining the True Self Through Self-Sacrifice

All of us are learning what Pisces are born to discover: Self-sacrifice can be a sacred act. By sacrificing those qualities in our nature that don't serve us, and developing and enhancing the qualities that do, we awaken to our Higher Nature, which is Universally Loving.

Pisces have a tremendous urge to merge with something that is greater than themselves. They yearn for an ultimate connectedness with something quite mystical and timeless—the oneness from which we all emanate. One way Pisces can accomplish that is by surrendering their own desires of how things should be, and, instead, going along with the natural flow of life. Another way is by practicing selfless service, or the act of giving of themselves so completely that they are able to step out of their limitations and realize their greater capacity.

In doing these things, Pisces tap into the fullness wherein they understand that they are bountiful, limitless and fulfilled. From there, they can reach out and assist others through the overflow of Universal Loving and compassionate understanding.

The Pisces Challenge: Sacred Sacrifice, Not Martyrdom

Pisces can learn the higher expression of self-sacrifice by involving themselves in the lower expression of self-sacrifice, which is martyrdom and victimization. Sometimes, Pisces mistakenly believe that they have to *give up everything*—including taking good care of themselves, or maintaining their healthy personal boundaries—even all they value, in order to be a good or caring person. But that's not the sacred self-sacrifice they are to learn: That's just plain *not* taking care of themselves.

Instead, Pisces are learning to sacrifice anything in their nature—or in their lives—that keeps them distracted, confined or separate from their Higher Self. As Pisces learn to sacrifice things like distracting fantasies, emotional indulgences, even fears, they more readily tap into their true essence.

In truth, the kind of self-sacrifice Pisces are learning to express takes nothing of value away from them. Instead, when Pisces practice sacred self-sacrifice they are given the rich rewards of expansion, awakening and empowerment.

The Pisces Key: Taking Care of Their Spirit

Pisces are the most uplifted when they realize that the highest act of service is serving themselves and their Spirit. When Pisces attend to aligning with and developing their own Higher Nature (and not just indulging their lower wants and desires), they are able to tap into their Divine Essence, which is magnificent. That fulfilled, they are most capable and wise in assisting others.

Some Things FISHy

Pisces' astrological symbol is Two Fish, facing in opposite directions and tied together in the middle. There are many ways to interpret Pisces' symbol, and that reflects Pisces' rich and complex nature. Just as their symbol can be approached from many levels, so can Pisces identify and express themselves on many levels. This makes them fascinating, as well as pretty much impossible to fully figure out.

One interpretation of Pisces' fish swimming in opposite directions reflects the "duality" in Pisces' intentions. Oftentimes, Pisces want to take two opposing courses of action concurrently. For example, they might adore their career as a designer, yet wonder if they should actually be a psychologist. Or Pisces will be drawn to beginning a new relationship, while still intending to remain loyal to the relationship they are already in.

An even deeper interpretation of Pisces' symbol addresses the dual nature of their awareness: Pisces are fascinated by the offerings of this world, yet feel equally compelled to "let it all go" in order to connect more deeply with their spirituality. Pisces are at once bound to this planet, yet yearning to soar to the Divine.

This duality in Pisces' nature gives them a tremendous range of perspectives. They can at once be very knowledgeable and involved in worldly matters, yet at the same time be very sensitive and developed in spiritual matters. By keeping their awareness of both the spiritual and material levels, Pisces are able to recognize the Divine Essence within everyone and every earthly thing. Thanks to this ability, Pisces can better assess what has real value to them and their evolution versus what is just action for action's sake.

Some Pisces feel they have to make a choice between their spirituality and their worldliness. They needn't. In fact, one of their life lessons is learning how to find a balance between the two. The most satisfied Pisces seem to find a way to go about matters of this world with an attitude that, no matter what they do—even if it's an everyday task—it's an avenue of spiritual awakening. So, Pisces make dinner, get promotions and raise their children, all with an understanding that they are spiritual beings living a human experience.

But this duality in Pisces' nature can make life challenging for them. Pisces can feel attracted to multiple directions (and people) much of the time. As they do one activity, another might seem more interesting or glamorous, and Pisces start feeling "pulled" in that direction. Sometimes, this can lead to Pisces doubting—or feeling ambivalent about—their choices, or fearing they might never be satisfied with what they choose. Or Pisces' urge to go in multiple directions can tempt them to let themselves become scattered or overcommitted, as they try to accommodate all of their interests.

When this happens, it's important that Pisces remind themselves that the magic of life doesn't come from chasing down and doing everything that intrigues them. Rather, Pisces create their own magic by being 100 percent involved and present in whatever they do. That allows them to fully experience the depth and specialness of even their most ordinary moments.

The UnderWATER World of Pisces

Pisces is one of the three Water Signs (Cancer and Scorpio are the other two). That means Pisces are most comfortable with the emotional side of their nature. Water gives Pisces a deep alliance with their feelings and those of others, which enables them to connect with other sentient beings.

The unique Piscean expression of the Water element is their ability to reach out to others with tremendous understanding and compassion. Pisces are most capable of empathically sensing and feeling what others are feeling, even if it's painful. Pisces understand that life involves a rich range of emotions—from joy to anguish and all points in between—and they accept that every emotion offers a valuable experience.

Being a Water Sign makes Pisces extremely sensitive and tender. There is a harmlessness about Pisces, in that it hurts them to see anyone or anything hurt. So they do what they can to treat all around them with a soft touch and gentle consideration (and they appreciate that kind of consideration in return).

However, Pisces' emotional vulnerability can sometimes open them to becoming deeply hurt. Thoughtless or hurtful words or acts of others, whether intended or not, can seem to go straight through to Pisces' heart and soul, wounding them to their very core. Whereas other signs can deflect or at least quickly recover from hurt feelings, Pisces take a while to heal. But they can. Usually, they do that by extending their compassion to themselves. It also helps when Pisces use another aspect of their inner wisdom: their ability to forgive, to let go and move on.

The MUTABLE Quality of Pisces: Flowing with the Changing Currents of Life

Pisces is one of the four Mutable Signs (Gemini, Virgo and Sagittarius are the other three). Mutability is the changeable quality that allows Pisces to adjust and flow in order to cooperate with whatever is going on. Mutability also seeks variety, and prompts Pisces to keep moving and exploring all that life offers.

Pisces' particular expression of Mutable energy is the ability to *adapt themselves emotionally* to the needs of their environment. They easily sense what feelings and attitudes are present in a situation, and emotionally join in so they can resonate with others and connect with them.

In fact, more than any other sign, Pisces is the most chameleonlike. They have an uncanny awareness that they can be anything (and nothing), and they fluidly become whatever is necessary to align with whatever is going on around them. So when Pisces are with one kind of person (or in one kind of situation), they can mold their expression to reflect that. Later, when they're with another kind of person (or in another kind of situation), they will adapt themselves to reflect that one.

This chameleonlike quality expresses itself in Pisces' versatile thinking. Instead of expecting that life should be black or white (like

Capricorn or Taurus), Pisces can see life as an endless spectrum of grays—and that even includes the way they see themselves. Pisces needn't stick to a rigid set of attitudes and expressions in order to feel genuine.

Interestingly, Pisces' chameleonlike ability works both ways: Many times, others will project traits and qualities onto Pisces that they don't (necessarily) inherently possess. It's almost as if Pisces are mirrors that easily reflect what others want to see.

Pisces is a **Transpersonal Sign.** That means Pisces go beyond just identifying with their own personhood, and, instead, identify with the greater whole. This whole depends on the individual Pisces: It can be just one other person, or their family, or the whole of humanity. Usually, Pisces use their *feelings* to connect with others. And they are good at it. When someone confides to Pisces that they are feeling a particular way, it's as if Pisces reach into a filing cabinet in their consciousness and retrieve a sort of memory of, "Ah! Yes! *This* is what they feel!"—whether or not they've actually had the other's experience personally.

The Depth of NEPTUNE

Neptune rules the sign of Pisces. Neptune governs matters that cannot be proven or entirely understood, but nevertheless exist: like spirituality, intuition, imagination, illusions, even physics. Neptune gives Pisces not only gifts in such areas, but also a predisposition to wanting to explore those areas more fully, and possibly even make a career of one of them.

Neptune also governs the seas and oceans, and that gives Pisces an affinity for huge, ocean-like feelings and experiences, as well as a love of the ocean itself. Just as a human can feel very small in relation to great bodies of water, Pisces can be aware of their tininess in relation to the great, powerful "unknown." This unknown can be powerful feelings Pisces sense from the world, or it can be the magnificent presence of Spirit.

As grand as these experiences are, they can also make Pisces feel insignificant. When that happens, Pisces need to remember that it's only their ego that feels insignificant: Their Spirit is great. When Pisces feel small, they're being challenged to connect with the grandness of their Spirit.

Neptune's rulership of Pisces gifts them with a *Developed Intuition.* Many times, Pisces know things before they happen, intuit the true feelings of others, or tell a friend where to find their lost pet. Pisces' intuition not only gives them helpful hints about how to navigate life, it goes even further to give them glimpses into the workings of the Divine.

Pisces regularly have inner experiences that let them know there's something grander than what humans normally acknowledge is going on here. That's a very special gift, indeed.

Neptune is also associated with glamour, and gives Pisces a taste for—and/or an ability to create—situations that are romantic, dramatic, special, magical and larger-than-life beautiful. The attraction toward sparkly glamour is a reflection of Pisces' spiritual urge to "go for the Light."

Glamour (every Pisces considers different things glamorous) can be really exciting and intoxicating for Pisces. But they need to remember to look past the illusions of glamour to see what it is really made from. Otherwise, in Pisces' sparkling intoxication, they could allow themselves to be hoodwinked by people and things that seem like something special, indeed, when, in truth, they are somehow artificial.

Neptune also rules illusion, and more than any other sign, Pisces have an *Understanding of the Power of Illusion*. They know that our perceptions shape a huge portion of what we consider reality. And Pisces know how to manipulate perceptions in order to shift current reality to make it (hopefully) better for themselves.

Photography (at which Pisces can excel) is a good example of this. A picture can tell a thousand words. Yet, change the angle, the lighting, the focus of any picture, and it tells a completely different story of the exact same event. Pisces know they can do the same with their consciousness. They can shift the focus, the "light," or the angle that they approach any situation from and change their understanding of it. Or they can change other people's perceptions of things by shifting the perspective as well. And they do, regularly.

Pisces are learning to guide their perceptions so they are uplifted and expanded by them. A wise man once said, "You'd be a fool to lose in your own fantasies." The same goes for Pisces' perceptions. If Pisces interpret their experiences as something bad or against them, they are not only working against themselves, it's likely they are perceiving incorrectly. If, instead, Pisces learn to perceive whatever happens as a valuable opportunity and gift provided so they can grow and develop, they are leveraging their perceptions to win.

Some Pisces get caught in the negative side of Neptune's illusions by becoming deceptive themselves. It's tempting for Pisces to sneak in a little white lie here and there, if only to make things (and themselves) more interesting. Or, Pisces can be so adept at conjuring up fantasies that they believe they can convince anyone of anything. They figure if no one realizes they've been untruthful, well, everything's okay. These Pisces can tend to lie to others, but they also lie to themselves. Then it becomes confusing to be them because they present themselves so differently from their reality that they lose touch with their inner core of identity. It works best if Pisces acknowledge to themselves that they're not stating the whole truth, so they can stay clear inside themselves.

The true lesson of illusions is that things aren't as they appear to be. For example, we may seem like we're bumbling humans, yet in truth we are great beings in human bodies that sometimes bumble. The challenge of Pisces is to go past the limits of the illusions of life and keep their eye on the spiritual truths. Whatever Pisces find these truths to be, they will involve loving and connectedness as a theme.

The Pisces Archetypes: Dreaming, Helping and Transcending

In order to support Pisces in accomplishing their mission of discovering the higher expression of sacrifice, Pisces (and those who are Pisces-like) will fulfill the archetypes of the Selfless Helper, the Dreamer and the Mystic.

The Selfless Helper

Pisces embody the Selfless Helper archetype because they have a profound drive to help others in need. If they see anyone—or anything—in need of assistance, they are right there, doing whatever they can to assist. Pisces are honored to provide this kind of service because being able to lend a helping hand or helping heart brings great meaning and purpose to their lives.

When Pisces act on their Selfless Helper energy, they tap into the abundant emotional and spiritual rewards that come from service. Pisces can give from such a pure devotion that they let go of their own ideas of how things should go, and, instead, connect with an intuitive sense of what's really needed. Service allows Pisces to tap into the resourcefulness of their inner core. When they do, they feel expanded, powerful and plentiful, and have all the energy they need to take care of themselves, as well as to assist others. That's a high state of consciousness—one that gives Pisces the feeling of connectedness to the whole. And that's what Pisces are truly after.

Really, selfless service is so magical for Pisces that they wonder why everyone doesn't practice it. It empowers Pisces and helps them to accomplish magnificent feats. Selfless service is a positive avenue by which Pisces can learn the joy of sacred self-sacrifice. The more they step out of themselves to give, the more they step into their greater selves. In doing so, they realize who they truly are.

One of the strongest motivations for Pisces portraying the Selfless Helper is their remarkable sensitivity to the weight of the world. Perhaps more than any other sign, Pisces is attuned to pain and suffering, which can seem so pervasive that Pisces feel they are the core of the human experience. Whereas some signs try to avoid recognizing pain and suffering (all the Fire Signs, for example), Pisces *can't help but notice it* because they resonate with it at a very deep level.

Pisces have a remarkable understanding of pain. Many have experienced pain and suffering as avenues for their own redemption. Pain's exquisite poignancy somehow connects Pisces to something greater than themselves. Pisces' Selfless Helper intends to help others use their own experience of pain as an avenue for redemption as well. And, because everyone suffers at one time or another, Pisces understand that pain can be a common experience, a bridge that spans the distance between people, bringing them together.

Pisces' awareness of their own pain and difficulties leads to tremendous compassion for the difficulties others face. Moreover, it prompts them, through their Helper archetype, to do something about it. Whenever they notice that anyone or anything is hurt or needs help, Pisces will use whatever resources they have to try to fix it. So professions that involve assisting others in some way can be intensely gratifying to them. All aspects of psychology, counseling (including addictions counseling) and healing are natural professions for Pisces.

Pisces certainly don't need to be in a formal setting to extend help to others. They can find countless ways to help out. Anything from being a compassionate friend, to offering a look of kindness to a troubled stranger, to jumping out of their car on a rainy night to rescue a stray dog will work to satisfy Pisces' Helper need.

Pisces' Selfless Helper archetype urges them toward redemption. They want to make an impact so the world can be a better place. So, they seek to bring upliftment and resolution to any areas where they see darkness or pain. Pisces are so driven to this, it can seem to others that they are on a crusade. They zealously try to help others redeem themselves from any bad choices or loneliness (even from bad hair days) by lending sincere support and encouragement.

But the truth is, each of us has to choose to redeem ourselves. So it works best if Pisces don't set out to actually redeem others, but, rather, to support them so they can redeem themselves. And, since not everyone wants to be redeemed, it's important for Pisces to understand that that's their individual choice, not an indication that Pisces haven't done—or tried hard—enough.

The challenge of having this powerful Helper archetype is that Pisces can believe they *have to* serve others, even if it's at the expense of attending to their own basic needs. Instead of giving what they can, while nonetheless taking good care of themselves, Pisces might exhaust their own personal resources in an attempt to take care of others.

Sometimes, it's guilt that motivates Pisces to help others. Because they are aware of another person's difficulties, Pisces can (mistakenly) think it's their obligation to rectify them. Other times, Pisces feel such sympathy for another's predicament, they'll try to help fix it just to gain their own relief. They can go to great lengths to alleviate another person's pain, even to the point of trying to absorb it themselves.

For the sake of their own mental health, Pisces need to make some sort of peace with their sensitivity to the needs and suffering of others. That way, their need to help does not become a compulsion. What some Pisces use to maintain their perspective is the understanding that each and every person has their own path to take, complete with the freedom to make choices. Some will make good choices, others won't. Suffering and pain can serve as powerful feedback that can teach someone to make a better choice. If Pisces try to take another's pain away, or alleviate it before they've gained the lesson they need from it, they might be robbing that person of their greatest teacher.

Sometimes, Pisces can go way beyond simply helping others to attempting to downright rescue them. Pisces might believe that others cannot handle the bad or difficult things they're experiencing. Pisces might feel they are stronger than the person going through the difficulty, or that their own need to rescue is more important than the person's need to work through the situation on their own. This can be exacerbated if Pisces believe that they and others are simply *victims* of situations, rather than cocreators of them.

When Pisces believe they have to rescue others, for whatever reason, it is entirely possible that they will initiate a crusade to assist those who don't necessarily want their help—or don't need it in the way Pisces are offering it. Sometimes, a Pisces will exhaust themselves by going to heroic lengths to try to rescue someone, who, in the end, just goes back to doing what they were doing (and recreating the problem) before Pisces came rushing in to save them from themselves. Had Pisces asked first, they might have found out their help wasn't wanted.

Another pitfall can be that others willingly take what Pisces are generously offering, but fail to give anything back in return. This can devastate Pisces because they were so sure that they could create a beautiful connection through helping.

Perhaps the best way Pisces can use their Selfless Helper energy is to intend to do what's for the Highest Good for someone. Of course, few of us know what the highest good really is. But that intention prepares Pisces to use their wisdom and compassion to support others in finding that place of strength within themselves to deal with their life's challenges the best way they can. Pisces' compelling loving presence alone can help others learn to make better choices (i.e., choices that produce more of what they want in their lives, rather than difficulty or pain). That way, Pisces needn't do anything to actually "rescue" others, but, rather, can hold the Light—and Vision—by which others can rescue themselves.

If Pisces overidentify with being a Helper, they can come to believe that their worth hinges on helping and rescuing others. When that's the case, Pisces can seek out others who need their help, merely to fulfill Pisces' own need for validation. If Pisces need to be needed, it can lead them to actually support other people's weaknesses just so they have something to help them out with. This can really keep Pisces—and the others concerned—stuck. Pisces can devote so much of their time and energy to trying to save others from their problems that they might neglect to deal effectively with their own. In fact, it's a Pisces' trick to try to put off dealing with their own issues by keeping their attention on those of others. It's good to be helpful to others, but Pisces have to be just as helpful to themselves.

In truth, the only person Pisces are really responsible for saving is themselves. They are learning to have compassion (not self-pity) for themselves, whereby they regard themselves as beings who have intrinsic value and worth. Pisces' job is to take excellent care of themselves, so they can have a full reservoir from which they can assist others. This isn't a self-involved kind of self-care, where Pisces are consumed by trying to satisfy every personal need and want they feel. Rather, it is a mission to care for their Spirit. That means doing those things that keep them healthy, balanced emotionally, and using their adept perceptions to notice the goodness that's all around them.

Sometimes, Pisces can believe that Selfless Helping involves suffering. Then, they'll think they have to become a martyr—or at least feel like one, in order to be good or spiritual. Pisces can then sacrifice everything—from their truth or their essence, to their savings account—in order to live up to this definition of service, hoping it will redeem another.

This is an error in approach. Pisces' primary calling is to take good care of the Spirit within themselves. If Pisces sacrifice what's truly them, they've given over the very thing they're here to develop and nurture. And if Pisces allow themselves to be martyrs, they have limited not only their freedom of expression, but also their avenues of being able to assist others. Someone who remains in an abusive relationship, for example, is far less free to reach out to others than someone who's unencumbered by that kind of oppression.

The flip side of Pisces' Helper archetype is the Victim, which *they* display when they feel that *they* are in need of being rescued. Pisces can feel their lives involve more than their fair share of suffering, which they don't deserve. They can wonder why bad things happen to them, while good things happen to others. This can lead to self-pity, where Pisces' focus stays on what's wrong, rather than on the redeeming lessons their difficulties could be offering them.

Feeling like a victim can even prompt a Pisces to act against their inherently kind nature; to be mean, even cruel, to others. They might think they have to be severe in order to keep themselves safe. Or they can justify aggressive behavior, thinking that others "deserve it" because they've been hurtful. But, in truth, being mean to others hurts Pisces as much as it hurts them. It not only perpetuates negativity, but also strikes against Pisces' own Spirit because they are so attuned to others and are so innately compassionate.

If Pisces find they are feeling like a victim or martyr, it's a signal that they need to evaluate their decisions and actions to see how they helped set that up. Pisces should ask themselves if they are choosing to put other people's well-being ahead of their own, to the point of neglecting themselves. Alternatively, they could look to see if their need to serve others is interfering with their need to serve their Spirit. Or, they could consider whether they think they are going to win extra spiritual points because they are suffering. Answering "yes" to any of these suggestions might indicate that Pisces is off course.

It's highly possible that Pisces have somehow glamorized being a victim. They can consider being a victim a higher or more evolved expression, because victimhood is neither selfish nor willful. But they must sacrifice that belief, because there is nothing noble about being a victim.

Pisces can believe that the suffering—through pain or withstanding burdens—can somehow strengthen them or help them more deeply access Spirit. And it can. But it's not the only approach. Suffering can break down the ego, so all that's left is the pure essence of who they truly are. Indeed, it can be a powerful approach to spiritual development.

However, there are more uplifting and expansive approaches to life's challenges. Pisces could make choices that involve grace and ease, means by which Pisces can arrive at the same high place. **Ultimately, it's up to Pisces to reach past pain and suffering into the joy and peace that is just as present. In doing so, Pisces act as brilliant lights of love and support, and that in itself awakens and redeems others.**

The Dreamer

Pisces personify the Dreamer archetype because, well, they are dreamy. Pisces' consciousness isn't limited by the mere reality most others agree on. They feel free to augment their experience of everyday life by using their imaginations to add extra zip and zing to whatever is going on. That elevates Pisces' experience of even the most ordinary acts of life, and helps them to connect with the bigger picture.

One of the ways Pisces use their Dreamer archetype is to dream up some great fantasies that spice up life and make it more magical for them. For example, Pisces could imagine themselves living another, more exotic kind of life, or enjoying a fabulous relationship with someone they've not even met—or even envision a different kind of world or culture around them. These dreams can be very real to Pisces because they understand that, if something is happening in their imagination it might be as valid as if it's happening in their real-life experience. **Actually, for many Pisces, there is a very thin line between fantasy and reality, to the point that it can many times be very questionable to them which is which.**

Connie, a very creative and spiritual Pisces, let me in on the simple key she uses to discern between her fantasies about how things could be versus her present reality. She asks herself, *Is this happening right now?* In doing so, she brings her focus into the present as it's happening, without dismissing the possibility of manifesting her fantasy.

Another way Pisces use their Dreamer archetype is through Magical Thinking. To Pisces, life is bursting with possibilities. Pisces can imagine things happening that others would argue just aren't possible. But that does not limit Pisces. They adhere to the motto, "If you can envision it, you can create it." Pisces' Magical Thinking doesn't bother with combing through facts or looking at what has been done in the past in order to evaluate if something can be done. Instead, it jumps from point A to point Z of fully imagined outcomes.

When Magically Thinking, Pisces are playing with life, trying to stretch it to find out where the limits are. Others (like Earth Signs) may find that frustrating because they judge that Pisces are just not being reasonable. What they fail to understand is, Pisces don't necessarily care if those things do happen, they just like considering them. The real point is that they might, indeed, be possible, and Pisces are right in envisioning them.

But problems can arise if Pisces let their Magical Thinking keep them from rationally thinking things through before taking action. Pisces might become so focused on what they imagine as possible that they neglect considering the practicality of what is actually needed.

My Pisces client, Sean, used Magical Thinking to envision himself making a fortune in the stock market. He spent hours dreaming and imagining what his life was going to be like when he had enough money to buy himself and all his buddies lavish gifts, and then have money left over for charity. So he gathered all his savings and invested them in three stocks he had good "gut feelings" about. Sean was so sure his choices were "winners," he didn't bother to research the stocks he decided upon. Unfortunately, those three stocks were only winners in his fantasy. In the real world, they were losers, and Sean lost his savings along with his imagined fortune. That devastated him, but it also taught him an invaluable lesson. Sean realized that, along with dreaming the big dreams, he also needed to investigate the facts. Now he's a very successful investor, who still gets good vibes about stocks, but he studies them before he buys.

Pisces' imaginativeness translates into prolific creativity. Most Pisces have a need to express their visions through some sort of art, and they are good at it. Music, painting and acting are all likely interests for Pisces, and make great career choices for them as well. Pisces need to express and dramatize the dreams that go on inside them. For Pisces, art is not necessarily only about making something beautiful (as it is for Libras): It's more about the act of transcending or merging. They love the act of creating because they are able to witness something that was once formless coming into form. And Pisces love the surrendering process it takes to create: the releasing of their own notions of what something could—or should—be, and discovering what it wants to be. Really, art is a completely magical, if not downright spiritual, process for Pisces. Pisces can paint and merge with the colors; or play music that moves them to the depths of their souls; or sculpt and marvel at an inanimate object "coming alive."

And Pisces are actors. Whereas some signs might use their egos to entertain (Leos, Geminis and Sagittarians, for example), Pisces act by losing their egos and becoming entirely enmeshed in the characters they portray. Pisces love becoming embroiled in the drama of another's life, because it connects them to the wholeness of the human condition.

Pisces' Dreamer consciousness makes them particularly impressionable. Because their vivid imaginations can entertain almost anything, they can *believe* almost anything. If someone says something is true, Pisces might wholeheartedly believe it, seeing no reason not to. This gives them a wonderful openness to all the possibilities life presents. However, it also sets them up to be duped.

Being impressionable can make Pisces gullible—especially if they don't check things out. Eager to believe what others tell them (or what they tell themselves), Pisces might not take the time to investigate the truth for themselves. They might even ignore the fact that what someone says—or what they promise—doesn't match their behavior.

(This can be especially troublesome in intimate relationships.)

So Pisces need to take extra care to make sure that what they perceive is accurate. Sometimes, they learn this the hard way through situations where others deceive them or take advantage of them. They can sputter an innocent, "But they said . . ." and seem stunned that others would fool them. In truth, someone just saw that Pisces' gullibility made them an easy mark. Pisces can feel blindsided by these kinds of situations, believing there was nothing they could have done about them. Then, Pisces might consider themselves victimized, and lose faith in their own ability to distinguish good people—and acts—from bad.

If Pisces believe their dreamy openness creates problems for them, they might shut it down. They can develop a type of "hardness"—a defense mechanism wherein they believe nothing and dream nothing, instead listening to everything with an ear of suspicion, even doubt. These Pisces are tough and resolve never to let anyone take advantage of them again. But, inwardly, they're disappointed and sensing something is missing. They are right. They've shut themselves off from the magic that's their birthright. That's what's missing.

This is a shame. It is the tapping into the magic and the openness to wonder that distinguishes Pisces from all others. Shutting that off not only makes life one-dimensional and unnecessarily rigid, it can also inhibit spiritual awareness.

It works much better if Pisces use their experiences of being "burned" to learn more about themselves. Pisces benefit from using any experiences of being taken advantage of (or fooled) to identify their blind spots, which others were able to capitalize on. That way, Pisces can understand how they got taken advantage of, remedy that without losing their ability to dream, and become wiser by learning from the error they made.

Some Pisces use their dreams and fantasies to escape being conscious of what's going on in their lives, rather than using them to augment what's going on. They hang out in their imagination to deny what's happening, or to space out on their commitments. Then, they're misusing the Dreamer energy. Sometimes, life can seem really harsh or simply boring for Pisces, so they'll help it along by imagining something better. But there is a difference between considering other options and not staying present with what *is*.

Getting lost in the Dreamer archetype can cause Pisces to be irresponsible to the life they have created. They might get so involved in their fantasies they can "forget" about facing their own challenges. Pisces might put off confronting a partner about a problem or fail to get a project in on time, because either they've done those things in their heads or they prefer their fantasies of things and just don't want to "mess it up" with the reality. Pisces can also space out doing the more ordinary, mundane things, thinking they're inconsequential. They can put off paying bills until they're past due, forget they promised to water a vacationing friend's plants, or figure they can be late for a dinner date—even if it's for *their* birthday. Although they can seem like little issues to Pisces Dreamers, these things make up the foundation of functional life.

Needless to say, if Pisces' Dreamer energy distracts them from their worldly agreements, those around them can be quite frustrated by what they consider to be Pisces' spaciness. Pisces might have spent the afternoon envisioning world peace, but what others notice is that they forgot to mail the tax return. *Who cares? It doesn't matter in the scheme of things,* Pisces think. But those around them (especially the Earth Signs) think, *I care!* They want Pisces to pay attention.

If Pisces find they are more interested in and attentive to their fantasies than their actual lives, they might need to evaluate the choices they have been making. Chances are, Pisces are not pursuing something they truly desire, or they have given up on a goal that might really be right for them. Or they have gotten themselves involved with something they don't like, and they're shirking the responsibility of getting out of it. Pisces' lives are their greatest canvas: If they don't like what they have created, it's up to them to change it to something that they do like.

Pisces also express this Dreamer archetype by needing time to just reflect. Whereas some signs have a need to always be doing something—to produce, to read, to think, to move—Pisces have an essential need to just *be.* When Pisces let themselves just "be," their consciousness can disconnect from the concerns of this world and begin to move toward expanded awareness. "Doing nothing" is actually doing something very important for Pisces: It is Pisces' time to connect with Spirit as they know it.

So Pisces need to take time to be with themselves. This is not necessarily napping on the couch, although that might work. It is more about activities that have a sense of "timelessness." Meditation, for example; or, fly-fishing where they watch the water rippling for hours; or, just wandering around a garden without feeling like they need to pull a weed. That's sacred time. Pisces need it. It heals and uplifts them.

Pisces' Dreamer archetype supports their spiritual growth by giving them the ability to dream God. By using their imaginative gift to imagine what God would be like, look like—what it would be like to rest in the Heart of God—they can prepare and open their consciousness to further aligning with God. Remember the saying, "Whatever a person holds in their heart they become." As Pisces hold the Divine in their consciousness, they are able to become it.

The Mystic

Pisces' Mystic archetype expresses itself through their need and propensity for transcendence. Pisces' consciousness expands beyond the limits of worldliness to tap into something quite expanded, even to the point of Divine Awareness. Pisces transcend in many ways, but with a common thread of spirituality: a timelessness, a wholeness and a sense of overall connectedness. There is boundaryless-ness in Pisces' consciousness that recognizes what mystics have reported throughout the centuries: We are all one. Even the most seemingly down-to-Earth Pisces report experiences of a profound merging, connecting and unifying presence. Indeed, it's that feeling of the Ultimate Connectedness that is the elixir of life for Pisces.

The Mystic expression of Pisces has a quality of selflessness wherein they transcend identification with their bodies, minds and emotions, and connect with a greater, more expanded aspect of their essence. Some call this their Spirit, or their soul; others simply relate to it as a loving feeling. However they explain it, Pisces have an awareness that they are much more than who their personality seems to be. This isn't the result of an overblown ego; rather, it is the result of Pisces stepping out of the boundaries of their egos to recognize reality from a higher perspective.

Part of the Pisces Mystic archetype stems from their being the final sign of the zodiac. Pisces have a sense that things are coming to completion. They feel they have one foot in and one foot out of this world—wherever that may be. (And some Pisces think that feet, in general, are out of this world, but that's another topic entirely.)

Many Pisces experience this connection to something beyond this Earth in the form of an inexplicable world-weariness, and a readiness to go on. Some don't know where that would lead them; others define it as meeting their Maker. This isn't morbid or rooted in a fascination with death (as it is with Scorpio). Rather, it's a resolve to transcend this world and move on. Those who believe in reincarnation often have the sense that they are very old souls, and would prefer to be done. Maybe it is their last life—or the last of a cycle of certain kinds of life experiences—but even the Pisces who believe we live only one lifetime have a yearning to go to distant horizons.

So Pisces' experience can have a bittersweetness: Pisces can feel they are looking at their beloveds for the very last time, or watching their last beautiful sunset, or listening to their final gorgeous melody—even when they're still teenagers. Many Pisces intend to live a life full of experiences, kind of like a checklist before they transcend. *Did I feel pain? Pleasure? Was I of service? Did I love?* They want to make sure they've partaken of every experience humanly possible.

Many Pisces undergo a mystical experience through a type of

dissolving: Who they think they are (i.e., their bodies and personalities) seems to disintegrate and give way to a sense that they're all Spirit—or Light or Love. Some Pisces experience themselves liquefying into Light or Energy. While these reports might be met with some skepticism from others whose sense of self is rocklike and solid (like Earth Signs), to Pisces, they are as real as, if not more real than, everyday reality.

Pisces can experiences mystical experiences through knowing a Universal Love that is so compelling, it overwhelms their personal boundaries, and expands them into a most intimate and compassionate understanding of their fellow human beings. They are intensely attuned to the rise and fall of humanity, from its heart-swelling heroics to its heartbreaking tragedies. It is as if the entire human march to evolve moves through their consciousness and opens their awareness of the great challenges we face. They are at once aware of both the incredible beauty and the great turmoil of life. This can allow Pisces to tap into what's called the Ocean of Divine Love and Mercy—an awareness of an exquisite compassion and an understanding of suffering as a purifying experience—in doing so, Pisces experience the Ultimate Connectedness they yearn for.

Of course, there are bound to be times in their lives when Pisces don't feel that Ultimate Connectedness. Rather, they feel very alone or separate—from their essence, others or God. That is extremely painful for any sign, but especially for Pisces, because they strongly sense they're missing something. And they are.

That's when school is in session for Pisces: They are learning to consciously reach back to the Spirit of who they are. When Pisces intend to connect with their Spirit (instead of something or someone else), they are going directly for their greatest power. If Pisces aren't sure how to connect with their Spirits, they can use their imaginations to envision that they are. (That's what it's there for, after all.) They can see themselves in alignment with the Divine One, however they imagine that to be. Some Pisces do that by thinking of something—or someone—they love completely. That opens them to the tenderness and vulnerability of the open heart, which can lead to them opening to Divinity.

Pisces' Mystic energy tends to feel intimate connections to spiritual figures. They can identify with the life of Christ, for example, whether or not they are Christians. Christ's life of pain, suffering and crucifixion can seem very familiar to Pisces, who feel their lives have a similar theme. And Pisces understand in their own lives (as in the life of Christ), how forgiveness and sacrifice ultimately lead to redemption. Pisces are also attuned to Buddha's message that one has to let go of desires to become free of suffering. Because of Pisces' identification with spiritual figures, it's important they focus on the ultimate, redemptive message that spiritual figures' lives signify. If they don't, Pisces can think the troubles spiritual figures experienced are necessary for spiritual awakening—and that's not necessarily the case.

Indeed, the concept of Grace is extremely important to Pisces. When they understand that they can be instantly absolved and uplifted through self-forgiveness and Divine assistance, they allow themselves to let go of suffering, and move toward transcendence. Life needn't be hard or arduous. At some point, Pisces have to choose Grace over pain.

The Mystic in Pisces can adore religions for their messages of hope, for the camaraderie of devotion, even for the pageantry of the music and ritual. Some Pisces devote their lives to one religious path, while others consider themselves practitioners of a combination of religions. Either way, Pisces reach beyond the precepts of religion to have a direct experience of the Divine. Most don't need a priest, rabbi or minister to serve as a mediator between them and the Divine One either: They go direct to the Divine on their own.

Pisces can have mystical experiences that are intensely private and known only to them. But, sometimes, they can have mystical experiences right in front of the rest of the world's eyes. For example, athletes that are in the "zone" might be accessing the mystical; so might the fisherman mesmerized by the sound of the water. Turn to watch the look on a Pisces' face during a concert, or even a touching news story, and you may spot them being uplifted and expanded to a Divine experience of compassionate loving that sends them into mystical spheres. Meditation is a direct highway into the mysticism Pisces seek because it allows them to release their attentiveness to the world and touch into other realms. Even if Pisces don't consciously identify what they do as meditation, they might practice a form of it all their own, nevertheless.

Some Pisces experience the Divine through the rapture of music or poetry, while for others, science is a doorway to expanded awareness. Pisces are the first to recognize the spiritual implications of physics research, for example. The fact that everything and everyone is made of the exact same material points to the oneness that Pisces already sense as a reality. Pisces have a natural inclination toward the study of quantum physics, particle physics and relativity theory (Einstein was a Pisces), because those fields verify the exquisite intelligence of life.

The Mystic in Pisces expresses itself through an urge to flow with life, rather than an attempt to control it. They love watching how life unfolds in its own magical way. They don't feel compelled to do things to improve upon the Divine Order; rather, they're curious to see what life will bring about in its own way—and its own time.

Because of that, Pisces can hesitate—or even resist—inflicting their will on what's going on. They feel it would be a shame to tame life, or impose a specific direction on to it, because they sense that there's a Divine Order in the process of becoming manifest. They enjoy witnessing how things work out and fall into place without much effort. Because of this, Pisces might hesitate to make a final plan, or finish things up, because they want to leave room for the serendipity of life to step in and influence matters.

In doing so, Pisces are able to transcend all structures and form. Instead of seeing people as their personalities—or situations as they appear, or even information as it presents itself—Pisces are able to see the grander spiritual dance that's taking place. They are able to go beyond appearances into the essence of the Divinity of whatever they encounter.

In that is a love of chaos. Pisces don't need to have things figured out, strategized or cleaned up. Rather they love the hurtling, wacky way life works on its own. The chaos of life thrills Pisces. They experience it as an exciting unraveling of infinite potential.

There is a "timelessness" about Pisces as well. Whereas other signs pride themselves on sticking to schedules, Pisces have a sense that things will work out fine whenever they do. Following the limitation of time contracts Pisces. They feel it imposes a false structure around the bounty of possibilities, and keeps Divine Order from manifesting naturally. The saying, "Nothing in Spirit is rushed," is one that Pisces fully understand.

This flowing strategy is right for Pisces, but can drive others crazy. Some signs might interpret Pisces' penchant for chaos, timelessness, and allowing matters to unfold their own way as a cop-out for not taking responsibility for their commitments. Whereas Pisces can be a few minutes—or even a few hours—late because they lost track of time due to a Divine Rapture they experienced while playing a piece of music, other signs might demand they cut the inner (and, to them, invisible) experience short to meet their commitments. Or Pisces can understand that there's plenty of time in which to complete a project, but that holds up others from satisfying the agreements they have made.

It isn't easy being a Mystic and operating in this world, but it's a challenge Pisces face. They have to become discerning about what is of real importance—for them and others. Sometimes, Pisces will realize an agreement or project just doesn't uplift them or bring any meaning to them, and decide to just let it go. That's fine; letting go is the essence of surrendering to life's greater plans. But Pisces need to remember that, just because they decide to let something go, doesn't mean others are letting go, too. Others may still see meaning in it. So Pisces need to inform others when they decide not to follow through on or complete an agreement, and renegotiate new terms so they don't leave others hanging.

Personally, Pisces express their Mystic archetype by identifying with a transcendent sense of self. They experience themselves as who they are, yet also as somewhat above or more expanded than who they are. Whereas Pisces can normally be quite easily hurt from other people's thoughtless remarks or actions, when they are in their Mystic mode, Pisces may not even recognize they've been wronged. Because they are connected with their Higher Self (that is their reality), they observe their personal Self as just a tiny aspect of the greater essence of who they are. So if someone sends them a zinger, Pisces see it as addressing something that isn't really them. Or they pull their consciousness or perspective high above what's going on and look at what's happening with a detached objectivity. It's kind of like how an astronaut would see the Earth from space: Instead of separate countries with various governments, they see a unified mass traveling through space. From that perspective, another behaving in an annoying fashion is not a big deal.

This ability to identify with the Transcendent Self also supports the Piscean ability to forgive. Forgiveness of judgments can be one of the most direct ways any individual can transcend. It frees up one's consciousness and allows greater loving and awareness to come in. Pisces have a penchant for forgiveness because they are able to uplift their awareness from their personality's take on what went on, to a higher perspective. Many times, Pisces understand that another's cruelty had absolutely nothing to do with them, but with the other person's pain. Then, they feel compassion for the other and all is forgiven. In doing so, they are able to let go of who's right and who's wrong, and return to what they value most: loving connectedness.

Forgiving and letting go are remarkable gifts. But, sometimes, Pisces try to shortcut this Mystic process by simply dissociating from their feelings, or going unconscious about what has happened. A Pisces might just space out or ignore hurts and wrongdoings—even abuse—thinking they are transcending them. But, in fact, they're just not taking care of themselves. Sometimes, Pisces need to extend compassion toward themselves, and demonstrate it by standing up for themselves when wrongdoings have been inflicted upon them. In that way, they champion the Spirit of who they are.

The Mystic archetype gives Pisces an interesting ego structure. They can at once feel great and grand, yet simultaneously like they're nothing at all. If it rains, Pisces can feel responsible, as if they alone made it rain (Leo does that as well). But Pisces can also feel as if they have no impact at all. For example, they can suppose that if they never showed up at work again no one would ever notice. (Leo would never think that.)

This concurrent over- and under-inflation of their sense of Self reflects the fluidity of Pisces' identity: They can feel they are, at once, everything and nothing. That's mystical, but the personal ego might not have a lot to hang on to.

This duality of importance/nonimportance is unique to the Pisces experience. So if they compare their sense of Self to how others define themselves, they will notice a difference. Other signs seem so sure about the qualities of their nature: They know just what they like, what they want, what specific goals they want to achieve. But Pisces don't always know that about themselves. They are full of contradictions and ambivalences. One minute, they want something; the next, they feel it's inconsequential. They might think a certain goal would be nice to achieve, and then think it might not be. Or in going for one goal, Pisces might fear missing out on achieving another that also looks interesting. This could cause a Pisces to feel less confident than other signs, as if they don't have what others have to succeed in life.

It's important for Pisces to understand and accept that there is something fluid about their identity, something in the moment that's never to be absolutely determined. They don't need the identity boundaries or sense of absolute clarity about whether or not an action or thought is correct. (Indeed, those things can be complete illusions anyway.) In fact, it is Pisces' "not quite knowing" who they are that prepares them to become enlightened about who they truly are. By not having a sense of how things should be, Pisces can be perfectly present with what is, and act with the knowing of the moment. That way, they are just as capable, if not more so, of making a positive impact on and difference in this world.

Because this Mystical—or spiritually transcendent—quality is so central to Pisces' identities, it is critical for them to find an uplifting and expansive avenue for developing it. Pisces have such a desire to merge into something greater, that they have to be careful about what they merge with. If they fail to develop the spiritual side of their consciousness, they can be tempted to simply merge with different, though not necessarily higher, experiences. Instead of relinquishing their personal will to the Will of the Divine, they can instead lose their will by becoming addicted to something.

If Pisces don't learn to connect with their natural transcendent consciousness, they can feel trapped in this painful one-dimensional world. Instead of merging with something uplifting, these Pisces can merge with suffering or pain, thinking that's all there is.

Because it can be so excruciating, and so lonely, Pisces can attempt to anesthetize themselves, turning to things that diminish their sensitivity, like alcohol or downers. They can justify becoming unconscious because they feel being conscious offers nothing but pain. But this is an illusion and a cop-out. When Pisces are consumed by pain, it's their signal that they haven't opened their consciousness to greater understanding and truth. It's likely that, instead, the illusion of being a victim is controlling them.

Or a Pisces might even seek out recreational drugs as a shortcut to the spiritual awareness they seek. But Pisces aren't truly lifted by using drugs to alter their reality because, in the end, they are only left with the same limited consciousness they started out with. Indulging in drugs is somewhat ironic for Pisces because, more than any other sign, theirs is capable of the kind of genuine transcendence that leads to a profound loving and joy that no drug can offer. But they have to learn to cultivate it.

If Pisces do realize they are wrestling with an overdependence, or even an addiction to alcohol or drugs, they have a powerful inner spirit that can help them kick it. By Pisces finding ways to connect to the greater whole—be it through service, creativity or spiritual pursuits—they are able to find what they are truly looking for: Mystical Flow and Unconditional Loving. That's what Pisces are born to discover and embody.

The Pisces Gifts: Becoming One with All

Compassion is one of Pisces' greatest gifts, because it allows them to play their part in the greater scheme of life. Instead of feeling like an individual cork bobbing on the sea of life, compassion gives Pisces the experience of participating in the rest of life's creations. This sense of being-in-it-together with the rest of humanity uplifts them and brings meaning to whatever they do.

Compassion also gives Pisces a tremendous sense of **Empathy.** Pisces don't fear emotions; rather, they willingly extend themselves to understand what others are going through. It's very important, however, that Pisces don't confuse empathy with sympathy. When empathetic, Pisces understand the feelings and challenges of others, and they bear validating witness to support others in their experience. Pisces' empathy says, "I know what you're experiencing is difficult, and I'll support you while you navigate your way through it." Sympathy, on the other hand, has a quality of joining in (kind of like Pisces' Helper becoming a Rescuer). Instead of supporting the other person, when Pisces are sympathetic, they will jump right into the emotional mud puddle with the sufferer. In the end, sympathy is not as helpful as empathy or compassion.

Pisces use their gift of **Sensitivity** in all they do. They have an ability to gather immense amounts of information about others, the environment, and even Spirit, through their remarkably attuned senses. Pisces use what their sensitivity shows them to become as kind, caring and healing in the world as they can be.

Pisces are **Emotionally Sensitive** to the feelings and needs of others in a highly developed way. They don't wonder—or even try to know—what others are feeling, they just know. Pisces have such a rich array of emotions within their own nature that they can easily recognize what others are feeling, because their emotions resonate with Pisces' own.

I call Pisces "Emotional Velcro," because of their tendency to pick up other people's feelings and hold them to themselves. It helps Pisces stay clear about what's going on with them versus what they are sensing from others by simply asking themselves, *Are these my own feelings or the feelings of someone else?* If they realize they are feeling the emotions of others, they can release them simply by intending to.

Remember: It is not Pisces' responsibility to resolve other people's feelings, even if Pisces are aware of them. If anything, it's best for Pisces to hold loving appreciation for others as they work to heal themselves. In doing so, Pisces are able to stand clear inside themselves, and vibrate at a frequency that can assist others in uplifting themselves. That's a great service.

Pisces are also **Psychically Sensitive.** They recognize and understand the deeper implications of matters and people—even have visions of what's to come, often without any clues. Sometimes, Pisces demonstrate their psychic sensitivity by "just knowing" what's going on with others. Just by looking at someone, Pisces might know if someone is pregnant, or getting a new job, or struggling with a secret. Or it may be an ability to see another's aura or sense where they have body pain.

This openness to the "psychic radio station" of life can sometimes result in Pisces feeling downright bombarded by the thoughts, feelings, premonitions, fears, and all the other subtle influences that are bouncing around in the atmosphere. Going to the local shopping mall or football game can become overwhelming or exhausting for Pisces because it's so psychically noisy. That's why it's always a good idea for Pisces to surround themselves with Light as they step into any busy—or contentious—situations. That helps them to deflect any unnecessary psychic debris. A book on psychic self-defense can be a valuable resource for Pisces.

Pisces are also **Energetically Sensitive.** They can feel the essence of the energies around them. Pisces can step into a room and get the vibe of what's really going on, or they can tap into the essential disposition of an animal, or discern whether someone—or something—has an inherently positive or negative charge. This gift allows Pisces to be incredibly attuned to the best way to approach things.

Pisces also have the gift of **Awe.** They can recognize the magnificence that's happening around them, even in the midst of what others would call "ordinary" reality. Pisces see the beauty, the acts of heroism, and the extraordinariness in people, things and situations that others might miss seeing. That's because Pisces want to—and are able to—see the Divine working through, and in, matters. Many Pisces don't necessarily interpret this as Divine; they just think something's remarkable. But behind that attitude is a willingness to see something grander than themselves, even to be made humble by what they see. Pisces' ability to be "awed" keeps them open to the magic and serendipity of life. They want life to be extraordinary, and awe puts them in a position to see how it truly is. Awe keeps Pisces appreciating everything that takes place as the remarkable occurrence that it is.

Pisces can many times be awed by other people's gifts. They can be truly impressed by what others do. This gives a tremendous support to the expression of others, because Pisces' respect encourages them. A Pisces will be the first to say, "You amazed me by what you did!" It's important, though, that Pisces don't use their awe of others to feel that they are less than other people.

Sometimes, Pisces can be so bowled over by the gifts and actions of others that they underestimate their own gifts and actions in comparison. This defeats Pisces. What works better is for Pisces to allow themselves to direct awe toward themselves, as well as to others. Not in an ego-impressed "I'm so great!" kind of way; that's not awe, that's self-aggrandizement. Rather, Pisces benefit from recognizing and respecting how the Divine expresses through them in its own amazing way, just as it does through others. Some Pisces do that by saying to themselves, *Spirit drew a magnificent picture through me today.* Or, *Spirit uplifted a loved one through me today.*

Pisces also have the gift of **Boundaryless-ness,** or an ability to step out of the limited experience of the ego Self in order to connect to everyone and everything else. Pisces can use boundaryless-ness not only for spiritual awakening, but also in a worldly fashion, by working cooperatively with others. Instead of thinking they've got to have their way, or capture the credit for what's done, Pisces understand that they can share and exchange ideas and efforts with others in a way that everyone taps into and benefits from. Pisces don't operate in a vacuum: They want to give and receive energy and inspiration. They know the whole is greater than the sum of its parts.

The Pisces Fears: See Me! . . . No, Don't!

Maybe more than anything else, Pisces **fear being invisible.** They can have a sense that they just aren't making an impact on the world around them, to the point of not being noticed or validated at all. This differs from those times when Pisces *make* themselves invisible as a way of "checking out" in order to be safe or create time for reflection. This is a feeling of being present in a situation, yet not being seen.

Sometimes, this takes the form of Pisces thinking they are not making a valuable contribution to the world. Just as the Jimmy Stewart character in the movie *It's a Wonderful Life* thinks his life doesn't matter to anyone, so can a Pisces imagine that they don't matter to others at all. They can fear their existence isn't significant enough to be important. They can think they don't have the kind of presence that captures other people's interest, or that has anything of value to offer.

In order to compensate for this fear, Pisces can do things they know would have a valuable impact, making themselves worthy of being noticed. This can be channeled into incredibly useful actions that can bring about attention and acknowledgment in positive ways. Pisces will ask themselves, *How can I get some attention here?* This is not merely attention but a sense of assurance that they are making a positive impact. For example, Pisces will provide useful services to those in need, as well as express themselves dramatically or creatively. They will generously give of themselves in every situation, making sure they contribute something that adds to the whole.

But, sometimes, Pisces can overcompensate for their fear of invisibility and do things that aren't necessary. For example, they might try increasing their visibility by rushing in to "save" someone—or something—as a way of having something of value to offer, instead of checking to make sure their help is wanted (or needed). This can lead to Pisces overgiving to—or over-rescuing—others, thinking that will get them noticed as valuable.

Other times, Pisces might do outrageous things in an attempt to ensure they'll be noticed. They might go for "negative attention" by annoying or riling people up just to get others to see them. So they become disruptive or incorrigible as a way of saying, *See me!*

Or Pisces might decide to withdraw from others, thinking others don't think Pisces count anyway. They can "disappear" and hide away. While doing so, they might be wishing others would try to draw them out, but, because of Pisces withdrawal, others might think they just want to be left alone.

The truth is, neither Pisces nor their contributions are invisible. They needn't do or be anything other than who they are to be valuable or noticed for the significant beings they are. In fact, when Pisces are feeling invisible or insignificant, it's because they are feeling that way toward themselves. They might not be validating their own expression, or acknowledging the importance of their own contribution.

It works best if Pisces continue to reach out and participate positively during the times when they don't feel noticed, and find ways to acknowledge themselves and their works to themselves. It might also help if they expressed their concerns of not being noticed. That gives them a chance to hear from others that they are, indeed, being noticed and valued. But, remember: It's not about others reassuring Pisces that they're significant; it's about Pisces reassuring themselves. Sometimes, it's just nice to have a reflection from one's world that one's presence does, indeed, make a difference.

Oddly enough, at other times, Pisces **fear becoming too visible.** They can fear becoming too noticed, too exposed, and being consumed by the world's needs of them. Pisces are so aware of other people's energies and projections that they can feel bombarded when they receive too much attention. It can overwhelm their sense of self, and even confuse their identities and their boundaries.

So Pisces can do things that create a sort of invisibility: a kind of shielding that deflects attention from themselves. Sometimes, they do this by being chameleonlike and blending in with their environment, so they don't stand out in any way. Other times, they do this by becoming extremely quiet, keeping their thoughts and opinions to themselves. Many times, Pisces will put on a sort of psychic "cloaking device," wherein they're there, but somehow others don't take notice of them.

All these strategies can serve to keep Pisces feeling safe and protected in situations they're unsure of. They also give Pisces time to reflect on what's right for them, or to become clear about their personal boundaries, physically and psychically.

But these can also be strategies for Pisces "hiding out" and not participating fully in what their lives are offering them. They might fear not being able to handle what's going on, or feel threatened by others scrutinizing them, and instead retreat to the background, allowing others to make the decisions or control matters. But that can prevent Pisces from growing and developing their own skills and opportunities.

What works best is if Pisces use the times when they are invisible as opportunities to retreat, refresh, replenish and get a useful handle on things. Then, they can feel more comfortable with whatever kind of attention they get because they are in touch with their inner core.

Pisces in Relationships: "Let's Merge"

Pisces adore relationships, yearn for them and invest themselves fully in them. Pisces love the connection and understanding that relationships offer, and they do their best to ensure they are good companions to others.

Pisces are usually quite social and enjoy a variety of types of people. Rarely snooty or exclusive, Pisces can find something interesting and worthwhile in almost anyone they meet. But they do like the unusual people—people with intriguing stories, people with quirks, people who need help, and people who try to shoo them away. They are curious about what makes others tick, and are fascinated by people just being themselves.

But, mostly, Pisces love people with whom they can enjoy a deep emotional bond. For Pisces there's nothing like emotional intensity or passionate exchanges with another. They want to feel something from others, perhaps even be transformed in some way by what they exchange. If they could they would merge completely with whomever they love. Alas, they cannot, but they will do their best to create the semblance of merging and revel in whatever sense of merging they can create.

Pisces are incredibly kind in relating to others, gentle and considerate of other's feelings and needs. They give of themselves fully (maybe too much so) and do their best to have compassion for others' shortcomings. In fact, Pisces can be so kind and understanding that they often allow others to behave poorly toward them because they can see the hurt that is driving the negative behavior. But that's no excuse. Pisces really serve the Spirits of both parties when they don't permit others to treat them poorly.

Pisces crave emotionally rich relationships, including relationships where Pisces (attempt to) help others. In doing so, they experience satisfying emotional connectedness. That's why they do it. However, sometimes, Pisces can be so uplifted by helping another that they confuse it with romantic love. I've counseled many Pisces who have found themselves committed to people who they realize they're bound to out of emotional concern, not because they are truly in love. Pisces have to check with themselves to make sure they are differentiating between being a partner and being a helper.

Pisces are the classic hopeless romantics! They love the swooning, the fantasy, the gentleness, and, especially, the emotional excitement that romance creates. They love the thoughtful details and the devotion to the beloved. Flowers, baths (Pisces are big on Water), candlelight, and "I just can't bear not being with you every moment!" declarations are right up Pisces' alley.

If you're trying to catch a female Pisces' eye, let her in on your feelings. She wants to know there's an emotional, passionate being inside of you that she can relate to and connect with. (However, sometimes, Pisces can fall for someone who is as unemotional and stoic as can be. With them, a Pisces will project a world of unexpressed feelings, thinking they're in so much pain they'd be a great project—someone they can help to release their feelings. Usually, this doesn't happen, leaving Pisces with someone who remains stoic and unsatisfying.) And let her know all your feelings, not just the "good" ones. She responds gently and lovingly to someone who wants—or needs—a little reassurance or cheering up. But that's just step one.

Step two, three, and so on are about romance and kindness, touching and sharing. She wants it all. And she'll give it all back. Cleverly, with a twist that will surprise you.

If you're trying to catch a male Pisces' eye, show him your tenderness and your ability to go to deep levels of feeling. He wants someone with whom he can feel safe with his sensitivity and his dreams. He's attracted to outer beauty, but compelled by inner beauty. A Pisces man looks past a prospective partner's presentation to see her soul. When he sees an element of magic, power or emotional strength, he knows he's in good company. Approach this man softly. No big come-ons, no sales pitch or parading what's so great about you. Rather, let him know that you are as sensitive to energies as he is, and show him that you know when to advance—and when to retreat.

And be romantic! He can't help but get caught up in the intoxicating trance of "what could be beautiful." Allow him to tell you of his dreams and tell him yours. Remember: This man is a Dreamer and a Mystic, and he wants something that feels extraordinary.

The Last Word on Pisces

Pisces may tend to dream their way through life seeking to discover their True Self. They only find it, though, by sacrificing their lesser Self.

About the Author

Phyllis Firak-Mitz, M.A., has enjoyed a flourishing astrology practice for over twenty years.

Using her unique blend of astrology with psychology (in which she holds her master's degree) and spirituality, she has counseled thousands of people from all walks of life, including many of Hollywood's top stars, Washington politicians and CEOs of Fortune 500 companies.

Phyllis makes frequent radio appearances, is widely published, and lectures throughout the United States on the practical ways in which astrology can be used to make everyone's life happier and more successful.